THE ARLEY ARCHIVE SERIES

C000176304

The Arley Archive Series is designed to illustrate the de[velopment of the north-]west of England in the centuries before the Industrial Revol[ution] [through] examination of the lives of the people living there. The core of the study is the Arley Estate in north Cheshire, a major landowner since 1200, where some unusually detailed records have survived. The first book described the residents and landowners of four townships on this estate in the mid-eighteenth century. The second volume, based on national as well as local archives, focused on north-western agriculture in the seventeenth and eighteenth centuries. Since these two volumes were written, the author has extended his research into the extensive archives of the Leicester family, whose Tabley estate adjoined Arley. Two of the seven households described in the third volume were based on Arley's archives and two on those of Tabley; the other three were derived from Lancashire sources.

This fourth and final volume, *Capital and Innovation*, describes the lives of a large number of people who lived in the area bounded by Warrington, Knutsford, Northwich and Frodsham between 1500 and 1780. The information in all four volumes combines to form a picture of the development of the whole society of this area. Using this portrait as an example of society in this region, reasons are suggested as to why the great innovations that brought about the Industrial Revolution occurred in north-west England and not anywhere else in the world.

Four Cheshire Townships in the 18th Century – Arley, Appleton, Stockton Heath and Great Budworth, Charles F. Foster, 1st. ed., April 1992, Arley Hall Archive Series, No. 1., 88 pp., 7 maps, 5 b/w illus., 25 x 17 cm., paperback ISBN 0 9518382 0 2. This is a unique snapshot of rural life in the eighteenth century. It details the lives of the residents of 8,600 acres in the four townships – from Sir Peter Warburton of Arley Hall to Jonathan Berry, a sheep shearer. Extraordinary details of these people's incomes and occupations have survived in rare tax returns, maps, rentals and deeds in the Arley Hall archives.

> 'An excellent book that deserves widespread attention.   *Archives*
>
> 'Contains much fascinating detail.'   *Agricultural History Review*
>
> 'This is a lovely book to look at as well as to read.'   *Open University*
>
> '…deftly done in a manner which is reminiscent of Richard Gough's 1700 account of Myddle … well worth the consideration of economic and social historians.' *History*

Cheshire Cheese and Farming in the North West in the 17th & 18th Centuries, Charles F. Foster, 1st ed., May 1998, Arley Archive Series, No. 2, 128 pp., 4 maps, 28 b/w illus., 25 17 cm., paperback ISBN 0 9518382 1 0. In 1650 the first ship loaded with Cheshire cheese sailed from Chester to London. So popular did it become that within a few years several pubs in London were called *The Cheshire Cheese*. This trade led to important changes in the shape of rural life in the North-West. In the course of charting these developments Charles Foster provides fascinating details about daily life on the farms, the people who worked the land and the men who sailed the ships between London and north-western ports.

> 'Achieves a level of precision in understanding the operations of both the estate and its tenantry which is rare indeed.' *Economic History Review*

> 'As interesting and informative as the previous one.' *Agricultural History Review*

> 'A picture of a changing rural economy at a local level which can hardly be bettered.' *Cheshire History*

> 'One of the most important pieces of writing on agriculture in northern England of recent years. *Historic Society of Lancashire and Cheshire*

Seven Households: life in Cheshire and Lancashire 1582-1774, Charles F. Foster, 1st ed., Dec. 2002, Arley Archive Series, No. 3, pp. xviii, 248, 5 maps, 4 col. 55 b/w illus., 25 x 17 cm. Hardback ISBN 09518382 2 9. Paperback ISBN 09518382 2 9. The descriptions of three major gentry households – Smithills from the 1580s to the 1600s, Tabley from the 1630s to the 1680s and Arley between 1740 and 1780 are contrasted with the lives of more ordinary people. The Fells of Swarthmoor were much engaged in business, Thomas Jackson and Richard Latham were brought up on 15 and 20 acre farms while George Dockwra lived quietly on a small pension as a lodger in a farmhouse. These detailed examples were designed to support and enrich the thesis set out in the fourth and final volume of this series.

> 'His forte is the precise accumulation of detailed evidence; his preference is for the quantifiable.' *English Historical Review*

> '… so much revealing information … on the social tiers below the county families' *Lancashire and Cheshire Antiquarian Society*

> 'I found particularly illuminating the career of Thomas Jackson, a three-life lease-holder.' *Agricultural History Review*

> '*Seven Households* is a very readable book, the sort you pick up and read from end to end just out of pleasure.' *Local Historian*

These books can be bought direct from the Arley Hall Press, Northwich, CW9 6NA. Prices including postage and packing:

	UK	Europe airmail rest of world surface	rest of world airmail
	£	£	£
Vol. 1. *Four Cheshire Townships*	6.95	8.00	9.00
Vol. 2 *Cheshire Cheese*	8.95	10.00	12.00
Vol. 3 *Seven Households* (paperback)	11.95	14.00	18.00
(hardback)	19.95	23.00	28.00
Vol. 4 *Capital and Innovation* (paperback)	16.95	19.00	23.00

Please send orders with a cheque or credit/debit card details to Arley Hall Press at the above address or email to: enquiries@arleyhallandgardens.com

CHARLES F. FOSTER

Capital and Innovation

– how Britain became
the first industrial nation

*a study of the Warrington, Knutsford,
Northwich and Frodsham area
1500–1780*

*Illustrations digitally realised
from the originals by*
PAUL ATKINS

with a foreword by
PROFESSOR
FRANÇOIS CROUZET

ARLEY HALL PRESS

Cover: The engraving of a river port shows Bank Quay, Warrington, in 1772 (Plate 22 in this book). The clock face was made by John Caldwell in Appleton in 1750 (Pl. 46). The lathe is from John Wyke's catalogue issued from his business in Prescot and Liverpool between about 1758 and 1782. This lathe is similar to that shown in Pl. 45 except that it includes a second centre for the turning of larger diameter pieces.

Planned for 2003 but published 2004 by
Arley Hall Press
Northwich, Cheshire
CW9 6NA
(Tel. 01565 777 231, Fax 01565 777 465
email enquiries@arleyhallandgardens.com)

ISBN 0-9518382-4-5

Typeset in Monotype Ehrhardt by
XL Publishing Services, Tiverton
Printed and bound by
Amadeus Press, Cleckheaton

Contents

Part I   The redistribution of wealth 1530–1670

4 The occupations of people in north Cheshire 1560–1646

5 Social changes and the distribution of wealth in the seventeenth century

Part II   The emergence of a business society 1650–1780

Part III   Comparisons

List of Figures

Note: all the above invoices are in the Arley archives

List of Maps

List of Plates

BETWEEN PAGES 14 AND 15

Foreword

Capital and Innovation is the last volume in the Arley Archive Series. It deals with the same area of northern Cheshire as the three books which preceded it, though with many glances at the larger region of north-western England. Whilst they were mostly concerned with the countryside and the people who worked the land or lived off it, this time commercial and industrial activities and the development of society as a whole are at the centre. We thus have a remarkable example of *micro-storia*, the in-depth study of a rather small area or social group, which uses all relevant sources and considers its subject from all possible angles. Moreover, his detailed analysis suggested to Charles Foster some answers to a *macro*-problem: why did the Industrial Revolution start in north-western England and nowhere else? Since this famous revolution indubitably was at first restricted to some districts, it does, indeed, have to be explained, not by considering British society as a whole, but by examining the society and culture of those districts.

Charles Foster has been fortunate in having at hand the treasures of the Warburton and Leicester Muniments, but he has also used many other sources, in Cheshire, in Lancashire and in London. And thanks to hard work, to scholarly skill, to a feeling for the past, he has written an outstanding book. After reading debates between cliometricians, conducted in an abstract empyrean inhabited by neo-classical models and regression analyses, it is refreshing to come down to grass-roots level and to get to know 'real' individuals and families, thanks to the lively vignettes which Charles Foster has drawn.

A major conclusion of the early books was that, in the seventeenth century and for most of the eighteenth, the 'Arley Hall Country' had a diversified rural society, which was markedly different from the 'classical' three-tiered system – large landowners, big capitalist tenants, landless labourers – which prevailed in much of England. Admittedly, from 1650 to 1750 the number of landowners and farms fell and the average size of farms increased. Nonetheless, by 1750, in the four townships around Arley Hall, 60% of the land remained in the possession of 194 freeholders and three-life leaseholders, whilst just 40% was in the hands of three major landowners. It was only from the Napoleonic wars onwards that the peculiar social structure of northern Cheshire gave way to the 'classical' pattern of southern and eastern England.

Foster has connected this diversified society with two developments which had started *c.* 1540: changes in the law and in property rights (which gave increased rights to farms' occupiers) and inflation, particularly of rents and land values. As a consequence, part of the landed wealth was transferred into new hands, and a large number of small and medium cultivators became owners of some capital. Thus a relatively numerous, 'middling sort' emerged within rural society. To Charles Foster, this was the starting point of the process which eventually blossomed into the Industrial Revolution in north-western England.

This society was strengthened by the development of a market economy, and a decisive change was the rise of dairy farming for making Cheshire cheese, which, from 1650 onwards, was exported to London by sea in large and increasing quantities. Cheshire farmers responded to market signals and also innovated (making 'thick' cheeses, thanks to new, heavier presses). Still, a good deal of their production was retained for local use: the consumption of cheese by the staff at Arley Hall in the 1750s and 1760s was 120 lbs per capita per year! The coasting trade to London and other places created new opportunities for traders, and, of course, Cheshire cheese is a splendid example of the early formation in England of a national market.

Actually, Foster sees the mid-seventeenth century as a watershed for the North-West, a view which fits with 'the divergence of England' after 1660, which D. C. Coleman and E. A. Wrigley have stressed. In Cheshire (and the North-West), a great variety of businesses sprang up, as members of the middling sort of landowners and landholders moved themselves – and their money – into trade and manufacture. It was once believed that many pioneers of the Industrial Revolution had come from 'yeomen's' families. Foster shows that actually they belonged to business families, which had previously moved from the land to the towns and business. This move had been helped by the habit in those families of dividing inheritances and of granting portions to children when they became adults. Younger sons used their portions to set up as traders, shopkeepers, craftsmen, carriers.

Foster sees this equal division of estates and granting of portions as a major aspect of the 'business culture' which developed among the middling ranks of society in the North-West, in contrast (this is a central part of his analysis) to the 'gentry culture' of the South, which gave all the family wealth to a single heir.

The gentry were born to fight and rule, not to work. Admittedly, many large landowners attended to their estates and Sir Peter Warburton played a leading role in the modernisation of the Weaver Navigation. Moreover, in the salt industry of Northwich, much of the capital invested before 1700 had come from major landowners, a group which had a long tradition in developing minerals found on their land. But, in the eighteenth century, they gave way to bourgeois investors. In the 1730s only three of the eight rock salt mines were operated by landowning families, and there were no landowners among the operators of the five brine saltworks. This confirms once more that nobility and gentry, far from playing a key role in the Industrial Revolution, as some writers have maintained, had actually been withdrawing from business enterprise since the seventeenth century. On the other hand, some capital from the land went into industry, but via small freeholders or leaseholders, who sold or mortgaged land, in order to set up a business, either for themselves or for their children. The sailcloth manufacturers of Warrington in the mid-eighteenth century are a good example. By analysing this move of both men and capital from the middling ranks of the agricultural sector to non-farming activities Foster has made an important contribution to our understanding of the relationship between agriculture and the Industrial Revolution.

He has also contributed to another debate, on the role of dissenters in the Industrial Revolution. This role was stressed by historians in the mid-twentieth century, but recently it has been pointed out that many eighteenth-century entrepreneurs were Anglicans. In Cheshire, Foster shows that many of the 'middling sort', who were of independent mind and position, were attracted by the radical forms of the Protestant religion and, after the Restoration, became Nonconformists. Eventually, in Warrington, over one half of the sailcloth manufacturers who obtained contracts with the Royal Navy in 1756/57 were Nonconformists; moreover five of the richest were Unitarians and two were Quakers. Foster does not adopt, however, the Weber thesis, but he stresses that Nonconformity strengthened business culture and prevented it from being overwhelmed by the dominant gentry culture.

In any event Warrington was a 'business town', its population lived from trading and manufacturing. And it was wealthy – 150 families owned £1,000 or more. Foster stresses that it was different from most towns in southern England and on the Continent. But it should be remembered that the sailcloth industry was a recent and artificial creation by Acts of Parliament. This fits well with Patrick O'Brien's view that the foreign and military policies of the Hanoverian state were a factor in the Industrial Revolution, but it also makes Warrington a rather special case. Moreover, the sailcloth industry was traditional in its technology and organization. As for the salt industry of Northwich, its technical revolution (coal-heated iron pans) had come in the seventeenth century.

Historians have looked for a trigger mechanism which generated the Industrial Revolution within the entrepreneurial society to be found in Warrington and other north-western towns. To Charles Foster things were simpler: the famous technical inventions around 1770 were a natural consequence of the evolution which had made north-western business society larger, richer and more sophisticated, and of the accumulation of much capital in the hands of many dedicated businessmen, who gave their chance to technically skilled people (and, as it is stressed in Appendix 11.1, innovation results from team work rather than from individual intuition). The Industrial Revolution started when the number of rich entrepreneurs had become large enough. Undoubtedly, the accumulation of capital and skills was a necessary condition of the Industrial Revolution, but one can wonder whether this was enough, even though the West Riding, with its many small landholders and clothiers, fits in well with Foster's views.

One can also wonder whether research on some industrialized continental districts would confirm England as the exception, the only country where 'ordinary people owned some capital'. These questions show that *Capital and Innovation* is a ground-breaking work, which will stimulate debate and research.

FRANÇOIS CROUZET
Emeritus Professor of Modern History
at the University of Paris-Sorbonne

Author's Preface and Acknowledgements

In 1967, when we were first married, my wife and I spent every weekend in a lovely old thatched farmhouse nestling in the hills above Honiton in Devon. It had a marvellous sitting-room, with elaborately moulded oak beams and joists in the ceiling, an oak panelled wall and a great wide hearth with carved stone cheeks. I often found myself wondering how the farmer who built the house in about 1600 had become rich enough to afford so much luxurious building work. One Saturday in Honiton I bought a paperback copy of *Old Devon* by W. G.Hoskins and began my historical enquiries. At Christmas and usually for one weekend each summer we went to stay with my wife's parents at Arley Hall in Cheshire. On one of these visits, no doubt stimulated by something I said about history, my mother-in-law produced from a cupboard a number of medieval charters. I learnt that this was just a fragment of the huge archive the family had accumulated over 800 years.

From these twin beginnings there slowly evolved the idea that when I retired from my engineering business I would devote myself to a study of the Arley archives. I was an unusual character to be doing historical research; people normally start as post-graduate students who have to produce a PhD thesis. I had specialized in history at school, but after getting a history Exhibition to New College, Oxford, in 1949 I switched to PPE and concentrated on economics. My career, too, followed a maverick pattern. After a year in an investment bank, I spent 10 years in the building industry, in the last six of which I ran my own firm. Five years back in the investment world, working on industrial finance, were then followed by 17 years, until 1987, running my own small precision engineering business.

In the 19 years between 1968 and my retirement from full-time business in 1987 history became an increasingly important leisure activity for me, and my interest always concentrated on social, economic and technical changes, rather than on politics or religion. I read as widely as I could in order to equip myself to under-stand the archives – studies of monastic and family papers, of parishes and towns, original documents like letters and diaries, and manuals of early handwriting so that I could read the documents. After I retired, I was able to draw the Arley papers out of the John Rylands Library, as they were still owned by my wife's family. I sorted them and catalogued them before returning them to the Library.

Most historical research projects start with a clearly defined object: for example to describe the growth of the cotton trade in Manchester. My aims were both wider and vaguer. I hoped that my varied background in business, technology and finance might enable me to find something in the records that earlier researchers had not noticed. My first discovery was the existence of exceptionally full details about the owners and occupiers of some 8,000 acres in the 1740s, which I described in *Four Cheshire Townships*. I was led to my second subject by finding the accounts of the cheese warehouse at Sutton, on the River Weaver opposite Frodsham, and this produced my second book – *Cheshire Cheese and Farming*. Early on in my study of the Arley area, I had learnt that the Tabley estate had always owned land that inter-locked with Arley land, and that the Leicesters also had a huge and largely unknown archive, so it seemed sensible to examine that too. There I found two sets of household papers with unusual details of everyday life that complimented the two sets at Arley. This encouraged me to look for other records of this kind and these eventually became the subject of my third book – *Seven Households*. These seven portraits of families were designed as examples to illustrate in detail and so to enrich the more general picture of the changes in north-western society described in my final volume.

This book, then, is the fourth and last in my Arley Archive Series. It began with my effort to understand the origins of the three-life leases by which all the tenants on these estates held their lands from the mid-sixteenth to the late eighteenth centuries and my discovery of the 1545 Tax Return among the Leicester archives. The great redistribution of wealth that my research revealed not only showed me how a business society grew up in the North-West but also suggested that the builder of my Honiton house had become rich as a beneficiary of the same phenom-enon.

In researching and writing this book I have had much assistance. Perhaps my greatest debt is to Tom Jackson, who spent 20 years researching the history of Warrington in the eighteenth century, before moving to Silloth near Carlisle. With amazing generosity he put all his files and indexes at my disposal – without them I could not have written the second half of the book. Not only did he give me all this material but he answered every enquiry I made and produced photocopies of new papers or gave me pointers to archives which I had not yet found. In addition to all this he read and corrected the typescript of these chapters, so he should perhaps be regarded as virtually a co-author of this part of the book.

I have also had substantial help from my friend Robert Steele, Head of Humanities at Great Sankey High School in Warrington. He drew my attention to the New Haven connection and more broadly to the influence of the Puritans in the Great Budworth-Warrington area. He found the Tithe prescription areas which are an important part of Maps 3 and 6 and he also kindly read the typescript and made helpful comments.

I must thank again three very kind friends who read the typescript of both my last two volumes and made many important and helpful comments which I hope the books have profited from – Michael Power, Colin Phillips and Martin Rosendaal.

I am most grateful to many other people who have done things for me that I couldn't do for myself. Paul Booth has clarified for me several conundrums I encountered in the early sixteenth-century papers. The staff in a large number of libraries and Record Offices have assisted me. I would particularly like to thank Peter McNiven of the John Rylands Library and Jonathon Pepler in the Cheshire Record Office who enabled me to study the great archives of the Warburtons and the Leicesters with such ease. I must also thank John Hodgson and Jill Groves who helped me to identify some of the townships in the 1545 Tax Return, whose names were partly missing in the manuscript. Hilary Chambers, Janice Heyes and their colleagues at Warrington Library and Museum were all very helpful both with their documents and their illustrations. I would like to acknowledge my debt to all the owners of the images listed on pp. ix–x and to thank them for their kindness in allowing me to reproduce them; also Cheshire County Council for permission to reproduce the documents in Appendices 2.1, 2.6, 3.4 B, 3.7 and 5.2.

I am extremely grateful to Professor François Crouzet for reading the typescript and for making many helpful comments, as well as for kindly agreeing to write a Foreword. I would like to thank my old school-friend, fellow historian and economist, Hector Hawkins, for taking an interest in this book and also for introducing me to Professor Crouzet. Paul Atkins has again made the book more attractive and interesting by creating marvellous images – some of them from rather unpromising originals – and Nick Scarle has drawn more of his beautifully clear maps. I am indebted to both of them. Amy Shaffer persevered wonderfully in typing the script and the terrible appendices. Roger Hudson's editorial skills improved the text in many places and his advice and encouragement were always a great support. My wife has done much more to help prepare this book for publication than she had to do for the earlier ones. I am most grateful to her for helping an ageing fellow complete the task he set himself so long ago.

Abbreviations

Add. Mss	Additional Manuscript
A.R.I.	Arley Receipted Invoice
Ag.Hist.Rev.	Agricultural History Review
arm.	armiger – a person entitled to bear heraldic arms
B.L.	British Library
C.R.O.	Cheshire Record Office
C.L.R.O.	Corporation of London Record Office
DCH	Cholmondeley Estate papers in Cheshire Record Office
DLT	Tabley Estate papers in Cheshire Record Office
D.N.B.	Dictionary of National Biography
EGR	Dunham Massey Estate papers in John Rylands Library, Deansgate, Manchester
Econ.Hist.Rev.	Economic History Review
H.S.L.& C.	Historic Society of Lancashire and Cheshire
I.P.M.	Inquisition *Post Mortem*
J.C.T.P.	Journal of the Commissioners for Trade and Plantations
J.H.C.	Journal of the House of Commons
L.& C.A.S.	Lancashire and Cheshire Antiquarian Society
L.P.R.S.	Lancashire Parish Record Society
Lancs. R.O.	Lancashire Record Office
O.S.	Ordnance Survey
Penrhyn Papers	at the University of Bangor Library
P.R.	Parish Registers
P.R.O.	Public Record Office, Kew
Record Soc. L.& C.	Record Society of Lancashire and Cheshire
Soc.	Society
Trans. R.H.S.	Transactions of the Royal Historical Society
VCH	Victoria County History
WCW	Will in Lancashire Record Office
W.I.	West Indies
WM	Warburton Muniments in John Rylands University of Manchester Library
W.P.L.	Warrington Public Library
Y.A.J.	Yorkshire Archaeological Journal
Y.A.S.R.S.	Yorkshire Archaeological Society Record Series

PART I

The redistribution of wealth, 1530–1670

CHAPTER 1
Introduction

One of the most significant events in English history occurred in the early sixteenth century. On the face of things, it was no more than a small change in the law which gave the occupiers of farms increased rights, but over the following century it transferred a large part of the landed wealth of England into new hands. The legal change was the creation of 'customary' tenants whose rents were fixed and who could not be ejected. By itself this altered little, but when combined with the great inflation in the market rental value of land in the same century, it put wealth into the hands of the tenants on a huge scale. This wealth was a windfall for the tenants but a loss to the Crown, the Church[1] and the old landed gentry on whose lands the tenants lived. One reason why the Monarchy in England became increasingly short of money at this time was that, whereas it was receiving a full market rent on its land at the beginning of the century, it was only getting 5%–10% by the end. When the Stuarts sold manors in the seventeenth century they usually received only 5% or 10% of their full value because their tenants 'owned' the rest. There was a large political dimension to this. The poverty of the Crown led to the increased importance of Parliament with its ability to raise taxes. The efforts of Charles I to govern without Parliament were a major reason behind the outbreak of the Civil War. The massive transfer of landed capital out of the hands of the traditional governing group in society that had occurred by then may have been an important reason why the Stuarts, unlike all other European monarchs, lost their civil war.[2] However, this book is not concerned with political history.

These important changes have been partly obscured from historians by the shortage of archive evidence. For reasons that I examine in Chapter 3, the Crown, the Church and the lawyers never admitted that in finding that 'customary' tenants existed they were in part inventing a 'new' custom, and the happy recipients of the new rights were not going to jeopardize them by exposing the fiction. The increase in market rental values, the second half of the cause of the redistribution of wealth, only became fully known when scholars obtained access to the archives of private landed estates in the last 50 years.[3] My research over the last ten years or so in the

---

1   Much of the land of the dissolved monasteries was held by 'customary' tenants. About 90% of the value of the monastic land retained by the Crown probably went to these tenants. How successful the customary tenants were in retaining their rights in land sold in the 1540s is not usually known.

2   The Spanish crown had only lost half of its territory in the Netherlands to the Dutch Republic a few decades earlier.

3   Kerridge, 1953 and Fig. 1, p. 57 below.

unusually detailed and extensive archives that have survived on two old Cheshire estates has enabled me to clarify their importance.

This book, then, sets out the evidence for the great changes in the distribution of wealth that occurred in the sixteenth century and describes their consequences in the seventeenth and eighteenth centuries in a small patch of country on the borders of Cheshire and Lancashire, at the eastern (or mainland) end of the Mersey estuary, roughly the area bounded by the towns of Warrington, Knutsford, Northwich and Frodsham (see Maps 1 and 4). This area includes most of the estates owned by the Leicesters of Tabley and the Warburtons of Arley, on whose archives much of the book is based. This was a geographically important area in the period 1500–1770, close to water transport and port facilities. The Port of Liverpool included the whole of the Mersey estuary and it had three main quays:[4] at Liverpool, Frodsham and at Sankey Bridges near Warrington. In the seventeenth century the last two, at the eastern end, were the most active and Warrington was the largest town. Only at the end of that century, when the larger ships used for Atlantic voyages became more frequent visitors to the Mersey, did the quays in Liverpool town become the busiest. Even then Warrington remained important because it was beside the navigable waters nearest to the great textile centre of Manchester.

The evidence for the redistribution of wealth consists of descriptions of large numbers of individual families. Chapter 2 examines the incomes of the two old major gentry families of Leicester and Warburton between 1362 and 1870. It is shown that during the three centuries from 1550 to 1850 they received less income from their lands than they might have done. In Chapter 3 we see that the Crown did even worse. At least 80% of the income and the capital value of an old Crown manor went to the tenants, thanks to the legal changes of the early sixteenth century.

The gains that the tenants made are illustrated by details of the lands occupied by the inhabitants of eleven different Cheshire townships:

Allostock	Nether Peover
Antrobus	Nether Tabley
Appleton	Over Whitley
Aston by Budworth	Sevenoaks
Cogshall	Sutton Weaver
Great Budworth	

The analysis describes the development of a new type of society, more equal than the societies that had existed earlier in Europe, or indeed that continued to exist on the Continent. Many more families both owned property *and* worked for their

4 In Customs jargon 3 'legal' quays.

living, with a different culture to that of the old landowning gentry who were only trained to govern and to fight. As their wealth grew in the sixteenth century, some of them started businesses. Trade expanded and new methods of doing things were introduced. Many more people acquired an education. In the seventeenth century some went to America, others settled in the West Indies. Their wealth enabled them to settle these new lands as individual families, not as part of a state- or gentry-financed organization, as occurred in most of the colonies established by other European nations. These new countries provided new products: sugar, tobacco and cotton from the tropical latitudes in the south; timber from virgin forests in the north. A great new trading system developed across the Atlantic, as English manu-factures were exchanged for the new products. A new, innovative, 'business' society came into existence.

By the 1770s this new society had brought about far-reaching changes on both sides of the Atlantic. In England it devised mechanical cotton-spinning and the steam engine, the two innovations which drove the Industrial Revolution. In America it made the United States the first great non-aristocratic, egalitarian, nation state. These two developments established the modern world. Cheshire and Lancashire, together with Staffordshire and the West Riding of Yorkshire, consti-tuted the area where this new society was created, and, by describing families in Cheshire and Lancashire between 1500 and 1780, I hope to provide an outline of its development.

The north-west of England was always different from the south and east. In the early sixteenth century it may have been poorer and less thickly populated. A well-known map of England in 1524–25 shows that the taxable wealth in the country was almost all in an area south and east of a line drawn from Gloucester to Hull.[5] The reason why the North-West had fewer inhabitants was because it was more difficult to grow grain crops there than in the warmer and drier South and East. It was pasture country and the main products of its farms were sheep and cattle. The plains of Cheshire and Lancashire were filled with small farms averaging about 30 acres each.[6] The families living on these farms in the sixteenth century produced almost all their own food and much of their own clothing[7] so their society was different from that in the south of England, where arable agriculture in common fields was the pre-dominant activity. The distribution of wealth in Cheshire and Lancashire in the

5 Hoskins, 1976, p. 28, but see below Ch. 3 (ii), p. 48 and Hoyle, 1987, p. xv, for evidence that the North-West may have been both under-counted and under-assessed to the 1524–25 tax returns on which this map is based.
6 See Ch. 3 below, pp. 45–9.
7 See Foster, 2002, Chs 1–3.

sixteenth century seems also to have been different from that in the South and East. Cheshire had its rich old gentry families, like the southern counties, but there were far fewer minor gentry and mercantile families occupying the middle ground between these rich gentry and the small farmers with few possessions. This was perhaps because there were only two towns with a substantial trade – Chester and Manchester.

The introduction of 'customary' tenancies and the rent inflation had different effects in the two halves of the country. In the south and east many of the small occupiers seem to have been bought out or edged out by richer men who wished to create large and profitable arable farms. By 1640 many small farms had disappeared and by the early eighteenth century rural areas consisted mainly of large commercial farms and considerable numbers of cottagers. Although this topic is outside the scope of this study an example is given in Chapter 11. The redistribution of wealth caused by 'customary' tenancies seems to have resulted, in the south and east of England, in the development of a society where perhaps 80,000 families owned freehold farms which were often let to commercial farmers paying a full market rent.[8] These farms formed the capital base of gentry families whose members usually pursued careers as officials, merchants, lawyers, clergy, and naval and military officers. In the North-West, by contrast, the small farms remained until the second half of the eighteenth century.

Before 1640 a few of the small farmers of the North-West became rich enough to educate their children for the Church, the Law and City of London companies – examples appear in Chapters 4 and 6. Many more expanded their business activities as traders, carriers, artisans and retailers, as examples in Chapter 4 illustrate. But the Civil War and Commonwealth period seems to have been a watershed in the North-West. Old customs and conventions that had inhibited technical and commercial change evaporated and people felt free to pursue business opportunities wherever they might lead. The families that were in possession of the many small farms each owned a small amount of capital. I suggest in Chapter 5 (iv) that as many as 25,000 families in the two counties may have had some capital by the 1660s. Examples of some of the great variety of business that sprang up are given in Chapters 7–10 and in my *Cheshire Cheese*.[9] By the middle of the eighteenth century many of these business families, much helped by the huge growth of trans-Atlantic trade, had amassed capital amounting to thousands of pounds and were busy investing it in every new technical and commercial project they could find (see Chapter 9). I suggest that it was the existence of so much capital in the hands of so

8 See Gregory King's tables, for example in Laslett, 1965, pp. 36–37 of the 1973 paperback.
9 See Foster, 1998, and also Foster, 2002, Chs 2, 3 and 4, for other businesses.

many dedicated businessmen that led to the famous technical innovations.

This leads me to the other main issue discussed in this book. Why were these families such enthusiastic businessmen? In trying to answer this question I seek to make a distinction between what I call 'gentry culture' and 'business culture'. The first was the way of life of the peerage and the landed gentry, the group that I usually refer to in this book as major gentry. The two families on whose archives much of the book is based form the two main examples of this group. The customs of these families – the way in which their capital was kept entirely in the hands of the head of the family and only very rarely divided when it passed from generation to generation, the manner in which they spent their incomes and treated their daughters and younger sons – are examined from several angles in Chapter 2 and in my *Seven Households*.[10] These were families who always had substantial capital but never engaged in trading activities. They managed farms, ran corn mills, exploited the minerals on their lands and did public service in Government and the military forces. Occasionally, a younger son might enter the Law, the Church or even a City of London company, but in the two families I describe the owners and their direct heirs never engaged in trade or manufacture. They were wise not to do so because their culture was not suitable. As Arthur Young wrote:

> I never knew a man of landed property, with the education and habits of landed property, attempt either [trade or manufacture] but they were infallibly ruined; or if not ruined, considerably hurt.

He goes on to suggest that

> the habitual inattention of country gentlemen to small gains and savings, which are the soul of trade, renders their success impossible.[11]

These families were the leaders of society, the highest status group in the land, so that many other families sought to join their group by adopting as many of their customs and attitudes as possible. This gentry culture spread widely beyond the families who actually formed the landed gentry; many successful businessmen in the South and East deserted business to become gentlemen.

Business culture had its roots at the other end of the social and economic spectrum. Most of the families who occupied farms in Cheshire and Lancashire in 1500 had been serfs (villeins or *nativi*) before the Black Death struck in 1350. The 'customary' tenants on all the estates whose papers I have examined did 'boon works' for their lord, they gave presents, such as hens at Easter, and they paid 'heriots' on

10 Foster, 2002, Chs 2 and 7.
11 Maxwell, 1950, p. 122.

their deaths. These were the badges of serfdom that went with their farms. These were families who worked for a living, a custom which they virtually all retained, however much capital they acquired, right up to 1770. As they grew richer in the sixteenth century and became more engaged in trading, they became less servile and more independent. This was reflected in an enthusiasm for reformed, 'Puritan', religion. Under the Commonwealth more extreme sects developed. The Quakers, who appear in my *Seven Households*, Chapter 4, and in Chapter 8 below, adopted practices which directly challenged gentry customs. They wore plain clothes instead of the brilliant colours favoured by the gentry. They kept their hats on at all times and addressed everyone as 'thou'. In this way they daily challenged the old hierarchical custom that every man should doff his hat to the gentry and call them 'Your Honour' or 'Your Ladyship'. After the Restoration the Quakers and many other 'Puritan' congregations were branded Nonconformists or Dissenters. Their meetings were obstructed, their ministers driven underground and their members' career opportunities were restricted. This powerfully reinforced their feeling of being different from the gentry and the Anglican clergy who dominated much of the South and East. Some of the business families described in Part 2 remained attached to their Nonconformist congregations after they made their fortunes; others never left the Established Church. Whether they were Nonconformist or not, north-western businessmen often continued in business for several generations.

Other strands contributed to the success of business culture in Cheshire and Lancashire. It was the normal practice in these families to divide their wealth approximately equally among all their children, male and female, and also to provide a 'portion' for each child when he or she became an adult. This custom probably predated the appearance of Protestantism and it contributed powerfully to maintaining a more equal society, in which a large number of families each owned a small amount of capital. In the South and East, gentry culture encouraged families to keep their capital in the hands of the eldest son who then used his influence to obtain posts in Government or the Church for younger brothers and sons. The suggestion put forward in this book is that it was the large number of capital-owning families in the North-West that allowed them to form a group strong enough to resist the lures of the status-dominated gentry culture, whereas, in the South and East, the smaller number of capital-owners, each on average richer than those in the North-West, were happy to join in a watered-down version of gentry culture.

Jane Jacobs has described the different ethical systems that form the foundations of 'business' society and 'government' society.[12] Each system gives support to

---

12 Jacobs, 1992. She calls them 'commercial' and 'guardian' syndromes.

people engaged in the appropriate activity – in business or in Government – but individuals with the 'wrong' ethical system for the activity they are pursuing are much less effective. Thus the major gentry, who were brought up in the ethical system suitable for government, did not do well in business. My 'business culture' includes Jacobs' 'business ethical system'. Historically, most human societies have been dominated by the 'government' ethical system and that could be one reason why they were usually slow at innovating their technologies. The development of the business society between 1500 and 1800 described in this book was an exceptional event that helps to explain why the north-west of England was able to improve its technology so rapidly.

The brief comparisons with other societies in Part 3 suggest that England was the largest European state in which wealth came to be owned by ordinary working families in the sixteenth century. The same phenomenon occurred in the western half of the Netherlands and seems to have been a major cause of the rapid technical and commercial developments there, which made it the most advanced European economy in the seventeenth century. There is some evidence from other European states[13] that local customs prevented the actual rents paid by tenants rising as rapidly as market values in the sixteenth century. Some tenants got richer and often became Protestants while monarchs, Church and nobles struggled to maintain their positions with stagnant revenues in an inflationary age. Some governments reacted to this by supporting the Counter-Reformation and by combining the efforts of the Jesuits with military force and a more active bureaucracy to re-establish the revenues which their absolute monarchies required. Others became Protestants but they too raised taxation. The victims of these policies were the small farmers who might have become businessmen. These states experienced sluggish technical and commercial development before the French Revolution. In France the land became widely distributed among a large number of nobles and urban bourgeoisie, but their culture was even more aristocratic than that of the English gentry. Internal trade did not develop as vigorously as in England and, as Arthur Young noted, there was no traffic in 1789 on 'one of their greatest roads within thirty miles of Paris'.[14]

The origins of the Industrial Revolution is a subject that has attracted many historians, economists and sociologists. The views of those who wrote before 1965 have been admirably summarised by R. M. Hartwell,[15] and many articles have been published since then,[16] but no consensus has developed. This book is not an analysis

---

13 See Ch. 11 below, p. 332.
14 Maxwell, 1950, p. 14.
15 Hartwell, 1967, pp. 53–80.
16 For example Wrigley, 2000, pp. 117–41, suggests that the development of the British coal industry was the key factor

of the origins of the Revolution, but a study of the social and economic development of a new type of society in a small area of the Mersey basin. From the analysis
of some unusually detailed archives two factors that have often been neglected
seemed to me so important that I have high-lighted them – the transfer of capital
into the hands of working families and the development of a culture that valued
business.

I have suggested that the society I describe in my area was typical, in many ways,
of the North-West and that it had more in common with society in the northern
colonies in America than with society in the south and east of England and in
Europe. Whether these suggestions are found to be convincing will depend on what
other historians discover when they draw pictures of other areas as detailed as the
one I have drawn in this book.

CHAPTER 2

Two Landed Estates: the Leicesters of Tabley, 1362–1832, and the Warburtons of Arley, 1500–1874

i) Introduction

This chapter describes these two landed estates[1] between the fourteenth and nineteenth centuries. The genealogy of the families is already well known from the work of Ormerod and others[2] so the various holders of the estates and their families are described only when their situation or behaviour affected the development of the estate and its income. The picture that emerges is that the incomes of the two estates were greatly reduced below what they might have been by the introduction of three-life leases in the 1540s. These three-life leases improved the gentry's position compared to other forms of customary tenure but nevertheless resulted in massive transfers of wealth from the landlords to their tenants.[3] Between the 1750s and the 1870s the estates slowly recovered their rights over their tenanted land so that, in that period, their incomes grew more than fivefold. This increase was at least as large as that obtained by most other groups in society and much greater than the rise in prices so these estates continued to occupy a dominant position in the country until 1914. The experiences of these two estates seems to have been common to many of the other old major gentry estates in Cheshire and Lancashire.

Much of this chapter describes changes in the incomes of the two estates. In the 150 years after 1355 as market rents doubled, their incomes also doubled, but after 1500, when market rents rose much more rapidly, they only enjoyed the benefit of the rise on the lands they farmed themselves. Their tenants got a large share of the higher values through the new system of three life leases. A gulf grew between market-related rents and the 'old' rents that the three-life leaseholders paid. This situation continued until the middle of the eighteenth century after which 'old' rents slowly disappeared and market rents became universal again.

The second subject that the chapter aims to illuminate is the way in which these major gentry families perceived their estates and their families, and how these perceptions determined the way in which they spent their income and treated their

---

1 See Appendices 2.1, 2.2, 2.3, 2.4. and Map 1.
2 Ormerod, 1882, Vol. 1. Leicesters, pp. 617–26, Warburtons, pp. 566–75.
3 See Ch. 3 (iii) and (iv), pp. 56–67. for a fuller discussion of the introduction of these leases.

children – what I call their 'culture'. From the many details of their behaviour we see the importance of the family name and of the big house in which they lived. For example when Peter Warburton of Arley found himself with six daughters and no son, he did not divide the estate between them and his many grandchildren. Instead he put it in trust for his great-nephews because they were named Warburton. Bequeathing it to a single male heir ensured that the estate was maintained as a single unit and not broken up. The same spirit determined the destiny of younger sons who were normally not given a share of the capital, but were encouraged to live on the estate, on a small allowance, so that they were available to inherit if the elder brother died. The example of Sir George Warburton, 1st Bt, carving off the manor of Winnington for his eldest son by his second wife, was a mark of his special affection for her and was a rare event in a gentry family. More typical examples of the lives of younger sons appear in the portraits of Sir Peter Leicester, 1613–78, and Sir Peter Warburton, 1708–74, in my *Seven Households*.[4] We see there that the basic expenses of the gentry way of life were not out of line with those of other prosperous people. Peter Leicester only paid £110 for his family's board and lodging in Dutton Hall, his mother-in-law's house, for the whole of the year 1648. This provided for himself, his wife and three children, plus four servants. After he had paid off his debts, most of Peter's large income of £1,000 a year was spent on his own and his wife's fine clothes, their coach with its horses and attendants and, most costly of all, the rebuilding of their house and the addition of an elegant chapel. These were all status symbols and his behaviour underlines the importance of status in gentry culture. The search for an improved status probably explains the Leicester family's continual pursuit of heiresses. To add another estate to the ancestral acres not only made the family richer, it also raised their status with other gentry. If the inheritance of the estate had to pass through a female it was important to ensure that the new owner adopted the old surname, in the way that the Byrnes changed their name to Leicester when they inherited Tabley. In all these accounts of members of the two families, we never find the owner of one of the estates or his immediate heirs entering into any career other than Government or military service. These families always owned large capital assets, but these assets were employed only in agriculture or mineral extraction, and they never invested either in a trading enterprise or in one trying to make or implement technical innovations.

ii) The Leicesters' estate

The marriage of Nicholas Leicester to the rich widow, Margaret Denbigh, in 1276 was the origin of the Leicester family's estate at Tabley. Margaret was the daughter

---

4 Foster, 2002, Chs 2 and 7.

Map 1. The main lands of the Leicester and Warburton estates.
All the townships identified in this map were in Bucklow Hundred except three on the southern edge – Witton, Nether Peover and Allostock – which were in Northwich Hundred. The last two are considered in detail in Chapter 5 (iv).

of Geoffrey Dutton, ancestor of the Warburtons of Arley. On her first marriage, he had presented her with two large farms in Aston by Budworth, called Wethale and Hield, and the manor of Nether Tabley (see Map 1). This manor was probably not very valuable at that time because the Hert or Heart family and others had 'charter' or 'freehold' land there. Charters usually fixed the rents forever at low levels but the occupiers of 'charter' land had military obligations which were valuable to their 'lords'. Nicholas and Margaret lived at Wethale. Their son Roger inherited their estate and added one-third of Over Tabley to it. Before he died in 1349 he had managed to buy all the 'freeholds' in Nether Tabley.[5] A survey and valuation of the estate in 1362 has survived (see Appendix 2.1). This shows the family living in a hall at Wethale surrounded by pasture, woods, and farmland. Most of their cash income came from a watermill and 27 tenants who were farming all the land at Nether Tabley and together brought in £19 19s 8d. Three freeholders and 15

5   C.R.O. Leicester of Tabley Papers. DLT/A14, A26, B13, B20.

tenants in Over Tabley contributed a further £6 13s 3d. There is no rental to tell us but these rents may have been lower than they were before 1349. In that year the Black Death arrived in England and as the death toll mounted there were fewer people to occupy the land. A striking example of the fall in rents after 1350 is provided by leases to Hield. In 1355, John Leicester granted a lease at £3 per annum to William Hield, his wife and their heirs. Later in the same year, in another document, the rent was reduced to £2 p.a.[6]

We can summarize the annual value of the estate in 1362 as follows:

Table 1. Leicester estate in 1362 (see also Appendix 2.1)

	Approx. area statute acres[7]	Annual rent or value £ s d	d per acre
Nether Tabley	1,107	19 19 8	4.3
Over Tabley	408	5 19 7	3.5
Hield	124	2 0 0	3.9
Wethale	264	3 15 4	3.4
	1,903	31 14 7	4.0

John Leicester was getting just £31 14s 7d a year from his 1,903-acre estate. At 4d per acre the annual market value of an acre of land was only the same as the 4d per day that a craftsman was paid. The other interesting fact revealed by this valuation is that the 1,844 oak trees on his lands were worth nearly £400. This may have been about the same as the capital value of the whole of the rest of his estate. Good oak trees were evidently scarce and valuable in this part of Cheshire in 1362.

The Leicester family seem to have established a family tradition of improving their estate in each generation. John Leicester fought under John of Gaunt in France in 1373–75. On his return he built the family's first house at Tabley in about 1380. This was his contribution. His children and their successors all added a little.[8] Then in 1465 the estate nearly doubled in size. Margaret, the wife of Thomas Leicester, inherited one fifth of the estate of her father, Robert Grosvenor of Hulme. As he had no male heir his estate was divided between his five daughters. The Leicester

6 DLT/B13/M13–15.
7 (a) The acreage is from the 1663 surveys (see Appendix 2.3). 70 acres of land in Over Tabley which was bought between 1558 and 1633 has been deducted. (b) In 1362 some land in these townships will have been woods, mosses/peat, and commons. Although not under the control of individual tenants it was as valuable to the community as their fields. (c) The O.S. measured 1,205 acres in Nether Tabley, but this included the lakes.
8 DLT/B20.

1. *Sir Francis Leicester, 1674–1742.*
Painted by Thomas Murray, in one of the elegant outfits in which he adorned fashionable London.

2. *Sir John Leicester, later the 1st Lord de Tabley.*
Painted by James Northcote, as Colonel of the Cheshire Yeomanry c. 1803.

3. *Tabley House.*
The only eighteenth-century Palladian country house in Cheshire.

4. *Peter Warburton, c. 1600.*
If he had had a son he might have been tempted to purchase an Irish peerage from James I as did other Cheshire gentry. On the other hand, perhaps it was his dislike of titles that made him decline the almost compulsory knighthood.

5. *Lord Alington.*

This fine portrait is thought to be of Lord Alington (*c.* 1642–85), father-in-law of Sir George Warburton, 3rd Baronet. He fought for the Hapsburg Emperor against the Turks in Hungary and is painted here in the clothes of an east European nobleman.

6. *Sir George Warburton, 3rd Baronet.*
A painting by Herman van der Mijn in about 1724, when Sir George's daughter married Sir Richard Grosvenor.

7. Arley Hall.

The new Hall built 1840–45. By 1840 Rowland Egerton-Warburton was enjoying the whole of the greatly increased income of the estate and he used it to build a new house designed by George Latham and closely modelled on the old Crewe Hall (partially destroyed by fire in 1866). This house had been built between 1615 and 1639 for another successful Elizabethan lawyer, Sir Randulph Crewe, Lord Chief Justice. The brick diaper work – a characteristic of the area – probably began almost as early as brick building itself. People discovered that they could make patterns with the black bricks, some of which were regularly produced in the hearths of the coal-fired kilns.

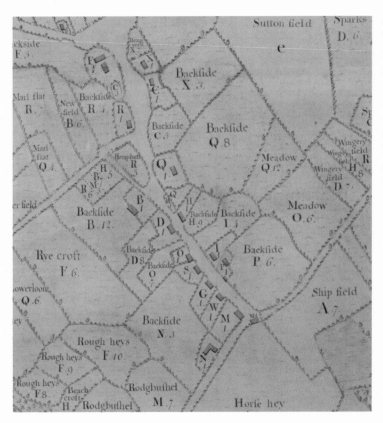

8. *Sutton Weaver.*
The village street as shown in the 1753 map. Each farm was given a letter and they are reproduced in Appendix 3.1. B1, C1, etc., always indicate the house and garden. Most houses had a 'backside' where the animals could graze close to the house.

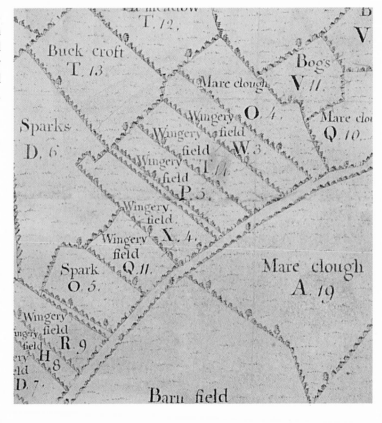

9. *Sutton Weaver.*
This detail of the Sutton map shows how the old common fields – Wingery and Sparks – were divided among the tenants.

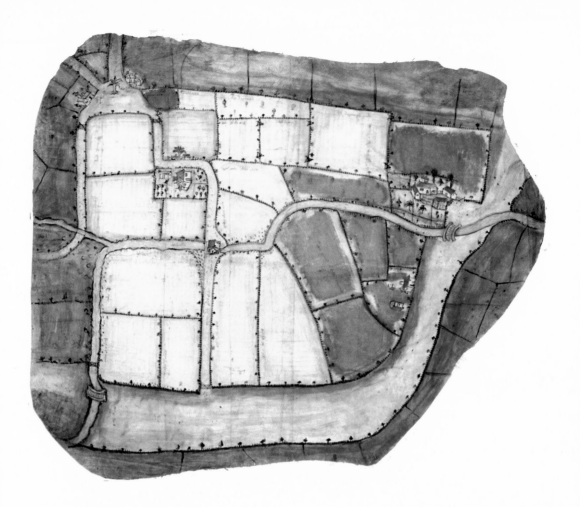

10. *The Cogshall estate in 1578.*

Notice the wide road to the south which was probably a 'Queens Highway' over which the estate had grazing rights. The packhorse bridges were not central so as to leave space for the ford beside them which was used by carts in the summer (see p. 133). The survey of this map was defective – see the correct shape of the estate in the shaded area of Cogshall in Map 3, p. 50. Compare this with the much more accurate map of Smithills in 1620 and T. Jackson's survey of 1649 (Foster, 2002, pp. 13 and 113) as examples of the technical advances in surveying skills and in instruments like theodolites, made in the late sixteenth and early seventeenth centuries.

11. *Burrows Hall.*
See text and also Foster, 2002, pp. 44–46 for the start of coal burning and the building of chimneys at Smithills in the 1590s.

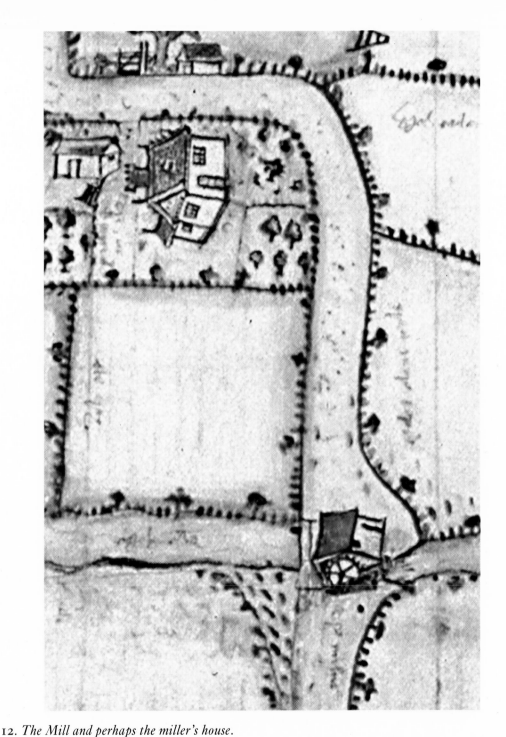

12. The Mill and perhaps the miller's house.
Was the miller a three-life leaseholder? Was this a corn mill or a fulling mill? (see p. 116–17).
Mills in the area were the subject of continuous craft-based innovation so that the great wheels
that powered the Titleys' new slitting mill at Partington in 1749 (see p. 256) will have been very
different to this simple installation.

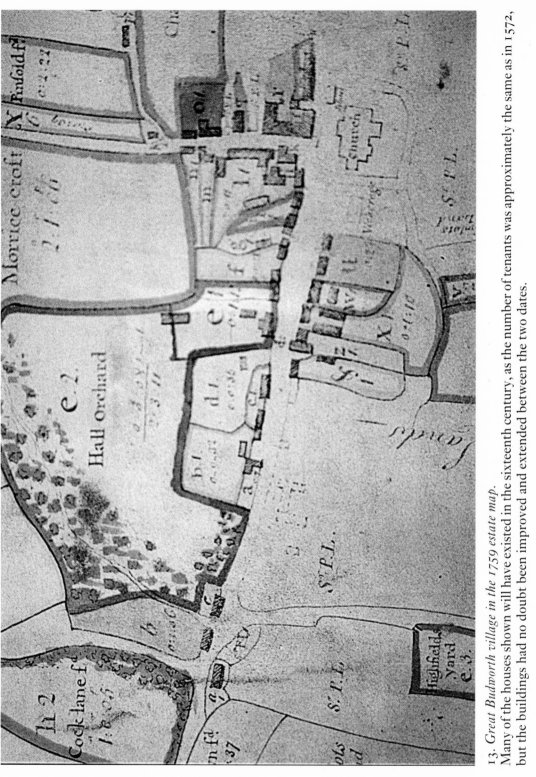

13. *Great Budworth village in the 1759 estate map.*
Many of the houses shown will have existed in the sixteenth century, as the number of tenants was approximately the same as in 1572, but the buildings had no doubt been improved and extended between the two dates.

family acquired half the manor of Nether Peover including Little Peover, one third of Over Alderley and one fifth of Allostock. They also obtained lands in Hope-by-Alstonfield in Staffordshire, which were sold piecemeal during the sixteenth century to provide the money to purchase other lands closer to Tabley.

The value of farmland in Cheshire had risen substantially by the beginning of the sixteenth century. This was probably because population numbers had recovered after the Black Death. In 1503 a valuation was made of the demesne lands in Nether Tabley, field by field. The total value came to £21 13s 8d p.a. Besides the demesne, there were 16 tenants living in the township. They paid rents of £16 7s 10d p.a. between them. So the total value of Nether Tabley had risen to £38 1s 6d.[9] This shows that the value of land had approximately doubled between 1362 and 1503.[10] In 1503 it was worth 8.3d an acre.

This change was not confined to Nether Tabley. A nearly complete rental of the whole estate in the year 1543 survives (see Appendix 2.2). This shows that the annual value of the '1362' estate had increased to £63 17s 9d, approximately double the £31 14s 7d it had been worth in 1362. The new estate inherited from the Grosvenors had rents of £30 8s 10d, making the annual value of the whole estate in 1543 about £94 6s 7d.

Up to this point it has been simple to set out the income of the Leicester estate. Two changes that occurred in the 1540s make it much harder to describe. First, there was a large increase in market rental values. Second, the tenants ceased to be lessees 'at will' paying a full market rent. They became three-life leaseholders. In these leases (which are described at greater length in Chapter 3, (iii) and (iv)),[11] the rent paid around 1530 remained fixed and became known as 'old' rent. Some of the increasing market value was reflected in a capital payment as each new 'life' was added to the lease. The annual list of tenant rents therefore ceases to tell the full story of the Leicesters' income because of the capital sums occasionally paid to add new lives. Full details about the capital payments have not been preserved in the archives.

The best evidence for the rise in market rents is provided by the rents paid for half the Hield farm. This farm, which had been let to the free (not serf) tenant William Hield in 1355, came to be divided between his two daughters. In 1500 the Leicesters bought one half back. Unlike the land occupied by the 'old' tenants, they usually rented out these 62 acres at a full market rent.

9 DLT/B13. The original in Latin is DLT/A72/2.
10 The progress of this rise can be seen in Leicester rentals of 1430, 1442–43, Edw. IV, 1485 and 1495–96 in DLT/B13 fol. 157–75.
11 A number of examples are given in Foster, 2002, Chs 3 and 5.

Table 2 sets out the rents they received for this land between 1355 and 1663, showing how these rents doubled between 1355 and 1503. They then increased nearly 19 times between 1503 and 1663. The really rapid rise occurred between 1543 and 1584. This phenomenon, often called 'the great Tudor inflation', happened all over Europe. In Chapter 3 (iii), p. 56, we examine how it affected different groups of people in the North-West. The rise in rents was much greater than that of food prices (which only increased 6½ times), while wages in the North-West merely doubled or trebled.[12]

Table 2. *Full market rent of half Hield, 1355 to 1663*

| | Rent | | | Rent per acre | | | |
	£	s	d	d (pence)		s	d
1355	1	0	0	3.9			
1503	2	0	0	7.7			
1543	2	5	0	8.7		s	d
1556	4	13	4	18.0	or	1	6
1584	18	16	4	72.8		6	1
1663	37	10	0	145.2		12	1

Sources: DLT/B84, B86, 5524/2/2.

Between 1543 and 1641, the Leicester family acquired a number of small properties. A farm in Wincham, adjoining their Tabley lands, was bought in 1548. In the same year they bought the freehold of a group of small tenanted properties in Great Budworth from John Eaton of Crowley. Before 1544 these had been owned by Norton Abbey (these properties are described in greater detail in Appendix 3.7, p. 100). It is likely that one attraction of this purchase was the prospect that a part of Budworth Heath might be enclosed. This happened soon afterwards and the estate's share was a new small farm adjoining Hield. In 1579 the family bought another one fifth of Allostock. Finally in 1601 they reacquired the other half of Hield. The sale of part of the Staffordshire lands seems to have provided some of the money for these purchases. The premiums, or 'fines', that the tenants paid to renew their leases may also have contributed.

Peter Leicester died in 1581 without male issue. Four days before he died he settled all the old Leicester family lands on his brother Adam. On the same day, Adam signed an agreement, no doubt after negotiations, to pay to trustees over a period of years the large sum of 3,200 marks (£2,133). The purpose of this fund was to provide portions for Peter's illegitimate children. If no agreement had been

12 Foster, 2002, p. 19.

reached the estate would have been divided between Peter's three legitimate daughters. Adam and the illegitimate family would have got very little. Peter's legitimate daughters inherited their mother's land in Staffordshire.[13]

The need to pay so much of the estate's income to this fund may have been the reason why Adam leased out parts of the Tabley demesne lands. Rough notes in an old rental suggest that he and his widow may have raised between £70 and £120 each year in this way between 1587 and 1611.[14] This demesne land was let in small parcels to 20 or 30 people. Many of the surnames listed are the same as those of Leicester customary tenants in Nether Tabley.

A remarkably complete view of the estate is provided by the survey and valuation of 1666 (see Appendix 2.3). This is part of the great archive left to us by Sir Peter Leicester (created baronet 1660), the famous Cheshire historian, who inherited the estate from his father in 1636. A more detailed account of his way of life is given in Chapter 2 of my *Seven Households*.[15] A number of surveys and valuations of parts of the estate survive from 1641 onwards. These all show similar values to those of 1666. This 1666 valuation therefore also provides us with a picture of the estate in 1641, on the eve of the outbreak of the Civil War. The document shows the area and value of every property on the estate and we know that the valuations were reasonably reliable.[16] The picture of the estate that emerges is shown in Table 3.

Table 3. *The Leicester Estate in 1666*

Type of land	Statute acres	True annual value £		Actual receipts £
Demesne	867	497	Rents paid and in kind	497
Tenanted	3,150	1,804		553
			Old rents – 203 Fines and heriots (one year with another) – 350	
	4,017	2,301		1,050

Source: Appendix 2.3.

13 DLT/B20, B57; Ormerod, 1882, Vol. 1, p. 622.
14 DLT/5524/2/2.
15 Foster, 2002, pp. 65–87.
16 See Foster, 2002, Ch. 3, p. 92.

The 867 acres of demesne lands yielded their full value. Part was leased at market rents, part was occupied by the family. The rents and services paid by the tenants of the remaining lands came to only £203 as against the true annual value of their lands of £1,804. Part of this was made up by the 'fines' and heriots[17] they paid when they renewed their leases.

These figures make it clear that in the Civil War period the estate had a market value of about £2,300 per annum and that the Leicesters and their tenants had shared the increase in wealth that the great rise in land values had created. Only £1,050 p.a. of the total was enjoyed by the Leicester family; the tenants, as a group, had rights to the other £1,250 p.a. This was a substantial capital asset which they had acquired between 1540 and 1640. However, despite this division, the Leicester family had also gained greatly from 'the Tudor inflation', their income from the estate in the 1640s being more than ten times what it had been in the 1540s. Sir Peter Leicester's careful delineation of the facts was probably done to enable him to calculate the price it was worth paying to acquire tenanted land. Throughout the seventeenth century the Leicester family were slowly increasing their demesne by buying land from tenants.

Sir Peter Leicester died in October 1678 and his wife in January 1679. Sir Robert, their son, died aged only 40 in July 1684. In these few years the shape of the family was greatly changed. Sir Robert's widow, Meriel (née Watson), was left with two young sons – Sir Francis, aged 10, Peter 8 – and a daughter, Meriel. Her parents were both dead but her grandfather, Francis Piggott, came to live with her at Tabley until he died in 1694. Her daughter, Meriel Leicester, received a portion of £4,000 on her marriage to Sir Pope Danvers in 1700 – a relatively large sum which suggests that the Leicester family now felt that they were considerably richer than they had been earlier. This may have been partly due to the long minority of Sir Francis and the acquisition, from his mother and grandfather, of the Watson and Piggott estates.

Francis and Peter Leicester went to Shrewsbury School in July 1685. That autumn they both caught smallpox at the school and Peter died. Francis was quickly removed by his mother and after Christmas, when he had recovered, she sent him to school in Manchester. In May 1688, before he was 14, he went to Eton where he stayed till December 1691.[18] He then broke with the Cheshire tradition of attending Brasenose College, Oxford, and instead went to St John's, Cambridge, from 1692–94, followed by two years travelling on the Continent. As a young man, he formed a close friendship with Peter Legh of Lyme who nominated him as Member

17 See Foster, 2002, p. 89, for an example.
18 DLT/B100.

of Parliament for the family seat at Newton, Lancashire, in 1715.[19] In London Sir Francis (Pl. 1) achieved the ambition of every young beau and married a rich young widow called Frances Thornhill. She was the only daughter and heiress of Joshua Wilson, from whom she had received the manor of Colton in Yorkshire, worth £350 p.a., and property in Sligo and elsewhere in Ireland worth a further £700 p.a.[20] After the sudden death of Bryan Thornhill within a year of their marriage, Frances was once more a rich and attractive potential bride. She was only about 22 when she married the 31-year-old Sir Francis Leicester in 1705. Unfortunately, they had only a single daughter whom they named Meriel. Lady Leicester died in 1716, aged 34.

In that year Sir Francis commissioned a survey and valuation of his estate, similar to that made by his grandfather in 1666 (see Table 4). His wife's estate was not included in this valuation but was settled separately on their daughter. Purchases

Type of land	Statute acres	True annual value (£)		Actual receipts (£)
Demesne	1,246	644	Rents	644
Tenanted	3,394	2,132	'Old' rents – 163 Fines and heriots (one year with another) – 300	463
	4,640	2,776		1,107

Table 4. The Leicester Estate in 1716

Source: DLT/B83

made with money from the Watson and Piggott families had increased the total area of the Leicester estate by 623 acres, and the true annual value had grown by £515. The demesne had increased by 379 acres. This had largely been achieved by not renewing leases on lands adjoining the old demesne. This new demesne accounted for all the £100 increase in annual income.

As heiress to all this property, Meriel would have been a very desirable bride. In view of her father's great friendship with Peter Legh of Lyme it is not surprising that she married his heir, Fleetwood Legh, in 1723. Two years later Fleetwood was caught in a storm while out hunting; the cold turned to pneumonia and within a week he was dead. At the time Meriel was expecting her second child and the shock was so great that she lost the child and nearly died herself.

19 He remained an MP until 1727.
20 DLT/B16 and B83.

Two years later when she had recovered, negotiations were begun for Meriel's second marriage. On this second occasion she was a slightly less rich bride because her mother's fortune was now in trust for her daughter by Fleetwood Legh. However, she was still a considerable catch, although possibly rather shy. After being introduced to one prospective young suitor she found the meeting so embarrassing that she wrote to her father asking him to choose a sensible man with a good estate for her.[21] The young man selected by her father was Sir John Byrne – a marriage which was to have a major impact on the fortunes of the Tabley estate.

The Byrne family had substantial property in Ireland and had acquired a baronetcy from Charles II. However, they had remained Catholics and under an Irish Act of 1704, Catholics were prohibited from inheriting land in Ireland. In about 1704, Sir Daniel Byrne had married Dorothy,[22] the only daughter of Edward Warren of Poynton in Cheshire, and a condition of the union was that the children should be brought up as Protestants in England. As a result Daniel and Dorothy's son, Sir John, had been able to inherit the Irish estates. The Warren family had originally proposed the match with Meriel and in 1729 the marriage took place on the basis that Sir John would sell his Irish estate and reinvest in land in Cheshire. It was agreed that if they had a son, he would take the name Leicester when he inherited Tabley. In the event, the sale of the Irish estate was deferred because several members of the Byrne family were still living there. Meanwhile, Sir John and Meriel lived happily together in Cheshire and produced five children, including two sons.

When old Sir Francis Leicester came to make his will, he made the proviso that the Byrne family, either Sir John or his sons, could inherit the Tabley estate only if they sold the Irish estate within two years of Sir Francis' death and reinvested in Cheshire lands. Whoever inherited then had to change their name to Leicester. This was all as already agreed so it raised no protests. But the unexpected happened. Both Meriel and her husband died before Sir Francis Leicester – in January and December 1741 respectively.[23] Old Sir Francis was by then so ill that he didn't realize the consequences of this disaster.

It was not until he died on 30 June 1742 that the lawyers read the will and realized that the Byrne heir was a boy of only nine who, as a minor, could sell nothing until he became 21 years old on 10 December 1753.[24] A private Act of Parliament had to be obtained to extend the time which he was given to sell the Irish estate to 23 January 1756.

---

21 DLT/C10
22 Born 26 April 1682.
23 DLT/D53 and D119.
24 DLT/D119.

In 1744 young Sir Peter Byrne added Leicester to his name and in 1753 he came of age. The value of his Irish estate had been estimated in the 1730s at between £50,000 and £60,000. By 1755 the growing confidence in the political and economic stability of Ireland had raised its value to over £100,000.[25] After the other members of the Byrne family had received their shares, more than £83,000 was available to invest in Cheshire lands.[26] This was a huge sum and it was difficult to find enough land for sale. The principal purchases were the manors of Marston and Witton and a large part of Over Tabley. These adjoined the old estate, but other purchases lay much further away. Between the 1750s and the 1830s there was a constant stream of land transactions due to a number of different factors. It was clearly desirable to concentrate the estate around Tabley, so distant lands, including parts of the ancient estate, like Over Alderley, were sold. All the nearby land that became available was purchased. Some old leases were bought from the tenants while others were not renewed. Farms were merged into larger economic units to be let at rack rents. Furthermore, agricultural rents were rising strongly throughout the period; by 1830, they were between two and three times higher than in 1750. As a result of all these changes on the Tabley estate, it is difficult to compare the size and value in 1830 with the figures for the earlier period. However, at its peak the estate extended to more than 10,000 acres and the rent roll reached more than £10,000 p.a.

Despite this wealth considerable debts were accumulated. Peter's son, Sir John (Pl. 2), created Lord de Tabley in 1826, lived very grandly and owed more than £130,000 at his death in 1827 which necessitated sales.[27] Luckily the estate had profited hugely from the development of the salt industry after 1760. The manor of Witton, which included much of the town and salt bearing lands of Northwich, had cost only £21,000 in 1757. In 1827 it was offered at auction for more than £100,000. With this sale and that of other outlying lands, including 1,000 acres in Allostock, the debts were brought under control and the estate reduced to about 7,000 acres. In 1832, the second Lord de Tabley inherited the Warren estate and added Warren to his family name. The full consequences of the marriage of Meriel Leicester and Sir John Byrne were at last realized after more than a century.

The great accession of wealth which the Byrne estate brought to the owners of Tabley was reflected in changes in their lifestyle. The old Tabley Hall in the Pool with its corn mills underneath was deserted in favour of the magnificent Tabley House, built between 1761 and 1766 to the designs of John Carr of York, which survives today (see Pl. 3). Sir Peter Leicester (he had by then dropped 'Byrne' from

25 DLT/D53.
26 DLT/D53.
27 More than £150,000 in one list.

his name) bought the lease to a house in Hill Street, Mayfair, from Lord Cornwallis in 1765 for £6,000.[28] After his death in 1770, Lady Leicester took her young family to live in this London house. Her son, Sir John, adopted an extravagant lifestyle, accumulating the enormous debts already mentioned. After Trinity College, Cambridge, he went on a grand tour around Europe in 1786–91.[29] Later he raised a cavalry regiment and became a friend of the Prince Regent. He bought a large collection of pictures by living artists and in 1826 he was ennobled as Lord de Tabley for his patronage of British art.

The Leicesters are a good example of a family who had built up a great estate by the middle of the nineteenth century through a long succession of good marriages. The honesty and moderation shown by the heads of the family in the important positions in local and national government into which their wealth carried them had made a valuable contribution to the development of English society.

iii) The Warburtons' estate

The Warburtons traced their descent from Odard, who appears in Doomsday Book living at Dutton on the River Weaver. Adam de Dutton, one of Odard's great-grandsons, assembled the Arley estate between about 1170 and 1210. His descendants became known as 'of Warburton' in the early fourteenth century after they had built their principal house there.[30] As a younger son Adam only received from his father the small manor of Sutton on the Weaver and he acquired much of the rest of the estate through his wife Agnes. After the death of her brother she became one of the heiresses of her father Roger, son of Alfred de Combray. Adam also bought lands including the manor of Great Budworth.

There appear to have been few sales or purchases of land between 1210 and 1572 when Sir John Warburton had a complete rental made of his 'freehold' estate (see Appendix 2.4). This document shows that the family's ownership of several manors had become only nominal as the legal system of land tenure had evolved in the medieval period. Apart from these manors, the estate had demesne lands and customary tenants on more than 10,000 acres. Some 1,200 acres of demesne land surrounded Arley Hall in Aston by Budworth. The family had built this house and made it their principal residence in about 1470. At Warburton Park, their earlier house, there was a demesne of about 300 acres and at Sutton Hall the demesne was 250 acres. The 'freehold' and customary tenants occupying the rest of the land paid 'chief' and 'old' rents of some £240 p.a. Parts of this substantial estate were leased

---

28 DLT/D409.
29 DLT/D155.
30 Ormerod, 1882, Vol. 1, p. 569.

to junior members of the family. Peter Warburton, Sir John's son and heir, lived with his wife and family at Sutton Hall while three of Sir John's brothers had life interests in various farms, including Hollin Hall beside Arley.

The only substantial addition to Arley's lands in this period was the Winnington estate. This happened in an unusual manner. Richard Winnington, the owner, married Joan Smith. He died in 1503, leaving two young daughters – Elizabeth aged 3, and Katherine, only six months old. Before he died he had settled his estate, the principal trustee being his wife's uncle William Smith, Bishop of Lincoln. By 1510, Elizabeth was the only surviving daughter and heiress. In that year the Bishop, as trustee, made a contract that Elizabeth should be married to Piers, Sir John Warburton's eldest son and heir. If Piers should die she was to marry the second son, John. When Elizabeth was 14 years old, Sir John would pay the Winnington trustees 80 marks (£53 6s 8d) every year until he had paid a total of 400 marks (£266 13s 4d). If she died the payments were to cease.[31] This was a risky contract for Sir John because if there was no child of the marriage to inherit the Winnington properties they would return to the Winnington family and he would have lost his money. Elizabeth and Piers were married in 1514 as soon as she was 14, but they probably did not live together immediately. Their son, John, was not born until 1523. Happily, he survived to inherit both estates. The Warburtons had thus acquired an estate of over 3,000 acres bringing in an income of about £120 p.a. and therefore probably worth more than £1,200. The Bishop had secured £266 to divide among other members of the Winnington family (see Appendix 2.4 for this estate).

In addition to their 'freehold' estate, the Warburtons acquired two leases in the sixteenth century on very favourable terms. One was from the Crown via the Duchy of Lancaster while the other was from the Church, in the shape of the Dean and Chapter of Christ Church, Oxford. We have already noticed how the value of Crown and Church lands was diminished by the appearance of 'customary' tenancies after 1540. These two leases show other ways in which the Crown and Church estates suffered while major gentry estates benefited.

The Duchy of Lancaster had long owned Northwood Park adjacent to Arley Hall. It was an old hunting ground of the Barons of Halton and was later to be known as the township of Crowley. In an official Progress around Duchy properties in 1476, this park had been discovered to be in a ruinous condition.[32] In 1502, the Duchy granted an 81-year lease to Sir John Warburton at a rent of £13 6s 8d p.a. This was approximately 2.3d an acre which was probably reasonable since only a small part was cultivated and the rest was old forest from which the useful trees had been

31 WM Box 1.
32 Myers, 1964, p. 8. See Map 1.

removed. In 1538 there still cannot have been much cultivated land there because the tithes were valued at only 10s a year. Evidence reviewed in Chapter 3 (vi) below suggests that, by the late 1540s, there was not enough land in the area to provide for the growing population. It would appear likely, therefore, that an area of some 1,100 acres in Crowley was divided into small farms before 1550. The remaining 300 acres would have remained moss (peat bog) or become roads. Unfortunately the Arley archives contain no rentals which would confirm this supposition.

In 1558 Sir John Warburton, grandson of the original lessee, paid £200 to extend the lease till 1656. He was to pay a doubled rent of £26 13s 4d p.a. after 1583.[33] The market rent of the Leicesters' farm at Hield in 1556 was 1s 6d an acre (Table 2, p. 16 above). If this was the value of the 1,100 acres of new farms in Crowley they were worth more than £80 p.a. and therefore had a capital value approaching £1,000. Sir John Warburton had thus renewed his lease from the Crown on very advantageous terms. In the only surviving underlease, dated 1623, Peter Warburton sold a 31-year extension of lease to Peter Richardson for £60. The rent of his 47-acre farm was £2 p.a. (10d per acre), plus boonworks and a heriot. There was also an obligation to provide a man with 'pike, corselet, morion, sword and dagger in time of war'.[34] If all the 1,100 acres had been re-leased around 1620 on these terms, Peter Warburton would have received some £1,300 in capital payments. The annual rents the tenants paid would have greatly exceeded the Crown rent.

The lease from the Dean and Chapter of Christ Church proved equally lucrative for the Warburtons, at the Church's expense. Young Peter Warburton inherited the Arley estate in 1575. One of his first acts was to purchase the lease of the tithes of Great Budworth parish. This was a large parish including some 35 townships and covering about 36,500 acres. In the Middle Ages the tithes had been owned by Norton Priory. The monastery had apparently found it difficult to get workmen to gather the tithes in such a large area and the farmers were only obliged to leave the tithe sheaves in the fields. The practice had therefore arisen for the Priory to sell the tithes in each township to a local farmer or landowner, who could conveniently gather the sheaves and cart them to his barn.

After the dissolution of the monasteries, the Court of Augmentations leased the tithes of Great Budworth for 21 years from 1537 to George Cotton for £82 2s 8d a year. The rectory of Great Budworth and this lease were later given to the Dean and Chapter of Christ Church, Oxford, as part of their endowment. In 1557 a new lease for 41 years at £82 2s 8d was granted to Elizabeth Shakerly, widow, of Hulme in Great Budworth parish. Ten years later, in 1567, Christ Church granted another

33 P.R.O. DL 42/32 f.330.
34 WM Box 48.

lease to Roger Daye of Eton, Berks, to run for a further 50 years after the expiry of the 41 years in the 1557 lease, still at the same rent of £82 2s 8d p.a.[35] Soon after inheriting in October 1575 Peter Warburton acquired these two leases, with the help of his friend, Peter Leicester, who seems to have discovered that they were for sale. We do not know, unfortunately, how much any of these people paid for these leases although a letter from Peter Warburton to Peter Leicester in 1575 would seem to suggest that he paid £200.[36] If this is correct it was a great bargain. The price of grain rose strongly after 1567. It climbed still higher after 1575, so it is no great surprise to find that this lease was valued at £1,300 in 1626 when Peter Warburton died. The lease still had 22 years to run, so with an interest rate of 8% this valuation implied a profit of £127 p.a. over the rent which Christ Church had been receiving (see Appendix 2.5 for a more detailed discussion).

The great rise in rental values that we have seen on the Leicester estate also occurred on the Warburton lands. The wealth that flowed in can be seen by comparing the inventory made after Sir John's death in 1575 with that made on Peter's demise in 1626, 51 years later (Pl. 4). The total value of Sir John's possessions was £773 while Peter's possessions were valued at £12,613. Of this just over £9,000 was in gold and silver including £8,445 in gold and silver coins. There were also the leases to Crowley and to the tithes valued together at £1,446. Peter's farming stock was not much different from his father's. He had 213 head of cattle, compared with his father's 209, but the value of both animals and grain had about doubled. £1,118 was invested in the farm in 1626 as compared with £450 in 1575.

Taking out the coin, the leases and the farm stock leaves a balance of nearly £1,600 for the contents of Arley Hall in 1626. This may be compared with the valuation of £323 in 1575. The only luxuries mentioned in 1575 were 18 cushions of tapestry valued at £3 6s 8d, and two cushions of purple velvet and cloth of gold at 13s 4d. Details in the 1626 inventory show the much more elaborate and costly way of life that had developed at Arley over these 50 years. Peter Warburton had a large collection of jewellery worth £45 and a great gold chain valued at the staggering sum of £122. There were Venetian glasses and Chinese dishes. In 1626 there were 952 oz. of gilt plate at 5s 2d per oz. and 835 oz. of ordinary silver at 4s 8d per oz. valued together at over £440, compared with the £100 worth of plate in 1575. Peter Warburton's wardrobe was extensive and included some 19 silk, satin or taffeta suits, 14 cloaks, 35 pairs of silk and 99 pairs of worsted stockings. The whole collection was valued at more than £128. He must have looked a proper gentleman in 'a hair coloured satin suit cut and raised, laced with silk and gold lace', enveloped in

35 Christ Church, Oxford. Great Budworth tithes.
36 DLT/B15 f.125.

'a silk grogren cloak lined with plash and six broad laces about'.

The satisfaction that Peter Warburton may have felt at the flourishing condition of the estate he was to bequeath may have been marred by the fact that, despite having six daughters, he had no son. To preserve this ancient estate in the Warburton family, he settled it on his grandfather's male heirs who were numerous. His great-nephew Peter, a young married man with two small sons, must have seemed a most suitable heir in 1625. Unfortunately, he died in February 1626. To try to prevent his six daughters, who were all married to local gentry, from wresting the estate away from the child heir, Peter altered his settlement to provide that all his money and chattels and the income of the estate during the minority should be divided among his six daughters and their husbands. Even these handsome gifts were not enough to deter them from trying. There is a letter at Arley from the children's mother to her kinsman the Earl of Bridgewater asking him to protect her children's estate from threatened lawsuits. Each of the daughters employed agents to manage their part and collect the rents.[37] No central administration appears to have been maintained and no manor courts were held. This jealousy between the six families seems to have been the reason why old Peter Warburton's inventory was produced in an exceptionally detailed manner. As historians we are able to profit from this.

Peter, the elder of the two children of the great-nephew, was married to the beautiful Eleanor Needham[38] when he was about 16 and she was 11. They never cohabited and he died at Oxford in 1641, aged 19.[39] His brother George came of age and inherited the estate about 1644.

One unfortunate effect of the failure to maintain an overall administration during the minority of George and his brother was that the estate lost control of Northwood Park – the township of Crowley. As the boundary of Crowley was only 100 yards from Arley Hall, it drew attention to the curious fact that the Hall was now extremely close to the edge of its large estate. This inconvenience to the Warburtons had resulted from Charles I's attempt to govern without Parliament. Charles had had to borrow heavily from the City of London Corporation in 1627–28. They demanded security so the Crown deposited property deeds with them, including the title deeds of Northwood Park. What had originally been conceived as a loan then became a sale. Amongst the property sold by the Crown was the freehold of Crowley.

37 WM Box 3.
38 Portrait at Tabley House, reproduced in Foster, 2002, p. 70.
39 These child marriages, like the Warburton/Winnington one mentioned earlier, were quite common in gentry families. The parties did not cohabit and the marriages could be annulled before they were consummated.

At the time this did not seem to matter as the Warburtons' lease ran to 1656, but in 1656, four men who had farms in Crowley – John Haslehurst, Richard Jackson, Thomas Mosse, and Robert Okell – contracted with the City to buy the freehold of Crowley on behalf of all the tenants and to sell each man his lands. The price was £6,250. Perhaps they found that some tenants didn't want to buy and were therefore unable to raise the money. In any case, they transferred the contract to Peter Brooke of Reddish, Esq, Robert Pickering of Moore, John Glendole of Chester, clerk, and John Fogge of Liverpool, clerk, who completed the purchase.[40] Robert Pickering, a lawyer, took Crowley Lodge, which the Warburtons had occupied, and kept a good farm around it. He renewed the leases of 13 tenants while about eight others bought their farms. Two investors, Richard Rutter of Moore and John Brotherton, bought large farms which they probably let at rack rent.[41] For the next 96 years the Warburton family owned no land in Crowley.[42]

Old Peter Warburton's six daughters had divided between them all the £12,613 worth of gold, silver and other possessions listed in his inventory. They had rented out all the demesne lands so that, with the rents and fines paid by the three-life leaseholders, they had enjoyed an income in excess of £2,000 p.a. between the six of them. They had also sold off outlying lands that had not been included in the Settlement and pocketed the proceeds. Young George Warburton inherited a bare estate in 1644 with no cattle, no crops and no furniture except what his mother could give him. He probably therefore continued to let much of the demesne. His tenants' desire to produce cheese for the London market may have encouraged him to build the cheese warehouse beside Frodsham Bridge in 1670.[43]

In 1641 George married Elizabeth, daughter of Sir Thomas Myddleton of Chirk Castle in Wales. They had two sons and four daughters before she died in 1650.[44] In about 1653 George married, as his second wife, Diana, daughter of Sir Edward Bishoppe of Parham, Sussex. They had no less than ten children, and after his death in 1676 she wrote a touching verse in memory of their affection for each other which can still be seen in Great Budworth Church. In 1673 Sir George[45] settled the manor of Winnington on Thomas, the eldest of his sons by Diana.[46] This was probably part of the arrangements for Thomas's marriage to Anne, the daughter of Sir Robert Williams. She and her sister, Gwen, were joint-heiresses of the Penrhyn estate in

40 C.L.R.O. Royal Contract Deeds 45.4, 45.5. See also Ashton, 1960.
41 DLT/B36.
42 Sir Peter Warburton bought Garland Hall farm in 1752.
43 Foster, 1998, pp. 7–8.
44 Myddleton, 1931, Vol. 1, p. 24.
45 Created Baronet in 1660.
46 WM Box 38.

North Wales. The Parliamentary influence of Gwen's husband, Sir Walter Yonge MP, and Sir George Warburton MP, combined with the doubtless legendary profits of the Winnington rock salt mines (see Chapter 7(ii)) seem to have been enough to secure the appointment of Jane, a daughter of this modest squire, Thomas Warburton, as Maid of Honour to Queen Anne. The story of her romance at court and marriage to John, Duke of Argyle, has been told by Lady Louisa Stuart.[47]

Peter, Sir George's elder son by his first wife, was married in 1673 to Martha, the only daughter and heiress of Thomas Dockwra of Putteridge, Hertfordshire.[48] Because his father's second family was living in Arley Hall, he settled in Hertfordshire and only visited Cheshire occasionally, even after he inherited in 1676. Despite this, he was conscious of the need to improve the income of the estate and with his manager he organized enclosures and the rearrangement of lands in Appleton. This created a number of large dairy farms to produce cheese for the London market.[49] When he settled the estate just before he died, he provided that three of these farms should always be let at full rack rents; the annual income of the estate was thus permanently increased.[50]

Peter and Martha had three sons. The eldest, Sir George, inherited Arley about 1698. In 1700 he married Diana, the daughter of a neighbour in Cambridgeshire, Lord Alington of Horseheath (Pl. 5), who became the heiress to one third of her father's large estate. Sir George served as MP for Cheshire between 1702 and 1722 although he never lived at Arley. The couple had inherited a house on the Thames in Hammersmith from her mother, a daughter of the Duke of Bedford, and they seem to have divided their time between this and the Hertfordshire estate. They had a son and a daughter before Diana died in 1705. After his son's death the following year Sir George sent his daughter to the country to protect her health and she was brought up with the estate manager's family at Aston Park near Arley Hall.[51] In 1724 she married Sir Richard Grosvenor of Eaton Hall, but they had no children and both were dead by 1732. With the death of all his legitimate children, Sir George (Pl. 6) and his large estate were in an interesting position. The Arley estate had been settled by his father in 1697 on the children of his three sons. Of these there was now only one survivor, Sir George's nephew Peter, a young man of 23.[52] Sir George now enjoyed ownership of all the Hertfordshire, Cambridgeshire, and

---

47 Home, 1899, pp. 1–20.
48 MP, St Albans, 1685.
49 Described in Foster, 1998, p. 14.
50 WM Box 38.
51 WM Box 24, Folder 2, Isaac Houghton's evidence.
52 Born 1708, Lilley P.R.

Hammersmith lands. At the age of 57 should he marry again and try to provide an heir? The course he actually chose was to install himself in a house in Albermarle Street, off Piccadilly, London, and to send his nephew Peter and his illegitimate son, Thomas Slaughter, to live in Arley Hall. Both young men were put on small allowances. Peter seems to have been introduced to other Cheshire families as Sir George's heir while Thomas Slaughter was given an ill-defined role in the management of the estate.

By the end of the 1730s, Sir George had sold all his estates in the south of England. Unlike the Arley estate which was settled on his nephew, he had personal ownership of these lands and he wanted to raise cash to give to his natural son, Thomas Slaughter. It seems to have been clear to everyone that he preferred Slaughter to his nephew and when he died in 1743 he left everything he could to him. All the contents of Arley Hall and the house in Albermarle Street, together with the family portraits and all his papers were given to Slaughter.[53] The total value was probably more than £50,000.

Thus in 1743 Arley was again inherited as a bare estate, this time by George's nephew, Peter, the 4th baronet. Out of the total area of about 9,609 acres[54], 2,116, let at rack rents, were bringing in about £1,200 (11s 4d an acre) and the remaining 7,493 acres, let on three-life leases, produced only £474 (1s 3d an acre). Sir George had contrived by clever legal moves to leave the estate with a debt of £6,000 to Thomas Slaughter. In order to discharge this debt Sir Peter sold Marthall, approximately 1,200 acres, for £8,800. The sale valued Marthall at only £7 6s 8d an acre, because all but about 80 acres was let on three-life leases. The valuation document (see Appendix 2.6) estimated the total annual value (rack rent value) of the land at £639 13s 8d (10s 8d an acre). At 30 years' purchase (the then going rate – equal to an interest rate of 3.3%) this would have implied a value of £19,190 (£16 an acre) for the whole estate if it had all been rack rent land. Three-life leases like this seem to have been still common on old estates throughout Cheshire and south Lancashire. By 1750 the land had been let on this basis for more than 200 years. Sir Peter Warburton had lived at Arley Hall with little money and no occupation for 13 years before he inherited. He may well have noticed that only a few of the three-life lease-holders were still farming and that many no longer even lived in the immediate area.[55]

In 1745 Peter married Elizabeth, eldest daughter of the Earl of Derby. They decided to stay at Arley, bring up their family there and live simply within their

53 Canterbury will, 1743.
54 Foster, 1992, p. 8. Foster, 2002, pp. 181–226, for the household of the 4th baronet.
55 See Foster, 1992, Appendix 2 (particularly 2.5).

income.[56] They seem to have formed a policy on the subject of three-life leases: that they would renew them only in Warburton and Great Budworth. These were both townships with a large number of smallholders and were intended to remain part of the estate. In Aston by Budworth and Appleton, the Warburtons would not renew leases on farmland. Instead they would buy any leases that were offered and any freeholds that came on the market. This would enable them to reorganize the land into economic dairy farms let on rack rents. In Pulford and in Sutton, which were both townships lying at some distance from Arley Hall, Peter would not normally renew leases. He hoped that this land would slowly rise to its full rack rent value as the leases fell in, and anticipated that the estate would have to sell these manors in the future. The proceeds would repay the mortgages they were going to have to take out to pay for their purchases of land in Aston and Appleton. The adoption of these policies meant that Sir Peter's income from 'fines' for renewing three-life leases was only one-third of what it might have been. His total income in the late 1740s was probably only about £2,000 p.a.[57]

Sir Peter pursued these policies with vigour. Income from new lettings at rack rents rose so that they were nearly £1 an acre by the time he died in 1774. However, farms were usually let for 14 or 21 years at a fixed rent so rising rents did not immediately affect the estate's income. At his death in 1774 the estate's income was approximately as follows:[58]

Table 5. The Warburton Estate in 1774

	£
Farms at rack rents	2,455
Value of demesne farm say	300
Old rents on 3-life leases	260
Fines on 3-life leases say	400
Mills and casual profits	325
	3,740
Less interest on £20,000 loans at 4%	800
Net estate income	2,940

Peter and Elizabeth's son, also Sir Peter, who became the 5th Baronet, sold the Manor of Pulford, near Chester, in 1778 for £19,000 in order to reduce the debts that his father had left him and to provide portions for his sisters' marriages. The

56 Lady Elizabeth's letter 25 July 1751. Arley Hall Large Box 7.
57 Foster, 1992, pp. 8–10.
58 WM Boxes 17, 18, 20 and 25.

valuation of Pulford in Appendix 2.7 shows that its 991 acres had a true annual value of just over £1,000. Because of the American War of Independence, the interest rate had risen to 4%. This meant that 25 years' purchase had become the going rate. Pulford would have been worth around £25,000 if it had been available for letting on new rack rents. That it sold for £19,000 (76% of full value) reflects the success of the policy of not renewing leases. 855 acres were either at rack rent or in leases with only one life remaining. This sale value compares favourably with that of Marthall in 1745 which realized only 46% of its full value because of the longer leases that existed.

Sir Peter, 5th Baronet, served as an officer in the Cheshire Yeomanry in the Napoleonic Wars. On the estate he continued the policies of his father. He bought more land in Aston by Budworth and Appleton and also provided portions for his sisters with money that he borrowed. To pay off all his loans he then sold the manor of Sutton in 1810. Unfortunately, the full papers have not survived but it appears from a valuation of that period that its 1,139 acres were estimated to have a rack rent value of £1,587 (£1 8s od per acre). It probably fetched between £30,000 and £40,000.[59] In 1813 when Peter died, the estate had a gross income of more than £7,200[60] which was more than double what it had been when he inherited 39 years earlier. He and his wife unfortunately had no children so he left the estate to the grandson of his sister, Emma, Rowland Egerton, then a boy of nine. Rowland's father added Warburton to his name so the boy was called Rowland Egerton-Warburton when he took possession of the estate in 1826, aged 21.

The policy of the two Sir Peters had been to obtain full possession of the main farms by not renewing the three-life leases, although they did renew the leases of smallholdings and cottages, particularly in Warburton and Great Budworth. In 1813 there were still 167 properties on these leases yielding total rents of only £130 p.a. As soon as Rowland's father, as guardian of his son, acquired control of the estate, he decided not to renew any of these leases. The annual rental value of the farmland reached approximately £1 10s 0 an acre by 1832[61] and did not alter much for the next 50 years. The estate income rose slowly from the £7,200 of 1813. The main farms were normally let on 14- or 21-year leases so it took some time for the new level of rents to be generally applied. The three-life leaseholds slowly fell in and by 1874 there were only 16 remaining. As these properties were relet at market rates, the estate income increased further so that in 1874 gross rents reached £14,000 p.a.

This was not all net income because the estate was now letting house property as

59 The receipts paid off a mortgage of £18,000 and Sir Peter had about £16,800 in cash and a mortgage at his death. The valuation is in WM Box 21.
60 WM Box 33.
61 See individual field valuations in WM Box 21/14.

well as land. To set against the gross rents was the cost of maintaining the buildings which had previously been the responsibility of the three-life leaseholders. The estate started to employ a large building staff. It is not easy to estimate the cost of building maintenance because Rowland also made substantial improvements to all the houses as they became his responsibility. If we put in a figure of £2,500 a year for maintenance of buildings, the net income of the estate's 7,500 acres in 1874 would have been £14,000 − 2,500 = £11,500.[62]

After about 350 years the estate had returned to a full market rent position on all its land. In 1525 the rent was about 8d an acre. By 1875 it had risen to £1 10s 0d, 45 times. Between 1540 and 1870 the money paid by the tenants was always less than the full market value of the land. From the 1560s to the 1620s the capital sums paid by the tenants as 'fines' for renewing their leases partly offset the low rents. Peter Warburton had built up a large cash sum by 1626 from these payments and the sharply rising value of demesne land. From 1750 to 1810 when the main three life leases of farms were not being renewed, the estate's income was correspondingly depressed. Fortunately for the estate owners in this period, their rack rents were rising strongly so that their total incomes rose gently.

These two estates seem to have been fairly typical of gentry estates in Cheshire and Lancashire.[63] Most of these properties were 'settled' by family trust deeds. Their 'owners' were legally only tenants for life. They could not sell the land, except as permitted by the Trust. Sir Peter Warburton, 4th Bt, had eventually acquired his estate outright because his uncle, Sir George, had refused to settle it on Peter's proposed brides and their children when he was the heir.[64] He in turn had trusted his son, Sir Peter, 5th Bt, to behave sensibly and had not wished to impede the necessary reform of the estate. His confidence was not misplaced.

The last Sir Peter, however, perhaps because he bequeathed the estate to a child, settled it on trustees so that Rowland Egerton-Warburton was only a life tenant. Sir Peter also left handsome annuities to his widow and his two sisters. He put the estate in debt to the tune of £15,000 to provide a legacy for his other married sister's family. The Egerton-Warburtons therefore did not have enough income to live at Arley for more than 20 years after his death and spent much of this period at Orleans in France

62 Rentals at Arley Hall.
63 Because the Leicesters bought so much land between 1750 and 1800, their archives include leases and court rolls from the Venables of Kinderton, Holford, Meredith, Brereton, Daniel, Warren, and Ashley estates in Cheshire. I have also examined some of the archives of the Earl of Derby, Legh of Lyme, and Scarisbrick estates in south Lancashire.
64 The estate had been settled by Sir Peter, 2nd Bt, on his three sons and their children in 1697. It was not possible to settle land on more than one generation of unborn children. Sir Peter, 4th Bt, was bound to acquire full ownership automatically unless he and Sir George, 3rd Bt, had agreed to resettle it before he inherited.

where living was much cheaper. See the new Arley Hall (Pl. 7).

In 1819 Rowland Egerton-Warburton was approached by Thomas Lyon, the successful businessman and banker of Parr and Lyon in Warrington. Lyon had a farm in Appleton and wished to acquire more land beside it so that he could build a new mansion. He also owned two or three farms in Crowley. He suggested that the Egerton-Warburtons exchange some of their Appleton lands for the Crowley farms. This proved an excellent arrangement for both sides. In the course of the next 50 years the estate acquired virtually the whole of Crowley paid for by the sale of lands in Appleton to the Lyons of Appleton Hall and the Parrs of Grappenhall Heyes.

The Arley estate was one of the largest in the Bucklow Hundred of Cheshire when it was created by Adam de Dutton before 1200. Apart from the acquisiton of Winnington there were no subsequent additions to the estate. On the contrary it slowly diminished in size and is now much smaller than it was, even in the nineteenth century. However, it is still in the ownership of the same family who acquired the original lands 900 years ago.

These two old major gentry families provide good examples of the stability of English gentry culture over hundreds of years. Many of the attitudes they had to their estates and their families when they emerged from the Middle Ages continued into the nineteenth century. They took a long view of their position as estate owners. The type of three life-leases they adopted in the 1540s allowed them to recover the full value of their lands in the eighteenth and nineteenth centuries. They were still the leaders of society at the beginning of the twentieth century and so had little reason to doubt that their 'gentry' culture had served them well.

There were about 100 major gentry families like this in the county of Cheshire. In the 850 years from the Norman Conquest to the outbreak of the First World War they ran the government of the county and represented it in Parliament. As is shown both in the stories presented here, and in the more detailed portraits given earlier,[65] these families normally married into other major gentry families in Cheshire or neighbouring counties, so most of them were related to one another. They met not only as families, but also at Quarter Sessions and the Assizes and at sporting events. Fear of being excluded from the group restrained the behaviour of members and allowed the establishment of the standards of moderation and compromise and of relatively honest and efficient government that became one of the characteristics of English life. As an élite group they had a powerful influence on the people around them so that their attitudes and values – their gentry culture – was a powerful social force.

65 Foster, 2002, pp. 65–87, 181–226.

Appendix 2.1. **Survey and valuation of John Leicester's estate in 1362**

	Annual value		
	£	s	d
Wethale			
The Hall with 61 acres (see note 2) of arable land and pasture land in the Park	3	15	4
Hield			
1 Free tenant: heirs of William Hield	2	0	0
Nether Tabley			
The watermill		10	0
Grazing in Ringwood	1	10	0
	2	0	0
Leaseholders			
Ralph, son of Hugo with Tack (see note 3)		15	4
Adam the smith with Tack	1	6	0
Adam Brandreth with Tack	1	15	4
Nicholas Webster with Tack		10	8
William Longford with Tack		18	0
Adam Radulhurst with Tack		15	8
William of Hales with Tack	1	8	4
William Hales, Junior, with Tack		10	0
John Godel with Tack		14	4
William Starthum with Tack	2	1	0
Vivian de Tabley with Tack		11	0
William Sonder with Tack		13	8
William Holden with Tack		14	4
William Burges with Tack		11	0
John Spendelow, chaplain, with Tack		6	0
Adam the cardmaker with Tack		7	6
William Bennet with Tack		13	0
Peter Dunne with Tack		8	0
William Litlour with Tack		3	0
John Litlour with Tack		5	0
John Yonnas with Tack		7	9
Hamo of Tofte with Tack		6	0
Richard the Baker with Tack		14	4
Richard of Watson with Tack		4	5
William of ——rthur with Tack		5	0
William Bote with Tack		3	0
John Robuk with Tack		6	0
Boons and autumn works		6	0
	£17	19	8
Total for Nether Tabley:	£19	19	8

Over Tabley

3 free tenants (list of names)		2 0
15 leaseholders (list of names) rents	5	11 3½
Boons and autumn works		6 4

Total for Over Tabley: £5 19 7½

Valuation of woods, Wethale

		s	d		£	s	d
In the park:	63 oaks worth	12	4	each	42	0	0
	103 oaks worth	8	0	each	41	4	0
	147 oaks worth	5	0	each	36	15	0
	210 oaks worth	1	6	each	15	15	0
In an orchard:	12 oaks worth	2	0	each	2	16	0
In the Lord's field:	102 oaks worth	1	6	each	7	13	0
	653 oaks total				146	3	0

Underwood and old fence pales   26 13 4

Total for Wethale: £172 16 4

Valuation of woods, Nether Tabley

	£	s	d
In Flittowe wood: 630 oaks	152	19	10
(similar list to Wethale with values of 10s to 6d per tree)			
In Kallerhey and various fields: 561 oaks	72	6	6
(236 valued at 10s to 2s; 325 at 6d)			

Total for Nether Tabley: £225 6 4

GRAND TOTAL: £398 2 8

Source: DLT/B82 and B84

Notes:
1. The original is in Latin. This is an abbreviated and simplified translation.
2. The acres in Wethale were Cheshire acres. See Foster, 2002, p. 62.
3. Sir Peter Leicester wrote a note in B84 saying that the rents of the lessees (terminarii) in Nether Tabley included their Tacks (short-term leases of parts) of the demesne lands.

Appendix 2.2. *The annual value of the Leicester estate in 1543 (rents paid plus value of demesne)*

		£	s	d	£	s	d
Nether Tabley	18 tenants	19	14	6			
	demesne (see note 1)	21	13	8			
Over Tabley	21 tenants	13	0	3			
Hield	2 tenants	3	5	0			
Wethale	6 tenants	6	4	4	63	17	9
Allostock	5 tenants	4	19	10			
Over Alderley	8 tenants	5	12	0			
Nether Peover	15 tenants	10	18	0			
Alstonfield	5 tenants (see note 2)	3	7	2			
Plumley	4 tenants	3	6	2			
Knutsford	3 tenants	2	5	8	30	8	10
Total value of estate:					**£94**	**6**	**7**

Source: DLT/D37/11 and B13 folio 166.

Notes
1. The demesne was not valued in 1543. To complete this Appendix, I have inserted the 1503 value. This should perhaps be increased by 11% in line with the rental increase between 1503 and 1543 shown in Table 2, page 000.
2. This township's rental for 1543 has not survived. The figure shown is from the 1554 rental.
3. See Appendix 3.2 for more details of Nether Tabley tenants, 1543–44.

Appendix 2.3. *Survey and valuation of the Leicester estate in 1666 (summary)*

	Statute acres	True value £	Rent now paid £	Value of services £
Demesne lands				
in Nether Tabley	720	376	376	
2 water corn mills	–	40	40	
in Over Tabley	122	68	68	
in Wethale	25	13	13	
Total demesne:	867	497	497	
Tenants				
19 in Nether Tabley	387	239	20	6
22 in Over Tabley	357	215	18	5
10 in Sudlow	200	120	5	3
4 in Nether Knutsford	–	20	6	–
7 in Wethale	239	123	15	3
7 in Hield	124	75	5	1
1 in Marston	80	40	1	1
1 in Pickmere	24	12	6	–
1 in Aston	24	11	1	–
13 in Great Budworth	57	46	4	1
4 in Northwich	–	22	11	–
5 in Plumley	88	55	3	1
23 in Nether Peover	385	231	18	6
10 in Little Peover	96	63	7	2
14 in Allostock	517	255	33	7
20 in Over Alderley	566	274	13	1
1 in Shurlach	6	3	–	–
Total tenants:	3,150	1,804	166	37
GRAND TOTALS:	**4,017**	**2,301**	**663**	**37**

Sources: DLT/D44. B81, B86 have similar surveys 1663–69.

Notes
1. The survey details each field of the demesne and each tenant's land. For details of tenants' land in Nether Tabley see Appendices 3.2 and 5.2. For details of tenants' land in Nether and Little Peover and Allostock see Appendix 5.1. For details of tenants' land in Hield see Appendix 3.8 and Foster, 2002, pp. 113–14. For details of tenants' land in Great Budworth see Appendices 3.7 and 3.8. For details of tenants' land in Aston by Budworth see Appendix 3.8.
2. Sudlow was a hamlet in Over Tabley township.
3. Nether Knutsford was the township in which Knutsford Town lay, so these were urban properties.
4. In Northwich, one tenant rented a salthouse, representing 3 wichhouses or 12 wallings of brine. The other 3 tenants rented shops or houses.
5. The tenant in Aston was the Berry family. Most of this farm was bought in 1668 by Thomas Jackson. See Foster, 2002, pp. 102–04.

Appendix 2.4. *The Warburton estate in 1572*

THE OLD WARBURTON ESTATE

Township	Lord of manor	Demesne acres (approx.)	Free-holders	Annual 'chief' rents £ s d			Lease holders	Annual old rents £ s d		
Warburton	√	300	6		7	8	39	27	11	7
Lymm	½	–	5		13	3	13	3	12	5
Aston-by-Budworth	√	1,200	9	2	5	2	26	23	1	5
Great Budworth	√	–	2		4	2	42	18	0	11
Comberbach	√	–	1		4	0	7		4	8
Appleton	√	–	10	1	0	3	26	26	3	0
Stockton and Hull	√	–	7	2	0	7	–	–		
Newton by Daresbury	√	–	8	2	0	5	2	2	16	0
Warrington (Lancs)	–	–					1	1	19	3
Sutton (Weaver)	√	250	1		9	2	22	17	9	11
Sub-total								120	19	2

THE WINNINGTON ESTATE

Township	Lord of manor	Demesne acres (approx.)	Free-holders	Annual 'chief' rents £ s d			Lease holders	Annual old rents £ s d		
Winnington	√	? 150					28	33	5	4
Northwich							13	17	7	8
Anderton							1	1	8	2
Witton							1	1	8	8
Lostock Gralam							1		12	0
Allostock	⅕						7	5	0	8
Hulse							1			4
Marthall	√		2		–		23	21	2	10
Pulford	√		6		2	4	17	24	18	3
Chester							17	14	11	11
Sub-total								119	15	10
Grand Total				9	7	0		240	15	0

Source: Ornamental rental in Arley Hall and WM Box 1

Notes

1 The old Warburton estate also included 'overlordship' of freeholders in Nether Walton, Stretton, Sale, Hatton, Over Tabley, Nether Tabley, Lithe ultra Dee, and Happesford. These rights seem not to have had commercial value by this date. Notice how the old Warburton estate, approximately 9,000 acres, only yielded the same 'old rents' as Winnington's 3,000 acres. Perhaps grand old landowners like the Warburtons were less interested in rents in 1500 than in the military service due from their freeholders. Compare this with the tendency for noblemen's estates to include many copyholders.

2 A number of the Warburton freeholders were owners of large neighbouring estates, who owed (but perhaps did not pay) small chief rents. Many others owned farms which paid larger chief rents.

3. The Northwich leaseholders included 6 men who were renting 7 salthouses. The other 7 had houses and land.

4. See Appendix 3.1 for more details about Sutton tenants 1539-1753. See Appendix 3.3 for more details about Appleton tenants 1545–72. See Appendix 3.8 for more details about Great Budworth and Aston by Budworth tenants, 1572–1628.

Appendix 2.5 *Great Budworth tithes, 1623–1761*

1. There is a list of the tithes paid for half a year in 1623.[1] 42 people paid a total of £110 12s 10 ½d, implying an annual payment of £221 5s 9d. The largest payments were by Mr Shakerly (of Hulme) and Mr Starkey of Stretton, who each paid £10. Mr Marbury paid £5 and Mrs Leicester £1 13s 4d. Roger Wright paid only 1½d. The area for which each person was paying is not specified.

There is no payment from the Warburtons. In the period 1537–63, they had paid £6 3s 4d p.a. for Budworth, Aston, Winnington, and Crowley.[2] They may also have paid a capital sum of £30 for a lease for years at a fixed rent. Including a reasonable notional contribution from the Warburtons, the total annual tithe collected will have been in excess of £230 p.a. This provided a surplus of about £148 p.a. over the fixed rent of £82 2s 8d. There was an obligation to maintain the chancel but the 1626 inventory valuation was probably a conservative one.

2. After 1648, Christ Church made their own arrangements to collect tithe.[3] The only figures in their file showing what they collected are:

    1696   £529 p.a.
    1726   £675 p.a.
    1761   £841 p.a.

The 31-year moving average price of wheat did not change greatly between 1620 and 1760[4] so it appears likely that £230 p.a. was a sadly low figure for the value of the Great Budworth tithes. In Peter Warburton's inventory of August 1626, his grain in the fields of Aston by Budworth was valued at £218. His demesne was only 41% of Aston by Budworth, so it would seem that £53 would have been a reasonable figure for Aston in the 1620s. In 1761 it paid £62. £53 is 85% of £62, so perhaps Great Budworth tithes were worth around £715 p.a. in 1623 (i.e., 85% of £841).

We are left with the feeling that Peter Warburton was charging his neighbours only about one third of the real values of the tithes they were collecting. Having enjoyed such low figures for so long before 1648, the gentry of the parish who gathered the tithes were reluctant to pay more. It took the Christ Church 'managers' a century to raise the sums to more realistic levels.

1 WM Box 2.
2 WM Box 1, Folder B, and Beamont, 1866, pp. 65–69.
3 See Foster, 1998, p. 68–9 for a detailed description.
4 Hoskins, 1968.

Appendix 2.6. *Valuation of Marthall, 1744*

Type of lease	Actual rent paid £ s d			True annual value £ s d			Valuation Multiplier	Value (£)
Rack rent								
2 tenants	44	3	8	44	3	8	× 30	1325
One-life								
3 tenants	3	8	11				× 7	24
				52	0	0	× 16	832
Two-lives								
8 tenants	10	7	11				× 10	104
				196	10	0	× 13	2554
Three-lives								
18 tenants	21	6	10				× 12	256
				347	0	0	× 11	3817
Totals:	**£79**	**7**	**4**	**£639**	**13**	**8**		**£8,912**

Source: Cheshire R.O. DET 3229/31 in Sir Peter Warburton's handwriting

Notes
1. The final agreed value was £8,880.
2. Observe that the multiplier used in the valuation declines from 30 for land let at the full annual value to 16, 13, and 11 for land where the purchaser will not get possession until 1, 2, or 3 'lives' have died.

Appendix 2.7 *Valuation of Pulford, 1778*

Type of lease	Area statute acres	Actual rent paid £ s d			True annual value £
Rack Rent					
8 tenants	318	268	8	0	309
One-life					
8 tenants	537	19	0	2	563
Two-lives					
3 tenants	136	6	16	9	139
Three-lives					
1 tenant	0.5		6	0	4
Freeholds					
2 chief rents			8		
Totals:	**991.5**	**294**	**11**	**7**	**1,015**

Source: WM Box 28

Notes
1. The agreed value was £19,000.
2. No capital values are given in the survey document.
3. Most of the farms on rack rents were let on 14- or 21-year leases at fixed rents which were below the current rental values.
4. The sale also included the advowson of the rectory. The glebe and tithes were valued at £100 p.a.

CHAPTER 3

Changes in the distribution of wealth in the sixteenth century

In this chapter we examine in detail the way in which most families who occupied land in 1540 acquired, in the following century, valuable property rights in their small farms. The old medieval society, in which the major gentry – the Lords of Manors – owned almost all the wealth and the mass of the population had very little, passed away. However, during the century a new group of poor people, owning little or nothing, developed underneath the propertied families who came to occupy a position in the middle.

We begin by examining the whole community in the Bucklow Hundred of Cheshire, through a study of their tax assessments in 1545. The different groups in this society are identified through their wealth. At the top was a small group of about 25 major landowners. At the bottom were some 1,500 tenants. In between were about 50 lesser families with an income from land and about the same number of families with similar wealth derived from other occupations – the Church, the Law, and trade. By comparing the taxpayers in several townships with the rentals of the landowners who owned these entire townships, it is established that the taxpayers were normally living on small farms with an average size of 30 acres. Virtually all the households living in these townships were taxpayers. It appears that there was not much relationship between the size of farms and the wealth of families. The richer taxpayers without a landed income were scattered widely over the Hundred, Knutsford being the only township with a concentration of traders. The portrait of this society is unusual in that it reveals almost no poor families unable to pay tax, at least in the rural areas owned by the big estates, though that may not have been the position in Knutsford and other towns, about which we have no information. It is clear from the rural rentals that there were no other rent-paying houses in the townships described here in detail.

The way of life on these small farms is described in this and the following chapter and in Chapters 1, 3, 4 and 5 of my *Seven Households*.[1] In 1545, every household had enough land to grow its own food and access to common land on which it could graze a cow, a pig and a few sheep, so that they were all self-sufficient. The common land also provided supplies of peat for fuel and timber to repair houses, carts and ploughs. An efficient household lived well, a hopeless one starved and fell apart.

1 Foster, 2002.

The tax-paying households no doubt contained old and disabled people who were not capable of supporting themselves.

The next section describes the impact on this society of the large increase in market rents after 1540. From about 8d an acre in the 1530s, rents rose to around 11s an acre in the 1630s. The freeholders and the tenants of the Crown were the two groups who did best. The tenants of gentry also improved their position significantly because they ceased to pay the full market rent. Instead, they had a privileged tenure as three-life leaseholders. The major gentry thus lost their commanding position and became merely dominant. An attempt is then made to explain how this transformation came about. An unexpected chain of events appears to have greatly diminished the value of the Crown's landed estate. When rents first rose Government ministers thought the movement was both transitory and undesirable and left rents fixed. For 20 or 30 years they seem to have been too distracted by religious questions to concentrate on the subject. When they did focus on it, in the 1560s, market rents were three or four times what they had been 30 years earlier. The Crown apparently decided that it could not risk the unrest that might be caused by asking for such an increase, so they did nothing and hoped for the best. One effect of these changes was a large increase in the number of freeholders. By the 1660s, perhaps as many as 500 families in Bucklow Hundred owned some freehold land.

From the analysis up to this point it would seem that almost every family living in Bucklow Hundred before 1540 had a small farm with enough land to grow their own food. After about 1540 there seems not to have been enough unoccupied land left for this pattern to continue. As the population grew, some families had to be accommodated in cottages with only a garden, so they had to buy food. The price of food rose about 6½ times in the century after 1540, while a labourer's wages only rose from 4d to 9d a day. Thus the position of those families dependent on their wages to buy food deteriorated badly. The lucky ones had a cottage and a garden to help them cope, but many of those without became vagrants and beggars.

The chapter ends with some illustrations of the way of life in the townships. The arrangements of the farms and the fields in Sutton Weaver in the sixteenth century are described. Many of the same families continued to live there until the eighteenth century. Around 1600 they divided up the old common fields to give each family their own land. A different view of country life is provided by a map of Cogshall in 1578 which shows the construction of the houses and the mill. Finally the changes in Great Budworth after 1540 are examined. The sale of the old monastic lands after the Dissolution of the Monasteries created a new group of independent freeholders at the top of village society. They too enclosed much of the common land and, like the inhabitants of Sutton Weaver, they did not use the land to provide more housing for the poor. The country had become the preserve of better-off people while the poor were crowded into the towns.

ii) The distribution of wealth shown by the 1545 Tax Return for Bucklow Hundred

The 1544–46 'lay subsidy' was the most comprehensive tax raised in Cheshire in the sixteenth century.[2] Every person having lands or goods valued at £1 or more had to pay.[3] There were different rates for lands and for goods and and all the rates were steeply raked. In this return, lands worth £20 p.a. or more paid 5%, while lands worth £1 p.a. paid only 0.83%, or 2d in the pound. There was no one with goods valued at more than £20. Those assessed at £20 paid at 3.3%, while the poorest people with goods worth only £1 paid 0.416%, or one penny.

Map 2 shows the townships in Bucklow Hundred and the number of taxpayers in each township in this return. Unfortunately, two 'membranes' (sheets) of the return have been cut out so that the figures for about 12 townships are missing. These townships have been left blank on the map. Altogether about 1,648 names appear in the return. These people were living in 57 townships extending over more than 60,000 acres. Who were these taxpayers? What can we discover about them?

A brief examination of the document shows that there were four main groups. Some 25 major landowners paid tax on lands assessed at more than £10 p.a. The Warburtons and the Leicesters were among them. There were 52 others assessed on smaller amounts of land. We know from other sources that all these people owned freehold land.[4] The other 1,571 taxpayers were taxed on their goods. There were only 58 people with goods worth between £10 and £20, so 1,513 people were assessed on goods worth £9 or less, of whom 1,270 had goods worth £4 or less.

In Appendices 3.1 to 3.4, the taxpayers in four of the townships are listed opposite the tenants in the same townships. From an analysis of these lists it appears that we can make the following statements:

---

2 34 and 35 Hen. 8 c.27. The return is in C.R.O. DLT/F64. There is a good discussion of the problems of interpreting these early Tudor tax returns in Hoyle, 1987, based on exceptionally good archives relating to the Yorkshire dales from Keighley to Sedbergh.

3 The rates are set out in the Statute and in Tait, 1924, p. xxvii. Collection was spread over the three years 1544, 1545, 1546. This return lists the tax collected in 1545. In 1544 the tax collected from all those with lands worth less than £10 or goods worth less than £20 were taxed at double the rates shown in the text. I am much obliged to Paul Booth for help over this.

4 These people were known at the time as charterers, because each had a document or charter that was his title deed. It specified how much rent he had to pay as 'chief' rent. As the amount of the rent was fixed, inflation in the sixteenth century made these rents insignificant. Their owners became known as freeholders partly for this reason and partly because they had originally been 'free' men not 'serfs'.

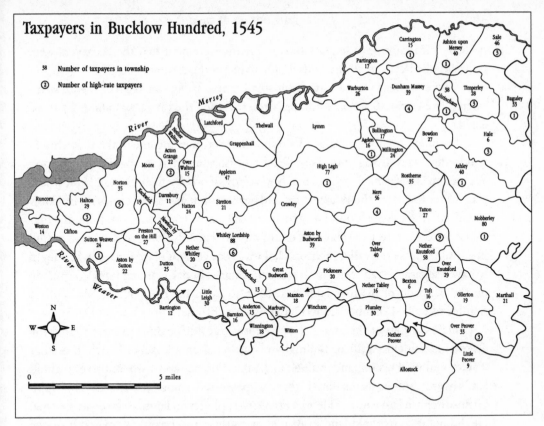

Map 2. Taxpayers in Bucklow Hundred in 1545 *together with Witton, Nether Peover and* Allostock in Northwich Hundred.

1. Taxpayers were normally the heads of all the households living in the township. For example, Sutton Weaver was a township wholly owned by the Warburtons so their tenants were the only inhabitants. Appendix 3.1 shows the 22 names in the rentals of 1539 and 1572, and the 23 taxpayers of 1545. A large number of the names are the same. The notes to the Appendices suggest reasons why the lists are not identical. The township of Nether Tabley, which was wholly owned by the Leicester family, provides a second example. The rental of 1543 is compared with the taxpayers of 1545 in Appendix 3.2. Apart from Peter Leicester himself, 15 people paid tax and 14 of their names appear in the rental. There are four other names in the rental but we do not know why. In the other townships there are substantial similarities between taxpayers and tenants, but there are also large disparities. An important reason for these is that the rentals are not contemporary with the tax return. In Whitley Lordship the rental is of the year 1526/7; in Appleton it is 1572. There were a total of 175 taxpayers in these four townships – more than 10% of the total in the whole tax return. The evidence may not be quite

perfect, but it appears adequate to support the statement that the taxpayers were normally the heads of all the households living in the townships.[5]

2. These families were all living on small farms. In Sutton Weaver the 22 farms ranged from 7 to 78 acres, while in Nether Tabley the range was about 17 to 60 acres.[6]

3. People normally paid this tax on the whole of their income in the township in which they were living. For example, Lady Elizabeth Savage paid tax in Sutton Weaver on lands valued at £140 p.a. She was evidently living in Sutton Hall, which she was renting from the Warburtons and her assessment was the largest in Bucklow Hundred. She was a widow and a trustee of the family lands. Her son John, the heir to the Savage estate, aged about 19 or 20, was presumably living in Rocksavage Hall in Clifton, across the valley. Sutton Hall was a convenient place for Lady Elizabeth to have a separate establishment. It was a fine house, built for young John Warburton on the occasion of his marriage in 1486/7 to Jane, the daughter of Sir William Stanley of Holt, Chamberlain to Henry VII and brother of the Earl of Derby.

Other examples of this practice make for greater difficulties in interpreting the original document. William Bellingham was living on a leasehold farm in Nether Tabley and paid tax on lands valued at £3 p.a. I do not know where these freehold lands were, but it seems likely that he possessed some.[7] In the case of John Grimsditch we know more. He was taxed in Appleton on lands assessed at £10 p.a. He did not own freehold land in Appleton, but was presumably living on his large leasehold farm there. The family also owned Grimsditch Hall in Nether Whitley and a large freehold in the Warburtons' manor of Newton by Daresbury, which paid an annual chief rent of £1 0s 2d. The family did not pay tax in 1545 in Nether Whitley, so John Grimsditch was paying in Appleton for all his lands. These two examples illustrate that freeholders were not only happy to own leaseholds as well as their freeholds, they were also content to live on their leasehold lands. It may be useful to observe that Appleton is close to Warrington and Nether Tabley is beside Knutsford. These men may have preferred the greater social life that probably existed near towns. Later we will find other small landowners living in rented houses in Great Budworth, possibly for the same reason.

4. Some families who owned freehold land paid tax on their goods because the Act required the Assessment to be on whichever category yielded the most tax to

---

5 Other sixteenth-century rentals of townships in Bucklow Hundred support this view.

6 These figures are calculated from the 1543 rental at 8d an acre – the average rent. The Norburys' farm, which was the largest in 1663, was then measured as 64 acres. In Whitley there were about 77 farms on 2,393 acres, which works out at about 31 acres each.

7 If we did not know from other sources that the Leicesters owned the whole of Nether Tabley, we might have thought Bellingham had a freehold in Tabley.

the Crown. For example, in the Warburtons' manor of Appleton, there were 17 freeholders as well as 26 leaseholders listed in the 1572 rental (Appendix 3.3). There were 47 taxpayers in 1545. At least five of the freeholder families, whose freeholds were presumably of small value, seem to have paid tax on their goods – a Dainteth, a Hill, a Johnson, a Warburton, and a Watt.

5. There seems not to have been a close relationship between the size of a farm and the tax assessed on the occupier. For example, in Sutton Weaver the goods of the families with the two largest farms, the Challoners and the Martins, were valued at only £1. Ralph Drinkwater, on a more typical 33-acre farm, had goods worth £10. Because of the steeply raked tax rates, he paid 3s 4d, whereas the Challoners and the Martins only paid 1d each. This disparity suggests that farming was not the main determinant of the wealth of these families. Their other occupations may have been more important.

The picture emerging from these statements is that the Tax Return lists almost all the families living in Bucklow Hundred in 1545. Except for a small number of gentry families and any poor families in the towns, they were all living on small farms. Most of these farms were probably leased from the gentry but some were freehold. The type of tenure does not seem to have been important for this tax in 1545. We can see why this might have been. The average size of the farms was 30 acres. Leasehold rent of 8d an acre made an annual total rent of £1. If the 'chief' rent paid by the freeholder was 4d an acre, his rent was 10s a year. His economic position was not greatly different to that of the leaseholders and the annual value of his freehold was only 10s p.a.[8]

A closer examination of the various groups tells us more about this society. At the peak of Bucklow society, both socially and economically, stood the large landowners. Appendix 3.5, Table A, lists the 25 people whose lands were valued at more than £10 p.a. The list is headed by Lady Elizabeth Savage (£140 p.a.), whom we have already met. The next two are Sir Peter Dutton (£133 p.a.) and Sir Peter Warburton (£100 p.a.). These three families between them paid tax of £18 13s 3d, or 21% of the £89 paid in the whole return.[9] The 25 landed families in Appendix 3.5 paid £47 12s 3d or 53.5% of the total. Below these major families there was a group of 16 people assessed at values between £5 and £10. Eight of these were junior branches of the main families, while eight had other surnames, such as Grimsditch mentioned above. At the base of the landed pyramid were another 36 people assessed on lands valued at £5 or less, of whom 21 had the same surname as one of the 25 major gentry. So the whole of the 'landed' society was quite a small group amounting

8 See Foster, 2002, p. 103 for Berry – a freehold paying a chief rent of 6d an acre.
9 Erasures and damage in the manuscript made all the figures approximate.

to only 77 households out of 1,648. Among these 77 there were less than 50 different surnames.[10]

There is evidence that the tax assessments substantially undervalued the wealth of taxpayers so we probably need to multiply the assessed values by between three and four times to get an idea of the actual values of the householders' goods and rental incomes. We have seen that the Leicesters of Tabley had a gross estate income of £94 p.a. (see Appendix 2.2) at this period.[11] £94 was 4.7 times the £20 value they were assessed at in Bucklow. The Warburtons had gross rents of about £250 p.a. In addition to their tenanted land they had around 1,900 acres of demesne.[12] This may have been worth about £100 p.a. in 1545. If these figures are right their total income was around £350 p.a., three and a half times their assessment of £100 p.a. The value of the Savage estate in 1532 has been calculated at between £321 and £548 p.a.[13] which would have been about three times the assessment of £140 p.a. This under-assessment seems to reflect the great separation of the North-West from the rest of the country. The Cheshire and Lancashire gentry had their own Palatinate Law Courts so they hardly needed to go to London. They evidently knew that London-based officials did not have any evidence of their wealth so that they were safe to understate it. As we shall see below (p. 54) it was different in Yorkshire and we know that London merchants' attempts at under-assessment were corrected by the Government.[14]

We have seen earlier that, of those who were assessed on their goods alone, the richest were the 58 people with goods valued at between £10 and £20. Who were they? Where did they live? We have also seen that the great majority of taxpayers were living on small farms, and a study of Map 2 reveals that they were distributed fairly evenly across the countryside. The large townships like High Legh and Mobberly had large numbers – 77 and 80; small townships like Daresbury and Keckwick had only 11 and 19. One township stands out as an exception to this rule. Nether Knutsford was not large but it had 58 taxpayers. The other numbers (in circles on the map) show the number of highly assessed taxpayers in each township. These too were widely distributed across the Hundred, 23 townships having at least one. There were nine in Nether Knutsford, much the largest concentration in the

---

10 Appendix 3.5, Table B.
11 The Inquisition Post Mortem (IPM) on John Leicester, in 1543, valued the Estate income at £63 p.a. DLT/B15, folio 163. There may have been jointures and allowances to younger sons of which we are ignorant. IPMs were held after the death of all owners of land held directly from the Crown.
12 Appendix 2.4.
13 Ives, 1976, pp.19–20.
14 Hoskins, 1976, p. 21.

Hundred. Knutsford was the nearest thing to a town in Bucklow and these highly rated taxpayers were presumably the leading traders there. A further 11 taxpayers there were rated between £5 and £9, so it would seem that Knutsford contained at least 20 families in business. The township with the next largest concentration of rich taxpayers was the Whitley Lordship (Map 3 and Appendix 3.4), with six altogether. We examine this unusual township in more detail shortly.

Two other neighbouring townships had an unusual number of these rich men – Norton with five and Halton with three. These seem likely to have been connected with Norton Abbey and the administration of the Hundred Court in Halton. Rather than traders, these people may have been lawyers and priests. The other group of highly assessed taxpayers occurs in a ring of townships around Altrincham – Hale with three, Timperley with three, Sale with three, and Dunham with four – a total of 13. Altrincham and nearby Hale had had 'urban' centres in the Middle Ages. It seems likely that these were both already small towns in 1545. Possibly rich traders preferred to live in the adjoining country rather than in the urban centres themselves.

The Whitley Lordship was the largest 'township' in Bucklow Hundred with 88 taxpayers in 1545. It was owned by the Duchy of Lancaster (the Crown). It was, in fact, at this period divided into six townships: Over or Higher Whitley, Antrobus, Middlewalk, Sevenoaks, Cogshall (see Map 3) and Crowley. This last, it will be remembered, had been leased to the Warburtons in 1502.[15] Its history was therefore quite different and it is not discussed here.

Two sixteenth-century rentals of the Whitley Lordship survive. The first, from 1526/7 (18 Hen. 8), is a list of the rents paid by 77 tenants (Appendix 3.4, col. 1). 59 of the taxpayers in 1545 had the same surname as one of the tenants 18 years earlier in 1526/7. This illustrates the continuity of the ownership of these tenant families. Many of the families continued to live in the Lordship throughout the sixteenth century. 26 of the 1526/7 surnames are also to be found, both in the 1595 rental and in the 1626 survey. Some 13 or 14 families lived on the same farms throughout. For example, Piers Lowton paid a rent of £1 1s 11d in 1526 and John Lowton was paying the same rent for the 36-acre farm in 1612. This survey shows that the size of the landholding that went with a farmstead varied from as little as seven or eight acres up to about 51 acres, the average being 31 acres.

There were 88 taxpayers in 1545, rather than the 77 one might have expected from the 1526 rental. One reason for this was that the Lordship included about 1,000 acres of freehold land. Apparently, in 1526/7 no chief rents were paid for this, but the 1595 rental includes six chief rents. Details about these freeholds are given at the end of Appendix 3.4. The extra 11 taxpayers of 1545 were probably living on

15 See page 23–4 above.

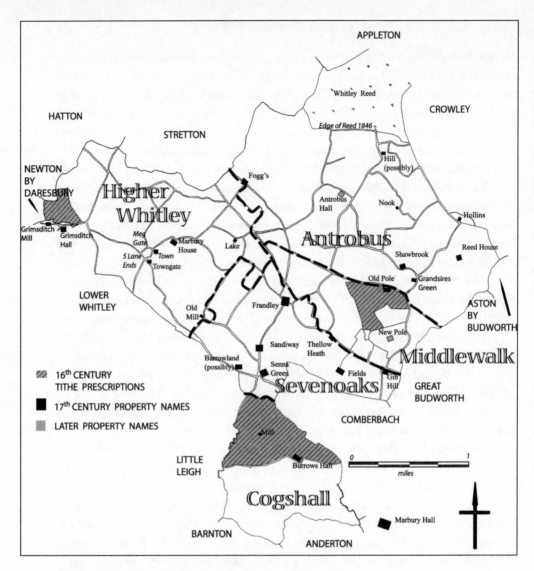

Map 3. *The Whitley Lordship and its five townships.*

Appendix 3.4 shows that there were 77 farmhouses and 41 cottages on the copyhold land in 1612 and probably 10–20 houses on the 1,000 acres of freehold. Most of these dwellings will have been on the same sites as buildings marked on nineteenth-century maps, but they are not shown here because until that century houses were usually named after their owner, e.g., Lowtons, etc. Only where there were several families with the same surname did houses get their own names, e.g., Eaton of the Pole; Daken of Hill, etc., so this is the character of the farm names marked. It can be seen that Higher Whitley was the only township with a village centre; all the rest of the houses were scattered among the fields. Antrobus Hall, a nineteenth-century name, may have been where the Venables and Antrobus families lived in earlier centuries.

Tithe prescriptions usually applied to gentry demesne lands over which the vicar had, in the fifteenth or sixteenth centuries, agreed that the 'small' tithes (on animals) would be a

these freeholds. The Whitley Lordship was all flat Cheshire plain land so it is not surprising that it was all fully settled by 1526/7.

Four of the nine freeholders we know of were major landowners – Marbury of Marbury, Massie of Rixton, Starkey of Stretton and Warburton of Arley. They paid tax elsewhere and they will have had tenants on their lands. Grimsditch paid tax in Appleton as we saw earlier. We know nothing of the taxpayers in the three families who may have owned smaller freeholds.

Only two families actually living in the Lordship paid tax on their lands. Robert Venables paid on a value of £20 p.a. This was the same value at which the Leicesters were assessed. We have seen on p. 48 that the Leicester estate at this time was worth about £94 p.a., and extended over nearly 4,000 acres. The Venables estate was presumably of comparable size. This branch of the Venables of Kinderton (near Middlewich) family had purchased the Antrobus family's lands in the Whitley Lordship in the middle of the fifteenth century. The Inquisitions *Post Mortem*, made after the death of Robert's son Thomas in August 1578 and that of 1583 show that the family had lands in 15 Cheshire townships as well as in Antrobus, Over Whitley and Cogshall.[16] The second person to pay tax in 1545 on his lands in Whitley was John Crosby, clerk in holy orders, whose land was assessed at £15 p.a. The Crosby family had one or more farms in at least six different townships in the area.[17]

As well as these two men with lands, there were six people in Whitley who paid tax on goods worth £10 or more. One is tempted to think that Richard Crosby (£15) and John Venables (£14) were junior members of the landed families. Two other men, Peter Colstenstock and Robert Eaton, were members of two large family

---

Map 3 continued

fixed annual sum so that a count each year was not required. They therefore provide evidence of the existence of ancient demesne lands.

The township of Middlewalk disappeared into Antrobus in the eighteenth century, probably because the Eaton family of the Pole acquired so much land in the township that there were no longer a sufficient number of householders to carry out in rotation the township duties of constable, overseer of the poor, etc. The boundary of Middlewalk is based on the surviving evidence of deeds, etc., and may not be correct.

The land covered with peat, which was the main fuel in the sixteenth century, was mostly in the low-lying areas bordering Northwood Park/Crowley (hence the name Parkmoss), through which flowed the Gale Brook which partly drained the Whitley Reed.

The ownership of land in these townships continued to be widely distributed and in 1785 over 100 individuals paid land tax there. Among the largest payers was Thomas Woolrich (see pp. 251–4) for three farms let to rack-rented tenants.

16 Ormerod, 1882, Vol. 1, p. 658 and C.R.O. CR 63/1/226/32.
17 IPM after the death of Thomas Crosby, who died 16 September 1595. C.R.O. CR 63/1/226/27. There was no freehold land in Whitley listed in this Inquisition.

groups. The Colstenstocks had five farms in 1526/7 and five members of the family paid tax in 1545. The Eatons had six farms and six taxpayers. Each family also had one member whose goods were highly valued: Robert Eaton's at £10 or £15[18] and Peter Colstenstock at £12. We don't know for sure what either man did. This Robert Eaton was probably the same as the man who married Ann, daughter of William Port of Ilam, Staffordshire, a brother of Sir John Port, justice of the King's Bench. This seems to make it likely that Eaton who lived at Sandiway in Sevenoaks, was a successful lawyer. He bought part of the Norton Abbey estate from John Grimsditch in 1544. Because this estate was held by knight service, it was the subject of an Inquisition *post mortem* after his death on 23 November 1557.[19] A Hugh Colstenstock was apprenticed in the Drapers' Company in London in 1498. The name is sufficiently unusual to suggest a connection between the Whitley family and the London textile trade. Of the other two rich men in Whitley – Thomas Highfield, £10, and Randle Richardson, £12 – we know nothing. That there were such rich people living on small farms in the middle of the country suggests that they had other occupations. The main road to London ran through Whitley so they may have been traders.

Before leaving the Tax Return of 1544–46 we need to compare the picture it has given us of Bucklow Hundred with the view it provides of two other areas. The return for the neighbouring south Lancashire Hundred of Salford is conveniently in print (see Map 4).[20] It discloses many similarities to Bucklow. There were a total of about 1,500 taxpayers in the surviving incomplete return. About 92 people were assessed on lands. The 22 richest paid £41 17s 0d of tax as compared with £46 2s 3d paid by the same group in Bucklow. There were about 91 people assessed on goods worth £10 or more, compared with the 58 in Bucklow. 39 of them were in the large town of Manchester/Salford which shows that it was presumably a much more substantial place than Knutsford. Many of them were also much richer. Adam Byrom was assessed on £80 in goods while ten others had their goods valued at more than £20. Manchester was a real trading centre and it was also a much more populous place than anywhere else. There were 256 taxpayers in Manchester and a further 51 across the river in Salford. With 307 in the whole urban area it had more than five times the population of Nether Knutsford with its 58 taxpayers. There

18 An erasure makes an uncertain reading.
19 Ormerod, 1882, Vol. 1, pp. 615, 657 and P.R.O. Ches/3/72 No. 4. This inquisition disclosed that he owned ten small farms. Seven were in Comberbach, which had belonged to Norton Abbey. He had one each in Budworth, Lymm, and Over Walton. His son Richard, who died in 1577, passed the same lands to his son John. IPM 7 January 1578. CR63/1/226/32. See Appendix 3.7 for the lands bought from Norton Abbey. The area of land mentioned in these IPMs is usually only roughly indicative of the actual size of the properties, and so is not quoted here.
20 Tait, 1924, prints the 1545 return for Salford.

Map 4. The North-West of England.

was, however, nowhere else in Salford Hundred that was recognisable as a town except perhaps Prestwich, where there were seven taxpayers assessed on £10 or more.

If these two Hundreds were broadly representative of lowland Cheshire and Lancashire we can say that it was a countryside of small farms averaging about 30 acres each. There were a small number of powerful landowners with great estates.[21] Substantial areas of demesne lands were attached to the great houses on these estates. Most of the small farms were lived in by their tenants, a few of whom were freeholders, though not economically very different from the other tenants. By 1545 the plains of the two counties were well filled up with these farms. There was little 'spare' land in those townships which we have examined in detail. There were only a few urban areas and there were large differences in wealth between the great landed families and everyone else. There was only a small middle group which, in Bucklow Hundred, consisted of 52 families with lands and 58 families whose wealth probably derived from the Law, the Church or trade.

How did Cheshire and Lancashire compare with other areas? Bordering Cheshire and Lancashire, across the Pennines, is the West Riding of Yorkshire and Ralph Smith has analysed the Tax Returns there for 1543–46,[22] (see Map 4). The first great difference that strikes one is that the Yorkshire gentry seem much richer than those in Cheshire and Lancashire, the richest being assessed on lands valued at £533 and £400. However this turns out to be an illusion resulting from the much more accurate assessments made in Yorkshire. Smith lists the assessments of six major gentry families in Yorkshire and then gives their incomes as revealed in other contemporary documents. Their six incomes total £1,473 and their six assessments add up to £1,226.[23] This seems to confirm that, for the reasons given earlier on p. 48, we probably need to multiply all the assessments in Bucklow Hundred by around three to make them comparable with Yorkshire. If we do this the numbers and wealth of the landed gentry seem similar on both sides of the Pennines.

The second great difference seems to relate to the different agricultural systems used on the two sides of the Pennines. Smith takes as an example the town of Selby, lying beside the Ouse in the heart of the great plain of the Vale of York. This was grand grain-growing country from which considerable quantities were often exported via the port of Hull. A survey of Selby, part of the estates of the former Selby Abbey, was made in 1540 and listed 220 dwelling sites and 236 tenants, but the tax return of 1545 only has 113 taxpayers and only 60 of their names occur in

21 The Wirrall Hundred return shows no gentry estates.
22 Smith, 1970, Ch. 3.
23 *Ibid.*, 1970, pp. 290–93; Cheshire had a long history of under-assessment. See Foster, 1992, p. 54 for under-assessment of the land tax, *c.* 1750.

the survey. The discrepancy between the number of dwellings and the number of taxpayers suggests that half the households in the town were too poor to pay tax and the reason that only 60 of the 236 tenants listed in the survey paid tax seems likely to be that many of the residents were not direct tenants of Selby Abbey, but were sub-tenants.[24] This contrasts sharply with the rural Cheshire townships we have examined where virtually all the tenants were both residents and taxpayers. Unfortunately we have no evidence for the town of Knutsford which may have been different, but let us first examine why the Yorkshire plain was so unlike the Cheshire and Lancashire plains.

In arable country like the Vale of York the nobility and the monasteries were more important as landowners than they were in the North-West. For example, seven of the ten largest landowners in East Yorkshire in 1530 were ecclesiastical, two were Earls and the last was the Crown.[25] Both they and the other gentry had large farms let to tenants. Smith lists 20 of them, *c.* 1535, which contained a total of 4,516 acres and so averaged 225 acres each.[26] Large areas of grain cultivation like this created a demand for large numbers of workers at harvest time. This seems to have led to the existence in arable country of large nucleated villages or small towns, where this labour force lived. When they were not required in the fields, these workers made textiles, rush mats or baskets or practised some other labour-intensive activity in their cottages. As plenty of grain was produced in these communities it was always on sale in local markets or elsewhere, so these workers did not need lands of their own. Half the inhabitants of Selby in 1545 were probably poor families of this type renting their cottages or even only rooms from richer men who were tenants of Selby Abbey. They were paid for their textiles or their agricultural work by the week or the month and bought their food in the town.

In Cheshire and Lancashire the farming system was quite different. As we have seen the land was all divided into small farms. The principal wealth of north-western farmers was always in their cattle. A cow was worth around 10s in 1500 so a two- or three-cow family are likely to have had a total wealth of at least £3 or £4.[27] If the gentry let their large demesnes, which at this period they probably only did when for some reason the family was not resident in the big house, they let them as grassland to their adjoining tenants.[28] Normally only 10% to 15% of the land in each farm was growing grain each year and the rest was pasture or meadow. Each

24 Smith, 1970, pp. 100–03.
25 English, 1990, p. 10.
26 Smith, 1970, p. 279.
27 Foster, 2002, p. 59, for later cattle values.
28 See, for example, Appendix 2.1 above where each of the tenants had a 'tack' of demesne land in 1362, or p. 17 above.

household usually grew just enough grain for its own use, and with its own farming equipment and animals of all kinds it was, at this period, a self-sufficient farming unit.[29] The families who constituted these households and owned everything on their farms therefore had valuable 'goods' in 1543–45 and it could be that, if they had been fully assessed, the lowest value for the goods of any household would have been £3 or £4, i.e., three or four times their actual assessment. This analysis seems to imply that there may have been few poor people in Bucklow Hundred in 1545. It certainly would appear from the evidence of rentals and surveys that there were very few in the rural townships although there may have been more in the towns. In section (vi) below the appearance of poorer families in the rural areas soon after 1545 is described.

The third great difference between the communities in the West Riding and in Cheshire and Lancashire was that land values seem to have risen earlier on the Yorkshire side of the Pennines, so that the small copyholds and freeholds on which many upland families lived had acquired a property value by 1545–46, as explained more fully in section (iv) below.

iii) The impact of the rent revolution on this society

It is well known that food prices rose sharply in the sixteenth century. They were 6.44 times higher in 1640–49 than they had been in 1450–99.[30] This used to be explained as the result of the influx of precious metals from the New World. This view has recently lost favour and has been replaced by the idea that growing populations put pressure on the food supply and forced up prices. The phenomenon was European-wide and there is evidence from across Europe that populations were recovering from the effects of the Black Death by the end of the fifteenth century. We have seen earlier (Ch. 2, Table 2, p. 16) that market rents on the Leicester estate rose from 7.7d an acre in 1503 to 12s 1d an acre in 1663. This was in line with general national trends as seen in Fig. 1.[31] which show that rents rose around 18 times in this century and a half. However, the wages of farm workers in the North-West only doubled from around 4d a day to between 8d and 10d a day. Our interest in this section is to examine how this substantial increase in the market value of land affected the various groups of householders whom we have identified as existing in 1545. In (vi) below we examine the effect of these changes on the poor.

We will start with the small freeholders because their position was the least

29 See Foster, 2002, Chs 1, 3, 4 and 5, farming sections.
30 Thirsk, 1967, p. 595.
31 South Midlands figures from Allen, 1988, p. 43; North Cheshire from Table 2, p. 16 and Table 4, p. 19; later from Arley estate valuations. See also Clark, 2002, pp. 281–308, for charity rental values, 1500–1914.

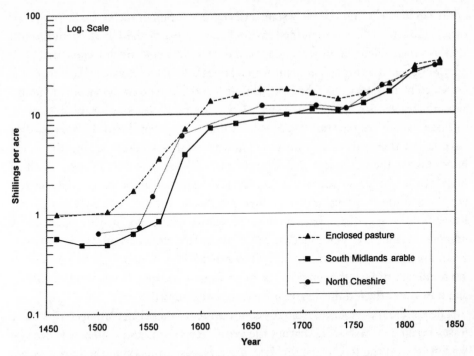

Figure 1. The full annual value or rack rent of agricultural land, 1450–1850.
Sources: *Enclosed Pastures and South Midlands Arable*, R. C. Allen, Econ. Hist. Rev., XLI 1 (1988), p. 43; North Cheshire, above Ch. 2, Table 2, p. 16 and Table 4, p. 19 to 1716. Arley surveys later.

complicated. These were people who usually held their land by charter from a major landowner. The charter normally stated the money rent payable or the gift to be made each year – for example, a barbed arrow, a pound of cumin, or a red rose. This 'chief' rent was therefore known to be fixed forever. These small freeholders did not usually have tenants. They seem to have employed the young unmarried children of other householders to do the farm work for them. Their workers' wages therefore only doubled in the century 1540–1640, but the value of the farm produce increased 6 times, so the profit of their farms grew greatly and reflected their increased values. Alternatively freeholders could rent out their land at market value by the year and enjoy the income. A 30-acre farm would have produced under £1 p.a. in 1500, but £18 p.a. in the 1660s; this group clearly prospered greatly.[32]

The second group to be examined is that of the other tenants of resident landlords like the Warburtons and the Leicesters. These tenants held their land 'at the will'

32 For example, see Foster, 2002, Chs 1, 3, 4 and 5, farming sections.

of the landowners into the early sixteenth century.[33] Sometime in the late 1530s or
early 1540s, for reasons examined in (iv) below, most of the Cheshire and South
Lancashire resident landowners converted their tenants into leaseholders. Each
man was given a written document which appears to have recorded the same terms
on which he had previously held 'at will'. It had the same rent, boon works, heriot,
and military service obligations. The leases were for 21 years or for the lives of up
to three named people (not necessarily in different generations). Consequently I
have called them 'three-life leases'. The earliest I have seen among the many
hundreds in the Leicester and Warburton archives was dated 1543. A small
premium or 'entry fine' seems normally to have been paid at the start of these leases,
but the amount is often hidden by such phrases as 'for a certain sum of money'.
Entry fines seem to have been a common feature of the old 'at will' tenancies. A
number of fines are mentioned in Sir William Brereton's accounts for 1531–33,
when his tenants were still 'at will'. They ranged from 10s to £3.[34] See Appendix
3.6 for details of how the 'entry fines' or premiums on these leases were calculated
and how they affected the wealth of tenants and landlords.

The picture that emerges from the complexities of these calculations is that these
leases became a method of sharing the great increase in land values between the
landowner and the tenant. In the first 50 years, say up to 1590, the tenants seem
likely to have received the benefit of rather more than half the increased market
value of their land. For the next 60 years, until 1651, when interest rates declined
to 6%, the landowners probably had the larger share. In the following century up
to 1750 the pendulum slowly swung more in favour of the tenants, as interest rates
declined to 3% to 4%. After 1750, landowners in Cheshire and Lancashire seem to
have worked to end this system of leasing and it largely disappeared on farmland
during the Napoleonic wars. This summary of the position of the group who became
known as three-life leaseholders shows that they did not gain quite so much as the
freeholders. The holders and purchasers of these leases were nevertheless a privileged group who were enjoying an above-average return on their investment in land.
They had a marked advantage over the man who rented land at the full market value.
We can see why some families retained their three-life leases over two or three
centuries.

Having defined the position of the majority of their tenants, we are now able to
examine how the rent rise affected the major resident landowners. As we have seen,
the Warburtons had some 1,900 acres of demesne lands and the Leicesters about
800 acres. Everyone in the landowner group had demesne lands on which they

---

33 See, for example, DLT/A72/2; Beamont, 1849, pp. 2–3; Ives, 1976, p.274.
34 Ives, 1976, pp. 165, 184, 195–96, 251–52.

enjoyed the full increase in market value. On their tenanted land they were less fortunate. Their freehold tenants may have paid below market rents in the fifteenth century, but in return they may have performed valuable military service in the Wars of the Roses. This military service ceased in the sixteenth century and, as we have seen, the freeholders received the benefit of the whole of the rise in market value of their lands. These changes significantly reduced the social position of major landowners, like the Warburtons, who had enjoyed prestige in proportion to the military force they could bring to a war.

We have just examined how the great estates shared the increased land values with their leasehold tenants. Both the Warburtons and the Leicesters had at least three times as much land let to leasehold tenants as they had in demesne, and this was probably common among members of this group. So the typical position of these families may have been that they enjoyed the full rise in land values on a quarter or less of their lands and about half the rise on the other three quarters.[35] This would have left them with an income of about half what they might have had if they had enjoyed the full rise in values on both these types of land.[36]

So far we have examined the positions of three groups: the freeholders, the three-life leaseholders and the major resident landowners. We now come to the group whose position is most difficult to explain, the tenants of the Crown. The 77 names of people paying rent in the Whitley Lordship (Map 3) in 1526/7 were those of tenants of the Duchy of Lancaster (see Appendix 3.4). The list was headed 'Tenants at will' in the same way as in the Leicesters' 1503 rental. For some reason, these tenants were not changed into leaseholders around 1540, as the 'tenants at will' of resident landowners were. They continued to pay the same relatively low rents. They went on transferring their holdings in the Manor Court in accordance with custom. They paid the same entry fines of one third of their annual rents. They became known as copyholders because their title deed might be a copy of the entry in the Manor Court record. The Whitley tenants, and others like them, whose customs included passing their holdings down to their children, became known as 'copyholders of inheritance'. In the 1560s the Duchy of Lancaster in London inquired into their tenure.[37] After that they appear to have been accepted as 'copyholders of inheritance', whose rents were fixed, who could not be ejected and who got richer with every rise in market rents that they did not have to pay.

---

35 It seems impossible to calculate the full income of these families, because inadequate records survive of the capital payments made by the leaseholders. Nor are there calculations of the interest accruing on these payments of rent in advance. This interest was an important part of the landlords' income when rates of interest were as high as 10% or more.

36 See the Leicesters' 1666 valuation in Ch. 2, Table 3, on p. 17.

37 P.R.O., DL 44/175 and DL 44/220.

By the time of the 1595 rental, freehold and copyhold land in the manor was separately identified. The confidence that people had in copyhold titles by the end of the sixteenth century is shown by the appearance of William Lyon, Bishop of Cork and Ross, among the 1612 copyholders.[38] This confidence was evidently shaken by James I's lawyers because in 1612 the copyholders made an agreement with the government to purchase their lands 'in fee-farm', which meant that they paid the old fixed rent forever and became effectively freeholders. They agreed to pay the King £2,300,[39] which was just under £1 an acre for the 2,393 acres of their farms shown in the 1612 survey. The 423 acres of commons and lanes were included, as it were, for free. The market value of the farm land in 1612 is likely to have been more than £5 an acre, so in one sense they bought the land for less than a fifth of its value.[40] In this manner the 86 small freeholds listed in Appendix 3.4, Col. 4 (the 1612 survey) were created. This was not the only example of this process in Bucklow Hundred. Old Duchy of Lancaster tenants in the townships of Runcorn and Moore became fee farmers/freeholders in a similar manner in 1628,[41] as did the old tenants of Shrewsbury Abbey in Thelwall.[42] In Lancashire the process took place on a much larger scale. The Honour of Clitheroe was a huge area of hilly country, perhaps 100,000 acres, comprising the forests of Pendle, Trawden, Rossendale and Accrington, owned by the Duchy of Lancaster, and including most of the old parish of Whalley. It was sold to its tenants for a total of a few thousand pounds in the early seventeenth century.[43] The Shuttleworth family were one of the fortunate beneficiaries of these events. The Fell family of Swarthmoor in Furness were another happy recipient of such windfall gains.[44]

Lands in the hands of the Crown were not the only ones sold to their tenants. A large part of Mobberley township was owned by a branch of the Talbot family of Grafton in Worcestershire who became Earls of Shrewsbury. Another part was

38 See D.N.B. The Lyon family seem originally to have been small freeholders in Rainford and Eccleston townships, near modern St Helens. See Ch. 7 (v) for another branch of the Lyon family.

39 See Ormerod, 1882, Vol. 1, p. 656 for the agreement. See WM Box 1, folder B for the receipt for the £2,300. Hoyle, 1992, pp.242–43.

40 See Foster, 1998, Appendix 8, for land values in the area. See Fig. 1 for rental values and Appendix 3.6 for interest rates.

41 Ormerod, 1882, pp. 674, 740.

42 *Ibid.*, p. 748.

43 Tupling, 1927, pp. 149–50. £3,953 was paid by the manors of Accrington, Colne, and Ightenhill in 1609, and perhaps £2,000 more later (p. 159). See also Whitaker, 1872, pp. 287–89; Farrer, 1912, Vol. II, pp. 377–88; Farrer, 1912, Vol. III, pp. 405–08. In the old royal manor of Rochdale, 41,828 acres, which was most of the parish of Rochdale, the inhabitants in 1626 were 300 freeholders and 240 copyholders. Fishwick, 1913, p. xv. See Map 4 p. 53.

44 Foster, 2002, Ch. 1 for Shuttleworths, Ch. 4 for Fells.

owned by the Radcliffes of Ordsall, Lancashire. Both these families sold their lands to their tenants in the early seventeenth century. Unfortunately, Sir Peter Leicester does not tell us why. He just lists the 59 freeholders who were there in the 1660s.[45]

iv) Possible reasons for the advantageous position of royal and other customary tenants

The legal position of these tenants was that they held their land 'at the will of the Lord in accordance with the custom of the manor'.[46] This appears to have been established in the late fifteenth century. A case in which the landlord had evicted tenants in order to enclose the land came before the courts in 1481. In a famous passage, Chief Justice Brian, replying to counsel who had suggested that copyholders could be evicted because they were only 'tenants at will', said: 'That was never my opinion … if the lord ousts a copyholder he will have an action of trespass on the case against the lord.'[47]

Although it is clear that this judgment protected copyholders from evictions designed to enable enclosures to be made, it was perhaps not obvious to contemporaries that it affected their rents. There is certainly evidence that the rents being paid by 'customary' tenants were market-related before 1510. We have seen that rent on the Leicesters' lands doubled from 4d an acre in 1362 to 8.3d an acre in 1503.[48] Between 1505 and 1507, the Duchy of Lancaster's commissioners reorganized the farms and raised the rents in the Honour of Clitheroe.[49] The Duchy of Lancaster's 77 tenants in the Whitley Lordship were paying an annual rent of £71 15s 4d for their 2,393 acres in 1526/7. This was 7.2d an acre (see Appendix 3.4). This was not too dissimilar to the market rent of 7.7d an acre at Hield in 1503, given above. The tenants of Norton Abbey in Great Budworth were paying about 7d an acre in 1535/6 (see Appendix 3.7). This evidence inclines us to agree with Sir Peter Leicester when he tells us that 'it appears by that rental, as well as by another of my own in Henry the Seventh's time that in those ages till Henry VIII, the ancient tenants in our county had generally no leases for lives, as now they have; and the rents which at this day we call old rents were in those former ages the utmost value of such tenements on the rack..'[50]

45 Ormerod, 1882, pp. 411–19. See pp. 63–4 for the Earl of Shrewsbury's lands in Yorkshire.
46 This was how they became known as 'customary' tenants.
47 Holdsworth, 1909, Vol. 3, pp. 177–78.
48 See Ch. 2, pp. 14–15.
49 Tupling, 1927, pp. 43–45.
50 Ormerod, 1882, Vol. 1, p. 536 (Altrincham). For the general proposition that the rents paid by the tenants before 1500 were market-related, see Chibnall, 1965, p. 103. Davenport, 1906, p. 78 shows rents falling unsteadily from 10.75d per acre in 1376 to 7.25d per acre in 1500. Howell, 1983, pp. 50–53.

There must then have been later judgments in the Courts of Equity that decided that rents and entry fines were controlled by the custom of the manor.[51] The cases in which these judgments were delivered probably did not come before the courts until after 1510 because it is likely that market rents across England were stable between 1450 and 1510 as shown in Fig. 1. However, after 1510, people living in counties on the south and east coasts of England must have become increasingly aware that the price of grain was rising. Table 6 reproduces part of an index of grain prices in the English market.

Table 6. Average price of all grains. Index Numbers 1450–99 = 100

Decade	Index number
1500–09	112
1510–19	115
1520–29	154
1530–39	161
1540–49	187
1550–59	348

Source: Thirsk, 1967, p. 857

This 'market' was created by ships moving grain along the south and east coasts to supply London and any other port area which required supplies. The steady increase in prices shown in Table 6 is likely to have led to a rise in the annual market value of land as farming became more profitable. Evidence that such a rise did in fact occur in the grain-producing areas of Yorkshire is provided by Ralph Smith in a Table which shows that the average rent being paid around 1535 by 20 large farms covering 4,516 acres was 15d an acre.[52] This was about double the 7d to 8d an acre that seems to have been the national rate around 1500. These farms were, no doubt, on demesne lands, but such greatly increased rent levels seem certain to have induced some landlords to try and raise their tenants' rents. Presumably some group of tenants took their case to court and gave the judges an opportunity to say that rents and entry fines were controlled by the 'custom of the manor'.

At the time these decisions probably did not seem greatly significant. The 1481 judgment had contributed to rural peace and the judges probably felt that extending the principle to cover rents and entry fines would help to maintain that peace. The rise in market rents might well prove transitory. Every manor had slightly different

51 A. W. B. Simpson, 1986, p. 163, quotes C. M. Gray, 1963, p. 34.
52 Smith, 1970, p. 279.

customs and it was rarely known exactly what they were because they were not usually written down. Some historians have suggested the custom of fixed rents and entry fines in some manors was centuries old. The evidence given above that rents were market-related before 1500 seems to contradict this view. It seems more likely that it was the stable market rent levels between 1450 and 1500 that created the custom.

A practice that had existed 'beyond the memory of any man alive' was a 'custom' in the view of many lawyers. The evidence in Fig. 1 suggests that by the 1520s and 1530s the inhabitants of many manors could claim that fixed rents and fines were a 'custom of their manor'. Some Yorkshire landlords reacted to these judgments by keeping rents stable and raising the entry fines of their customary tenants, claiming that their entry fines were not fixed by custom. Whereas rents were paid twice yearly, entry fines were only levied every decade or two, so people's recollections and records were much poorer. Other landlords found other ways of keeping their rental income in line with the market. On the Clifford estates in the 1540s a number of tenants bought tenancies by warranty that replaced copyhold tenure.[53] Eight monasteries in the area granted a total of 195 leases between 1527 and their dissolution.[54] Other landowners including the Duchy of Lancaster did nothing, but continued to grant tenancies in the Manor Court at the usual rents and entry fines. It would seem likely that it was the tenants of this last group of landlords who appeared in the 1545/6 Tax Return for the West Riding assessed on lands valued at £1 to £4. There were 1,358 Yorkshire people in this category in the 1546 Return[55] and their existence marks the third great difference between the returns in Yorkshire and Cheshire, as there were only 14 people in this group in Bucklow Hundred. These small landowners were heavily concentrated in some parts of the West Riding. They do not seem to have been numerous in the plain of the Vale of York, but were mostly in the upland areas that formed the clothing districts around Halifax, Huddersfield, Wakefield, Leeds and Bradford, Knaresborough Forest near Harrogate, and in the Sheffield area (see Map 4). In these areas they comprised more than 50% of the taxpayers in 1546.[56] It seems likely that many of them were copyholders of the small farms which are found in later records to have existed in these areas.[57] A 30-acre upland farm worth 2½d an acre in 1500 had an annual rent of 6s 3d. By 1546 the land might have been worth 1s an acre making a total of £1 10s 0d,

53 Ibid., 1970, pp. 79–80.
54 Hoyle, 1989, pp. 111–37.
55 Smith, 1970, pp. 97, 110.
56 Ibid., 1970, p. 112.
57 Some of them may have been small freeholders.

so that the copyholder owned property worth £1 3s 9d p.a. The statute imposing this tax specifically included property rights of this kind.[58]

If this analysis is correct it establishes that by 1546 there were a large number of copyholders on the estates of the Duchy of Lancaster and the Earl of Shrewsbury (landowner of much of the Sheffield area) who had become property owners because their rents and entry fines had not been raised. In Cheshire and Lancashire, market rents may not have risen much before 1540 as shown in Graph 1 because grain prices in these counties were not closely linked with the market on the south and east coasts.[59] No copyholders were regarded as having property in 1545. But the rise in market rents around 1540 will have warned Cheshire and Lancashire landowners that they had better do something about their tenants-at-will before they became property-owning copyholders. If they looked across the Pennines, or probably at any grain-growing area in southern or eastern England, where market rents had been rising for 20 or 30 years, they would have learnt that giving their tenants leases was one way of controlling the position. However it happened, the evidence is strong that they seem to have decided, around 1540, to move from the system of transferring tenancies in the Manor Court to a system of documentary leases. There were three likely benefits for the landowners:

1. By using phrases like 'for a certain sum of money', they ensured that the entry fines were always uncertain and hence variable.
2. By making the leases for 21 years or the lives of named people, they set a term to the length of the leases.
3. By setting out the terms of the tenure in detail, they prevented litigation about the customs of the manor.

These leases achieved these objectives. They effectively insulated the landowners against the possible unpleasant effects of tenure according 'to the custom of the manor'. At the same time, they preserved the spirit of the judge's ruling that tenants should continue in their holdings at the old rents and on the other old conditions.

The Crown, the Church, and a few other non-resident landowners, who often belonged to noble families, did not follow this example. Their tenants continued to transfer their holdings in the Manor Court, as we have seen seems to have happened in the West Riding. Why had these landlords not put their tenants on leases? The answer has to come in two parts. Firstly, North-west England may well have been the last area to experience the rising annual value of land. Secondly, this group of large landlords owned land all over the country and they had to behave in the same

58 Smith, 1970, pp. 106–07; 37 Hen. 8 c. 25; see Foster, 2002, Ch. 1, p. 56, for an example in upland Lancashire.
59 See Foster, 2002, pp. 24–25.

way to all their tenants. The Duchy of Lancaster's Cheshire and Lancashire tenants became copyholders because the Duchy's tenants in the West Riding and elsewhere were already copyholders. It was not possible for the Duchy to put its upland tenants in Lancashire on leases while their neighbours across the border in Yorkshire were copyholders.

This reasoning may explain why the Duchy was one of the few landowners in Cheshire not to convert its tenants into leaseholders, but it does not help us to understand why they had not given their tenants in the south and east of England leases many years before. The answer to that seems to be that, in the 1530s and 1540s, the Crown, the Church and the nobility were all engaged in a campaign to keep rents and all other 'customs of the manor' unchanged. One reason for this campaign appears to have been that the government was nervous of agrarian discontent. They knew about the Peasants' War of 1524–25 in Germany. The Pilgrimage of Grace in 1536 had exposed the government's weakness in the face of mass movements. Ket's rebellion in Norfolk in 1549 and Wyatt's rising in Kent in 1554 showed that they were right to be nervous. Complaints about enclosures, evictions, raised rents and entry fines were made in all these movements.[60] The government hoped that, by protecting the position of the customary tenant, they would preserve the peace and prevent rebellion. Three examples of their campaign will suffice.

First, in 1548 the Duke of Somerset, the Lord Protector, had a special Act passed to enfranchise his own customary tenants.[61] Second, a special prayer was authorised by Edward VI 'that they that possess grounds ... remembering themselves to be thy tenants, may not rack or stretch out the rents of their lands; nor yet take unreasonable fines ...'.[62] The third and most famous example occurs in Bishop Latimer's first sermon preached before King Edward VI on 8 March 1549. He described the Leicestershire farm which his father had rented for £3 or £4 a year in 1497, and for which the farmer in 1549 was being charged £16 p.a. This farmer, he said, was 'not able to do anything for his prince, for himself, nor for his children, or give a cup of drink to the Poor'.[63] The existence of these views among government and Church leaders also helps to explain the extremely favourable terms on which the Warburtons acquired leases granted in the 1550s. It will be remembered (from p. 24) that Sir John Warburton bought an extension to his lease to Crowley from the Duchy of Lancaster in 1558 for £200. It turned out to be worth at least £2,000. His son bought a lease to the tithes of Great Budworth, granted by Christ Church, Oxford in 1557, which also became very valuable.

60 Tawney, 1912, pp. 318–37.
61 2–3 Edw VI, c12.
62 Quoted in Tawney, 1912, p. 175.
63 Latimer's Sermons, *Everyman*, p. 85.

It could be that some Government and Church leaders wanted to protect customary tenants so as to spread wealth more widely in society. Others among these powerful people no doubt felt in the 1520s, 1530s and the 1540s that the rise in rents was likely to be modest. Rents had not changed greatly since 1200. They expected that when the social tensions had died down and life was quiet and peaceful again, they would find a way to bring their tenants into line with other tenants who were paying market rents. As we have seen, these hopes were false. The political situation remained turbulent throughout the reigns of Edward VI and Mary. By the early 1560s, when Elizabeth had established a calmer atmosphere, market rents in Cheshire had approximately quadrupled to 3s an acre. Royal and old monastic tenants in Cheshire had enjoyed fixed rents for 20 to 25 years while market rents had risen sharply. They were strongly opposed to losing their privileged position. The judges, no doubt, were subjected to much royal pressure, but by the 1560s, the tenants were also a rich and more powerful group. Most Crown and old monastic tenants were recognised as 'copyholders'.

It seems, therefore, that the government and the Church are likely to have played the major role in protecting the customary tenants. They are likely to have persuaded the judges to extend the established concept of holding 'in accordance with the custom of the manor' to cover the entry fine and the rent which had probably been previously left to market forces expressed in the phrase 'at will'. The landowning gentry everywhere endeavoured to protect themselves from this legal alteration, as we have seen happened in Yorkshire. They were right to be alarmed since the new law was indeed likely to reduce their incomes. The new documentary leases adopted in Cheshire and Lancashire, however, kept open their ability to raise entry fines. This allowed them to share the increased market rental values with their tenants. After more than 200 years and in significantly different social and economic conditions, the terminable character of leases for lives allowed the Cheshire gentry to return to letting their land at market rents in the nineteenth century.

The long-term outcome for the Crown was less satisfactory. In the 1560s, the Crown investigated the possibility of raising rents. The Welsh marcher Lordship of Bromfield and Yale seems to have been a case that set a precedent for other Lordships in the area. Although the tenants' case was not without legal defects, the government in 1562 seems to have turned away from a major confrontation. In return for some minor concessions, they gave the tenants new 40–year renewable leases that effectively gave them the equivalent of a freehold title.[64]

James I's lawyers drew attention to the many anomalies in the legal positions of royal tenants and appeared to threaten them with expensive legal actions. This

64 Hoyle, 1992, pp. 202–03.

persuaded some groups, like those in Whitley, to pay 10% to 20% of the value of the land to secure confirmation of their titles. Many of the Honour of Clitheroe tenants followed the same route. Others declined to settle. Appendix 8.1 briefly describes two groups in Wensleydale, Yorkshire. One lost much of their land in legal proceedings in the seventeenth century, while the other obtained the freehold of their land after making only a small payment. The Crown had controlled a huge landed estate when it added the monasteries to its traditional lands at their dissolution in 1536. Some it sold in the 1530s and 40s at market prices[65] and some were given to courtiers and favourites. Charles I gave large numbers of manors to the City of London in the Royal Contract of 1627.[66] Many of these had copyhold tenants who became freeholders at the Restoration. It could well be that a much larger part of the royal estate of 1537 passed to the customary tenants than was sold or given away to courtiers. This study has only investigated the history of ownership of a few areas in the North-West that belonged to individual families. If the same pattern of events occurred nation-wide, the total area of land transferred from the Crown to customary tenants may have been very large. The suggestion advanced here is that the king and his ministers, together with other noblemen and church leaders, encouraged the judges to promote rural peace when ruling on land law. The judges decided to do this by extending the 'custom of the manor' to include rents and entry fines, so giving many tenants security of tenure at fixed rents. The Crown was never able to reverse these judgments which had the effect of giving most of the Crown estate to its tenants.

v) The larger number of freeholders in Bucklow Hundred in the 1660s

While it may be difficult to explain exactly how the tenants of Bucklow Hundred enjoyed windfall gains, it is much clearer that large numbers of tenants benefited. Some were tenants of traditional Crown lands; others had been tenants of monasteries or of estates forfeited to the Crown. They were joined in their good fortune by some of the tenants of non-resident noblemen and gentry. Altogether there were enough fortunate tenants to make a change in the shape of Cheshire society. Because of the huge areas of royal land in the Lancashire hills and the large forfeitures of estates in the north of the county after the Pilgrimage of Grace, the changes in Lancashire society were probably even greater. However, we have a better historical guide for Cheshire.

In Bucklow Hundred, we can measure the great increase in the number of freeholders because Sir Peter Leicester provided several lists of their names. In 1662,

65 A detailed description of one sale is given in Appendix 3.7.
66 Ashton, 1960; C.L.R.O. Royal Contract Deeds in large quantities.

he made a list of the 'freeholders who are to appear yearly at the Assizes at Chester'. The first 28 names he described as those of 'the better sort of Gentry'. These names include 18 of the families of those who were assessed at £10 p.a. or more in 1545. This shows that there had not been great changes in the major families. The list continued with 166 names of 'freeholders and gentlemen who have lands of inheritance'. These were apparently only the richer freeholders because in his book (reprinted by Ormerod, 1882), he noted almost 200 more freeholders having lands in particular townships. For example, only 11 names from Appleton appear in the freeholder list, but 21 names of charterers are printed.[67] In the urban centres of Altrincham, Hale and Knutsford, his patience was exhausted by the number of charterers. He did not list their names; he just noted there were 20 in Altrincham, 23 in Hale and more than 40 in Knutsford. Sir Peter made a further list of the Fee-farmers[68] in Whitley on which he wrote 'whether these Fee-farmers are to appear at the Assizes yearly?'. This list is in Appendix 3.4, and has 90 names. He made yet another list of 27 fee-farmers in Runcorn.[69]

The list of fee-farmers in the Whitley Lordship is interesting because it includes an estimate of the annual value of each owner's land. Sir Peter put a conservative value of 8s 3d p.a. on the average Whitley acre. The Survey of his own 4,000-acre estate in 1666 yielded an average annual value of 11s 3d an acre.[70] Nevertheless, these values give us an idea of the capital value of the land owned by these 90 people. Its total annual value was £1,051. At the going rate of 18 years' purchase, the total capital value of these fee-farmers' lands was £18,918.[71] A good farm like William Gandy's at Frandley in Sevenoaks, worth £30 p.a., had a value of £540. Even a field worth £2 p.a. had a capital value of £36.

Only about eight of the families who had paid James I to secure their titles in 1612 seem to have still owned exactly the same land in 1662, one of them being Isaac Hollinshead in Antrobus. Most of the families had divided or sold part of their land, while others like Gandy had bought land. In 1612 it seems likely that most of the farms were the family homes of their owners and only 11 owners were letting their land. By 1662 these farms seem to have become the capital investments of a group of families living across north Cheshire. About 25 of the owners are listed as living outside the Lordship; others may not have been at home much. We have seen that

---

67 See footote 4, p. 44 above, for the meaning of this word.
68 See p. 60 above, for the meaning of this word.
69 All these lists are in DLT/B36.
70 See Ch. 2, Table 3, on p. 17.
71 See Appendix 3.6 and Clay, 1974, p. 175.

Thomas Jackson did not occupy his farm in Aston by Budworth for many years of his long life.[72]

Sir Peter Leicester also made a list of 55 copyholders in Halton. As we have seen, they were virtually freeholders. When all these lists of freeholders are added together and some allowance is made for double counting, it seems likely that there were about 500 freeholders in Bucklow Hundred in the 1660s. This represents quite a social and economic revolution compared with 1545, when we found only 76 people paying tax on their land. Perhaps about half of these new freeholders had acquired their land from old royal, monastic and noblemen's estates which had allowed or caused their tenants to become copyholders of inheritance[73] who bought their freeholds. Some of the rest may always have been small freeholders and the huge rise in land values made these freeholders much more visible. The second development was the growing sale of freehold land by the old gentry. Many old tenants grew richer through the increased value of their three-life leaseholds or their freeholds. Some families made money from the expansion of business that got underway in the second half of the sixteenth century, as we will see in the next section. The richer families were potential buyers of freehold land from gentry who wished to sell. There were, no doubt, many reasons why gentry did sell. For example, on the Warburton estate, Peter Warburton's settlement of 1626 preserved only the main, long-owned manors in trust for his great-nephew. Outlying lands and recent purchases became the property of his daughters. Examples of their sales appear in Chapters 7 and 9. In whatever way they had acquired their lands, there cannot be much doubt that freeholder families constituted an important political, social, and economic force in Bucklow Hundred in the 1660s. Perhaps in the North-West 'the rise of the gentry' was the rise of the freeholders.

vi) A new problem: the poor and the building of cottages

We have analysed how the Rent Revolution affected the position of four groups of people who had rights to land. It is now time to see how it affected that part of the population which had rights to only very small amounts of land, or to no land at all. In the pre-1545 rentals of Sutton, Tabley, and Whitley (Appendices 3.1, 3.2 and 3.4), the smallest annual rent was three or four shillings. At 7d an acre, these were probably tenements with at least five acres of land. It seems likely that, in the fifteenth century, Cheshire and Lancashire landlords did not create smaller holdings than this. Perhaps there was no need. In the 1465 survey of the land in

---

72 Foster, 2002, pp. 91, 95–96.
73 See p. 59 above for the meaning of this phrase.

Warrington belonging to Sir Peter Legh,[74] some 20 houses with gardens were described as empty or ruinous. There was apparently no pressure at this period from new families seeking houses.

When every family in a rural township had enough land to grow its own grain, there was no supply problem in the country. Even in towns like Warrington, it seems that in 1465 almost every tenement had enough land to grow its own food. It was only in bad harvest years that people had to tighten their belts and share out what grain they had grown between them.[75] Large towns like Chester and Manchester were no doubt dependent on some supplies coming in from the adjacent country. However, in these places there is evidence that rich townspeople owned farms nearby and organized the farming to provide food in the city. The inventories of leading citizens usually included substantial stocks of cereals and animals.[76] From this analysis it follows that the market in grain was small. Most households had their own supplies and there is little evidence of grain arriving in the ports of Chester or Liverpool.[77]

As the population grew in the sixteenth century the number of families without land increased. This was because the land in many townships was already fully occupied. Sutton Weaver and the Whitley Lordship provide two examples. It was not possible to provide new families with enough land to grow their own food. Cottages, with only enough land for a garden, were built for these new families. They had to hope to make enough money working in another occupation to buy their food from those who had land. Then the fact that food prices were increasing much faster than wages had its effect and created a group of people poorer than anyone had been before 1530. Here are three examples of what happened in townships in this area:

1) Great Budworth
a) Cottages
Before 1536 the Warburtons and Norton Abbey[78] owned the whole village. Norton Abbey had two tenants on its demesne land and 11 customary tenants in 1536 (see Appendix 3.7 for details). The customary tenants were paying annual rents of between 3 and 11 shillings each. The Crown sold Norton Abbey's lands in Great

---

74 Beamont, 1849.
75 An example is given in Foster, 2002, Ch. 1, pp. 24–26.
76 For example, Aldersay, Mayor of Chester, 1547. Woodward, 1967, Appendix B shows the value
   of agricultural goods included in the inventories of shoemakers, saddlers, glovers, and tanners.
   Willan, 1980, pp. 40–47.
77 Woodward, 1970, pp. 66–69.
78 Norton Priory was made an Abbey in 1391. Greene, 1979.

Budworth in 1544. In 1548, Peter Leicester of Tabley bought the freehold of eight of the 11 tenancies. These transactions are described in detail in Appendix 3.7. The Leicester estate rental for 1555 is given in Appendix 3.8, Table B. By this time, the Leicesters had 14 tenants with properties and three more with only boatrooms (see p. 72). Four of these tenants were old Abbey tenants on their original lands and two were new families with old Abbey holdings. The other two old Abbey holdings had been divided. The Leicester estate had also received about 18 acres in the new enclosures (see p. 80) on which there were eight new tenants. Four of them were paying 2 shillings or less rent, so they are unlikely to have had more than a cottage with a garden. The three tenants of boatrooms presumably had no land at all.

The earliest surviving rental of the Warburton lands in Great Budworth is dated 1572. It is set out in Appendix 3.8, Table A.[79] This lists 28 leaseholders paying annual rents of between 3 shillings and £2 17s 8d, and 11 paying less than 3 shillings. Three more were paying for boatrooms. The 11 tenants on small rents probably only had a cottage and a garden. These rentals suggest that the households living in Great Budworth before about 1544 were only the 11 Norton Abbey tenants and the 28 tenants, plus two freeholders, on the Warburtons' land. These 41 families all had at least five acres of land each.

By 1572 there were in Great Budworth five freeholders,[80] 42 Warburton tenants, and 17 Leicester tenants, making a total of 64 families.[81] Of them, 15 were living in cottages without enough land to grow their own food, and six had no land at all, only boatrooms. These 21 families made a large increase in the market for grain. As grain prices rose over the decades and their wages rose less,[82] they became steadily worse off. In years of scarcity, their position was untenable – they could not afford to buy at all and were then dependent on the charity of their better provided neighbours.

b) Boatrooms and Budworth Mere

Fishing in Budworth Mere (see Map 6) was no doubt one of the occupations of the earliest settlers in the area. The idea of limiting access to a certain number of people who had a licence to fish, called a 'boatroom', does not seem to have existed in 1536, as there were no small rents of that kind in the Norton Abbey rental. By 1546 or 1547, when the butcher John Eaton of Crowley bought three boatrooms as well as the lands of the eight old Abbey tenants, the scheme of boatrooms had been created

---

79 Except the two freeholders who appear in Appendix 2.4.
80 See section (vii) p. 79–80 below.
81 We know most of these were residents because their names appear in Manor Court rolls and in Parish Registers, see p. 141, and some appear in wills and inventories, see p. 127.
82 See above, p. 56.

(see Appendix 3.7). The Leicesters acquired these three in 1548, the Warburtons had three and the Marbury family on the other side of the Mere had four.[83] There may have been other freeholders who also had some. Some of the men who were shown paying rent of 3s 4d to the Leicesters and 1s 6d or 3s to the Warburtons seem not to have been the same men who rented the farms. Several had the same surnames and may therefore have been relations. As they had no houses, they apparently lived with their relations or as lodgers elsewhere. The difference in the rents may be accounted for by the inclusion of the hire of the boat itself. The man paying 3s to the Warburtons has 'for a boat and a boatroom' written after his name.[84] An extraordinary document has survived in the archives of both the Leicesters and the Warburtons – a list of the rules that the fisher families who rented boatrooms had to obey in 1553. It is printed in Appendix 3.9.

More attractive career options than fishing in Budworth Mere were evidently available by 1641. The value of Leicester boatrooms had halved compared with 1604 (see Appendix 3.8, Table B). In the Leicester survey of 1666, John Anderton was renting a small holding of nine and a half acres in Budworth and all three boatrooms. The pressure that had led ten or more men to seek to maintain themselves (and perhaps their families) by fishing in Budworth Mere had evidently evaporated by the 1660s.

2. *Warrington*

The Legh family of Haydock and Bradley, Lancashire, and Lyme Park, Cheshire, owned one half of Warrington in 1465. Their survey of this estate in that year[85] indicates that virtually all the properties had agricultural land attached to them. The other great landlord in Warrington at that time was the Botelor family of Bewsey Hall, whose properties later passed into the hands of the Earl of Leicester. He commissioned a survey in April 1587, soon after he came into possession. This showed that there were 57 tenants holding between them some 530 acres of agricultural land. Of these, 29 had holdings of more than five acres while the other 28 had smaller plots. Nine of them had less than one acre. In addition to these tenants, there were 22 cottages with very little land between them. There were also four shops and ten fish yards. So there were perhaps a total of 64 families with less than five acres. This survey seems to confirm the Budworth evidence that in urban places there was a substantial growth in the number of families living without enough land to grow their own food.[86]

83 IPM on James Marbury, 29 Jan 4 Elizabeth.
84 1572 Rental at Arley Hall.
85 Beamont, 1849.
86 Typed copy of survey, WPL, MS 1174/2.

3. The Whitley Lordship

The smallest annual rent paid by any of the 77 tenants in Whitley in 1526/7 was 3s. The average rent per acre was 7.3d, so 3s was probably the rent of a 5-acre plot. At that time there was probably only a single house on each property. The 77 farmhouses noted in the 1612 survey were probably on the same sites as the farmsteads of 1526/7. By 1612 there were also some 40 cottages. When had they been built and why?

The value of tenancies in the Whitley Lordship rose rapidly in the sixteenth century. They were recognized as copyholds of inheritance by the time of the 1595 rental. They became 'freeholds' in 1612 by the payment of approximately £1 an acre. These developments increased the wealth of the traditional tenants and attracted well-off newcomers. By 1595 the Ward family of Capesthorne Hall (south of Wilmslow) who had intermarried with the Venables family, had acquired three of these holdings. Their tenants in 1612 included John Walthall, gent. People like him and traditional tenants of freeholder background like the Crosbys, the Eatons, and the Greggs did not cultivate the land with their own hands, but employed servants to do it. By 1600 they seem to have preferred an arrangement whereby their farm servants did not live with their families in the main farmhouse. Providing a separate cottage for those who had served for a number of years allowed the servants to marry, and helped to alleviate the pressure to provide homes for new families. Thus many of the cottages in 1612 seem to have been on the farms owned by the richer people. By 1612 some of these cottages had become detached from their farm-houses. For example, the Allen family were freeholders of Greenhills in neighbouring Nether Whitley. A member of the family had had a copyhold farm in Over Whitley in 1595 and perhaps for more than 50 years before that. Presumably they had built a cottage for their farm servant. By 1612 they had sold the copyhold farm and only retained the cottage and three acres with it. It is no surprise to discover in the 1612 survey that the farm which Reverend William Seaburne, Rector of Thornton, had bought had a cottage. He died in the farmhouse in 1607.[87] From all this, it seems reasonable to conclude that most of these cottages were built in the 50 years before 1612. This was another way in which the pressure of the growing population was accommodated.

A final strand of evidence that shows the fierce demand for a place to live at the close of the sixteenth century is provided by the list of cottages at the end of the 1612 survey. These nine cottages were all described as encroachments on the common. That is to say, their occupants had no legal title to be on the land. The continued existence of these cottages depended on the forbearance of the Steward of the Manor. The fact that four of the occupiers had surnames that were the same

---

87 Will 1607.

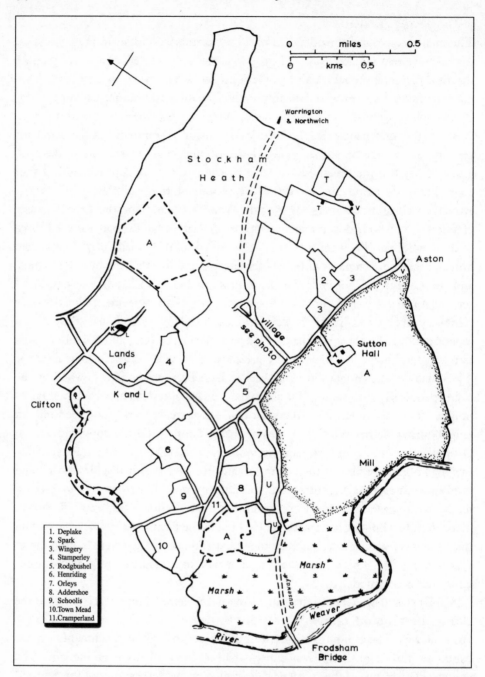

1. Deplake
2. Spark
3. Wingery
4. Stamperley
5. Rodgbushel
6. Henriding
7. Orleys
8. Addershoe
9. Schoolis
10. Town Mead
11. Cramperland

Map 5. Sutton Weaver – a simplified version of the 1753 map omitting the field boundaries.
    At the top, the high ground of Stockham Heath is shown as it was before it was enclosed
and divided up around 1600. The demesne lands of Sutton Hall are marked A and the
demesne's share of the common land enclosed on the heath and beside the Marsh are

as those of tenants suggests they had been allowed to set up these shacks because of some connection with the Manor. The land consisted only of a garden or a hemp-yard. The occupiers were evidently growing hemp and a few vegetables and they sold the processed hemp to buy grain. Rents were nominal because these people were probably as poor as anyone could be.

At least these people had somewhere to live and something to do. At the end of the sixteenth century there were people who had neither. The parish registers of Great Budworth record that from the 1570s to the 1620s one or two poor vagrants were buried every year. 'A poor cripple', 'a beggar's child', they were strangers whose names were not recorded or perhaps not known. In years of high grain prices or epidemic disease they were more numerous. There were nine such burials in 1597 and another nine in 1598. In both years they constituted a tenth of the burials in the parish. The great Elizabethan Poor Law of 1601 was dealing with a real problem.

vii) Developments in the Cheshire countryside in the sixteenth century

Three unusual pieces of evidence allow us to learn more about the people who lived on the small farms:

1. The township of Sutton Weaver

The Warburtons owned the whole of the township of Sutton. Both a map and a detailed field-by-field survey and valuation have survived.[88] These were not made until 1753, but due to the extraordinary continuity of tenant families in Sutton, we can get a good idea of the position 200 to 300 years earlier. Map 5 is a simplified version of the 1753 map, and photographs of the original map are printed on plates 8 and 9. Appendix 3.1 lists the Sutton farms in 1753 with the area and annual value of each holding. Sutton Hall had demesne land of 257 acres and there were 22 tenant farms which occupied virtually all the remainder of the township. There were six cottages, five of them near the wharf. All these cottages were built in the seventeenth or eighteenth centuries after the wharf and cheese warehouses were

---

Map 5 continued

indicated. The farms T and V, which were enclosed earlier from the Heath, are shown with their land beside their houses as are the two farms K and L. Farms U and E had smaller amounts of land beside their houses near the Marsh. All the other farms originally had strips in the common fields which were exchanged and consolidated around 1600 so that, for example, 20 strips became five small fields. Some of the unusual names of the old enclosed fields numbered 1 to 11 are given. These fields were mostly in fairly level areas and were probably originally used for arable or meadow.

88 WM Box 21.

constructed.[89] Five of the main farms had been occupied by the same families since 1545, and the lists demonstrate more generally that there had been little change in the tenant families in the two centuries before 1753.

Using the map and Appendix 3.1, we can reconstruct some of the history of Sutton township. It was a place that had been settled early. Its position opposite the old royal town of Frodsham and the river crossing at the mouth of the Weaver indicates its geographical importance. Like other old villages in Cheshire, it was a nucleated settlement with a village street containing most of the houses. Originally it had a number of common fields in which the villagers had strips and a common meadow, also in strips. Right up to 1753 it had marshes grazed in common. This arrangement of a village street and common fields in Sutton may be contrasted with the layout in the Whitley Lordship. Only one of the townships in the Lordship had a village and common fields – the township of Over or Higher Whitley. In the other four townships shown on Map 3 all the farmhouses, each surrounded with its fields, were distributed over the land. This was evidently the newer pattern of settlement. Most of the land of Sutton sloped gently down from the high ground (170 ft or 52 m) of Stockham Heath to the river. This heath seems to have been still common grazing land in 1572. Between then and 1628 the whole township was enclosed and the common fields were divided up. An amount of about 8d an acre was added to the annual rents for this extra land. This was what caused the increase in rents shown in Appendix 3.1.

The 1753 survey provides an example of the variety of land values in a township. The farms belonging to the houses in the main street were worth about £1 an acre in 1753. These values included the benefit of the use of Sutton Marsh, so without the Marsh each acre was only worth an average of £0.85. Nevertheless, this was the best land in the township and was presumably the first brought into use. When the Anglo-Saxon or Norman lords had established their demesne at Sutton Hall, they had to make do with the second grade of land, worth about £0.71 an acre in 1753. Sometime in the medieval period, a large ring-fenced property around K and L on the map seems to have been created on the worst land in the township, worth only £0.62 an acre in 1753. This was probably a 'freehold'.[90] The Warburtons evidently reacquired this land before 1539 and divided it into two roughly equal halves. Its different character is shown by the facts that these farms did not participate in the general enclosure made between 1573 and 1628, nor did they have any share in the Sutton Marsh grazing. The old rent of only 5.7d an acre probably reflected the poor quality of the land.

89 See map and text in Foster, 1998, p. 7. Leases in WM Boxes 4, 5.
90 Some of the charters listed under Sutton in Beamont, 1866, may refer to this land.

It was probably between the thirteenth and fifteenth or early sixteenth centuries that the four farms that did not have houses in the main street were established. By this period the idea of nucleated villages had been abandoned in Cheshire, and farmhouses were erected in their own fields. Farms 'T' and 'V' were created on the high ground that had probably been part of Stockham Heath which was only worth £0.65 an acre in 1753. The other two farms, 'U' and 'E', were made on the fringes of Sutton Marsh and were worth as much as any old village land. Improved drainage technology may have permitted these last two farms to be made.

These four farms probably represent efforts to make the maximum possible use of the township's land and with the creation of these four farms, the township was in a sense 'full'. The tenants were evidently not keen to give up any more of their 'common' land for development as additional farms. They seem to have preferred to divide it among themselves and they agreed to pay extra rent and presumably extra entry fines to do this. The reorganization and enclosure will have significantly increased the agricultural output of the township.

2. *The Cogshall estate in 1578*

The best evidence I have found of the construction of the houses and the arrangement of fields in north Cheshire in the sixteenth century is a map of a freehold estate at Cogshall in Whitley Lordship. The map (Pl. 10) was made about 1578 in connection with a legal action.[91] It shows a freehold, and possibly part copyhold estate of 173 acres[92] called Hall of Burrows. In October 1555, Richard Massie of Rixton, Lancashire, Esq. had sold it to his cousin Ralph Massie for around £1 an acre. The details of the 1578 lawsuit are unimportant, but the detail of the map is interesting.

In 1846 the estate was called Cogshall Hall. The main house was then, as it still is, near Senna Green (in the top left-hand corner of the old map), and the land was described as the ancient demesne of the Hall. The old site of the Hall (or capital messuage) is now known as Brook Farm. The name, Hall of Burrows, was presumably derived from a family called Burrows who owned it before the Massies. The two or three families called Burrows who lived in Whitley Lordship in 1526/7 may have been relations of this earlier family. The main house (Pl. 11) is shown as a single-storey hall, with a door and one large window on the south side, which was evidently heated by a fire in the centre of the room, the smoke from which escaped through the lantern shown on the ridge of the roof. The three smaller buildings surrounding the Hall were presumably the kitchen, stables/cowshed and the barn.

91 P.R.O. DL1/108.
92 Acreage from 1846 tithe map.

The courtyard was enclosed with a pale fence. Around the Hall are green-coloured areas with trees, which were probably gardens and orchard. The whole estate was divided into fields bounded by hedges in which large timber trees were grown at regular intervals. The brown-coloured land presumably represented the arable. Measuring these brown fields with the aid of the tithe map gives an area of only 27 acres. Even 30 acres would be less than 20% of the estate. This seems to confirm what many inventories suggest, that growing corn was a small part of Cheshire agriculture. Farmers concentrated on producing cattle by using their land as pasture and meadow. The concentration of the arable round the house suggests that this land was kept arable. The 'up and down' husbandry – ploughing up grassland for use as arable for a few years – with its better fertility was probably not yet being practised because ploughs were not strong enough.[93]

Several other houses are shown. The one near the mill (Pl. 12) was similar to the Hall, but slightly smaller. It was shown with a back addition as well as a lantern to allow the smoke to escape from the roof. It had a single outbuilding, but a good-sized garden or orchard. The man who looked after and operated the mill would presumably have lived in this house. The mill itself is shown as a small building beside a large undershot wheel. The stream is not drawn much wider on the west than the east side, so there was evidently no dam and little water storage on the west side. Without this facility, the mill can have operated only periodically after rain, as the stream is a small one.[94] On the south side of the map is a long, wide field between the two bridges. This is coloured differently to the estate and to the adjoining lands, and so was probably common (or waste) land over which the estate had grazing rights. This was the sixteenth-century road, the modern road occupying only a part of this wide field.

This map gives a good impression of the physical appearance of rural north Cheshire in the 1570s. In Chapter 1 of my *Seven Households* it appears that brick hearths and flues built in the walls probably only began to be constructed in this area at the end of the sixteenth century. This technical innovation allowed a first floor to be inserted between the ground floor and the roof timbers, as noted in Thomas Jackson's house in the 1650s and as shown in Thomas Millington's house, both in Chapter 3 of *Seven Households*. The fields on the map are shown in a similar manner to that used in the seventeenth-, eighteenth- and nineteenth-century estate maps. The 1846 tithe map shows many of the same fields and hedges. The areas of common or waste land that existed in the sixteenth century did not survive so long.

93 See Foster, 2002, p. 43, for a description of ploughs in the 1580s and p. 115 for 'up and down' farming in the 1650s and 1660s.
94 The mill site can still be seen. There was a dam in the nineteenth century.

In this map such areas were the wide road and Senna Green. Areas of this type were usually enclosed sometime between 1550 and 1750.[95]

3. The development of Great Budworth

Map 6 shows the township of Great Budworth as it probably was around 1550. The blank area was the part owned by the Warburtons and their two freeholders. The edged and shaded areas were those owned by the successors to Norton Abbey.[96] In 1544, all the land in Budworth which the Abbey had owned was sold by the Crown to John Grimsditch (see Appendix 3.7 for details) who had already arranged to sell it. John Hall and Edward Malbon were the Abbey's tenants on the two halves of its old demesne land and they each bought the freehold of their farm. Each contained about 60 acres. George Arrowsmith bought his nine acres and Thomas Anderton

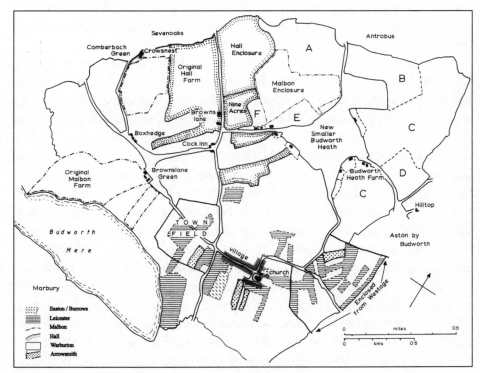

Map 6. Great Budworth township about 1550 showing the new enclosures.
See the text and Appendices 3.7 and 3.10 for full details. A–F are the Warburtons' new enclosures. A and B are 2 farms of 20 acres each, C is Budworth Heath Farm. D is new Hilltop Farm land. See Pl. 13 for the High Street in 1759.

95 See Sutton Weaver above and Great Budworth below. Also Foster, 1998, pp. 14–17.
96 See Appendix 3.10 for details of the sources used to create this map.

bought the five he was renting from the Abbey to add to the Crowsnest freehold which he held from the Warburtons. This was probably about eight acres. Eight of the Abbey's old customary tenants became tenants of the Leicesters of Tabley, while one remained under Robert Eaton.

Between 1548 and 1555[97] these freeholders and the Warburtons, as Lord of the Manor, agreed to enclose a large part of Budworth Heath and part of the Westage or Aston Heath. These common heaths were less good land than the old village fields, some of which were of exceptionally good quality. The map shows the two 30-acre shares that fell to the Halls and Malbons. It also shows the land that the Leicesters and two of the new small freeholders had as their share of the enclosures.[98] The Warburtons' share of the new enclosures was about 170 acres. They made a new large farm of 88 acres that came to be known as Budworth Heath Farm. John Acson bought a three-life lease of it (see Appendix 3.8). The Warburtons seem to have made two more farms of around 20 acres each as well as adding fields to a few existing farms including Hilltop in Aston.

After the sale of the Abbey lands and the enclosure of much of the Heath, Budworth became a different place. Before 1536, the Abbey and the Warburtons had owned the whole township. Everyone living there was a tenant of one or the other. Except for the two small Warburton freeholders, everyone was paying a full market rent for their land. After 1555, Budworth society was headed by two new large freeholders, the Halls and the Malbons. The Arrowsmiths and the Andertons had smaller freeholds. The vicar of Budworth had a good living at a great distance from his patrons at Christ Church, Oxford. John Acson, with his 88-acre three-life lease, was nearly on a level with the Halls and Malbons. These six probably made up the leading group in the village who were independent of the two large landlords, the Warburtons and the Leicesters. As land values rose in the second half of the century, the five property owners came to possess substantial capital. While they were enclosing a third of Great Budworth, the freeholders could have decided to use some of the land for cottages for the growing number of families in the area. They decided not to do so. There was apparently a united view among the richer members of this society that it was undesirable to create too many dwellings for poor people. This enclosure will have increased agricultural output, as did the one in Sutton.

* * *

97 See Appendix 3.7.
98 The land owned by the Andertons of Crowsnest and the Sutton freehold seems to have been the land north of Boxhedge and the tongue of land between the two roads there. We do not know the division between them. Hugh Crosby owned Gib Hill and the Sutton freehold in the 1670s, having bought both from the Suttons (WM Box 3). These two properties seem to have had their share of new enclosures, by arrangement with the Warburtons, out of Boxhedge land.

In the sixteenth century, the character of rural townships slowly altered. Before 1500 their poorest inhabitants were at the bottom of society. Such country people were, however, not badly off as each family had a little farm of at least 5 acres. Because some land was usually unoccupied rents were nominal. Most people worked for themselves, but if they worked for other people wages were good. They produced their own food and most of their own textiles. Each family probably acquired a few skills and did work for their neighbours, who worked for them in return. However, this was not a wealthy society because the technology was simple and there was little specialization of labour and little trade.

An example of the obstacles to trade is provided by the story of Warrington Bridge. The first bridge was built before 1305 and it certainly lasted till 1339. A second bridge was built between 1364 and 1369 and was still standing in 1397. How long it lasted we don't know, but it was no longer in existence in 1465.[99] There was no bridge from then until 1495 when it was rebuilt by the Earl of Derby, the largest landowner in Lancashire. If there had been any great volume of trade passing over the bridge before it fell, it would surely have been replaced more quickly. The movement of Lancashire cattle to the south and east would have been severely limited by the lack of a bridge. This was, no doubt, one reason why the rents in the Honour of Clitheroe were as low as 2.5d to 4d an acre in 1505.[100] The great sixteenth-century trade in Warrington was in textiles, made of hemp and flax grown on the Lancashire plain. This is likely to have been only a small business in the fifteenth century, and, indeed, trade only developed slowly in the sixteenth century. In the 1580s the Shuttleworths at Smithills were still buying only a few items that were not produced locally.[101]

The sixteenth century also brought the new problem of the presence in villages and towns of poor cottagers and vagrants who did not have either work or a cottage. Thus the family on a small farm in a rural township found themselves no longer at the bottom of society. Such families had ceased to pay rack rents; instead they held their farms by the financially privileged tenure of three-life leasehold. They grew richer and they participated increasingly, alongside the newly enriched freeholders, in the development of trade. By the early decades of the seventeenth century, as we shall see in Chapter 4, some families living in country townships had amassed substantial capital through trade. By limiting the number of cottages built in these rural townships, country society ensured that it was composed of fairly well-off but socially equal families.

99 Ormerod, 1882, Vol. 1, p. 602.
100 See Foster, 2002, Appendix 2.1, for Clitheroe rents of 4d per Lancashire acre = 2.5d per statute acre. This was raised to 4d an acre in some land in 1505–07, see p. 61 above.
101 Foster, 2002, Ch. 1, p. 42.

Appendix 3.1. Sutton Weaver tenants and taxpayers, 1753–1539

Map letter	1753 Map and Survey Tenant	Area (statute acres)	Annual value £	Annual rent £ s d	Other tenant families in order 1753–1628	1628 Rental Name	1572 Rental Name	Annual rent £ s d	1545 Tax Return Name	Value of goods £	Value of lands	1539 Rental Name	Annual rent £ s d
A	Sutton Hall demesne lands	257	183	Let at rack rent £170 p.a.		Farmed as demesne	Farmed as demesne		Savage, Elizabeth, widow		Value of lands 140 p.a.	Farmed as demesne	
B	Hough, Thomas	36	33	1 6 0		Hough	Hough	1 1 8	Hough	1		Hough	1 1 8
C	Hough, Thomas	7	8	7 4	Musket, Barker	Pierpoint	Challoner	5 4	Challoner, Thomas	1		Challoner	5 4
D	Hough, Thomas	28	28	1 6 2	Higginson	Moore	Moore	1 2 0	Moore	3		More	1 2 0
E	Hough, Thomas	30	30	1 10 6	Wright	Worrall	Worrall	1 0 0	Worrall	1		Worrall	(damage)
F	Okell, Robert (higher house)	30	29	17 6	Williamson, Pierson	Hough	Moore	13 4	Moore	3		More	13 4
G	Okell, Robert (lower house)	23	20	13 6	Dallam	Okell	Okell	9 4	Okell	1		(damage)	9 4
H	Okell, Robert	19	19	12 8		Okell	Okell	8 6	Okell	4		Jenkinson	8 6
I	Okell, Robert	34	31	1 3 4	Dutton	Weston	Allen	19 2	Allen	4		Allen	9 2
K	Okell, George	76	47	1 16 11	Williamson, Hough	Challoner	Challoner	1 16 8	Challoner, John; Challoner, Richard	1; 1		Challoner and Barker	} 3 13 4
L	Okell, George	78	48	1 16 11	Barker, Farrer	Martin	Martin	16 8	Martin	1			
M	Mulliner, Thomas	33	33	1 5 2	Miller, Williamson, Sarratt, Wilcockson, Pickering	Cheshire	Drinkwater	1 0 0	Drinkwater	10		(damage)	1 0 0

N	Starkey, James	27	28	1 1 0	Edwardson	Barlow	Barlow	16 10	Barlow	4	Barlow	16 10
O	Starkey, James	19	20	1 12 6	Shaw family till 1749	Shaw	Shaw	12 5	Shaw, Thomas / Shaw, Margery	1	Shaw	11 3
P	Jackson, Mary, widow	14	14	12 0	Allott	Worrall	Cooke	4 1		1	Cooke	4 1
Q	Taylor, Thomas	31	32	1 2 11		Roughsegge	Roughsegge	18 9		5	(damage)	18 9
R	Okell, Thomas	20	21	15 5		Potter	Potter	11 3	Potter	1	Potter	11 3
S	Morres, Hugh	13	15	13 6	Lawrenson, Dallam	Johnson	Lawrenson	9 4	Lawrenson	1	Bradburne	9 damage
T	Harper, Thomas	52	40	19 7		Harper	Harper	14 5	Harper	5	Harper	4 5
U	Gee, Nathaniel	38	38	1 12 4	Jennings	Hale	Hale	8 2	Hale 1	1	Hale	1 8 0
V	Mainwaring, Thomas	28	21	13 5		Kirkham	Kirkham	9 2	Kirkham	2	(damage)	(damage)
W	Hale, John	11	13	11 4		Hale	Hale	7 2	Hale	5	Hale	7 2
X	Cartwright, James	18	15	9 4	Anderton	Tollett	Challoner	5 7	Bradburne / Carker, Robert / Carker, Ellen	2 / 4 / 1	(damage)	5 5
TOTALS		922		£22 10 4				£17 7 10				

Sutton Marsh 103

Woods, lanes, cottages, pits, and five acres freehold 111

Total 1,136

Ordnance Survey 1,189

Sources 1539 Rental – I.P.M Sir Peter Warburton, 21 July 1550 (Arley Hall)
1572 Rental – WM Box 2 and Arley Hall
Remainder – WM Boxes 2, 4, 17 and 21
Tax Return DLT/F64

Notes

1. In 1753 in addition to these 22 farms there were six cottages, each with under one acre, mostly near the bridge. The earliest of them first appears in a rental of 1716.
2. The same annual rents were paid for each holding between 1628 and 1753.
3. All farms except 'K' and 'L' included 'Cowgates' in the 103 acres of Sutton Marsh.
4. There are 24 names in the 1628 rental which suggests an error.
5. There are 24 taxpayers' names in the 1545 return.
6. To aid comparability across the centuries, the spelling of names in this and other tables has been standardized.

Appendix 3.2. *Nether Tabley tenants and taxpayers 1543–45.*

1545 taxpayers	Value of Lands £ p.a.	Value of Goods £	Rent payers 1543	Annual rent £	s	d
Bellingham, William	3		same as taxpayer	1	2	8
Brock, John		4	same	2	0	0
Brooke, John		3	same	1	2	0
Broome, Geoffrey		4	same	1	7	0
Broome, John		3	same	1	5	0
Faulkner, John		4	same	1	2	4
Foxley, George		2	same	1	6	8
Leicester, Peter, arm.	20					
Norbury, James		9	same	1	16	4
Ridgway, John		4	same	1	3	8
Shaw, Edward		1	Henry Shaw		16	0
Simcock, Ralph		3	same		16	0
Warburton, John		1				
Widder, Robert		4	same		13	6
Wilkinson, Thomas		3	same		18	10
Wolmer, Charles		3	same		11	10
			Huchinson, Humphrey	1	18	8
			Moberly, John	1	3	4
			Reade, John		4	0
			Simcock, Roger		6	8
			TOTAL	£19	14	6

Sources: Rental DLT/B13, folio 166; Tax Return DLT/F64.

Notes
1. Members of the Warburton family appear in other Tabley rentals of this period (e.g., 1554) paying a rent of 4s a year. The omission of a Warburton from this rental may be a clerical error.
2. Humphrey Huchinson appears in no other rental.
3. Moberly, Reade, and Simcock all appear in other rentals. It is possible that a) their lands were actually in neighbouring townships, where they were taxed. The Simcocks had a farm in Marston where two Simcocks were taxed. These lands could have been included in the Tabley rental for administrative convenience. There is a note that one of the rents included lands in Plumley. A John Mobberley was assessed on £4 goods in Plumley. Or, b) the tenants may have lived in another township and so have been taxed there. c) John Reade may have been too poor to be taxed.

Appendix 3.3. *Appleton taxpayers, freeholders, and leaseholders, 1545–72*

Taxpayers 1545	Lands £ p.a	Goods £	Freeholders Leaseholders 1572	Leasehold annual rent £	s	d	F'hold chief rent s	d
Berry, Richard		1	*Brooke, Thomas of Norton, arm.*				15	1
Caldwell, John, Jnr	6		Caldwell, Thomas, Jnr	2	4	5		
Caldwell, John, Snr		4	Caldwell, Thomas, Snr	1	1	1		
Caldwell, Thomas		4	Caldwell, Richard		13	5		
			Clayton, John de Shepcroft				1	8
Clayton, John	2		Clayton, John		8			
			Clayton, trustees for Dennow				10	0
Cragge, Thomas		5	*Crosby, Thomas for Henshall*				6	3
Dainteth, Henry		3	Dainteth, John		8	0		
Dainteth, John		3	*Dainteth, Thomas*				Rose	
			Davies, heirs of William				Rose	
			Dewsbury, Peter	1	3	10		
Foxley, John		4						
Gamond, Cecilia		2	Gamond, Thomas and George		19	1		
Gamond, Richard		6	Garratt, Thomas		2			
Gatcliffe, Richard		1	Gatcliffe, John	1	6	3		
Gatcliffe, Thomas		1	*Gregg, Ralph of Bradley*				Rose	
Grimsditch, John	10							
Grimsditch, Thomas		4	Grimsditch, Thomas	2	1	5		
Grimsditch, William		1						
Hankinson, Peter		1						
Hankinson, Robert		1						
Harper, William		3						
Hayton, Dosse		1						
Hatton, Thomas		1						
Hatton, William		4						
Hill, Peter		2	*Hill, Peter*				9	2
Janion, Elizabeth		2						
Johnson, Peter		1						
Johnson, Thomas		1	*Johnson, Thomas*				1	7
Latchford, Robert		5	Leigh, William		19	8		
Marbury, Richard	2		Marbury, Richard of Burleyheyes	1	6	8		
			Marbury, Richard of Walton				3	4

Name	Tax	Name					
Middleton, Ralph	3						
Millington, Robert	3						
Moore, James	2						
Newall, Christopher	6						
Newton, George	2						
Normandie, William	1	Normandie, William	1	1	5		
		Percival, Peter				Rose	
		Percival, Peter	1	15	1		
Reddish, Elizabeth	2	Reddish, Thomas	1	12	1		
		Reddish, Ralph		6			
Renshaw, William	3	Richardson, Anne, widow	1	16	4		
		Rogerson, Robert		11	3		
Sankey, Peter	4	Sale, Ralph		9	6		
		Savage, Sir John					3
Sayer, Henry	5	Sayer, Robert and Joanna	1	15	4		
Sayer, Robert	6						
Shaw, Ralph	1						
Starkey, Richard	10	*Starkey, Thomas, arm. of Stretton*				3	7
		Starkey, Robert		13	6		
Stockton, Geoffrey	2						
Stockton, John	1						
Twiss, John	4	Venables, Anthony	1	10	6		
Warburton, Margery	3	Warburton, John	1	14	1		
Warburton, Hamon	2	*Warburton, Hamon*				2	0
		Warburton, Thomas of Partington				3	0
Watt, James	4	*Watt, Thomas*				2	11
		Watt, John		11	9		
		Watt, Thomas		6	0		
		Yordsfoot, Thomas		3			
		Yordsfoot, Thomas				4	4

Sources: Tax Return DLT/F64; Rental WM Box 2 and Arley Hall.

Notes
1. 'Arm.' is the abbreviation for Latin '*armiger*' = possessing an heraldic coat of arms.
2. Freeholders' token rents are marked 'Rose' here.
3. See Foster, 1992, pp. 39 and 41 for maps and pp. 67–74 for survey of Appleton in 1744. See Foster, 1998, p. 14, for enclosures in the seventeenth century.
4. Some freeholders may be unrecorded in the 1572 Warburton rental. A Hatton, a Middleton, and a Millington all paid tax on goods in Appleton in 1545. All these families had small freeholds in 1666. Robert Millington who paid tax on £3 worth of goods, seems to be the same man who appears in the 1580 Heralds Visitation under Millington of Appleton. (Harleian Soc, Vol. 18, 1882, p. 179.) A deed in WM Box 62 suggests the Stockton family owned land in Stockton before 1600.

Appendix 3.4 The Whitley Lordship tenants, taxpayers and owners, 1526/7–1662

Table A.

1526/7 Tenant	Annual rent £ s d	1545 Taxpayer	Value Land Goods £ p.a. £	1595 Tenant	Annual rent £ s d	Survey 9 June 1612 Tenant	Farm houses	Cottages	Statute acres	Annual rent £ s d	Additional information
Amery, John	13 8	Allen, Richard	3	Allen, John	1 3 11	Allen, John, gent.	–	1	3	3 3 4	tenant – John Goulden
Anderton, William	6 7	Nicholas	3	Anderton, William	4 5	Anderton, William	–	–	15	4 5	
Antrobus, Richard	13 4	Antrobus, Sibella	4								
		Ashton, Thomas	5								
		William	2								
Barber, Thomas	1 4 3	Barber, Geoffrey	1	Barber, George	12 5	Barber, William	1	–	20	12 6	
Bennett, William	1 18 0	Barlow, William	4	his wife	1 8	Barlow, John	–	1	6	3 4	
Richard	1 8 0	Richard		Thomas	11 11	Bennett, widow and her son Thomas	1	–	28	18 7	
Burrows, John	8 3	Bennett, Peter	5	William	12 6	Burrows, Hugh	1	–	21	10 7	
Piers	6 0	Thomas	3	Bennett, Christopher	1 5 0	Humphrey	1	–	21	10 11	
Piers	10 6			William	18 7						
				Burrows, Hugh / Humphrey / and Ellen Hale	10 11						
Carrington, Thomas	1 8 4	Caldwell, Geoffrey	4	Caldwell, Geoffrey (for Hastie's lane)	2 0	Caldwell, Geoffrey	–	–	3	2 0	
Colstenstock, Richard	1 8 4	Colstenstock, John	5	Thomas	14 2	Coppock, Thomas and his wife Eme	1	–	11	10 0	in Cogshall
Thomas	3 14 11	his wife	4	Colstenstock, Ann	1 8 10	Cocker, Ann, widow and her son John	1	1	7	4 11	tenants – herself and Thomas Telier
Thomas	1 9 7	Peter	12	John	10 4	Crosby, Hugh, gent.	3	2	148	4 11 8	
Thomas	6 7	Thomas	2	Peter	14 4	Hugh, gent.	1	–	34	1 1 6	tenant – Robert Richardson
Thomas	1 18 8	William	2	Cooke, Cecily	1 9	John, gent.	1	2	51	1 8 11	
		Crosby, John, clerk	15	Cocker, Peter	4 11						
		his wife	4	Crosby, Jane	4 11 8						
		Richard	15	Thomas	1 8						
				Hugh	1 10 0						
Daniel, Randle	15 1	Daniel, Agnes	4	Daniel, John	15 0	Daniel, Ann, widow	1	–	25	15 0	
Daken, Geoffrey	19 5	Daken, Peter	6	Daken, Thomas of Hill	19 6	Daken, Thomas of Hill	1	1	32	19 6	
Dewsbury, Thomas	1 3 10	Dewsbury, Randle	4	Thomas of Town	1 4 6	Thomas of Town	[1]	[1]	[40]	[1 4 6]	mss damage
				Dainteth, John	6 0	Dainteth, John	–	–	15	4 5	
				Ditchfield, Peter	1 8	Ditchfield, Peter	–	1	3	2 6	

1526/7

Tenant	Annual rent £ s d
Eaton, John (Heyton)	1 5 9
John	8 0
Hugh	19 7
Robert	1 4 4
Robert	9 0
Thomas	18 5

1545

Taxpayer	Value Land Goods £ p.a. £
Eaton, George	6
Lawrence	4
Richard	2
Robert	10 (or 15)
William	4
William	3

1595

Tenant	Annual rent £ s d
Eaton, Edmund	1 3 11
George of Pole	1 9 0
Hugh	1 2 7
John	2 4
Peter	9 6
Richard of Lake	5 1
Richard of Barrowlane	15 3
Richard, clerk	11 4
Robert and Geo Vernon	2 1 10
Robert of Lake	1 0 1
Thomas and M. Dainteth	1 2 8

Survey 9 June 1612

Tenant	Farm houses	Cottages	Statute acres	Annual rent £ s d	Additional information
Eaton, John of Sandiway, gent.	2	2	68	2 0 4	
John of Sevenoaks	1	1	20	10 6	
John son of Edmund	1	—	21	13 0	
Alice sister of John	—	—	6	3 0	now wife of Hugh Key
Ann sister of John	—	—	2	2 1	now wife of John Monks
Katherine sister of John	—	—	2	2 1	now wife of Peter Fernley
John of the Hollies	1	1	19	11 0	8
Richard, clerk	1	—	11	8 6	vicar of Gt Budworth
Richard, clerk	1	—	21	18 2	vicar of Gt Budworth
Anne, widow and Richard	—	[1]	[10]	[6 0]	
Richard of [Lake]	[1]	[1]	[8]	[5 1]	
Richard	1	—	21	15 3	1 cottage, tenanted by his sister, in reversion.
Thomas of Reed	2	1	38	1 15 3	
Thomas of Shawbrook	1	2	38	1 2 8	
Thomas of Sevenoaks	1	—	26	17 4	
William	1	1	21	12 11	Wm and Richard half each in reversion after death of George Eaton
Richard, vicar of GB	1	1	21	12 11	

Survey 9 June 1612

1526/7 Tenant	Annual rent £ s d	1545 Taxpayer	Value Land/Goods £ p.a.	1595 Tenant	Annual rent £ s d	1612 Tenant	Farm houses	Cottages	Statute acres	Annual rent £ s d	Additional information
Fernley, John	19 4	Fernley, George	4	Fernley, George	1 1 2	Fernley, Margaret and her son George	1	—	8	4 7	
John	4 8	Richard	4	Sibil	4 4						
Thomas	1 2 7	Roger	1	William, Jnr	4 7						
		Thomas	1	Foxley, Thomas	19 9	Foxley, John	1	—	34	19 9	
Green, John	7 0			Gandy, William	4 0	Gandy, William	1	1	23	13 11	
Goulden, Robert	18 0	Goulden, Elizabeth	1	Goulden, Randolph	13 4	Goulden, Randle	1	—	21	13 4	
Grimsditch, Randle	4 6	George	9	John	4 0	Gregg, Thomas, gent.	1	—	25	13 2	tenants Edw Hill and Richard Mere
				Grimsditch, John	19 7	Thomas	—	3	25	4 0	turbary
				Gregg, Thomas	2 0	Grimsditch, John, gent.	—	—	26	19 7	son of Thomas
Hankinson, William	1 2 7	Hall, Hugh	2	Hankinson, John	1 8 8	Hankinson, John	2	1	72	2 6 2	1 messuage in possession 1 in reversion
Highfield, John	19 1	William	5	Haste, John	9 0						
John	15 8	Hankinson, John	1	Hewett, Thomas	4 0	Harper, William	—	1	5	4 6	tenant Wm Knowles
		Hayes, Jacob	2	Thomas, clerk	6 8	Hayes, Nicholas, gent.	1	1	19	10 0	
		Highfield, Thomas	10	Hickson, Robert for part Haste's	4 0	Hickson, Robert	—	1	5	3 1	tenants Thos Eyes and Peter Barlow
				Highfield, Thomas and his mother	15 4	Robert	—	1	1	3 6	
				Hollinshead, Mr and George Venables	1 8 6	Highfield, Thomas	1	—	25	15 4	
						Hollinshead, Edward, son of Edward H, clerk	1	1	44	1 8 6	tenant Humphrey Cherry
Jackson, Robert	18 11	Jackson, John	1	Jackson, Peter	19 1	Jackson, John	1	—	34	19 1	
		Janion, Richard	2	Janion, John	1 4 0	Janion, Thomas	2	1	40	1 4 0	
		Johnson, Hugh	2	Key, Katherine	13 8	Key, Randle	1	—	21	13 8	
Lowton, Piers	1 1 11	Lowton, Thomas	4	Lowton, George	1 1 11	Lowton, John	1	—	36	1 1 11	
				Lydiate, John	6 4	Lyon, Wm Bp of Cork and Ross and his son Wm Lyon	1	—	11	3 8	tenants Humphrey Frere & Jane Page

Survey 9 June 1612

1526/7 Tenant	Annual rent £ s d	1545 Taxpayer	Value Land Goods £ p.a. £	1595 Tenant	Annual rent £ s d	Survey 9 June 1612 Tenant	Farm houses	Cottages	Statute acres	Annual rent £ s d	Additional information
Marbury, Robert	17 6	Massie, Edward	2	Marbury, Thos, arm.	1 2 6	Maddock, George	1	–	17	[10 0]	mss damaged
Massie, Wm arm.	1 11 0	Randle	3	Massie, George	1 10 1	Marbury, Thomas Esq	1		42	1 2 6	tenant Richard Eaton of Lake
Moore, John	14 3	Millington, Richard	1	James	17 6	Thomas Esq	1	1	68	1 15 4	in Cogshall
Robert	3 0	Moore, Geoffrey	3	Millington, John	1 1 3	Peter, gent.	1		47	1 8 10	
Robert	10 9	Thomas	1	Moore, George	10 10	Massie, Edmund	1	1	37	2 1	in Cogshall
				John	4 0	James	1		19	10 10	in Cogshall
				Ralph	14 3	Millett, Sibil, widow	–		7	4 0	
						Millington, Mrs Margaret	2		38	1 3	tenants Richard Eaton and Richard Richardson
Newall, Geoffrey	1 0 7	Newall, Geoffrey	4	Newall, wife of		Moore, John	–	[1]	[6]	[4 0]	mss damaged
John	5 6	wife of Peter	1	Geoffrey	10 0	Thomas	1	1	23	14 5	
John	1 0 10			John	1 5 0	Thomas	1	1	23	[15 1]	'for Stockton's house'
Richard	10 0			Robert	1 0 8	Newall, John	1	1	42	1 7 0	
William	18 4			Norcot, Thomas	6 1	Richard	1		36	1 0 8	
						William	1		19	10 0	
Okell, Henry	1 4 5	Okell, John	3	Okell, Eme	10 0	Norcot, Thomas	1		12	6 1	
Peacock, Peter	11 5	Peacock, Richard	1	Peacock, John	1 5 3	Peacock, John the elder	1		7	5	
Simon	19 3	Roger	4	+ son		Margaret and her son John					
		Thomas	1	Richard	12 2	Richard	1		42	1 [5 6]	mss damaged
Pemberton, Robert	12 4	Pemberton, Margaret	3	Pemberton, Thomas	1 8 10	Pemberton, Robert	2		57	1 16 1	
Robert	1 8 4	Robert	4			Thomas	1		8	5 4	
Pennington, Henry	11 3	Pennington, Jacob	3								
John	1 1 1	Peick? John	2								
Percival, Ralph	5 4										
Ralph	1 0										
Pickering, Piers	9 0	Pickering, Hugh	8	Pickering, Hugh	1 9 6	Pickering, Hugh	2		51	1 13 5	
Piers		wife of William	2	Peter, Snr	1 8 4	Peter the elder and William his son			50	1 10 5	
				Peter	?1 2 2?	Peter the younger	1		47	1 8 4	
Pimlot, William	1 0	Pimlot, William	2								
Poole, Richard	13 8	Poole, Richard	1	Poole, John	18 2	Poole, John the elder	1		44	1 3 7	a barn and 3 bays (an old encroachment)
Robert	1 3 3	Thomas	1				–		–	1 1	
Poole, William		William									

1526/7

Tenant	Annual rent £	s	d
Richardson, Randle		5	1
Robert	1	5	0
Savage, Randle	1	17	4
Randle		16	4
Smith, Richard		18	1
Starkey, Geoffrey	1	7	0
Stockton, Geoffrey		15	5
Thomas		6	5
Venables, Piers	5	13	7
Richard		3	0
Vernon, William	1	1	8
Warburton, Piers, arm.		8	6
Watt, Geoffrey		8	4
Richard	1	4	5
Woodnit, Elizabeth		4	1
Robert		19	9
Worrall, Thomas	1	2	1
John			
Wright, Henry		5	3
Peter			
Worsley, Robert			
Yannis, John		9	2
Total rent	**£71**	**15**	**4**

1545

Taxpayer	Value Land £ p.a.	Goods £
Richardson, Randle		12
Sankey, Geoffrey		2
Shakeshaft, Hugh		1
wife of Roger		1
Southern, Thomas		3
Thomas		3
Starkey, Richard		1
Stockton, Catherine		1
Peter		1
Robert		4
Venables, John		14
Robert	20	
Robert, Jnr		4
Warner, John		1
Richard		4
Watt, Peter		9
Whitley, Robert		1
John		2
Woodnit, Humphrey		2
John		2
Worrall, John		4
Peter		2
Worsley, Robert		4
Yannis, Thomas		1

1595

Tenant	Annual rent £	s	d
Richardson, John	1	1	8
Peter		10	0
Peter	1	5	0
Starkey, Thos, arm.	1	6	11
Stockton, Richard		15	1
Travers, Bryan (paid by Richard Dutton)		3	7
Warburton, Peter, arm. copyhold		10	0
Ward, William, gent., copyhold	3	18	4
Whitley Thomas		4	1
Woodnit, Richard		19	10
Worrall, Thomas	1	2	1
Worsley, Robert		3	9
Total rent	**£74**	**19**	**7**

Survey 9 June 1612

Tenant	Farm houses	Cottages	Statute acres	Annual rent £	s	d	Additional information
Richardson, John	1	1	36	1	1	8	cott has 1½ acres in Cogshall
Peter the younger and the elder	–	1	40	1	5	0	
Seaburne, William	1	1	42	1	5	0	tenants Ann Cocker widow, George Plumpton, John Gerard, & Richard Tiler
Starkey, Thomas Esq	1	2	42	1	16	8	
Thomas Esq	–	–	4		4	1	Turbary in Hades Moss
Warburton, Peter Esq	–	–	34		18	6	
Ward, Mrs Elizabeth, widow	3	1	114	3	18	3	tenants John Waltall, gent., William Gandy, John Barlow, widow Massie, Thomas Telier
Whalley, William	1	–	3		1	9	
Whitley, Thomas, gent.	1	–	6		4	1	
Woodnit, Richard	1	–	33		19	10	
Approximate totals, including estimates where mss is damaged:	77	41	2,393	£73	13	9	

9 cottages on the Common with gardens or hempyard. All were encroachments:

	Rent	
	s	d
Barker, John	1	
Bennett, Elizabeth	1	
Bennett, Thomas	Nil (a 'poor' cottage)	
Cross, Robert	4	0
Fernley, Thomas	1	1½
Lidyate, Katherine	Nil	
Nixon, Margaret	1	
Pickering, George	1	0
Pointer, Ann	1	

Notes

A) To 1526/7 Rental   *Source: P.R.O. DL 43 5/15*

1. The document is marked Tenants at Will.
2. The spelling of names varies in the originals, e.g., Heyton for Eaton. The spelling of names has been standardized here so they read across from 1526 to 1612.
3. The rental is for a half year. All rents have been doubled to make them annual.
4. After the 77 tenants' names and rents shown here, there is a list of 26 rents due at Michaelmas. Excluding the
£13 6s 8d due from Peter Warburton for Northwood Park (Crowley, see above, pp. 23–4) the list totals £4
13s 1d. All except three of the names are those of tenants. They were probably for turbary (peat) or timber.

B) To 1595 Rental   *Source: P.R.O. DL 44/537.*

1. As well as P. Warburton's rent of £26 13s 4d for Northwood Park, this document lists the following chief
rents:

	£	s	d	
Peter Warburton, arm. barbed arrows		1	4	
Thomas Marbury, arm.		1	0	(This may have been the freehold in Cogshall listed in his father's IPM 35 Eliz.)
Thomas Starkey, arm.		7	0	
Thomas Grimsditch			4	
Robert Venables, gent.	1	10	0	
Thomas Brassie and Amer his wife		1	2	
	£2	0	10	
Also, Thomas Grimsditch for Old Mills		10	0	

2. The rents listed include some 35 payments between 1d and 4d for 'encroachments'. These odd pennies have
been added to the rent in the list printed here.
3. George Massie listed as a copyholder was also the freeholder of Burrows Hall (see p. 77) in Cogshall in his
IPM 41 Eliz.

C) To 1612 Survey   *Source: P.R.O. DL44/903*

1. The survey has additional information about the copyholders' tenure, which includes the following:
a) Cogshall paid £20 every 21 years for the 'town tacks.'
b) A heriot of the best good was due at the death of every copyholder.
c) The entry fine was one third of every man's rent.
d) The Commons were 'over 200 (Cheshire) acres' (423 statute acres), of which 80 Cheshire (169 statute)
acres were lanes and highways. The rest was moss (peat-bog) and full of pits with common of herbage.
2. All major tenancies included a Moss Room (an area in the Moss from which they could take turves – peat).
These were mostly in 'Parkmoss'.

D) Tax Return: DLT/F64.

Table B. *Fee-farmers in Whitley Lordship listed by Sir Peter Leicester, 1662*[1]

The owners in each township are listed separately so that some indication of the where-abouts of the sixteenth-century farms is possible. See also Map 3.

	Annual value of land		
	£	s	d
Antrobus			
Anderton, Richard of Boxhedge (no house)	6	12	0
Ashley, Thomas of Swineherd	1	6	0
Barber, Peter	10	0	0
Barlow, Christopher; about 1½ acres*	[1	10	0][2]
Peter	15	6	8
Colthurst, Millington of Sandley Bridge in Little Warford cum Marthall	8	6	8
Eaton, John, called Sprat, Quaker	30	0	0
Peter	5	0	0
Richard	11	6	8
Thomas of Shawbrook	16	12	0
Fernley, William, now in possession of widow Eaton of the Pole	2	13	4
Fogge, Mr of Liverpool (no house)	67	6	8
Gandy, William of Frandley – the Chapel ground	2	0	0
Gregg, Mr of Bradley in Appleton	3	0	0
Haslehurst, Richard, cottage in possession Richard Woodworth	1	6	0
Richard, about six acres no house*	[6	0	0]
Hollinshead, Isaac	20	0	0
Leadbeater, William, now in possession J. Cooke	13	6	8
Massey, Richard of Helsby	2	13	4
Moss, Peter	26	13	4
Newall, John, the elder	6	13	4
John, the younger	8	13	4
Okell, Robert of Crowley, about 1½ acres*	[1	10	0]
Pickering, Peter, Mr Marbury of the Mere and Hugh Crosby of Gibhill, trustees of	29	6	8
widow of Pickmere, now in possession of Thomas Eaton of Shawbrook	[2	0	0]
Robert, of Thelwall and Crowley, lawyer, for Ashwood	9	6	8
Pope, Mrs of London, now in possession of Geo. Partington	6	12	0
Richardson, Richard of Middlewalk	6	12	0
Venables, Robert, Mr	24	0	0
Total	345	13	4

1 After the tenants bought their lands in 1612, they continued to pay the ancient rents which were called Fee-farm rents. When Sir Peter wrote at the head of the list '? whether these fee-farmers are to appear at the Assizes yearly' he was asking whether these new freeholders were to be treated the same as the old ones who paid 'chief rents'. DLT/B36.

* These have been taken as Cheshire acres.

2 Brackets indicate a blank in text. The figures have been estimated on internal evidence.

Cogshall

Ashton, Mrs[3]	40	0	0
Greene, Thomas of Sandbach, now in possession of Richard Percival	4	13	4
Lowe, George of Hartford	1	2	0
Marbury, Thomas of Marbury Esq	40	0	0
Massey, Edmund	23	6	8
Piggot, Edward	10	0	0
Pownall, Thomas of Barnton	2	13	4
Richardson, John	13	6	8
Total	**£135**	**2**	**0**

Middlewalk

Basnet, Joseph for the Horseshoe	6	13	4
Cheshire, Thomas of Halton (no house)	5	13	4
Crosby, Peter	16	0	0
Eaton, Mrs, of Ireland	12	13	4
widow, of Pole lane	18	13	4
Foxley, William	6	13	4
Jackson, Peter of Yorkshire, minister	10	0	0
Lowton, Thomas	12	0	0
Nield, Thomas for Burtonwoods House	2	0	0
Norcot, Thomas of Northwich, Quaker	7	6	8
Robinson, – for Pemberton's lands	20	0	0
Warburton, Sir George of Arley	10	13	4
Total	**£128**	**6**	**8**

Over Whitley

Burton, John of Stretton (no house)	2	0	0
Crosby, Hugh, Quaker	20	0	0
Daken, Thomas	12	0	0
Ditchfield, John of Statham in Lymm	13	6	8
Dutton, John of Shepcroft in Appleton	20	0	0
Eaton, John, the younger of the Lake, Quaker	12	10	0
Robert of the Lake	15	0	0
Mrs of Ireland, in possession of Thomas Dewsbury	2	0	0
Grimsditch, Mrs of Grimsditch	10	0	0
Jackson, Thomas	8	0	0
Marbury, John, Quaker	6	0	0
Middlehurst, Margaret, of Stretton, widow	13	6	8
Moores, Thomas, in possession of John Jackson	6	13	4
Thomas of Tarvin, in possession of Jo Wilkinson	1	7	0
widow	10	0	0
Peacock, – , John Wilkinson and John Peacock trustees for	29	0	0
Richard	20	0	0
Pickering, Peter, Quaker	18	13	4
Peter, of 5 lane ends	2	0	0

3 Ormerod, 1882, p. 655.

Shaw, John, Quaker	5	o	o
Starkey, Ralph of Newton, gent, 5 small tenements in lease	[10	o	o]
Venables, Robert of Antrobus in possession of Robert Baxter	3	6	8
Woodnit, William	12	13	4

Total	£252	17	o

Sevenoaks

Bennett, Thomas, a papist	7	6	8
Burrows, Peter	6	13	4
Crosby, Hugh of Gib-hill, Sectary[4]	6	13	4
Eaton, George	11	6	8
John, of the Fields	6	13	4
Robert, of Barrow land	13	6	8
Foxley, Thomas	10	13	4
Gandy, John, Quaker	10	o	o
William of Frandley, Quaker	30	o	o
Highfield, Thomas of Senna Green	10	o	o
Janion, Thomas	23	6	o
Key, Thomas	8	13	4
Lowe, George, of Hartford, in possession of Thomas Wilcockson	30	o	o
Richardson, Richard of Antrobus	6	13	4
Venables, Peter of Lostock Gralam, in possession of Thomas Eaton	7	6	8

Total	£188	12	8
Grand total for fee-farmers	**£1,050**	**11**	**8**

If Mr Fogge had gained his land by drainage since 1612, we need to deduct £67 6s 8d from this total to find the value that Sir Peter attributed to the 2,393 acres of the 1612 survey: £1050-11-8 – £67-6-8 = £983 ÷ 2393 = 8s 3d an acre.

Notes

1. *The amount of freehold land in the Whitley Lordship*
   The Ordnance Survey measured the land as follows:

	Acres
Antrobus including Middlewalk	2,114
Cogshall	520
Higher (Over) Whitley	1,020
Sevenoaks	631
	4,285

The 1612 survey (col. 4 above) measured the copyholds at	2,393
The 1612 survey measured the Commons and roads at	423
and in the Tithe Map (1844) the waters of Whitley Reed covered	309

In Sir Peter Leicester's list of fee-farmers in 1662 (above) Mr Fogge of Liverpool owned land worth £67 6s 8d. This was probably low-lying land near Fogge Farm that he had drained since 1612 by lowering the level of Galebrook. The average value that Sir Peter attributed to the land in 1662 was 8s 3d an acre.

At this rate Mr Fogge's land was	164
Total	3,289

4   Same as Quaker in Over Whitley?

So: Ordnance Survey   4,285
    Less fee-farm, etc.   3,289
    Freehold   996

2. *The freeholds in the Whitley Lordship*
The total area of freehold land in 1612 was probably about 996 acres. The principal owners were:

Venables family, probably the largest freeholders. Their main house was probably on the site of Antrobus Hall. This name was given to the site in the nineteenth century when the Antrobus family reacquired the land. The Venables family had bought the land in the fifteenth century from the Antrobus family.

Marbury family of Marbury. Their land probably adjoined Marbury Hall (see IPM 35 Eliz).

Starkey family of Lower Hall, Stretton. Their land probably adjoined their Stretton land.

Warburton family of Arley, whose land probably adjoined Great Budworth and Aston by Budworth.

Grimsditch of Grimsditch. Their 'tithe prescription' land was probably freehold (see Map 3).

Eaton of the Pole family whose land included their 'tithe prescription.'

Massie family – the Burrows Hall estate in Cogshall was said to be part freehold and part copyhold (see pp. 77–8 and Pls. 10–12 and IPM 41 Eliz).

Brassie family – location unknown.

Whitley family – see IPM 28 Eliz.

Notice that the Eatons and Massies paid no chief rent. The other chief rents were small. They appear not to have been regularly paid in the 1520s. There are similarities with the Warburton freeholders in Appleton in 1572 (p. 86).

3. Deeds in C.R.O. D 5494 suggest the following locations for some of the fee farmers lands:

1615 John Peacock was at the Old Mill in Higher Whitley.

1641–80 The Hankinson and Hollinshead families had land near the Nook in Antrobus.

1658 Thomas Daken owned a house beside 'Meg Gate' at the start of the lane leading north-west from centre of Higher Whitley village.

1662 Richard Peacock had lands near the village centre.

1662 William Leadbeater had a house in Barber's Lane, Antrobus.

1666 John Moore owned 'Towngate' in the centre of Higher Whitley village.

1671 Richard Woodnit owned land south of the centre of this village.

1677 John Marbury was probably at Marbury House in Over Whitley.

before 1682 The Pickering family owned the Reed House, Antrobus.

1732 Barlows were at Grandsire Green.

Appendix 3.5. *Families paying tax on their income from land in 1545*

Table A. People paying tax on lands valued at more than £10 p.a. in 1545

	Value of lands £ p.a.	Tax paid £	s	d
Savage, Lady Elizabeth, widow (of Rocksavage)	140	7	0	0
Dutton, Sir Peter (of Dutton)	133	6	13	3
Warburton, Sir Peter (of Arley)	100	5	0	0
Aston, Thomas, arm. (of Aston)	66	3	6	0
Legh, Sir John of Norbury Booths	55	2	15	0
Leicester, Sir Ralph of Toft	50	2	10	0
Carrington, John, arm. of Carrington	40	2	0	0
Daniel, Thomas, arm. of Over Tabley	40	2	0	0
Talbot, John, arm. of Mobberly	34	1	14	0
Ashley, George, arm. of Ashley	34	1	14	0
Holford, Thomas, gent. of Plumley	30	1	10	0
Mere, William, arm. (of Mere)	20	1	0	0
Carrington, John, Jnr, arm. (of Carrington)	20	1	0	0
Leicester, Peter, arm. of Nether Tabley	20	1	0	0
Marbury, James, arm. of Marbury	20	1	0	0
Starkey, Thomas of Stretton	20	1	0	0
Legh, Robert, arm. of High Legh	20	1	0	0
Booth, Elizabeth, widow of Dunham	20	1	0	0
Venables, Robert of Whitley Lordship	20	1	0	0
Hayes, Thomas (of Litley), Aston by Budworth	20	1	0	0
Domville, Margaret, widow (of Lymm)	17		11	4
Touchet, Thomas of Nether Whitley	17		11	4
Crosby, John, clerk, of Whitley Lordship	15		10	0
Millington, William, gent. of Millington	13		8	8
Venables, Hugh, gent. of Agden	13		8	8
Total:		£47	12	3

Notes
1. The place associated with each family comes from the township in which they paid tax, except where I have supplied it (in parentheses). Six of these people were Commissioners who were separately listed. The Domville widow was living in Marbury. The status, i.e., arm.(iger), gent., etc., also follows the tax return.
2. The only name missing from this list is Mainwaring of Peover. I have not discovered why.

Table B. Surnames of other 'landed' families in Bucklow Hundred in 1545

1.	Arderne	11	Grimsditch
2.	Bellingham	12.	Hanmer
3.	Bold	13.	Hulse
4.	Bowden	14.	Kelsall
5.	Caldwell	15.	Massey
6.	Clayton	16.	Parker
7.	Cluworth (Clough?)	17.	Partington
8.	Cocker	18.	Walton
9.	Culows	19.	Wilkinson
10.	Gleave	20.	Woods

Appendix 3.6. *Calculation of the entry fines (or premium or capital value) of three-life leases or leases for years*

The rate of interest on mortgages or other secured loans in England was as follows:

	%
Up to 1624	at least 10
1624 to 1651	8
1651 to 1704	6
1704 to 1713	5.5
1713 to 1720	5
1720 to 1730	4.5
1730 to 1772	4

Notes:
1. This table is a simplified version of Allen, 1988, pp. 33–50.
2. Before 1624 legal problems with security made loans much less common than they later became.

The payment of an entry fine or premium for a lease is a payment of rent in advance. The payment earns interest. The mathematical calculations depend on the rate of interest and the length of the lease. These have traditionally been available to non-mathematicians in the form of tables of which the following is a skeleton example:

Multiplier for purchasing leases for terms of years

Number of years	Rates of interest		
of the lease	10%	6%	3%
7	4.9	5.6	6.2
14	7.4	9.3	11.3
21	8.6	11.8	15.4
50	9.9	15.8	25.7

Source: Price, 1771

Example: to purchase a lease for 21 years of a property whose annual rent is £10 when the interest rate is 10%, should cost: multiplier 8.6 × £10 = £86.

After leases for 21 years or three lives were introduced in Cheshire in the sixteenth century, a typical calculation in 1575 might have been:

Farm of 30 acres. Old rent @ 8d per acre =	£1	0	0
Annual cost of boons and heriot,	say	15	0
Market rent in 1575 was 5s 0d an acre (from Fig. 1 p. 57)			
Annual market rent of farm, 30 acres × 5s =	7	10	0
Less old rent and boons	1	15	0
Net rent to be purchased	5	15	0

Cost of 21-year lease	8.6 × £5.75 = £49.45
Cost of three-life lease – say 50 years	9.9 × £5.75 = £56.95

It can be seen that these two costs were similar. 21-year and three-life leases were often thought to have the same value at that period.

In 1652, the cost of buying a three-life lease to this farm should have been:

30 acres rent	@ 11s per acre	= £16. 5
Less old rent and boons as above		1.75
Net rent to be purchased		£14. 75

Multiplier 15.8 × £14.75 = £233.

It can be seen from these two examples that the prices of leases were low in the middle of the sixteenth century, and steadily became much larger. Tenants enjoyed a benefit from the rising values. For example a three-life lease, purchased in 1550 for a small sum when market rents were about 2s per acre, became steadily more valuable as market rents rose sharply in the next 50 years. After market rents stabilized in the 1620s, this advantage dwindled away. After 1651 they began to enjoy a new advantage as the multipliers used by landlords did not match the mathematical calculations.

We do not have sufficient information on the two Cheshire estates to know the multipliers used in the sixteenth century. The figures for entry fines that survive suggest that old tenants paid small premiums to renew. Newcomers buying three-life leases may have had their fines calculated with a multiplier of as much as 9. In 1637–42, the Earl of Bridgewater's surveyors were seeking a multiplier of 10 for a 21-year lease and 11 for a new three-life lease.[5] This was the correct figure for a 21-year lease at 8%. A three–life lease should have had a multiplier of around 12. In 1716 Sir Francis Leicester re-leased most of his estate to raise money for his daughter's dowry. His surveyor used a multiplier of 12 for three lives. The multiplier should have been between 16 and 18 depending on the ages of the lives. The highest multiplier for three lives I've seen used in Cheshire was 14. At 4% it should have been 19–21. R. C. Allen found that freehold property was normally bought to yield up to 1% less than the rate of mortgage interest. It could reasonably be argued that the same interest rate should have applied to these long three-life leases. At 3% the multiplier used for three lives should have been between 22 and 26, depending on the ages of the lives.[6] The

5 Hopkins, 1962, p. 23, note 1.
6 All the 'correct' multipliers come from the tables in Price, 1771.

'multiplier' concept used here is similar to the 'number of years purchase' concept often found in discussions of the value of freehold land.[7]

These figures indicate the scale of the advantage enjoyed by the leaseholders. They also explain how the fines paid by the Jackson and Latham families were calculated.[8] The multipliers used for adding one or two lives to leases in Cheshire in the eighteenth century were in proportion to those used for three lives. A multiplier of 1½ or 2 was often used for adding one life, and one between 5 and 7 for adding two lives. There was also a negotiation between landlord and tenant. It was widely known in the eighteenth century that the multipliers used were too low. Custom prevailed over reason till Price's book and a wider interest in annuities changed the traditional view.[9]

Appendix 3.7. *Sale of Norton Abbey lands in Great Budworth and Comberbach in 1544*[10]

1. On 1 July 1544 John Grimsditch bought from the Crown for £226 and a 'chief' rent of £1 4s 1½d

	Annual rent[11]			#
	£	s	d	
Great Budworth				
a) Clerkes House (tenant John Hall)	2	6	0	
b) Newstead (tenants Edward and William Malbon)	2	0	7	
c) Eleven customary tenants				
Thomas Anderton		3	0	
Ralph Newall		6	8	1, 2
Edward Shakeshaft		5	6	1, 2
Emmote Dutton		4	0	1, 2
George Arrowsmith		11	0	
Elizabeth Ackson		6	8	1, 2
George Wider		4	0	2
Hugo Barlow		8	4	2
Hugo Forster		3	8	2
William Heyworth		4	4	2
George Burrows		3	8	1
Total for 11 tenants	3	0	10	
Fishing for three boats in Mere				2

7 It is important to note that the 'number of years purchase' concept only gives a true value of land if the 'annual market value' is the figure that is multiplied. In Crown documents of the sixteenth century the value of old rents was often used. Estimated land values based on old rents are subject to very large errors. See Hoyle, 1992, p. 18, for a table of such values.
8 Foster, 2002, pp. 100 and 156.
9 See also Richard, 1730; Richards 1739; Laurence, 1730; Kerridge, 1953; Clay, 1981.
10 DLT/B15, folios 111 to 119.
11 P.R.O. Ministers Account 1535/36. Sc6 Hen VIII/409.

Comberbach

a) 10 customary tenants

Robert Marbury		11 4	
George Hulme		10 0	
Randle Wirall		5 8	1
Humphrey Shakeshaft		14 0	3
Agnes Walker		6 8	1
Randle Lowe		6 8	1
Lawrence Percival	1	5 0	1
Roger Grimshaw		10 0	1
Thomas Highfield		8 0	3
George Eaton		9	1
Total for 10 tenants	4	18 1	

Notes

1. Clerkes House will have originally been the residence of the monks from Norton Priory. It was later known as Brownslane Farm and is now Brownslow Farm. Newstead was known as Brownslane Green Farm and is now known as Brownslow House. It was evidently built later than Clerkes House. Both farms were originally the demesne land of the Priory. It was probably all worked by serfs before 1350. After the Black Death the land was probably divided into two and let for money rent.

2. The following tenants in Budworth bought their freeholds from John Grimsditch at prices unknown: John Hall, E. and W. Malbon, Thomas Anderton, and George Arrowsmith.

3. On 14 July 1545 John Grimsditch sold to Robert Eaton of Over Whitley for £82 4s od:
   a) Great Budworth – 5 tenants marked with #1 in the list above.
   b) Comberbach – 6 tenants marked with #1 in list above.

4. In 1546 or 1547, John Grimsditch and Robert Eaton sold to John Eaton of Crowley, butcher, son of Lawrence Eaton for an unknown sum the 8 tenants and the boatrooms in Great Budworth marked #2 in the list above. Robert Eaton appears to have retained the freehold of G. Burrows tenement. See IPM 23 Nov 1557.

5. Between June and October 1548, John Eaton sold to Peter Leicester all his tenancies in Great Budworth for approximately £55, including legal expenses.

6. Comberbach:
   a) Marbury of Marbury bought the two tenants marked #3 according to Sir Peter Leicester.[12]
   b) What became of the other two tenants is unknown.

7. Calculations of the value and acreage of these lands:

a) Value

Robert Eaton's purchase of £4 1s 3d worth of annual rent for £82 4s od gives us an approximate price of £1 for every 1 shilling of rent. These rents were not the only return to the landlord. The tenants will also have owed customary services or 'boons', entry fines and heriots as well as suit of mill and court. The total return that Robert Eaton received on his investment was probably between 8% and 10%.

b) Acreage

In the early sixteenth century, many farms had rights over extensive common land. The enclosure of parts of Great Budworth Heath between 1548 and 1555[13] gave the farmers greater control over

12 Ormerod, 1882, Vol. 1, p. 615.
13 One piece of evidence for this dating is the increase in the number of the Leicesters' tenants between these dates. The other is the appearance of two large rents in Budworth in a Warburton rental of 1555. These seem likely to be rents from the newly enclosed land.

land they had always used so it is most meaningful to assess the area of farms after these enclosures.[14] The map on p. 79 shows that after enclosure the area of land was:

	Approximate acres
Hall family at Brownslane Farm	90
Malbon family at Brownslane Green Farm	90
Leicester family[15]	56

Using this valuation and these areas, we can construct the following table of the Grimsditch purchase which may represent the approximate shape of the transaction:

	Rent			Approx. capital value	Approx. statute acres
	£	s	d		
10 tenants in Comberbach	4	18	1	£98	200
11 tenants in Budworth	3	0	10	£61	80
Hall farm	2	6	0	£46	90
Malbon farm	2	0	7	£41	90
	12	5	6	£246	460

From this table, one can say:

a) The Abbey rents seem to have been about 7d per acre. Grimsditch bought the land at an average of 10s per acre. The village properties and their houses seem to have been more valuable per acre than farm land.

b) John Grimsditch probably made a modest profit on the transaction.

Note also:

c) The way in which the Crown's 'chief rent' of £1 4s 1½d was divided into six parts, several of which correspond with the sales Grimsditch made, suggests that Grimsditch's role was that of a broker for the two Eatons, the Halls, the Malbons, and the other purchasers.

d) The Leicester tenants in Budworth continued to pay the same 'old rents' they had paid to Norton Abbey, but they held their land on life leases. On 26 February 1574 John Lachford paid £8 for the lease that William Heyworth had for the lives of himself and his wife Elizabeth.[16] See Appendix 3.8 for Leicester rental of 1555.

14 The final enclosure of Budworth Heath in 1809 only enlcosed about 27½ acres. WM Box 74.
15 DLT/D/44/6.
16 DLT/B15, folio 113.

Appendix 3.8. *Rentals of Great Budworth and Aston by Budworth, 1555–1641*

A. Warburton rentals of Great Budworth

Table 1. *Leasehold tenants paying 3s annual rent or more*

1572 Name (28 tenants)	Annual rent £	s	d	1625–28[17] Name (36 tenants)	Annual rent £	s	d
Acson, John	2	17	8	Acson, Thomas	2	16	8
Anderton, Thomas		8	2	Anderton, Thomas		8	2
Anderton, Thomas and Starkey, Oliver		11	4	Anderton, William, Snr		7	8
Anderton, William		13	0	Anderton, William		13	0
Archer, Richard		10	3	Archer, Richard		10	3
Barber, Henry	1	12	0	Barber, Peter		16	0
Crosby, Thomas	1	6	4	Crosby, John	2	6	8
Dainteth, Chris		13	0	Dainteth, John		13	0
				Dewsbury, Richard		13	4
				Durling, John		4	4
Dutton, John		8	4	Dutton, John		8	4
Eaton, Peter		3	0	Eaton, Peter		3	6
				Eaton, Richard, Snr		4	0
				Eaton, William, Snr		3	0
				Eaton, William		3	8
French, J. and Dutton, P.		18	6	French, William		18	6
French, John, Jnr		7	3	French, Hugh		6	7
Heath, R and Sutton, J.	1	2	0				
Hebson, William		6	0				
				Highfield, Lawrence		10	8
				Kennerdale, Peter		16	0
Kerfoot, James		5	0	Kerfoot, James		11	0
Lawton, John		4	4	Lawton, John		4	3
Lawton, William		4	4	Leather, James		10	3
Leigh, Richard		4	0				
Leigh, Robert		6	0	Leigh, Robert		6	6
Mason, Thomas		3	7	Mason, Richard		3	7
Millington, Robert	1	2	10	Millington, Robert	1	2	10
				Pimlow, James		7	3
Ridgeway, Thomas		9	1	Ridgeway, John		9	1
				Ridgeway, Alice, widow		3	0
Shakeshaft, William		9	4	Shakeshaft, Richard		3	0
Starkey, John		blank		Starkey, John		4	4
				Starkey, Oliver		3	8
				Sudlow, William		14	0

17 Three names omitted in the 1625 rental have been supplied from the 1628 rental.

The redistribution of wealth

	£	s	d		£	s	d
				Sutton, Joan, widow	1	4	2
Underwood, Peter		9	0	Underwood, William		9	0
Warburton, John		6	8	Warburton, Robert		6	8
Wirrall, Hugh		4	0	Wirrall, Hugh		4	0
Widder, Peter		6	7				

Note: the spelling of all names has been standardized

Table 2. *Cottagers, fishers, and other leasehold tenants paying less than 3s annual rent*

1572				1625–28			
Name (14 tenants)	Annual			Name (14 tenants)	Annual		
	£	s	d		£	s	d
Anderton, John		1	0	Anderton, John		1	0
				Ashton, Thos		1	0
				Beardsley, Roger		1	0
				Bennett, Thomas		1	4
Caldwell, William		1	0	Brodhurst, Ralph		1	0
Dewsbury, Ralph		1	0	Dewsbury, John		1	0
Duckworth, John		1	0				
Eaton, John			6	Eaton, Peter		1	0
Eaton, Thomas of Dene		1	0				
Eaton, Thomas of Heath		2	8	Forshall, John		1	0
French, Sibill		1	0	French, Thomas			8
Robinson, Arthur		2	0	Hale, William		2	0
Shakeshaft, Edward (boat and boatroom)		3	0	Pimlow, John		1	6
Shakeshaft, William (boatroom)		1	6				
Starkey, Richard		1	0	Starkey, Ralph		1	0
Starkey, William		1	0	Sutton, Joan, widow (boatroom)		1	6
Underwood, Peter (boatroom)		1	6	Underwood, William (boatroom)		1	6

Sources: 1572 Rental, Arley Hall; 1625-28 Rental WM Box 2

B. Leicester rentals of Great Budworth

1555 Name	Annual rent £ s d	1604 Name	Annual rent £ s d	1641 Name	Annual rent £ s d
Ackson, T.	6 8			Anderton, J.	5 0
Barlow, E.	8 4	Barlow, widow	5 0		
Barlow, T.	10 0	Bennett, H.	4 0	Bennett, W.	4 0
Cocker, R.	3 4	Cooke, widow	1 4	Bretton, T.	6 8
Coppock, M.	4 0	Coppock, R.	4 0	Coppock, R.	4 0
Dutton, T.	4 0	*Dutton, W.	4 0	Dutton, W.	4 0
Eaton, J.	3 8	Eaton, H.	3 8	French, J.	5 0
		Eaton, T.	5 4	French, P.	16 8
		Key, T.	5 0	Fryer, H.	5 4
Newall, S.	6 8	Newall, C.	6 8	Highfield, R.	3 0
Norden, A.	2 0			Massey, R.	2 0
Peacock, R.	2 0	Peacock, widow	2 0	Price, A.	2 0
Robinson, C.	5 0	Rowley, R.	16 8		
Ryder, J.	2 0	Shaw, widow	3 0		
Shakeshaft, J.	6	Starkey, O.	6	Williamson, J.	8 4
Warburton, J. gent.	4 0	Worrall, R.	8 4	Worrall, T.	3 8
	£3 2 2		£3 9 6		£3 9 8
Boatrooms					
Astle, T.	3 4	*Dutton, W.	3 0	Dutton, W.	1 6
Robinson, R.	3 4	Pimlow, W. (2)	6 0	Anderton, J.	1 6
Milner, R.	3 4				
Totals	£3 12 2		£3 18 6		£3 12 8

Sources: 1555 rental DLT/D401; 1604 DLT 5524/2/2; 1641 DLT B/84

* Same person.

Note

1. The area of Leicester lands in Great Budworth in 1663 was 57 acres. It was presumably only about 40 acres before the enclosure *c.* 1550. Seven of the 14 holdings had less than two acres of land in 1663.

C. Warburton rentals of Aston by Budworth

	1572				1626			
Name		Annual rent			Name		Annual rent	
	£	s	d			£	s	d
Main farms								
Bretton, R.		14	0		Bretton, T.		14	0
Bretton, W.		10	3		Bretton, J.		10	3
Birch, P. and W.		16	0		*Walker, J.*		16	0
						(15 year lease)		
Birchenhead, R.		14	0		*Davies, R.*		13	10
						(6 year lease)		
Dewsbury, G.	1	6	10		Dewsbury, J.	1	6	10 }
							2	0
Dewsbury, T.		11	2		Dewsbury, T.		11	2
Forest, J.		11	0		Forest, P.		11	6
Forest, T.		12	0		Forest, G.		12	0
Forest, W.	1	3	5		Forest, J.	1	3	8
Gandy, J.	1	4	4		Gandy, J.	1	4	4 }
								4
Jenkinson, P.		14	4		*Barker, R.*		14	4
Jenkinson, P.	1	6	8		Jenkinson, R.	1	1	0
Key, W.	1	2	0		Key, J.	1	2	0
Leigh, J.		14	8		*Widder, G.*		14	8
Lawrenson, R.		14	0		Lawrenson, W.		14	0
Massey, G.	1	0	0		Massey, G.		19	7
Massey, R.		10	4		Massey, R.		10	6
Pickering, R.	1	0	0		Pickering, W.	1	9	3
Starkey, J.	1	0	4		Starkey, J.	1	0	4 }
							0	8 }
Venables, M.	1	0	0		*Kennerdale, J.*	1	2	6
Cottagers and small holdings								
Awen, T.		1	0		Birchenhead, G.		2	4
Bridge, J.		1	0		Bradburne, N.		3	3
Birchenhead, E.		1	0		Dale, W.		1	0
Hayes, J.		2	0		Norbury, W.		4	0
					Partington, J.		1	4
							2	8
					Shakeshaft, W.		6	8
					Woodward, P.		1	4

Sources: 1572 Rental Arley Hall; 1626 WM Box 2

Note:
1. Five new tenants in 1626 (in italics) have been allocated to the old farms based on the rent. Only Kennerdale does not match.

D. Leicester rentals of Aston by Budworth

1602 Name	Annual rent £ s d	*1641* Name	Annual rent £ s d
Wethale			
Cooke, R.	4 0	Cooke, widow	4 0
Griffith, R.	1 10 0	Griffith, J.	15 0
Key, R.	1 10 8	Key, A.	1 10 8
Leicester, J.	1 6 8	Leicester, W.	1 6 8
Poole, R.	3 8 8 (rack?)	Johnson, J.	15 4
Robinson, J.	4 4	Robinson	4 4
Venables, P.	15 4	Key, J.	15 4
	£8 19 8		£5 11 4
Hield, probable three-life leases			
		Jackson, T.	10 0
Jackson, widow	11 0	Jackson, widow	11 0
Kirkman, widow	1 0 0	Kirkman, J.	1 0 0
Leicester, widow	1 1 6	Leicester, I.	2 0 0
Percival, R.	10 8	Leicester, I. (boatroom Pickmere)	1 6
Whalley, W.	1 2 0	Whalley, R	1 2 0
Hield, probable rack rents			
Coppock, R.	1 13 8	Coppock, fowl meadow	2 0 0
Dutton, W. and others	2 16 8	Coppock, gorsty meadow	2 0 0
Key, T. Batefield	2 13 4	Coppock, Butty meadow	3 0 0
Key, T. meadow	1 8 0	French, P. Oxhey	2 0 0
Leicester, widow	6 13 4	Leicester, I.	7 18 6
–, –, house	6 8		
–, –, wayer (weir?)	3 4		
–, –, chief rent	10 0		
Rowley, R. Oxhey	1 2 4		
Williamson	11 0	Williamson, J	1 0 0
Williamson, wayer (weir?)	3 4		
Totals	£22 6 10		£23 3 0

Sources: 1602 DLT 5524/2/2; 1641 DLT B/84

'weir' = boatroom? Or weir on the stream between Pickmere and Budworth Meres?

Appendix 3.9. *Rules for fishing in Budworth Mere, 1553*

'An order taken by the Lords of Budworth Mere for fishing and what every fisher shall have belonging to a boate and a Boatroom, Dated 26 March 7 Edw 6 [1553].'

Imprimis to a Boat and a boat-room 12 Breme Powches
    of Dace Powches – 8
    of Parle Codde Pouches – 8
    of Fagots – 8
    Two rowe of Dace Nets
    One rowe of Breme Nets.

Item that every fisher do locke his boat before the feast of Saint George next comming.

Item that no fisher set any net in the Mere from St George's day until Michaels day.

Item that no fisher shall drawe none of his fellowes geare, nor take none of hisfellowes stakes.

Item that no fisher shall fish with noe Eele-speare, the tyme of Breme fishing.

Item that no fisher shall use any fishinge before the sunne-risinge and after sunne-settinge, onely in the Dace Rydde when fishers use to let downe for Eeles.

Item that noe fisher shall lend his boate to any man to rowe in during the whole yeare.

Item that no Fisher shall use any Breme Powches but such as hee shall lay in the Mere the time of Breame fishing; and such xii powches as he will stand unto for the Breame fishinge.

Item Every Fisher to lay no Dace Powches in the Mere at the Rydde tyme, but such 8 as he will fishe with all the yeare after.

Item if any fisher be so bold as to break any of the Articles above rehearsed, then the Lord of the Water, under whom he doth fishe to exempt and put him from fishinge in the said Mere for ever.

Source: Wm Box 24, folder 4; DLT...B15.

Appendix 3.10. *The map of Great Budworth*

The tithe apportionment for Great Budworth of 1844 shows those fields which were the subject of ancient prescriptions in lieu of tithes. Those fields formed the two large farms of Norton Abbey, which were bought by the Hall and Malbon families in 1544, and the lands which were allotted to those farms by the enclosures made about 1550. The history of these two farms is also described by the deeds 1663–1859 in WM Boxes 71–74 and by the Warburtons' estate map of Great Budworth in 1759 and its survey book in WM 21. These deeds show that each of the two original 1544 farms received a share in the enclosure of Budworth Heath. These shares are shown in this map. In 1844 the Belmont estate owned both shares.

The rentals in WM Box 2 show that the large enclosures marked A, B, C, and D were in existence by 1555. The C farm (Budworth Heath) had the boundaries shown in the Map by the time of the 1572 rental, because its rent of £2 17s 8d remained the same until 1759. These boundaries are copied from the 1759 map. This map has also been used to draw the new smaller Budworth Heath. By 1759, seven cottages with gardens had been built around its edge and on the road from Brownslane. We do not know when these were permitted.

We also do not know when the small farm marked E was enclosed. The field marked F belonged to the Cock Inn. The nine-acre enclosure beside it, shown belonging to the Hall of Brownslane farm, has been conjectured to have existed before the enclosures *c.* 1550 in order to make the acreage of the new enclosures proportionate to the area of the two old Hall and Malbon farms. If this is correct, the nine acres, F and E were all enclosures made before the *c.* 1550 enclosure. This is made to seem likely by the fact that the new 'Malbon' enclosure does not abut the road except beyond E.

The Leicester estate lands shown in Map 6 appear in their estate map *c.* 1760, and the map accompanying the sale particulars of 1834. Their rentals indicate they did not buy or sell Budworth land between 1548 and 1834. Budworth was an old village with common fields. The largest of them, the town field, is shown on this map. These common fields persisted till about 1730, when sentences that suggest common rights disappear from the Manor Court rolls. Normally the early leases only describe the farms as 'previously in the occupation of', and do not describe the individual fields. However, in 1703 Charles Henchman, who had been vicar of Great Budworth since 1699, bought a lease from the Leicesters. As he was not a native, he evidently insisted on having full descriptions of his land written into his lease. So we discover that the holding he was buying consisted of a hempyard and a croft, plus ten lounts or lands in eight different fields around the township.[18] This holding was described as previously John Anderton's (see Appendix 3.8, Table B for it in 1641). The total was 9½ acres for which the rent was five shillings p.a. The three boatrooms were an extra 4s 6d p.a. Henchman paid a total of £86 for a three-life lease.[19] There must have been a lot of consolidation of these lounts by exchange or barter to arrive at the much larger fields shown in the 1759/60 maps. However, neither the Warburton nor the Leicester archives contain any papers that give any indication of how these common fields disappeared. The location of the lands of the two smaller freeholders who had bought from the Abbey is derived from the 1759 Warburton map.

Map 6 is also interesting because it must depict the land that Geoffrey, son of Adam de Dutton (ancestor of the Warburtons) gave to Norton Priory in the time of Henry III (1216–72).[20] As well as giving the Priory a large area of demesne which became the Hall and Malbon farms, he evidently gave them a number of serfs and their houses and lands in the common fields. It is noticeable that many of the houses were grouped around the Church, so the serfs presumably looked after the Church as well as tilling the Priory's demesne land. Many of the details on this map, such as the roads, have been copied from the 1759 map, and such details may have been different in 1550, for example, the roads may have been wider.

18 DLT/D9/6.
19 DLT/D44.
20 Ormerod, 1882, Vol. 1, p. 605.

CHAPTER 4

The occupations of people in North Cheshire, 1560–1646

i) Introduction

The last chapter demonstrated that a large number of families in north Cheshire acquired property rights in the farms they lived in which provided them with a capital asset. Not only did they receive an income every year from this asset, but as owners of wealth they were creditworthy. Their neighbours could deal with them with confidence. In this chapter we see how this capital helped to open up new occupations and careers for some families. During the second half of the sixteenth century developments in the local economy and advances in its technology created a growing business community so that, by the 1620s, there was a substantial number of families with assets of a few hundred pounds, and a few with more than a thousand.

Much of this section is based on the evidence of some 120 wills and inventories. Most of the people whose possessions were described in these documents lived in one of the townships we have examined earlier. These were Aston by Budworth, Great Budworth, Nether Knutsford, Nether Tabley, Sutton Weaver and the Whitley Lordship. These townships contain more than 11,000 acres (4,500 hectares). With the exception of Knutsford, they are all townships in which we know the names and the area of farmland 'owned' by almost all the leaseholders and freeholders. For virtually every family mentioned we have information additional to the will and inventory. Evidence from a wide range of other sources has been used to supplement the information in the inventories.[1] One of the most frequently used sources is my book, *Seven Households*[2] and the seven families described there are listed in Note 2 below. These portraits of their households are extremely detailed and, on many occasions, amplify, extend and explain the information in the inventories. The seven families and their houses are mentioned in this chapter without further reference.

---

1 All the Cheshire wills cited are in the Cheshire R.O. They are referenced under the name of the deceased and the year of probate. This was normally the same year as the death and the making of the inventory. Where this information is given in the text no further reference is supplied.

2 The Shuttleworths of Smithills and Gawthorpe 1582–1621, Sir Peter Leicester of Tabley 1613–78, Thomas Jackson of Hield, Aston by Budworth, 1622–1707, the Fells of Swarthmoor Hall 1673–78, Richard Latham in Scarisbrick 1716–67, George Dockwra in Aston by Budworth 1741–57 and Sir Peter Warburton of Arley 1708–74; see Foster, 2002.

We begin with an examination of the textile industries. These probably employed more people than any other activity. Hemp and flax were grown everywhere in the lowland plain of Cheshire and Lancashire. Processing the fibres into linen, twine and ropes, a poorly paid occupation, seems to have been the main employment of the poorer section of the community. The country areas produced most of their own requirements while the supplies reaching the market may have been made mainly in the towns. The principal markets seem to have been the people who lived in the Pennines to the east, the Welsh hills, and in the midland plain as far south as Buckinghamshire. Woollen cloth, made from the fleeces of sheep kept in the north Cheshire plain, was probably used by many local people in the first half of the sixteenth century. However, the large businesses that had been built up by the woollen drapers in the area before 1610 suggest that locally-made cloth was being superseded before the end of the century. A number of these drapers made considerable fortunes by buying better-quality cloths from manufacturers in other parts of England and selling them in north Cheshire.

Some of the freeholders, copyholders and three-life leaseholders sent their children to school for long enough to qualify them for jobs in the learned professions and the City of London companies. Fathers usually divided their wealth equally between all their children, so the younger sons of the richer parents had an opportunity to enter these occupations while other families specialized in the Church or the law. Examples are recorded of individuals who achieved success in all three areas.

There is evidence that there were retail shops in Great Budworth by the early seventeenth century. A grocer sold imported spices, dried fruits and also mercers' wares, such as ribbons and imported cotton and silk cloths. A second specialist mercer's business apparently offered stiff competition in these lines because the grocer's business was transformed into a candle manufacturer. Budworth had a tailor, a butcher and a blacksmith, occupations that also existed in the country townships. None of the Budworth businesses was on the scale of those in Knutsford, where in the early seventeenth century there were several families with more than £1,000 employed in leather, grocery and cloth retailing businesses. These rich business families also owned small farms in the country townships on which they sometimes lived.

Almost every inventory in this study lists farm animals, grain, and husbandry equipment. Some writers have assumed that the deceased owners of such possessions were farmers whose main occupation was agricultural work. The evidence presented here suggests that only the least well-off people in this community did manual farm work. The better-off employed servants to do the work for them while others let their land at halves (sharecropping). In practice, much of the work was probably done by teenagers. Some of the better-off farm owners may also have been active in the commercial side of farming, dealing in cattle, horses and grain.

The families living in the country were probably engaged in a wide range of occupations. There were numerous horses on these farms, fed by the grass which grows particularly well in Cheshire. Transporting trade goods or building materials were clearly rapidly growing businesses in this period. From carrying coal or lime, it was a short step to dealing in these commodities. Other men found occupations in the building trades, in leather, or in metalworking. The Smithills accounts show that experts in all these fields were living in country townships during this period. The evidence from this group of inventories is that occupations were not mentioned in wills even when the deceased clearly had one. When the value of the chattels listed in the inventories is added to the value of the property that some of these people owned, we learn that, by the early seventeenth century, many families had substantial assets. It is unlikely that so much money could have been made by farming their little holdings. Though we do not know what their occupations were, it seems likely that many of these families had made a success in some kind of business.

ii) Textiles
a) Hemp and flax
Almost every inventory made in these townships included hemp and flax.[3] These products are mentioned as seed, as crops growing in the fields and as crops that had been harvested, but not yet threshed. After processing they appear as yarn, tow, hards and as finished cloth. The tools – brakes, swingles, heckles, cards, and spinning-wheels – are almost as common. On old surveys and maps, small fields called hempyards are shown next to virtually every farmhouse. Growing and processing the fibres are mentioned in the earliest five account books described in my *Seven Households*. There can be no doubting the almost universal cultivation of these two crops in lowland Cheshire and Lancashire before 1650. It is more difficult to discover whether people were growing and processing them just for use in their own households or whether they were also producing for sale. The Fell and Latham families certainly seem to have consumed most of what they produced and evidence of a trade in linen is rare.

Roger Harper of Dutton, who died in 1594, was the only person in the area whom I found described as linen draper in his will. He had eleven cattle and three horses, like many farmers. In linen he had:

3   See Foster, 2002, pp. 26–38, for detailed descriptions and illustrations.

	£	s	d
sheets and other linen	2	0	0
linen cloth	2	13	4
yarn	2	0	0
hemp and flax		7	0
hempseed		8	0
teare of hemp and flax		5	0

This list is similar to that in a dozen other inventories. Were they all linen drapers? We know that several of my seven households aimed to keep a stock of linen cloth and they also usually had fibre at various stages of processing. There is therefore nothing in this inventory that clearly shows Roger Harper to have been a trader in linen. It is possible that his business, like that of William Benson, the harden buyer and friend of the Fells, was to collect linen from the makers in the area and sell it to the carriers on the London road. This could have involved him in holding only small stocks.

I only found the will of one man described as webster – Hugh Wright of Great Budworth who died in 1639. His loom, warpstock and 'all things belonging' was valued at £1 6s 8d. His hemp yarn, 'both whitened and unwhitened', was valued at the unusually high figure of £10 10s 0d. His other business assets were two pieces of new linen cloth at 15s 0d, and a little tow at 2s 6d. 45 people owed him a total of £6 8s 1d. He was probably weaving some customers' own yarn into cloth as well as weaving linen for sale from yarn he had bought. Looms, however, appear in other inventories. George Lowton had one (p. 126 below). Thomas Fearnley of Whitley had '2 looms with healds and reeds 13s 4d' when he died in 1616. George Fearnley of Whitley had '40 slippings of sale yarn £1' in 1613. Thomas Pemberton of Whitley had five or six different kinds of yarn valued at a total of £6 17s 10d in 1595. These examples suggest that at least part of the output of these men was sold.

From the detailed description of the processing of hemp and flax and the prices paid by the Shuttleworths it is clear that the work was poorly paid and the value of the finished cloth was low. A piece of common cloth 20 yards long by one yard wide may have been worth between 10s 0d and £1, depending on quality. Such a piece may have taken 40 to 60 days to make, most of the time being spent on spinning, done by the women. Harvesting and processing hemp and flax and making things from the fibres probably occupied more working days of both women and men than growing their own food crops. We have seen that there were very poor people living in hovels on the waste in Whitley trying to make enough money to buy their food. They could grow enough hemp to keep themselves busy all year on less than a third of an acre. It is likely, therefore, that production for sale was carried on in the poorer households, the necessary equipment being cheap enough for poor people to acquire. It may be just because we have no inventories of these poor people that we have no evidence of the activity.

Hemp requires a deep, rich soil. With adequate manuring, it could be grown on the same land year after year. This is probably why 'hempyards' were usually small fields close to houses where waste products of all kinds could conveniently be used as manure. Flax also requires good land but does best when not grown in the same soil more than once in ten years.[4] Hoole, where the Shuttleworths grew all their hemp and flax from 1582 to 1621, has top quality agricultural land. They were so impressed with it that they bought more land there in the 1580s and 1590s to supply their house at Gawthorpe. It follows that there would have been a market for hemp and flax and products made from them in the areas where they grew less well, such as the Pennine hills. For example, in 1536, only the three chapelries in the Ribble valley paid tithes on flax to Whalley Abbey. The eight chapelries in the hills paid tithes of lambs and wool but nothing else.[5] It is likely, therefore, that from an early period the hemp and flax grown in the plains, and the cloth, twine, and ropes made from it were exchanged for the wool and woollen cloth produced by the flocks and the people who lived in the hills. This trading probably accounts for the development in Cheshire and Lancashire of towns situated where the plains meet the hills. These towns run from Lancaster in the north to Macclesfield and Congleton in the south. Manchester had the most favoured position in the centre and, as we have seen, it was already a large trading centre by 1545.

The hill country, then, was one market for the hemp and flax products of the north-west plains. Another market seems to have been the inland counties of the midlands and the south. One reason for this was that these inland areas of England were furthest from the cheap imported linen that was available to coastal towns. The cheapest linen products of every kind seem to have been produced in France and Germany, probably because wages there were lower than in England. The more technically sophisticated process of bleaching was often done in Holland, and the cloth exported from there to England. So, except for the few pockets of linen production in central and southern England, such as the Fens of south Lincolnshire,[6] north-western linens were competitive in all these inland areas.

Between the 1570s and the 1630s, linen products from the Leyland Hundred of Lancashire were carried by 'chapmen'[7] or 'linenmen' from that area and sold in the hills of north Staffordshire and Derbyshire, and further afield, around Coventry

---

4 Charley, 1862, p. 44.
5 Lowe, 1972, p. 8.
6 See Thirsk, 1967, p. 177 for these areas.
7 A man who bought in one place and sold in another.

and in many places in Northamptonshire, Oxfordshire, Buckinghamshire and Bedfordshire.[8] Men from the Ormskirk and Wigan areas also sold linens in these places and in Denbigh and Ruthin in North Wales. A Warrington man sold cloth as far south as Newbury in Berkshire.[9] Sack-cloth was also sent by Manchester merchants to London in large quantities. Isabella Tipping had 140 packs in London, worth £128 in 1598, and Richard Nugent had over £200 worth of canvas there in 1609.[10] Both these were probably coarse hempen cloth of the type made at Smithills. It may have been used for packing woollen cloth for export.

All this evidence is derived from the inventories of men who died while still active in business. The inventories record outstanding debts for the cloth they had recently sold. From its nature such evidence must be rare and the fact that so much has survived suggests that this trade was substantial. I have found no inventories including such debts owed to people in my townships. However, the London road running south from Warrington Bridge through Whitley and Great Budworth was carrying much traffic returning to London after bringing foreign goods to the North-West. It is likely that these chapmen and carriers bought linen for the return journey. Warrington, where chapmen bought supplies for the journey south through Cheshire, was probably an important linen centre because of this trade. The remoter areas further north in Leyland Hundred will have had less of this passing traffic. Perhaps, therefore, they had to find chapmen among their own people in order to sell to distant markets.

If this analysis is correct, there was a large market for north-western hempen and flaxen goods. Producing for this market may have been one of the principal occupations of the poorer leaseholders. It was no doubt an even more important occupation for cottagers. Some of these, living near Arley, were still engaged in it in the mid-eighteenth century, making ropes, twine, and nets. For the old, the disabled, men without skills or capital, and their unmarried sisters, it may have been almost the only occupation available. When the Latham daughters were not gardening or helping with the harvest or other agricultural work, they were spinning. However, in the Cheshire and Lancashire plains, these poor country people may not have been sufficiently numerous to produce any great quantity of goods for the market. The 'textile districts' that developed in and around the towns where linen was traded were probably the main sources of supply. The inventories analysed by Lowe showed much more activity around Blackburn, Clayton le Dale,

8 Withersby, 1998. We do not learn what the return loads of these carriers were. They must have earned their share of the costs of these long journeys.
9 Lowe, 1972, pp. 58–59.
10 Lowe, 1972, pp. 54–55.

Manchester, and Ashton-under-Lyne than I found in Cheshire south of
Warrington.[11] The analysis in Chapter 5 (iii) below of where the poor were able to
live may help our understanding of why these areas became textile producing
districts.

One final point needs to be made about the hemp, flax and linen industries in the
sixteenth and seventeenth centuries. In many successful textile-manufacturing
industries, such as the Florentine woollens of the fourteenth century, West of
England woollens from the sixteenth to the nineteenth centuries and Warrington
sail-cloth described in Chapter 9 below, the main employers bought the fibre – wool
or flax – in bulk and 'put it out' to women to spin in their own homes. At no time
did the women own the materials themselves. This practice put the spinners in the
power of their employers and tended, over the long term, to depress their wages to
very low levels. In Cheshire and Lancashire by contrast, since the inhabitants of
every farm and cottage grew the plants themselves, there was no need to 'put out'
fibre. In towns, raw fibre, grown locally, was bought by people for heckling and
spinning.[12] Linen yarn was also imported from Ireland because local spinners could
not produce enough. The tradition that weavers bought their own yarn was so strong
that Robert Birch sold Irish yarn to weavers who later sold the finished cloth back
to him.[13] It seems that hemp and flax fibres were not 'put out' for spinning in
Cheshire and Lancashire until they were imported it from the Baltic countries at
the end of the seventeenth century. The export of Cheshire salt to those countries
at that period revealed that Baltic fibre was often cheaper than home-grown (see
Chapters 7 and 9 below).

b) Wool

It was a common practice in Cheshire and Lancashire to keep a few sheep on each
farm. 15 of the 36 inventories for the Whitley Lordship listed sheep, and a small
amount of wool or woollen yarn often appears. This part of north Cheshire is not
good sheep country, because the wet and boggy clay land often causes disease in
their feet. The purpose of keeping sheep seems to have been simply to provide wool
for use in the household. The yarn seems to have been woven into woollen or linsey-
woolsey cloth (half linen, half wool). Thomas Fearnley, who died in Whitley in 1616,
had a pair of shearman shears as well as two looms. Even better evidence of woollen
cloth working is provided by the inventory of William Whalley of Aston, who died
in 1616. He had:

11 Lowe, 1972, pp. 46–55.
12 Phillips, 1985, pp. 104–09. John Robinson was owed money by at least 51 people for hemp and
   flax. Almost all debts were under £1. One of the smallest was for 4 lbs of flax for 2s 3d.
13 Lowe, 1972, pp. 53–54.

	£	s	d
Furnaces and all things in and belonging to the dyeing house	15	0	0
Dyeing wares	2	5	0
Iron gear for the mill and other necessaries thereto appertaining		5	0

He was a three-life leaseholder in that part of Hield which the Leicesters bought back from the Suttons in 1601. His holding, beside that of Thomas Jackson is marked on a map[14] which also shows how the mill was fed by a small stream coming down from the Aston Park area. It would seem likely that the mill was used both to grind corn and to full the cloth before it was dyed. A good supply of water from the stream was also useful in the cleaning and dyeing processes. Little industrial operations like this may have been widely spread around the rural area when every family was making its own woollen cloth.[15] Most of the seven families arranged for their wool to be spun and blankets and other coarse woollens to be made for them. The Lathams also made linsey-woolsey. Four inventories we are about to examine suggest that the custom of producing woollen cloth at home and having it fulled and dyed in these little local works was in decline by the time William Whalley died. Commercial woollen production was stealing the market from homespun so that when Thomas Jackson surveyed Hield in 1663 the mill was in decay.

Three of these four inventories are of woollen drapers who died between 1610 and 1614 and had presumably been building up their businesses in the 30 or 40 years before that. The largest was that of Henry Burges of Knutsford, who died in 1612. Over 70 items of stock in his shop were listed,[16] most of them various types and colours of woollen cloth, but there were also accessories like hose, ribbons, lace, and garters. Their total value exceeded £230, but this sum was dwarfed by the £1,025 of debts owed to him.

Burges did not have a monopoly of the woollen drapers' business in Knutsford. George Antrobus, who died in 1614 at his house in Nether Tabley, had shops in both Knutsford and Warrington. His stock was smaller with some 60 items valued at more than £130. The money owing to him was just over £300, and his executors made a list of the debtors, who came from all over this part of Cheshire. Several lived in Warrington and Knutsford, of course, but people in Rostherne, Dunham, Bowdon, and Mobberly are listed as well as Northwich and Davenham, Hulme,

14 See Foster, 2002, pp. xvii and 94.
15 Linen was much more difficult to dye than wool, and the evidence I have found suggests that it was rarely dyed.
16 Several inventories of this kind are in print. That of Nicholas Elcocke of Stockport, who died in 1620, has lists of stock and debtors that have much in common with those of these three drapers. See Phillips, 1992, pp. 159–71. Unlike Elcocke, the three described here all had farming possessions.

Warford, and Chorley. Thomas Hall, a draper in Congleton, appears as well as tailors in Grappenhall and Lymm. Knutsford and Warrington seem to have become the centres from which these woollen products from all over England were distributed. The third woollen draper whose inventory has survived is Thomas Eaton of Whitley Lordship who died in 1610, but he seems to have given up trade some time before his death. It is possible that his shop, if he had one, was not in Whitley. His stock of woollens was worth only £18. He still had debts outstanding of £98, but he had succeeded in getting in enough to make his hoard of ready money up to £215.

It would seem likely that many of the Knutsford trading families stayed in the town developing their businesses between the 1540s and the 1620s. Acson, Antrobus, Burges, Hough, Millington and Swinton are the surnames of six Knutsford traders who died and left us inventories between 1561 and 1617. All these are among the 15 surnames of the 20 largest taxpayers in 1545. We know also that the Antrobus, Burges, Hough and Millington families owned small farms and town property in Knutsford during this period.[17] Henry Burges was probably descended from the John Burges of Knutsford whose goods were assessed at £7 for the 1545 tax. George Antrobus' ancestor may have been either Richard, whose goods were assessed at £10, or William, who was assessed at £7. The large sums of capital in these businesses by the 1610s seem to have arisen from their great growth and profitability in the previous 30 or 40 years, as well as from the undervaluation of the businesses in 1545. For example, Thomas Acson of Knutsford was assessed at £5 in 1545. When he died in 1561 he had £10 worth of wares (unspecified) in his shop and another £8 4s 1d worth of farming and household equipment. By 1570 when she died, Sibel Swinton, probably related either to William Swinton, assessed at £16 in 1545, or Thomas, assessed at £5, had drapery, grocery and gloves worth £103 in stock, as well as debts owing to her of £40 in a total inventory of £256. The rapid growth of these businesses seems to have been the result of two developments. On the demand side, we have seen that all those with a stake in land had enjoyed rapid rises in their incomes in the second half of the sixteenth century. On the production side, it is evident that the cloths which these merchants were able to offer were much more attractive to consumers than anything they could make and process locally from their own wool.

The fourth inventory concerned with woollen textiles is that of Thomas Dewsbury of Aston by Budworth, a tailor who died in 1609. He was the leaseholder of a 12-acre holding now called the Old Shop, which his descendants retained till the eighteenth century.[18] His inventory lists two mares and a colt, two calves, and

17 See below pp. 124–5 and notes.
18 Photo and story in Foster, 1992, pp. 25–26.

other farming and household goods worth some £9, but he also had tacks[19] valued at £26 13s 4d and was owed £47. He described himself as a tailor in his will but the only other sign of his business was the possession of a pair of tailor's shears and a pressing iron worth 1s 6d. As we have seen in *Seven Households*, it was the woollen cloth for outer clothing that was made up by tailors at this period. His 25 debtors were presumably his customers and appear to be mostly from local families. The most socially distinguished was Mr John Hayes of Litley who owed 15 shillings,[20] but some customers spent much more than this. For example, George Key owed £5 as did Peter Barber.[21] At least some country people were evidently smartly dressed in the first decade of the seventeenth century.

The evidence presented here suggests that wool textile manufacture was never more than a household activity in this part of north Cheshire. In the seventeenth century it was a declining activity, as cloths made in the manufacturing centres around the country offered superior quality at competitive prices and the growing wealth of the population of the rural areas allowed many of them to wear better quality clothes.

iii) Occupations requiring schooling: the Law, the Church and City of London companies

In the earliest will and inventory to survive from Sutton Weaver we find clearly set out one of the main features of the behaviour of the small property-owning families – the family's wealth was usually divided among all the children. John Drinkwater was the son, or at least the heir, of Ralph, whose goods had been assessed at £10 in 1545 (see Appendix 3.1). He died in 1575, leaving a widow, three sons and several daughters of whom only the eldest son, Ralph, was over 21. John's inventory, made in 1575 and totalling £68 11s 8d, contained only farm and household possessions, including 15 cattle, 1 mare and 20 sheep. His will divided his wealth between his wife and his son Ralph, on condition that they make payments to the younger children. This trust was to be supervised by John's brother Robert and his brother-in-law John Wall. The two younger sons were to be kept at school until they were each 'set to an occupation' and each was then to be given £10. Each daughter was to be given £20 when she made an approved marriage. Young Ralph inherited the three-life leasehold and it is clear that he could only meet his obligations to maintain his siblings by hard work and great economy for several years. If money had to be found quickly, he would have to borrow. He might have done this by selling a 'tack'

19 See below and pp. 129–30.
20 See Appendix 3.5.
21 See rentals for these families in Appendix 3.8.

or lease of some of his land for a period of years. Such provisions for younger sons and daughters were common in this community. Another of the 11 pre-1642 Sutton wills to survive is that of John Hale who died in 1597. His younger son George was to be kept at school for a further four years and then given £20 by his mother and elder brother.

Two later Sutton wills and inventories reveal another characteristic of these documents. They normally avoid mentioning the occupation of the testator even when he had one. John Woodfen (Woodfine) who died in 1613 is described in his will, written in May, just as 'of Arley', while the inventory says 'of Sutton'. The will explains that he owned the lease of the farm in Sutton on which his uncle Richard lived. The following year his uncle Richard died and also left us a will and inventory. None of these documents mentions that both Richard and John were lawyers who had acted as Stewards of the Warburtons' Manor Courts and had participated in the management of the Arley estate. Richard followed Peter Warburton as Steward of the Courts in 1588 when the latter began his rise in the legal hierarchy, which was to carry him to be Chief Justice of the Common Pleas.[22] In 1604 John married Emma Ap Hugh, whose brother Robert was another Arley estate manager.[23] The 1608 will of Peter Barber of Whitley was written by John Woodfine, who probably had a general legal practice in the area similar to that of Thomas Jackson 50 years later.

John owned a small copyhold in Halton which was probably convenient for his appearances in the Hundred Court there. The arrangements about housing for the family, which were made in these wills, illustrate the flexibility of seventeenth-century life. John left a widow and two daughters, who became owners of the lease while Richard left a wife who was 'old and simple'. Richard's niece Alice and her husband William Hough were to continue to live in the house and manage part of the farm so as to look after her. John's widow and daughters were to occupy the other part of the house and the farm, and the girls were to be maintained in Sutton until they were 16. John left chattels valued at £113 while Richard's were worth about £70.

Some of the families in these townships chose the Church rather than the Law as their occupation. The Eaton families of Whitley seem to have established a tradition of sending their sons to the universities to become priests.[24] Between 1561

---

22 D.N.B.; Ormerod, 1882, Vol. 2, pp. 704–05.

23 These two Woodfens were probably related to Lawrence Woodfen, who had a 55-acre freehold in Weaverham. They owned Allen's leasehold in Sutton. Appd. 3.1.

24 Appendix 3.4 lists a number of Eaton properties in the Whitley Lordship between 1526 and 1612. The Old Pole is mentioned in the 1595 rental but does not seem to be in the 1612 survey, which suggests that it may have been a freehold. The ancient tithe prescription (Map 6) also suggests this.

and 1601 one or possibly two Richard Eatons were vicars of Great Budworth although little is known of them.[25] Robert Eaton who went up to Brasenose, Oxford, in the 1570s and became BA in 1577 was rector of Grappenhall, 1582–1621 and Rector of Mobberly from 1595 to 1620. His eldest son Samuel succeeded him at Grappenhall, and his third son Richard was vicar of Audlem. At least two of his grandsons were also Churchmen.[26] Richard Eaton, born about 1563, went to University College, Oxford, in 1581[27] and became vicar of Great Budworth in 1604, dying in 1616. Richard owned properties in Whitley, which are described in his will, 1617[28] which seem to have been those shown in the 1612 survey (Appendix 3.4). Three of his six younger sons went up to Cambridge between 1620 and 1630. His eldest son Theophilus was apprenticed in the City of London, becoming a Freeman in 1611. He then spent the next 25 years as a merchant in London with the Eastland Company. In 1637 with his brothers Samuel and Nathaniel he went to Massachusetts. Theophilus was one of the founders of the New Haven Colony in 1638, serving as its governor from 1643 until his death in 1657. Nathaniel became the first master of Harvard in 1637 but was disgraced in 1639. Samuel returned to England and founded the Congregational Chapel in Duckinfield, Cheshire, in the 1640s. Little seems to be known of Jonathon, the third and youngest Cambridge-educated son.[29]

Richard Eaton, the vicar of Budworth, 1604–16, was not the only resident of the area to apprentice his son to a City of London company, although Theophilus had the most distinguished career that we know about. The City of London registers of Freemen were destroyed in the great fire of 1666 so all that exists for the period before then is a fragment dating from 1551–53. However, of the 881 names in this list, some 22 came from rural Cheshire.[30] Analyses of apprentices in surviving registers of individual companies show that in the middle of the sixteenth century about 50% of City apprentices came from the northern counties. This declined to

But it is not listed by Sir Peter Leicester as an ancient freehold (Ormerod, 1882, Vol. 1, p. 656), nor does it appear in any Inquisition Post Mortem. Perhaps it was held from the Venables estate. It appears to be an example of the misty nature of some small freeholders in the sixteenth century.

25 Ormerod, 1882, Vol. 1, p. 611.

26 Foster, 1891; Ormerod, 1882, Vol. 1, p. 657, Note 'e'. Robert, the rector of Mobberly, was not the eldest son of Robert of Sandiway in Barrow Lane, who bought part of the Norton Abbey lands. Robert of Sandiway's lands (1PM 23 Nov 4, 5 Philip and Mary) passed to Richard, who was 27 in 1557 when he inherited. He passed the lands (1PM 7 Jan 20 Eliz) to John, who died in 1617 (1PM 3 Oct 1617).

27 Foster, 1891.

28 New Haven Colony Historical Society, 1901.

29 D.N.B. for Theophilus, Samuel, and Nathaniel. Foster, 1891; Venn, 1922–27.

30 Welch, 1908.

30% in the last quarter of that century. By the end of the seventeenth century the percentage of those entering City companies who came from the North had declined even further to between 10% and 15%, suggesting that commercial opportunities in the North had evidently improved greatly over this period.[31] Appendix 4.1 lists the names of 16 young men who were apprenticed to City companies by fathers resident in the area of this study. It is the result of a short, random trawl through some of the registers of only four companies. Three of the fathers came from old landed gentry families while five were the children of three-life leaseholders. The rest were the offspring of copyholders or freeholders. This suggests that apprenticing children to City companies was a luxury that only the richer property owners could afford. Thomas Jackson's family's experiences[32] illustrate the costs of joining even minor companies. Freemen of London did not always practise their trade there. We happen to know that Richard Malbon did, because he is described as 'draper of London' in probate papers of 1623. We see more of him and Theophilus Eaton and their emigration to America below at pp. 180-1.

These City of London registers indicate that business families were more numerous than is shown by probate records alone. George Antrobus, the Knutsford woollen draper whose inventory we examined, was not the only Antrobus in the trade in Knutsford. Henry Antrobus, a Merchant Tailor, was his brother and their father had also been in the trade in Knutsford. Between 1569 and 1662, no less than nine men called Antrobus belonged to the Merchant Tailors' Company in London and the Knutsford business was probably assisted by relations based in London and St Albans. In 1612, George Antrobus the woollen draper bought a house in Knutsford from Thomas Antrobus. Thomas had probably inherited this from his uncle Henry Hough, who had been a mercer in Knutsford. Thomas had been admitted to Lincoln's Inn in 1571-72. He prospered in the Law, was MP for Andover, 1603-04, and bought a large house near Petersfield in Hampshire.[33]

iv) The development of business in Great Budworth

The two earliest wills and inventories which mention occupations in Budworth are those of a tailor and a butcher. However, this is more likely to be because they both had the same surname than because they were the first two businessmen in the township. The Pimlow (Pimblowe) family were not traditional residents of Budworth. William Pimlow, the butcher, who died in 1610, had a wife called Jane and a daughter named Ellen. They were probably the same as the Jane Pimlow and

---

31 Wareing, 1980; Thrupp, 1948, pp. 389-92.
32 Foster, 2202, pp. 97-08 and 109.
33 Antrobus, 1929, p.9.

Ellen, daughter of William Pimlow, who were each left a legacy of £1 by Katherine Hall, widow, of Brownslane Farm. Katherine and her late husband John had had no children, so he had left his estate to Thomas Hall of Latchford.[34] Jane was presumably a relation and the Pimlows may have been rack-rent tenants of part or all of Brownslane Farm. This would have provided a sound basis for a butcher's business. The inventory contains no information about the business except that 'the reversion of grease for this year' was worth £2 10s 0d, which might refer to a trade in tallow. The inventory of his brother, the tailor who died in 1609, had no reference at all to his business. Both had typical farm and household possessions. James Pimlow, probably another brother or a son, acquired a small Warburton leasehold before 1625. The Pimlow family were to prosper in Budworth. Thomas was one of the richest tradesmen there in 1663 and he alone paid tax on goods in the subsidy of that year. In the same year, William, who was in business as a cooper, bought the first little piece of the freehold land that the family owned in the eighteenth century.[35]

The first real business inventory is that of the shop kept by Richard Dewsbury who died in 1612. The main trade seems to have been in expensive goods imported into London and carried up to Cheshire by packhorse.[36] He sold spices – pepper, cloves, nutmeg, cinnamon, ginger and turmeric – chemicals and metals – alum, verdigris, aqua vitae, quicksilver – and foods – sugar, currants, almonds and hops. He also sold manufactured goods, possibly not made in the North-West in this period: paper, pins, soap, starch, steelglass, tobacco pipes, and pairs of scales and weights. Finally there was mercery: ribbons, buttons, silk thread and lace, fringe, cotton yarn, and light cloths like fustian, jeans, perpetuana and buckram. His whole inventory, including farm and household goods, was worth £103. As well as retailing these purchased goods, Dewsbury had a 'candle trough and frame for making candles' valued at 2s.

Spices and dried fruits had been bought in London and carried up to Lancashire by the Shuttleworths in 1590. Sir Peter Leicester continued to buy them in London in the 1650s.[37] The appearance of a shop retailing them in a small place like Budworth by 1600 seems to confirm the growing wealth of the small freeholders and leaseholders. After Richard's death the business seems to have been carried on by John Dewsbury, perhaps a brother. He allowed the retailing side to lapse, but he developed the candle-making. When he died in 1621, the business was represented in his inventory by two items:

34 John Hall ws 1602, Katherine ws 1608.
35 Foster, 1992, pp. 23–24.
36 Woodward, 1970, pp. 69–72.
37 Foster, 2002, p. 82.

all rendered tallows and candles	£40	0s	0d
in wicke yarne		15s	0d

Richard's three sons, John, Ralph, and Nathaniel (aged 17 to 12) were asked to live together with John's widow Ellen on the combined family wealth (at least £149) 'so long as they will be ruled by her'. Nathaniel was evidently the most obedient, because he was still selling candles to Sir Peter Leicester in the 1650s. The elder two brothers seem to have taken their portions and gone elsewhere.

Perhaps the reason John Dewsbury gave up the mercery business was that there was now another mercer in Budworth. John Dutton died in 1621, leaving a stock of 'mercery wares' valued at £27 10s 0d. He owed £28 9s 6d to eight people who were probably suppliers including Mr William Anderley of London and was himself owed some £65 by 57 people who appear to be locals. The net worth of his chattels was over £124.

There are only two more inventories of Budworth residents before 1646 that mention business assets. William Hough, who died in 1635, cannot have been the first blacksmith in Budworth, but his is the only inventory to list a blacksmith's tools. Humphrey Fryer's inventory of 1634 does not even list trade goods, unless 8s worth of linen cloth 'at the webster' was such. But 19 people owed him a total of £22 11s 6d, which was surprising if he were not trading. These two people and Hugh Wright the linen webster (see above, p. 113) were not leaseholders, so their presence in Budworth in the 1630s may be evidence that the leaseholders were already sub-letting by this period.

These Budworth men had much smaller businesses than people in Knutsford. We have seen that in 1612 Henry Burges had over £1,250 invested in his woollen drapers in Knutsford. Other Knutsford men also had substantial businesses. James Millington, who died in 1608, was a tanner whose inventory totalled £256, including £130 worth of leather and debts of about £70 owed by 21 people. His farm and household goods made up the balance.[38] Robert Burges, who died in 1616, seems to have been a tawer[39] rather than a tanner of leather. He had a great variety of skins – deer, horse, sheep, calf – but apart from the £65 owed to him and £66 in cash, his main asset was some land recently purchased from Peter Daniel, Esq. for £447. He was a well-off man who already owned five small farms in the area and eight houses

38 He was probably related to Robert Millington of Nether Knutsford, who died in 1588 owning four small farms in the country and 13 properties in Knutsford (1PM 30 Eliz No 5) who in turn was probably descended from John or Ralph Millington who paid tax on goods assessed at £5 and £4 in 1545.

39 An alternative treatment for skins which produced soft, pliable leather for clothes. See Foster, 2002, p. 51 for a description.

in Knutsford,[40] and was probably in the process of retiring from business. Henry Hough was a mercer and grocer[41] whose stock of these goods was valued at £387 when he died in 1617. His wife was the sister of Robert Burges, mentioned above, and this was no doubt the reason why his inventory also included the remaining stock of debts of the two Burges businesses I have just described. His inventory totalled over £2,000, including some £1,588 of business assets.

v) Farming

We have seen that all the freeholders and leaseholders in these townships (except cottagers) had sufficient land to enable them to grow their own food. There are no surviving wills or inventories of cottagers, so it is not surprising that virtually all these 120 inventories include farming possessions. How was this farming being carried on? Who was doing the manual work? In this section the different types of landowners are examined in succession to see what the surviving evidence tells us.

Beneath the 'landed gentry' families of Bucklow Hundred, whose names are given in Appendix 3.5, Tables A and B, the top group in rural society were the freeholders. A number of people who died in our townships before 1620 were members of this group. Seven wills and inventories survive which were made by the three Budworth families of Hall, Malbon, and Anderton. These wills show that the value of a family's farming possessions was related to the size of their farm.

Humphrey Hall of Brownslane (now Brownslow) Farm died in 1578. On his 90-acre farm he had six oxen valued at £3 3s 4d each, ten cows worth £16 13s 4d, and a dozen other young cattle. He had five horses, 30 sheep and £37 worth of grain making up a total inventory worth over £160. As well as his lands in Budworth where he lived, he had small freeholds in Mere and Plumley and a leasehold in Over Tabley, which seem to have been let to tenants. His relations mentioned in the will were all from well-off families – Middlehurst, Broome, Swinton, Eaton, and Anderton.

The inventory of William Malbon of Brownslane Green made in June 1580 reveals a similar picture. He too had about 90 acres, and on it he had six oxen, 11 cows and a dozen other cattle. An unusual possession was a lease of the tithes of Middlewalk in Whitley Lordship. He left legacies to several servants and he also had some well-to-do relations. He asked Richard Eaton, vicar of Budworth, to supervise his will. Eight people owed him money for grain, and one for the hire of a cow. His other debtors included John Hall of Brownslane (son of Humphrey

---

40 IPM 20 Sep 1617 and 26 Aug 1619.

41 He was probably descended from either Godfrey Hough, assessed at £13 in 1545, or Robert, assessed at £8.

above), who owed £7, and the vicar, who owed £5 10s 0d for a quilt.

The third freeholder, Thomas Anderton of Crowsnest, had a smaller farming stock when he died in 1587. He had no oxen, only seven cows, one heffer, three horses and nine sheep. His grain was worth only £15 18s 0d. There were about 20 acres with Crowsnest, but he had several 'tacks' or leases of land for periods of years. He died unexpectedly without making a written will at which time some 35 local people owed him money totalling £26 9s 2d. Some had been lent money, others owed for agricultural produce or work, or cow hire.

In Whitley, Richard Allen, who died in 1580, was farming on a similar scale to Humphrey Hall. In Aston, the only representatives of this group were Thomas Fernhead of Lymm and John Reading. Both were young men in the entourage of Peter Warburton at Arley Hall. As they lived in the Hall they had no farming equipment, but their inventories include such things as gold and silver coins, rapiers, daggers and swords.

Next to the freeholders in wealth were the copyholders of Whitley. The 33 pre-1620 inventories of members of this group all include evidence of farming. The following two fairly typical examples show that the value of farming possessions varied with the size of the farms. The lists of other possessions give the only clues we have as to their occupations.

1) George Lowton (Lawton), who died in 1602, was the owner of an estate of 36 acres (Appendix 3.4). His inventory, made in February, includes:

	£	s	d
6 cows and 13 other cattle	29	13	4
3 mares	5	0	0
14 sheep	1	10	0
pigs, geese, and hens	1	17	0
oats, barley, hay, etc.	29	6	8
waines, wheels, plows, yokes, fellies, ropes, etc	9	0	0
firewood, turfs, coles	1	0	0
wichwood	1	10	0
30 slippings yarn and other flaxen yarn	1	10	0
all hemp, flax, and toe	3	0	0
sacks, pokes, twillsheet	1	0	0
wool		8	0
1 weaving loom		4	0
2 spinning wheels		2	0
12 ells of canvas cloth		9	0
tack for 1 year		10	0
tack at rack rent		1	0
Debts due to him:			
Richard Broomfield of Northwich for wood and a walme	2	4	8
John Key for cow hire		3	4
Ralph Scot for cow hire		2	0

Humphrey Eaton for corn		4	6
3 others (reason unspecified)	5	18	5
Military equipment:			
harness, caliver, and pistolett	1	0	0
The usual furniture and supplies in the house			

His son John, who died in 1614, had similar possessions, including £45 worth of cattle and horses, and £6 8s 4d worth of hemp and flax in various stages.

2) George Barber, whose inventory is dated 1 July 1609, probably farmed about 20 acres (Appendix 4.4). He had fewer farming possessions than Lowton. The principal ones were:

	£	s	d
1 ox	3	0	0
5 cows	13	11	8
7 other cattle	9	16	8
4 horses	6	0	0
corn	11	0	0
a tack for years	10	0	0
another tack		12	0

There are two inventories of three-life leaseholders from Great Budworth and 13 from Aston by Budworth making a total of 15. The leaseholders occupied 1,635 acres of land in these two townships as compared with the 2,393 acres occupied by the copyholders of Whitley. The fact that 33 copyholder wills survive, compared to only 15 written by the leaseholders, may be because the copyholders were much better off and the wills of poor people are always more rare than the wills of the rich. The leaseholders' farming possessions varied considerably. John Starkie (Starkey), who died in 1611, had a leasehold in Aston of between 30 and 40 acres.[42] He also had 'tacks' of land, valued at £102 13s 4d. His cattle, valued at £72 13s 4d, would have needed all this land and the total of his inventory was £274 4s 4d. Richard Bretton, who died in Aston in 1588, had only about 20 acres of land, with six cattle, valued at £7 15s 0d, and three horses in a total inventory worth only £22 8s 0d.

Six of the Budworth residents who left inventories before 1620 were probably not leaseholders of either of the big estates. We have seen that the two Pimlows may have been tenants of the Halls of Brownslane. Richard Dewsbury, the grocer/mercer (see above p. 123) may not have possessed the three-life lease that his descendants owned in 1625. Thomas Holes, who died in 1617, may have been a shoemaker as his inventory included 'awls, last and iron £1 10s 0d'. All had a few cattle and some grain. They were presumably paying a rack rent in order to have

42 Appendix 3.8.

sufficient land to grow their own food. The four mentioned above were all businessmen; indeed perhaps the other two were as well. We may be examining a group
of people who had decided to set up their businesses in Budworth and were renting
sufficient land from non-resident, property-owning families to make their food
supply secure.

Who then was doing the manual work of farming on the land of these groups of
residents? We have seen above that William Malbon left money to several servants
suggesting that the freeholders with the larger farms employed people to cultivate
their land.

In my *Cheshire Cheese*, the labour required to cultivate a 65-acre farm in the mid-
eighteenth century is analysed in detail.[43] The information about sixteenth-century
farming at Smithills suggests that the changes in these manual operations between
these two centuries were not very great. We also learnt that five of the eight farm
workers there in 1587 were teenagers. In the late seventeenth century the Fell family
at Swarthmoor managed a freehold farm, only slightly larger than those of the Halls
and Malbons, with an adult man and a number of teenage assistants. It seems likely,
therefore, that families like the Malbons and the Halls were also employing an adult
servant and one or two teenagers. Appendix 3.4 shows that the farms in the Whitley
Lordship were smaller than these, but by 1612 some 40 cottages had been built on
them. The purpose of these cottages seems to have been to provide housing for the
labour force required on the farms. A man like George Lowton (extracts from whose
inventory were given above), who had a copyhold farm worth about £140 and
another £100 worth of chattels, may not have wished to spend much of his day on
manual labour when he could have a servant to live in his house and do the work
for £2 or £3 a year.

The three-life leaseholders as a group were probably less rich than the copyholders, but we have seen that some of them, like John Starkey and the Tabley
manager, Thomas Jackson, at the height of his fortunes, were as well off as any of
the small freeholders we have encountered. The account books of Jackson and
Latham have also shown us that having servants was not the only way to avoid cultivating your land with your own labour. Thomas Jackson let his whole farm at rack
rent for several years. Later he contracted with people to grow arable crops at halves
– a practice known as share-cropping. Latham hired his neighbours to do specific
jobs for him in return for cash. It seems likely that all these groups of landowners
used all these different methods when it suited them. Some like Latham and his

family seem to have done part of the farm work themselves.[44] Thomas Jackson employed his nephew John Griffith, whose father had a neighbouring leasehold, to plough for him.

A practical consideration that should be mentioned is that land was sometimes owned by people who were unable to work it, such as women, children or older men in poor health. The main farming jobs, holding the plough, cutting and stacking the hay, reaping and harvesting the corn and maintaining the hedges and ditches were physically demanding and could only be done by fit, strong people. Therefore most of the farming work must always have been done by teenage boys and young, healthy adults. Such people were not usually the owners. Fit young men and teenagers lived in the houses of richer people as their servants. Poorer leaseholders and cottagers probably farmed their own land themselves and also cultivated their neighbours' land on lease at rack rent, or by sharecropping, or for cash by the day or by the task. So if the freeholders, copyholders and richer three-life leaseholders did not do much farming work themselves, what did they do? We have seen that a few were in the Law or the Church; were the rest sitting idly at home or were they pursuing the other occupations described in the next section?

Before we move on we should notice that a common feature in the inventories of this area are 'tacks' or leases for years. Richard Worrall, who died in 1611, owned several. Other examples of testators in Budworth owning tacks are: J. Pickering, 1602; W. Pimlow, 1610; W. French, 1617; J. Dewsbury, 1621. Richard Worrall's tacks included:

Black hey for 3 years worth	£6 os od
Starkey's meadow for 5 years worth	£5 os od
Pickering's land for 9 years worth	£36 os od
Kerfoot's land for 1 year worth	£1 os od

These seem to have been leases of one or more fields for periods of years. The question that arises is: how had Worrall acquired these lands? Why had Pickering and Kerfoot sold him leases of their land? We do not know, of course, the exact reasons. Any man could have got into debt and have been forced to sell something

---

44 The diary of the Reverend Peter Walkden 1733–34, Chipping Local History Society, Lancashire, (ed.) 2000, gives a very similar picture. The diarist, a Dissenting minister with a small and uncertain salary, lived on a 40-acre upland farm paying a full market rent. He employed a boy, who lived in the house, to do much of the farm work, but his adult neighbours did the heavy work of ploughing, reaping and digging for him at a daily wage. Like the Lathams, he and his family helped with the farm work when they had time. He earned additional money by using his horses, which he had to have for the ministry, to transport coal and lime.

to repay the debt. However, wills may provide a clue. A feature of many wills was the obligation imposed by testators on the person to whom they left their land to pay capital sums to other people – typically their sisters and younger brothers. Selling a lease to parts of the land for some years seems to have been a method used to make these payments. Rich men like Worrall would invest in these leases and get their return from the rent that working farmers paid them each year. These leases are sufficiently common in inventories to make it clear that there was an active market in rack-rented land and in leases for years. When leaseholders renewed their leases with the old gentry like the Warburtons, they knew the annual value pretty accurately and they also understood the favourable terms on which custom allowed them to add new lives to their leases.

If the men who sold 'tacks' were often leaseholders who needed to raise cash for portions for their siblings, what if anything, do we know about those who bought 'tacks'? Richard Worrall had a three-life lease of about 11 acres in Budworth from the Leicesters. As with almost all these small 'owners' we have no information about his occupation. He or his father had owned this leasehold since 1566 but it seems unlikely that such a small holding had generated the £232 17s 0d worth of chattels listed in his inventory in 1611. It seems more likely that he was a successful businessman. Of the other Budworth testators listed above who owned tacks, we have seen that Pimlow and Dewsbury were businessmen. J. Pickering was a resident who did not own a leasehold, so he may well have been in business. The French family had leased the Cock Inn from the Warburtons since at least 1534.[45] So perhaps the buyers of tacks were often businessmen and large freeholders. Perhaps John Starkie of Aston had acquired much of his £274 of chattels in business before he invested £102 of it in tacks. Richard Worrall certainly moved in the upper social circle in Budworth. In his will he left many legacies. One was to his cousin, Lawrence Marbury of Marbury, another was to Richard Eaton, vicar of Great Budworth, and a third was to his servant, Joan Cooke, who had evidently been looking after him. His largest gift was £20 for the founding of a free grammar school in Great Budworth, or at least for building a schoolhouse.[46]

Before we leave the subject of agriculture, we need also to consider the business side of farming – buying and selling the cattle and the produce. From the fifteenth century, if not earlier, there was a market in London and the South-East for Cheshire cattle. Noblemen sent drovers from the South-East into the western counties, Wales and the North to buy cattle.[47] There were also drovers based in

45 Beamont, 1866, p. 14.
46 This appears to be the origin of the old schoolhouse in Budworth churchyard. See also Cox, 1975, p. 52.
47 Skeel, 1926, pp. 136–40.

Cheshire who moved cattle to London. This skilled and responsible business was regulated by the government. The value of a herd to be driven to London could exceed £100. Thomas Perceval, apprenticed to the Skinners' Company in London in 1497, was the son of Roger Perceval, a drover from Daresbury, just north of the Whitley Lordship.[48] Drovers may have continued to operate until at least the middle of the seventeenth century, when the Toke family of Kent bought Cheshire oxen at Bartholomew Fair, London, at £5 4s 0d each.[49]

On the other hand, as trade and markets developed under Elizabeth the work of drovers may have been imperceptibly superseded by the slow drifting of cattle from the North and West to the South and East through the medium of local cattle markets. We have seen examples of this at Smithills. The Shuttleworths often bought cattle well to the north in Blackburn, Colne and Preston, and their sales were normally in Wigan or Salford to the south. In the mid-eighteenth century, the Warburtons normally bought Scottish cattle in south Lancashire, and they always sold their surplus stock to dealers further south – in Knutsford and Budworth. Farmers of all sizes were involved in this trade. We have seen that Latham, with a normal stock of only two cows, was continually dealing, so it is likely that large farmers like the Halls and Malbons, with herds of 30 animals, bought several each year in Wigan or Warrington and sold a similar number in Knutsford or Congleton. In this way animals in peak condition could arrive on the outskirts of London although they had been bred in Lancashire. This was a technical improvement on droving but unfortunately we know very little about this business because by its nature it never appears in inventories.

The same is true of the other farming business, the sale of produce. We have seen how the Fells sold the surplus from their farms at local markets when the demands of the household were unusually small. Only rarely, when a man died suddenly like Thomas Anderton in 1587 (above p. 126), were the extent of his agricultural sales revealed by the debts he was owed. These were special sales on credit to his neighbours. The Smithills and Fell accounts show that sales at markets were for cash. This business side of farming was probably among the occupations of owners, even when they did none of the manual work on the farm. For example, Thomas Shuttleworth always rode north himself on cattle buying expeditions.

vi) Other occupations

These wills and inventories do not mention a wide range of businesses. I have noted over 40 occupations in the section of the Shuttleworth accounts dealing with

---

48 Skinners Register, Folios 1–13 (1496–1500).
49 Skeel, 1926, p. 141.

supplies and services (and more in the section on textiles)[50] but only six of them appear in the inventories. It seems likely that many more wills were originally written than those that are preserved in Probate Court records. It was expensive to get probate[51] and, in many cases, inheritors will probably have taken possession of the chattels, as they did of landed rights, in full confidence that no one would dispute their right. It is a characteristic of many wills admitted to probate that they incorporated a 'trust' element; for example, the executors may have to make payments to children when they reach a certain age. This may have been an important reason why a particular will was actually registered with the Court and has therefore survived. Furthermore we have seen that it was customary, in pre-1650 society, for families to stay in the same type of occupation for several generations. Sons will therefore have inherited their father's tools and stock without the need for probate.

Some 14 of the 40 occupations noted at Smithills were concerned with building. These included the well-known building trades, such as carpenters and plumbers. There were also people who created building materials like brick-makers and sawyers. Eight occupations involved working with leather and another seven or eight with metals. People following all these occupations will also have existed in the townships surrounding Arley and Tabley. The richer people will have been in trades like plumbing and glazing, which required some capital to carry stocks of materials. Cleverer men will have been in organizing roles such as those leading the teams of builders on larger jobs. Some trades like mill-wright required particularly skilled, intelligent, resourceful people. All these occupations, as well as those connected with textiles, will have been the principal livelihoods of many lease-holders and cottagers.

A distinctive feature of north-western life was the importance of the transport trades. Virtually all inventories include horses, frequently, there are more than would be justified by farming needs alone. For example, George Barber (see above, p. 127) had four horses on his 20-acre farm and Richard Worrall also had four on his 11 acres in Budworth. These horses were undoubtedly kept for transport. At Smithills they used regular carrier services to London in the 1580s as well as 'cross' services to Chester, Manchester, Halifax and York, but such services were only a fraction of the total horse traffic on the roads. Wool and linen textiles were always on the move from the North and West to London and the Midlands. We can be confident that the majority of horses used in journeys to the South and East were based in the North-West because grass was cheaper and more plentiful there. It appears that pasture and hay were always scarce in the South and East.

50 Foster, 2002, Ch. 1, pp. 41–53.
51 Sarah Fell paid £2 9s 10d for two administrations after the death of her sister Bridget Draper (Account book 22 May 1678). Richard Latham paid £1 1s 10d to prove his sister's will.

As well as these main trade routes, there was a steadily growing volume of local traffic, much of it connected with building. At Smithills in the 1580s, many materials were still available 'on the site'. However, as the new bricks and mortar became popular, first for the hearths and chimneys required for coal-burning fires, and then for walls, more transport was required. To obtain bricks in north Cheshire it was necessary to bring coal from south Lancashire and to build a kiln. As peat (turf) became scarcer, more coal was used for fuel.[52] Sandstone had to be carried from local quarries for foundations and flagstones of special quality for paving. As stocks of local timber dwindled, supplies could only be obtained when woods were felled further away. Brick walling also required sand and lime. All these are heavy materials requiring much greater horsepower to move them than do textiles and spices.

To some extent economies in horsepower could be obtained by the use of the wains and carts which are a common feature of inventories (see Lowton p. 126). However their use was restricted on many routes to spells of dry weather in summer when fords were passable. It will be seen from Map 7 that, in 1618, that there were only eight cart bridges over rivers in the whole of Bucklow Hundred.[53] This map suggests the pattern of traffic. Seven of the eight cart bridges crossed the large rivers – the Mersey, the Weaver, and the Bollin – allowing carts to cross these rivers all the year round. During the summer carts could also cross minor streams at fords. We know that Cheshire people could ford the Mersey at Hollin Ferry in Warburton with their carts in the summer to fetch their coal supplies from Lancashire pits.[54] In winter, carts often stuck in the mud so horses were better for moving goods, but, at this time of year, even lesser rivers were dangerous, so horse bridges had been built over them. See Pl. 14.

In 1618 it would probably have been possible to drive a cart from Cheshire to London during the summer, but in winter only strings of packhorses could make the journey.[55]

Local industries like the salt-boiling in Northwich, described in Chapter 7, made heavy demands on local transport. Boiling the brine in lead pans was a quick job done periodically by women. The main work (and expense) was gathering and trans-porting the wood fuel required, and carrying the finished salt to distant markets. Many local people were involved in this. Lowton's inventory (p. 126) lists

---

52 Are the 'coles' in Lowton's inventory (p. 126) charcoal or mineral coal? See Foster, 2002, Chs 1, 2 and 7 for changes in building and fuel.
53 DLT/B47 end pages.
54 WM Box 23, folder 5.
55 See also Hey, 1980, pp. 59–102.

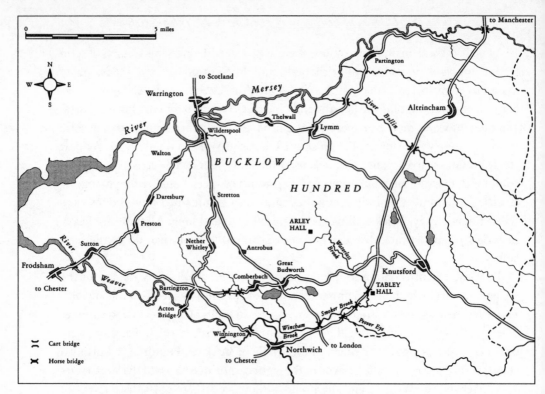

Map 7. The eight cart-bridges over rivers in Bucklow Hundred in 1618.
There were also 29 horse-bridges but only six of them are marked on this map as it would take a lot of research to be sure where all the others were. The two drawn in Pl. 10 (the map of Cogshall in 1578) are shown, together with three on the main road from Chester through Northwich to Manchester, and one on the main north-south road from Warrington to London. These last four suggest that even main roads were not usually passable for long-distance cart journeys in winter in 1618.

'wichwood', the local name for suitably sized wood. It also suggests that supplying wood or horses was a regular activity of his, because he was owed £2 4s 8d for wood, and a 'walme' of salt by Richard Bromfield, whose family included some of the principal citizens of Witton/Northwich.[56] One Thomas Anderton, salter, occurs in several inventories.[57] He was probably a member of the Budworth family and was probably a carrier of salt for sale. His business appears to have failed about 1610, since among Richard Worrall's debts, described as 'probably desperate' in 1611, was £42 11s 4d owed by Thomas Anderton, salter.

　　These examples show that a number of copyholders and leaseholders are likely

56 DLT/D241 for sixteenth century leases; Lawton, 1979, pp. 188, 235.
57 E.g., W. Pimlow, 1610.

to have been engaged in transport work. If they had land on which to keep horses they were halfway to a business, even if it was only hiring out their horses to the carrier. From carrying goods it is only a short step to dealing in them.[58] Travelling about the country provided knowledge of suppliers and markets. It may well be that transport and trading activities account for the considerable wealth that some lease-holders acquired before 1630. A few examples can be quoted to illustrate this fact. The Roughsedge (Roughstich) family of Sutton occupied a farm of 31 acres (Appendix 3.1). Ralph Roughsedge, who died in 1584, left chattels valued at about £32 to his widow and their son and five daughters. 50 years later, the inventory of another Ralph, who died in 1630, showed that he was then worth £296. Among the Warburton leaseholders in Aston by Budworth was John Starkie, who had a similar-sized farm and chattels valued at £274 in 1611. Richard Massie, who died in 1615, had a leasehold of only about 15 acres, and his inventory lists 'tacks' worth £78 in a total value of £218. William Key's farm was, like John Starkie's, around 30 acres, but his inventory included debts owing to him of £100 in a total of £222 in 1618. We have seen above that Richard Worrall of Budworth's inventory was worth £232 17s 0d in 1611. It seems much more likely that these people had made these substantial sums of money by trading than by cultivating their land more assiduously than their neighbours. These trading activities were unlikely to appear in their inventories except in the form of cash or debts.

In this chapter we have seen a few of the ways of making a living that happen to be recorded in surviving documents about the inhabitants of a few townships in north Cheshire. If one examined the same type of sources in the area of south Lancashire north of Warrington one would find a different range of occupations, because many people there worked in the coal-mines and in the numerous metalworking industries that sprang up on the coalfield. If one chose instead a group of townships near Manchester many occupations would be connected with the growing textile industry there. All these different areas would confirm the development of a business community in Cheshire and Lancashire in the century before the Civil War. Another important measure of this is the steadily declining number of youths from the area, seeking a business career, who felt that they had to go to London to find one. In the period 1486–1500 the opportunities in business in the North were apparently so bleak that more than 61% of City of London apprentices came from the northern counties. We have seen that this proportion declined in the sixteenth century and in the 40 years before the Civil War it was only 20%.[59] The increasing

58 See Foster, 1998, pp. 79–80, for the Widder brothers, who crossed this line.
59 Wareing, 1980.

attraction of a business career in the North-West was already evident by 1640.

The particular custom followed by many of these new property owning families, that parents should divide their wealth approximately equally among all their children, had a significant effect on the growing business community. We have seen that some men, like Burges and Millington in Knutsford, made enough money in their businesses to be able to add more landed investments to the original urban holdings or small farms their families possessed. The land they were able to buy usually consisted of a number of the small freehold farms that were typical of the area. When their lands came to be divided among their children or grandchildren, one or two of these small farms made suitable separate inheritances for their descendants. In this way they did not build up large estates like those of the major gentry, which they might have been tempted to do if their lands had been held in a single, large, economically efficient block. This continuous division of their estates by parents kept the pattern of the small farms with separate owners that we will see was still characteristic of Bucklow Hundred in the Restoration period. Other historians have noticed the connection between small property owners and the development of business. R. Smith commented on it in the cloth-manufacturing districts of the West Riding of Yorkshire, such as Halifax and Bradford, and among the metalworkers of the Sheffield district.[60] Joan Thirsk has traced a connection between the survival of the custom of 'partible' inheritance and the growth of rural industries, *c.* 1600.[61] The tendency for small property owners to use their capital in business was probably almost universal, but it was the concentration of such property owners in the North-West that made the industrial development of that area outstanding.

60 Smith, 1970, pp. 119–22.
61 Thirsk, J., 1961.
62 See Antrobus, 1929.

Appendix 4.1 *Some apprentices from north Cheshire at the City of London companies of Carpenters, Drapers, Merchant Tailors, and Skinners, 1497–1656*

Name	Company	Year of Apprenticeship	
Antrobus, George	M-Tailor	1601	son of Henry of Knutsford, cloth merchant
Antrobus, William	M-Tailor	1617	son of Henry of Knutsford, apprenticed to George Antrobus above
Antrobus, Thomas	M-Tailor	1627	son of the George Antrobus above
Antrobus			Six others were made Free of the M-Tailors between 1569 and 1662.[1]
Caldwell, Matthew	Carpenter	1656	son of Matthew of Appleton, collarmaker
Dutton, Edward	Drapers	1635	son of Richard, arm.
Eaton, George	Drapers	1618	son of John of Sandiway (in Whitley?)
Key, John	M-Tailor	1583	son of Richard of Budworth
Millington, Thomas	Skinners	1497	son of Thomas of Appleton. *See Note 1.*
Middlehurst, Thomas	Carpenter	1656	son of John of Grappenhall
Martin, John	M-Tailor	1615	son of William of Sutton
Malbon, Richard	M-Tailor	1604	son of William of Great Budworth
Nixon, George	M-Tailor	1583	son of John of Whitley
Richardson, Hugh	M-Tailor	1605	son of Ralph of Crowley
Starkey, Thomas	M-Tailor	1606	son of Lawrence of Stretton
Warburton, Thomas	M-Tailor	1612	son of George of Crowley, arm.
Warburton, Gabriel	Drapers	1617	son of George of Crowley, arm.

Note 1. Both father and son were probably ancestors of the Thomas Millington mentioned in Foster, 2002, pp. 101–03.

1   See Antrobus, 1929.

CHAPTER 5

Social changes and the distribution of wealth in the seventeenth century

i) Introduction

The Civil War period was a time of change in the social habits of the people of rural Cheshire. Until the war the great majority of families brought up their children on the small farms they had occupied since the fifteenth century. This behaviour pattern broke up during the 20 years 1640–60, so that these families were much more frequently non-resident in the Restoration period. Economically active members of these old families more frequently sought their careers elsewhere and other families, who had earlier been landless poor people, came on to these farms to work the land and to pay a full rack rent. The land was increasingly occupied by a new class of tenant farmers paying a full market rent. This converted the small farms into income-producing investments for their former occupiers, whether they were freeholders or three-life leaseholders. The farms became capital assets that supported the credit of their 'owners' and could also be mortgaged if capital was required. The new businesses started by these small capitalists helped to increase the range of jobs available and provided employment for everyone living in the area, so that the problems of begging and vagrancy gradually disappeared. The evidence for this picture slowly emerges from the detail in sections (ii) – (iv) of this chapter.

In section (ii) the information in the parish registers of Great Budworth is brought together with that in the rentals of several townships. The size of the population in the Budworth area is found not to have changed greatly in the period 1575–1645. The three-life leaseholders were mostly still living on their farms. The copyholders/freeholders of Whitley Lordship were different because they were richer. The parish registers indicate that they were drifting away from their farms in the first 30 years of the seventeenth century. We begin to see that the growing wealth of these country families, combined with developments in the economic life of the area, was drawing young people away to new careers. Section (iii) examines the influence of the Manor Courts in keeping the poor from settling in the country. In the period up to 1625 the leaseholders who dominated these courts upheld the ancient rules against strangers, but the price to pay for this was that it stifled economic development. Great Budworth remained a village, whereas Knutsford became a thriving town as well as a place of resort for the poor.

The final section (iv) is about the distribution of wealth in Cheshire in the 1660s. From an analysis of tax returns and estate surveys it is calculated that there may have been as many as 25,000 capital-owning families in the two counties of Cheshire and Lancashire. This represents an unusually wide distribution of wealth – much wider than in 1545 or in 1900.   The first part brings together details of the Poll Tax of 1660 and the Hearth Tax of 1664 with surveys and valuations of properties. In two townships in Northwich Hundred (see Map 1), the assessments for tax of individuals are compared with the valuations of their property. This demonstrates that the Poll Tax was normally levied on the income derived from capital assets. This allows us to divide the households in the Hundred into four groups. At the top were 21 major gentry families who each owned capital in the range £6,000–£60,000. The bottom group, containing about a third of the households, were poor families owning a maximum of £15 or £20 each. In the middle were two groups – in the richer one were families owning between £100 and £5,000 with an average of about £368 per family, and in the poorer one families had between £20 and £100 of assets with an average of about £50. Both of these capital-owning groups – the richer and the poorer – contained about one third of the total number of households in the Hundred.

If these townships and the Northwich Hundred are representative of Cheshire, the society in the county in 1660 was very different from what it had been in 1545. The picture of that society obtained from an analysis of the 1545 tax return of Bucklow Hundred (in Chapter 3 (ii) above) showed that there were only about 110 families with a little capital standing in the middle ground between the 25 major gentry and the 1,500 families whose wealth varied between about £3 and £30.[1] In 1660 perhaps about two thirds of the families owned enough capital to occupy a place in this middle ground.

In the second half of this section, the people who paid the Poll Tax of 1667 in Nether Tabley are compared with the survey and valuation of the farms in the township, made the year before. This shows that several of the leaseholder families were represented by widows and retired men who were being looked after by servants. Leaseholders bringing up their families on these farms were by this period in a minority. Eight families of 'strangers' – i.e., not leaseholders – had moved into the township. It seems likely that they were farming most of the land as sub-tenants on rack rents. Thus the old manorial controls had broken down. It would seem likely that those members of leaseholder families who were economically active had gone off to pursue other careers. The period of the Civil War and the Commonwealth appears to have been the time when the traditional settled society, in which families brought up their children on the old family farm, gave way to a new world of greater fluidity and enterprise.

1 These 1,500 families were assessed on goods of £1 to £10, but we estimated that these assessments were probably only about one third of the real values.

ii) Rentals and Parish Registers

I have spent a good deal of time with the Parish Registers of Great Budworth, hoping to learn something about the lives of people in the sixteenth and seventeenth centuries, by bringing together the information in the registers with that in the rentals and other archives of the Warburtons and the Leicesters, but I have found out little. I will not bore the reader with the detailed problems but, in general, there is too much uncertainty about people's identities – too many people with the same surname and often the same Christian name as well. What I have learned can be briefly stated.

First, we can perhaps say something about the total population in the Great Budworth area. In the period of 70 years from 1577 to 1646, the average number of baptisms each year was 78 and the average number of burials was 79.[2] Except for a few disastrous years, both baptisms and burials were between 60 and 100 each year. It would seem, therefore, that the total population living around Budworth did not alter greatly in this period. The people who registered their births and deaths lived in the townships near the church which served a total of 22 townships at this period. The people living on the outskirts of the parish used other churches. However, even the locals were not always assiduous about registration. Between 1560 and 1576, and again between 1646 and 1651, there was substantial under-registration.

We learn a little more by examining the evidence about individual townships. Warburton and Leicester rentals of Great Budworth and Aston by Budworth in Appendix 3.8 show great continuity in the tenant families. In the Warburtons' 1626 rental and the Leicesters' 1641 rental of Aston by Budworth, there are 30 different surnames. Between 1601 and 1648 the registers record births to people with 26 of these surnames.[3] There were 62 fathers bearing these names and they produced 221 children. This is an average of 3.5 children per father. If we extract the surnames of the seven cottagers and examine them separately, we find that there were 15 fathers in this group who between them had 34 children, an average of only 2.3 per father. This seems to accord with the weaker economic position of the cottagers. As well as the 221 children produced by the leaseholders, a further 134 children were born in Aston in this period to 70 other fathers. 95 of them were born to 31 fathers who had an average of three children each. Some of these fathers were probably the tenants of the eight freeholders in the township. Others were probably the rack-rent tenants who came to live on the Arley demesne after 1626 when it was leased out by Peter Warburton's daughters. There is even more uncertainty about the 39

---

2 In the 52 years of burial records I examined.
3 The name of the township in which the father lived is only recorded from 1601. The wives' names are never given.

fathers who each produced one child in Aston. One was an estate manager under Peter Warburton, another was his cook, and three were gentlemen staying in the Hall, but of the rest we know nothing.

The position in Great Budworth was similar to that in Aston. All but three of the surnames of the leaseholders and freeholders are represented among the men who fathered children. There were 116 fathers with property-owning surnames and they had 372 children between them. The impossibility of sorting out the families in more detail can be illustrated with the surname Anderton. People with the name Anderton owned one freehold in Budworth called Crowsnest, three Arley lease-holds, one Leicester leasehold, one Arley cottage or boat, and one Leicester boat – a total of seven properties. There were 12 Anderton fathers – three called Thomas, four Williams, two Johns and three with other names. Altogether they produced 46 children, but which father came from which property is impossible to establish.

As in Aston, there were plenty of fathers who were not freeholders or lease-holders. 74 men in Budworth fathered 146 children. We know something about only a handful of these people. One of them, John Key, was the schoolmaster in the old brick school that still stands in the churchyard.[4] He had four children in Budworth between 1617 and 1624, but where he lived we do not know. Richard Lowndes was a gentleman who seems to have decided to bring up his family in Budworth rather than on his own leasehold in Mobberley.[5]

So in Budworth we have counted some 518 children, 372 of whom were probably born to families with property rights in the township, 72 % of all the children born in this period. In Aston the children of the leaseholders represented only 62% of the total, but the Arley demesne and the freeholds were a large proportion of the land in that township. Despite all the uncertainties, the registers do seem to tell us that most of the leaseholders were still living on their farms in these two townships until the Civil War.

It is even more difficult to learn anything precise from the registers about the families who lived in the Whitley Lordship. We have seen in the 1612 survey (Appendix 3.4) that, at that date, about 14 of the 77 farmsteads were occupied by tenants. The number of freeholders living on their farms seems to have continued to decline. 134 of the children born in the period 1601–12 were fathered by 48 men whose surnames were the same as those of the owners of the farms. In the decade 1613–22 31 such fathers produced 110 children and from 1623 to 1632, 33 such fathers had 85 children.[6]

4 See Foster, 2002, p. 90.
5 Will, 1626.
6 The children were first grouped under their fathers. Then entire families were allocated to the decade in which most of them were born. I stopped the analysis 20 years after the survey.

One final point that the registers confirm was the weak position of the poor. We have seen earlier that the average number of burials each year in Great Budworth was about 79. The worst year in this period was 1588 when 161 people were buried, 111 of them dying in the first five months of the year. At Smithills 1586 and 1587 were years of poor harvests and high prices.[7] That estate sold barley to neighbours and employees at prices of up to 7 shillings a bushel in the autumn of 1587, and then seems to have run out of supplies for sale. This was about three times the ordinary price. They sold no oats in 1587 because they seem to have disposed of all their available supplies in 1586. Great Budworth is only about 25 miles from Smithills so, putting all the information together, it seems likely that many of the 157 people who died in the nine months between early September 1587 and the end of May 1588 succumbed to starvation or starvation-related diseases. In June 1588 when the new season of vegetables became available, the number of burials dropped to normal levels of six or seven a month.

iii) The poor and the development of Budworth and Knutsford

When much of Budworth Heath was enclosed around 1550 (p. 79 above), the opportunity to provide cottages for the poor was not taken. This was not the only thing the property owners did to avoid having poor people living in the township. The Warburtons held a Manor Court for their tenants (including freeholders) in Budworth, Aston by Budworth, and Comberbach once a year from 1580 to 1625.[8] Much of the court's time was devoted to mundane matters like keeping buildings and ditches in repair and not letting animals eat other people's crops. However, a more socially significant theme appears in the record of almost every court. Poor people, who were not tenants, must not be allowed to settle in the township although there was evidently no objection to rich immigrants. Richard Lowndes of Mobberley, whom we met earlier, p. 141, seems to have rented a good house and farm there. His inventory, including leaseholds in Mobberley, totalled £395.

Tenants were fined for two different offences:

1. Having inmates or lodgers

Women who were pregnant were particularly discouraged from moving in because their child, if born in the township, would be the responsibility of the ratepayers all its life. For example, in December 1581 a widow was fined for keeping a 'wandering woman' in her house and in October 1582, four people were fined 6s 8d each for

---

7 See Foster, 2002, pp. 24–7. 1586 was a bad harvest year all over England; see Hoskins, 1964, p. 46.
8 WM Box 6.

keeping pregnant women in their houses. These offences continued throughout the period. In 1619 Elizabeth Houghton was fined 6s 8d for keeping her daughter in her house, 'great with child'. However, it was possible for responsible people to avoid being fined. In 1605, the court recorded a memorandum that Mrs. Anne Eaton had the consent of the Lord of the Manor to keep a woman in her house, as long as she lived, 'to bear her company'. In 1625 it was ordered that any person taking an inmate should enter into a bond of £40.

2. Having sub-tenants or 'setting their grounds' to strangers, or 'going halves' with strangers

The Leicesters' tenants in Budworth and Aston attended that family's court at Nether Tabley which followed the same rules as the Warburtons' court.[9] Budworth seems to have been a sufficiently socially compact society for it to be impossible to keep the existence of lodgers or farming under-tenants secret. Once they were known, people felt able to announce their presence in open court. Fines were imposed and the practice was halted.

These measures seem to have been effective in keeping the poor out of Budworth. There was a price to pay for this: the place remained a village. The records of the court suggest that there was much building in Budworth in the 1580s and 90s when 'Encroachments on the waste' were common. These seem usually to have been caused by building part of a house on what was deemed to be the old public road. With its position on the London road running south from the bridge in Warrington, Budworth could have become a significant-sized town, but it never did.

This is in marked contrast with what occurred in Knutsford. By 1667 it contained more than 40 charterers or freeholders.[10] This division of responsibility between so many landowners may have been part of the reason why Knutsford became a resort of the poor. At the Quarter Sessions on 8 July 1663, the Justices decided to collect a tax in the whole county of Cheshire for the relief of the Poor in towns where they were so numerous that the inhabitants of those towns were unable to provide for them. The largest part of the tax, £70, was allotted to Knutsford (£52 to Nether and £18 to Over Knutsford). The next largest grant in Bucklow Hundred was £30 to Altrincham. The largest sum given outside this Hundred was £40 to Stockport.[11] The congregation of the poor in urban areas seems to have been fairly usual in the north of England in the seventeenth century. A survey of Sheffield made in 1615 gives more details. The total population of the township was 2,207, of which:

---

9 DLT/B15 states the same rules in 12 Henry 7 (1496/7).
10 Ormerod, 1882, Vol. 1, pp. 488–91.
11 DLT/B36.

       100 were householders paying poor rates
       160 were householders not able to pay poor rates
     1,222 were the children and servants of householders who could live without poor relief
      725 were begging poor dependent on charity
     2,207 [12]

The characteristics of the rural culture that have emerged from our analysis of the inventories and the seven families' accounts provide clues about how this structure of society evolved. The custom was to provide portions for younger sons and daughters and to send them out into the world. Sons whose career failed or daughters who married against their parents' wishes or who were widowed early could quickly descend into poverty like some of the Jackson family and they were not usually allowed to settle in the country areas.

The large number of vagrants and people hoping to be allowed to be lodgers probably reflects the generous instincts of country-dwellers. They were relatively well off and they had good supplies of food, so they may often have been kind to beggars. However, the Manor Courts maintained discipline and forced the vagrants to go to the towns and seek work. The other area that attracted poor young people was the hills. On these thinly populated lands with distant manorial control, it seems to have been possible to erect a shack and make a living in wool spinning, quarrying, etc.[13] The availability of this labour force encouraged business development in the hills and the towns. The main occupation of the poor in Cheshire towns was probably the processing of hemp and flax, the raw fibres being retailed by shop-keepers.[14] The production of thread probably developed as a speciality of Knutsford in this period. It was required in a large number of different forms from coarse, strong fibres used in saddles and shoes, to the finest grades used for sewing and lace-making. In the middle of the eighteenth century the town was famous for this trade, but it seems to have migrated to northern Ireland by 1800.[15]

iv) The Poll Taxes of 1660 and 1667 and the Hearth Tax of 1664
a) The 1660 Poll Tax and the 1664 Hearth Tax

A picture of Cheshire society in the 1660s can be obtained from the Poll Taxes of 1660 and 1667. The Tabley archives contain surveys and valuations that enable us to understand how these taxes were assessed. A detailed view of the distribution of wealth in this society appears from this analysis. The Poll Tax of 1660 was the most comprehensive national tax levied between the 1540s and the Land Tax of the eigh-

12 Hunter, 1869, p. 148.
13 Swain, 1986.
14 Phillips, 1985, pp. 104–09.
15 Aikin, 1795, p. 422; Foster, 1992, p. 24 for P. Penney, thread merchant, bankrupt 1764.

teenth century. Unfortunately only fragments of the return from Bucklow Hundred survive, so it is not possible to make direct comparisons with the 1545 tax described in Chapter 3. However, the return for the adjacent Northwich Hundred is one of the most detailed among those that have been preserved.[16] The Tabley estate owned land in this Hundred (see Map 1), so we can study that return.

The tax was levied on three separate groups of people: 1) All single men and women aged over 16 paid one shilling. Married couples also paid a shilling; 2) Those whose income exceeded £5 p.a. paid 2% of it; and 3) The major gentry, together with doctors and senior lawyers paid fixed sums ranging from £10 for esquires to £100 for dukes. Let us examine how this worked in Northwich Hundred. There were a total of 4,655 tax-charges. 21 people paid the fixed sums of £10 or more. 1,100 paid on incomes of £5 and more. About 1,060 married couples paid one shilling per couple, and 2,474 single people paid one shilling each. We will see later that these taxpayers were living in 21 gentry households, 850 rich households, 903 medium households, and 811 poor households.

The 21 people who paid the fixed charges were gentry similar to those who lived in Bucklow and are listed in Appendix 3.5. For example, Lord Brereton paid £40, Peter Venables, Baron of Kinderton and Sir Willoughby Aston, Baronet, paid £30 each. All the others paid £10 as esquires, except Dr David Roach of Congleton. Two widows only paid one third of what their husbands would have been assessed for if they had been alive. These fixed charges were only roughly related to actual incomes. £10 is 2% of £500. Many esquires will have had income of more than £500 p.a. We know that the income of the Warburton and Leicester estates was approximately £2,000 p.a. and £1,000 p.a. respectively at this period.[17] The heads of both these families became baronets in 1660. They would therefore have paid £30 each. 30 is 2% of £1,500 p.a. – so Leicester paid at 3% while Warburton only paid at 1.5%. The total amount of tax which was collected by the 21 fixed charges in Northwich was £270. This was about 35.6% of the total of £759 collected in the whole Hundred. This was less than the 53.5% paid by the leading 25 families in Bucklow in 1545, but the two figures cannot properly be compared. It can be clearly seen, however, that the leading gentry families were still a powerful force in the community in 1660.

Who were the 1,100 people who paid on incomes of over £5 p.a. and how were they assessed? The Act[18] charged tax on 'Every person that can dispend in Lands, leases, money, stock or otherwise of his or her own proper estate'. What did people

16 Lawton, 1979.
17 See pages 17 and 27.
18 12 Chas II c9.

understand by these words in 1660? In Appendix 5.1, B, all those who paid Poll Tax in Nether Peover in 1660 are listed in alphabetical order on the left of the page. On the right, against those who had property is shown the landlord, the area (if known) and the annual value of every property in the township. Thus the first entry shows that Thomas Ampson paid tax at 2% on £5 p.a. and had a three-life leasehold of 13 acres worth £8 10s 0d p.a. Of the 21 people who paid tax on more than £5 p.a. only two are not shown in these surveys to have had a property.[19]

In Appendix 5.1,C 22 Poll tax payers in Allostock are matched with their properties. It would seem, therefore, we can say that in these two townships the assessments were usually made on property. Most of the annual values were between two and three times the assessment. Thus Thomas Buckley had a three-life lease of 39 acres valued at £25 p.a. His income was assessed for tax at £10 p.a. Where the value of the property was under £10, usually only the standard one shilling Poll Tax was paid. Thus Hugh Bradshaw had a freehold worth £4 p.a. and Edward Foxley had a leasehold worth £6 p.a., but neither paid more than one shilling. People who leased property and paid a rack rent or market (near market) rent for it were not charged more than a shilling either. In Allostock for instance, the Stubbs family were old three-life leaseholders of the Leicester estate. It appears that in the 1650s they had been unable to pay the full capital sum required to renew their leases at the 'old' rents. Sir Peter Leicester seems to have allowed them to stay on their farms by arranging new leases under which they paid about 60% of the full rack rent. In 1663, they were paying rents of £12 p.a. and £11 10s 0d p.a. for their two farms, whose full annual values were £17 and £20. They seem not to have been regarded as having an income as great as £5 p.a.

In Sandbach, a number of traders were assessed on the value of their stock.[20] For example, John Langard, skinner, was assessed on a stock of £150, and John Hall, tanner, on stock of £100. The tax they paid shows that the charge was based on £9 p.a. for Langard and £6 p.a. for Hall. This means that the assessors assumed they were making 6% profit per annum on the value of their stock. In Congleton, Mrs Penelope Bradshaw was reputed to have a portion of £1,500.[21] The assessors assumed she could get interest of 5% on her money, and charged her tax on £75 p.a.

These examples show that land, trading stock and cash were all assessed. No doubt many assessments were made on a mixture of all three types of assets. We have seen that Thomas Jackson had both a three-life leasehold and money lent at

19 However, we know of two or perhaps four properties that did not pay tax. These discrepancies probably arise from the surveys having been made in 1663 and 1676.
20 Lawton, 1979, p. 62.
21 Lawton, 1979, p. 30.

interest. On the other hand, we have also seen that the family capital had to be divided with widows and younger children. Families could also have debts. In the townships, the assessors probably knew about each family's circumstances so that an individual's assessment took account of all these factors.

There are sets of title deeds to a number of properties in Northwich Hundred in the Tabley archives. The estate did not own these properties in 1660, but acquired them in the middle of the eighteenth century. These deeds also tend to show that the 1660 assessments were probably a conservative view of the wealth of these capital-owning families. Here are two examples.

Appendix 5.1,D gives details of some of the transactions in the Restoration period in the five farms in Allostock, which were sold by the Arley estate in 1678. Robert Higgenson, skinner, paid £155 in 1667 for a three-life lease of his family's 27½-acre farm. He bought the freehold in 1678 for another £107. He sold two fields to the Amson family for £75 in 1678 and the rest to them in 1685 for £255, so the total freehold value was £330 probably worth about £18 pa. Robert himself only paid tax of one shilling in 1660, but John who was probably his father was assessed at £14 p.a. The Whishaw family, whose leading member, Hugh, was only assessed at £6 p.a. in 1660, bought the lease of the Statham family's 34-acre farm before 1678. In that year, Joseph Whishaw bought the freehold of both farms for £410. The two farms totalled about 72 acres probably worth over £40 p.a., so their combined value after 1678 was probably more than £700. The family continued to own them till the mid-eighteenth century.

The second example is the Ralph Whalley family of Stanthorne. In 1660, Ralph Whalley appears as one of the richest men in the Hundred after the old major gentry. He was assessed at £80 p.a. and was evidently living in a large house (perhaps Spittle Hill House) attended by five servants. In 1575, his ancestors had had a three-life lease from the Brereton family of a 174-acre farm in Stanthorne. They may have made their money on this farm or in some other activity like the salt industry – we do not know. In 1664 he bought from Lord Brereton the manor of Stanthorne, including his own and other tenanted farms, for £2,750.[22] All these examples seem to make it clear that the people who paid the 1660 Poll Tax had significant capital and that the tax was normally assessed on the income received from these capital assets.

If we examine the 1664 Hearth Tax of Northwich Hundred alongside the Poll Tax, it allows us to get a clearer view of the wealth of this society. The Hearth Tax

---

22 DLT/D29 for Whalley leases; D46; D439; D35; a 1662 survey of Stanthorne manor is unlisted. In Ralph Whalley's will of 1598, he left the lease of a wichhouse of five leads in Middlewich to his eldest son Ralph.

listed 2,585 households. 811 were exempt while 1,774 paid tax. The Act[23] exempted households that occupied a house worth less than £1 p.a. and owned land and goods worth less than £10. We have seen that assessments normally favoured taxpayers, so it seems likely that households owning up to £15 or £20 pounds worth of assets were exempt from Hearth Tax in Northwich Hundred.

The Poll Tax tells us more about the 1,774 households who paid Hearth Tax. 1,100 properties were assessed to Poll Tax at values of £5 p.a. or more. Most of these were the homes of three-life leaseholders and small freeholder families. The richest freeholders had more than one property. Philip Pritchard, the richest man in the Hundred who was not the head of a major gentry family, was assessed at £105 p.a. for his house and land in Bostock, where he lived. His salt-works in Leftwich was assessed at £200 p.a., and he also owned a farm in Wharton, charged at £6 15s od p.a.[24] Some men had even more properties. As well as his house in Northwich, William Bentley owned four small farms in nearby townships. His total assessment on all five was only £39 p.a. He was unusual as most of the people whom I have traced as multi-property owners had only two farms. An example of a family owning two properties occurs in Appendix 5.1. Thomas Holford, gent., was living in Allostock in 1660 with his adult son Mathew and daughter Elizabeth on a 68-acre farm worth £36 p.a. He was assessed at £20 p.a. His son Mathew owned a leasehold in Nether Peover worth £12 p.a. and was assessed at £5 p.a. It is difficult to be certain in identifying such people, but it appears likely that there were about 850 households who owned property valued at £5 p.a. and more. Some of these property owners were not resident in the Hundred. Both the Poll Tax and the Hearth Tax seem to have been levied on non-residents.[25]

If we deduct those 850 households from the 1,774 who paid Hearth Tax, we are left with 924 households whose wealth was between the £20 that was the maximum exempt households are likely to have owned and the capital that gave rise to an assessment of £5 p.a. or more. From an examination of the values in Appendix 5.1, it would seem that £100 of capital was probably the minimum that was assessed at £5 p.a. The households in this middle group, then, had capital of between £20 and £100. Some households with £150 may have been lucky enough to avoid being assessed at £5 p.a. This analysis allows us to construct the following profile of the wealth of Northwich Hundred society:

23 14 Chas II c10.
24 See Ch. 7, p. 200.
25 John Oaseley paid Hearth Tax in Great Budworth in 1673–74. In a lawsuit in 1673, it was implied that he had never lived in Budworth and had always let his two farms at rack rents. WM Box 3. Perhaps non-resident owners paid Hearth Tax unless they had made their tenants liable for it in their leases.

Table 7. The wealth of Northwich Hundred in the 1660s

Number of households[26]	%	Social group	Likely income from capital £ p.a.	Likely capital assets £
21	0.8	Major gentry	300–3,000	6,000–60,000
850	32.9	Richer families	8–500	100–5,000
903	34.9	Medium families	1–10	20–150
811	31.4	Poor families	Nil–1	Nil–20
2,585	100.0			

We can see how this distribution worked out in Nether Peover. 42 households paid Hearth Tax, 41 paid Poll Tax. 21 people were assessed to Poll Tax at £5 or more. These would have been in the 'richer' families group above. 11 other people owned smaller properties. They were among the 'medium' families. They would have been joined in this group by some of the families who paid both Poll and Hearth Tax but did not own any property – for example, the two families of Peter Kinseys. They were probably living in the houses of some property owners who were non-resident – Richard Millington and Mrs Ann Pemberton may be examples. Those who lived in the cottages formed part of the group of 'poor' families in Nether Peover.

The Poll Tax can tell us more about this society. The property owners assessed at £5 or more were concentrated in the rural townships like Nether Peover and Allostock. Odd Rode contained many 'richer' families; there were 57 of them in the township and only 18 medium and poor ones. Most of these 18 families were probably living in farms belonging to non-resident owners because the Hearth Tax only listed 61 households. In the towns, the position was reversed; the poorer people were concentrated there.

Here are the figures for four towns:

Table 8. Rich and poor in four towns

Town	Taxpayers assessed at £5 p.a. and over	Married couples assessed at less than £5 p.a.
Congleton	116	161
Middlewich	19	74
Northwich	16	59
Sandbach	53	74

26 A detailed examination of the Poll Tax return suggests that only 500-600 of the richer families were resident. 200-300 of the richer families' households listed here were therefore headed by a non-resident owner. When examining the 1667 Poll Tax later we will find that a number of 'resident' property owning families were only represented by a widow or a retired man.

In addition to the 850 richer families with their 1,100 properties assessed at £5 p.a. and more, the Poll Tax lists 1,060 married couples and 2,474 single people. These last two formed the medium and poor households. The 1667 Poll Tax return for Nether Tabley (Appendix 5.2) shows us some examples of single people. One category was the adult (over 16 years old) children of the householders. Only one of the richer families, the Philip Wrights, had children living with them. But seven of the less rich families had their adult children at home. This probably represents the pattern we have seen earlier. The better-off families apprenticed their children to an occupation; the less well-off trained them at home in a craft often connected to the building industry, such as carpentry. Six of the richer families had non-family members in their houses. These were probably servants and farm workers. Only four of the less rich had such people who may have been lodgers. Those single people who were not part of such 'families' in the rural townships formed many of the poor households in the towns.

We may conclude by considering the wealth of the whole society. The 850 families whose 1,100 properties were assessed at £5 p.a. and over paid a total of £313 in tax. As the tax rate was 2% at this time, this means that they were assessed as having a total income of £15,650. If the rate of return they were receiving on the capital is conservatively estimated at 5%, these 850 families possessed capital with a total value of £313,000. On this calculation the average wealth of these families was £368 each. The wage of an agricultural worker was about £11 p.a., while craftsmen got between £15 p.a. and £20 p.a. £368 was therefore a substantial capital sum in relation to all manual workers. Moreover, we have seen that the assessments may well have understated these people's real incomes, so it is possible that, between them, they owned capital worth half a million pounds. The £313 of tax they paid was about 41.2% of the total of £759 collected in Northwich Hundred. Their share was greater than the 35.6% paid by the 21 major gentry who were assessed at the fixed 'rank' charges. Because of the different types of assessment we are not able to say which of the two groups owned the greater wealth in total.

We can use these figures to estimate the number of capital-owning families in Cheshire. There were seven Hundreds in the county, so that if the Northwich Hundred pattern existed in the others, there were 7 × 850 = 5,950 rich families and 7 × 903 = 6,321 medium families. This makes a total of over 12,000 capital-owning families in the whole county. Lancashire was a larger county, so there were probably a total of more than 25,000 capital-owning families in the two counties in the Restoration period.[27]

27 P.R.O. E179 250/4 contains a very full 1660 Poll Tax return for Blackburn Hundred, Lancs, which has many similarities to the Northwich Hundred return.

The most surprising conclusion to emerge from the analysis of these tax returns is that such a large proportion of the population owned a significant amount of capital. 68% of households owned capital assets of more than £20. £20 p.a. was a top craftsman's annual wage in the 1660s (p. 150 above), so two thirds of households owned capital worth more than a craftsman's annual wage. We saw that in 1545 about two thirds of the taxpayers (1,063 people) in Bucklow Hundred had goods assessed at £3 or less. These assessments were probably only a third of their real wealth so all these taxpayers owned capital of less than £9 while a craftsman's wage at that time was £8 or £9 a year.[28] So in 1545 two thirds of households had less capital than a craftsman's annual earnings, whereas in 1660 two thirds of households had capital exceeding the £20 that a craftsman then earned per year.

In the late nineteenth century, the annual earnings of an equivalent skilled worker were around £75 p.a. Estate (death) duty records show that only about 10% of those who died each year had assets exceeding £100 (the bottom limit of the tax).[29] Therefore, it seems unlikely that, in 1900, more than 20% or 30% of families had capital assets exceeding £75. The evidence from Northwich Hundred appears to show a completely different position in the 1660s from that which existed a century or so before or two centuries later. In Cheshire, wealth seems to have been unusually widely distributed in the seventeenth century.

b) The 1667 Poll Tax return for Nether Tabley

Some exceptionally detailed records made and collected in this period by Sir Peter Leicester have survived at Tabley. In Appendix 5.2 are the survey and valuation of Nether Tabley made in 1666, and the details of the people paying Poll Tax there in 1667 and Hearth Tax in 1664. This gives a good picture of who lived in every house in the township and the size and value of the farmland that went with each house. The tenants lived in 18 houses, 15 of which were farms with more than five acres while three were only cottages with gardens. The only tenant paying a full rack rent was Ann Birchenhough on her 12-acre holding. Richard Eaton was paying half the market rent for his cottage. Although full details of all their leases have not survived, it is likely that all the others had bought three-life leases. Five of the seven large farms of over 30 acres were still inhabited by descendants in the male line of the leaseholders of 1543 (Appendix 3.2) – Broome, Faulkner, Norbury, Ridgeway and Wilkinson. Ann Antrobus, widow, had succeeded to the farm which had been owned by George Antrobus, woollen draper, who died in 1614 (see p. 117). He had inherited this leasehold from his Broome mother, whose ancestors had been on that

28 6 Hen VIII c3.
29 Money, 1910, income duties, p. 23; estate duties, pp. 52–55.

farm in 1543. There had been some reorganization of the smaller properties in these 123 years. One notable feature of the picture in 1666/7 was that only four of the farms were inhabited by a lease-holding family who might have been able to do the farm work. Only the Broome, Faulkner, Houghton and Wilkinson families included an adult man and wife with the same surname as the leaseholder. In three farms the principal resident was a widow – Antrobus, Carter and Ridgeway. Ann Antrobus was attended by her servant Margaret Cragg, and Andrew Pue with his wife Joanne were also living in her house. It seems likely, from the evidence of wills and leases describing divided farmhouses,[30] that Ann and her servant were living in one part of the farmhouse and the Pue family was living in another part. The Pues were not described as servants, though they may have shared the kitchen. They were probably farming the land on a rack rent and they may have paid part of their rent to Ann in the form of food grown on the farm. The Act provided that the children, under 16, of those poor people not paying Poor Rates did not have to pay the Poll Tax. It is possible, therefore, that the Pues had their children living with them in their part of the house. Ann Antrobus would have paid the rates on the whole property.

Elizabeth Ridgeway seems to have lived with her daughter, Dorothy, while the Rowlands family did the farming. Margery Carter perhaps employed one of the families in a cottage or smallholding to look after her farm. Peter Norbury was probably living in a similar fashion to these widows. His finances were frail and he was unable to provide the money to renew the lease in 1683. After some legal and financial manoeuvring he surrendered the lease in 1694.[31] The old and younger Robert Merrimans, attended by their servants, also seem unlikely to have been doing farming.

So the picture that seems to emerge is of the leaseholders as a property-owning group who were not themselves usually working the land by this period. Members of their families, often old people, were still living in the family houses, together with servants and farm workers. The latter were sub-tenants rather than employees. The economically active members of the lease-holder families may often have been engaged in occupations that took them away from the old family home. Thomas Jackson, described in my *Seven Households,* did not live in the family home between

30 See above p. 120 for the Woodfen family of Sutton. Another example is in a lease of 1742. Richard Key, the Leicesters' leaseholder in Wethale, Aston by Budworth was a clockmaker. He let his 75-acre farm to John Starkey for £47 a year for three years. He reserved to himself the room he lived in, the Yewtree garden, the little house garden and the fruit of two apple trees. DLT/D26. See also Foster, 1992, pp. 35–36.

31 DLT/D42.

1639, when he was 17, and 1656, when, aged 34, he moved in with his wife and children.

The list of the inhabitants of Tabley Hall illustrates some of the customs of communal living. One group was the family – Sir Peter Leicester, his wife and their three unmarried children. Staying with them was their eldest daughter, Eleanor, and her husband, Ralph Leicester, heir to the Toft estate, and their second daughter, Elizabeth, married to Samuel Birch. The group of seven people at the end of the list are a mystery. They were neither family nor servants. Mr and Mrs Beverley were evidently of gentry status, because they were described as 'Mr' and 'Mrs'. We know nothing about the others. The only explanation one can offer is that there appears to have been a custom in gentry families to give accommodation in their houses to people they liked or to those to whom they felt they had an obligation.[32]

The 20 servants were carefully listed, with their wages, because they were paying tax at the rate of 1s for every pound of their wages. This tax on servants' wages seems curious to us in the twenty-first century. In my *Seven Households*[33] it was shown how the cost of benefits in kind – food and beer – received by the Warburtons' servants in the 1760s was greater than the annual wages of an agricultural worker. Servants also enjoyed free housing, free heating and free working clothes. Their cash wages were therefore either spent as pocket money or saved towards their married life. Manual workers, who were paid by the day and paid rent for their cottage or their part of a house, were significantly worse off. They, no doubt, thought it right that the rich servants should be taxed.

On a smaller scale, life in the large farmhouses seems to have had some of the same communal character as life in the great houses. The widow, Hannah Faulkner, lived with her son, William and his wife, who were probably newly married, as they had no children. Hannah also had her father in the house and a Mrs Ellen Cotton, of whom we know nothing. She had no servant, unlike several of the widows in the village, perhaps because her two unmarried daughters were still at home. They may have borne the burden of looking after the household. The old Manor Court prohibitions preventing tenants from 'setting their grounds' to strangers seem to have been relaxed by 1667. The township seems to have been the home of quite a number of 'strangers'. The Henry Heyes, John Robinson and Robert Wittar families seem not to have had tenancies or been Tabley people unless their wives were Tabley girls. Robert Faulkner may have been a member of the Tabley family, but Pearson,

---

32 Sir Francis Leicester seems to have provided a home at Tabley for an old Cambridge friend called Roger Kenyon (DLT/B50). There was a similar figure at Arley in the 1750s – Mr Lawrence (Arley vouchers).

33 Foster, 2002, p. 204.

Allen, Pue, Rowlands and Smethley were not surnames that occurred in Tabley rentals or Manor Court rolls. All these people seem to have been under-tenants paying rack rents. These eight or nine families seem likely to have been doing the farm work on a number of the tenant farms – indeed it may be that they were doing virtually all the work on these farms. As the three-life leaseholders took up other occupations, such people were inevitably drawn in to farm the land. They evolved into the tenant farmers on leases of 7, 14 or 21 years who produced cheese for the London market on a growing number of Cheshire farms from the 1660s onwards.[34]

The pressure of an over-large population in these rural townships seems to have eased somewhat at this time. In 1647 the population of Nether Tabley was 141 proper inhabitants plus 12 'inmates' or lodgers, making a total of 153.[35] In 1667 only 117 people paid Poll Tax. There may have been some more children who did not pay the tax as the Act exempted the children of the poor who did not pay rates. The four families who were living in and probably working the large farms belonging to Ann Antrobus, Peter Norbury and Elizabeth Ridgeway are all listed without children, but they could easily have had ten children between them. The only other couples in the township who had no children were probably newly married, because they were either living with their parents or their parents were still living nearby. The children of the four families living on the big farms may have raised the total population of the township into the 130s but that would still have been between 15 or 20 less than 20 years earlier. The only other inhabitants who did not have to pay Poll Tax were those in receipt of alms. The town book of Tabley shows that, between 1677 and 1700, the annual cost of maintaining the township's poor was usually only between £3 and £4. One or two people were paid one shilling a week for a few months, perhaps to assist them over an illness. A few clothes were bought for children and old people, but there do not seem to have been any poor people living in the township who were wholly reliant on charity.

The accounts in the town book were approved each year between 1677 and 1679 by the signatures of a number of the householders. This provides an unusual vignette of the degree of literacy among these well-off people at this time. Of the ten householders whose names appear, only three were able to sign their own names:

William Faulkner
William Merriman
Robert Ridgeway.

---

34 Foster, 1998, pp. 9–17.
35 DLT/B33, p. 122.

The following only made a mark:

> William Broome
> Christopher Houghton
> Robert Merriman, Snr
> Peter Norbury
> Everard Sharman
> Robert Wilkinson
> Thomas Wood

Most of these people appear in Appendix 5.2. All but one of their families owned three-life leases of their farms[36] so they owned a significant amount of capital. If this sample is representative, it appears that two out of three of these small capitalists were illiterate in the late 1670s.[37]

This chapter brings to an end Part I of this book which has revealed the great transfer of wealth that occurred in the century from 1540 to 1640. The Crown, the Church and the gentry lost part of their rights over their lands to their tenants, who were the occupiers of the many small farms in north Cheshire. Chapter 5 has shown how this resulted in an unusually wide distribution of wealth in Cheshire in the 1660s. The property rights of the freeholders, copyholders and three-life leaseholders in the small farms gave these families a capital asset that they were able to use to support their careers elsewhere. In Chapter 4, the growing involvement in business of these families has been sketched in from the rather thin material available in inventories. The more detailed information in my *Seven Households* provides a broader view of the life-styles that may have characterized these country-based families. In Part II, we see what some of these small capitalist families did for themselves and for the economy of the area in the 130 years from 1650 to 1780.

36 Everard Sharman bought a lease after 1667. Of Thomas Wood, I know nothing.
37 See also Ellin Barnes, who was illiterate when she married Thomas Hough in 1676 (see Ch. 8, below, pp. 238–9).

Appendix 5.1. *Nether Peover and Allostock: the payers of Poll Tax in 1660 and Hearth Tax in 1664 compared with the freeholders, leaseholders and tenants*

This appendix is in five parts:
A. Introduction
B. Nether Peover
C. Allostock
D. Sale of the Warburton farms in Allostock, 1678
E. A note on the use of the words 'gentleman', 'yeoman', and 'husbandman'

A. Introduction
(a) Nether Peover
1. In the seventeenth century, Peover consisted of the two townships of Over Peover and Nether Peover.
2. In Nether Peover, the land north of the Peover Eye brook was known as Little Peover and the rest was Great Peover. Little Peover was in Bucklow Hundred, and Great Peover was in Northwich Hundred. Only the Poll Tax return of 1660 for Northwich Hundred survives.
3. The names listed below are all those who paid Poll Tax in Great Peover, i.e., that part of Nether Peover in Northwich Hundred.[1] Every person over 16 paid one shilling, except husbands and wives who counted as only one person. Those assessed on incomes of £5 p.a. or more paid 2% of their income.
4. There were four landlords who leased property in Nether Peover. In the list below, their names have been abbreviated as follows:

Leicester of Tabley	L
Cholmondeley of Holford	C
Holford of Holford	H
Shakerley of Hulme	S

The Leicester tenants are known from a 1663 survey and valuation,[2] which provides both area and annual value for every property. All owned three-life leases. The other landlords, tenants and annual values are known from a survey of 1676.[3] This does not give the acreage of each leasehold, but the approximate area can be calculated from the observation that the average value per acre was usually between 11 and 12 shillings. Where the leaseholder's Christian name differed from the taxpayer's, the former is noted in the list. All tenants had leases for lives at 'old rents' except where noted.
5. The Poll Tax lists payers in groups which are thought to represent households.
6. We have noticed above p. 152 that houses were often shared. Those without property were presumably living in part of one of the property owners' buildings. Table 1 is the main list of the Poll Tax and Hearth Tax payers. It is followed by Table 2 – people who did not pay Poll Tax but who did pay Hearth Tax in 1664, and the property they had; Table 3 – people who were not chargeable to Hearth Tax but who may have occupied some of the properties listed below; Table 4 – properties listed in the surveys for which

1 Lawton, 1979.
2 DLT/B86.
3 DLT/B14, folio 133.

no obvious taxpayer has been found; Table 5 – cottages on Peover Heath.[4] These lists demonstrate the difficulty in reconstructing where poor people lived and exactly how poor they were, even when archives provide much more information than is usually available.

(b) Allostock

1. The township of Allostock had been divided between the five daughters of Robert Grosvenor of Hulme *c.* 1474. In 1660, of these five parts:

	In list
2 were owned by Leicester of Tabley	L
1 was owned by Warburton of Arley	W
2 were owned by Shakerley of Hulme, of which we have no survey	omitted

There were also seven freeholders. Two had tenants about whom we know:

Mainwaring of Over Peover	M
Venables of Antrobus in Over Whitley	V

Listed below, therefore, are only those Poll Tax payers who were freeholders or lease-holders of the four landlords of whose property we have a survey.[5]

2. Finally, there is a short list of property owned by the above landlords whose occupants in 1660 cannot be identified.

Abbreviations in the following tables:

dau	daughter
husb	husbandman
lab	labourer
sing	single
sp	spinster
wid	widow
yeo	yeoman,
N.C.	not chargeable to Hearth Tax

4 DLT/B14, folio 138.
5 DLT/B14, folio 10–14, pp. 47–52.

B. Nether Peover

Table 1. The *Poll Tax payers in 1660, the Hearth Tax payers in 1664 and the value of the property they owned.*

1660 Poll Tax payer	Assessed income £ p.a. (Note 1)	Landlord	Statute acres	Annual value £ s d			No. of hearths taxed in 1664
Ampson, Thos, husb	£5	L	13	8	10	0	2
Baguley, Ellin, wid *See 'properties' below*	£5						1
Bradshaw, Hugh Alice, wife		Freehold		4	0	0	1
Buckley, Thos, husb	£10	L	39	25	0	0	1
Bromhall, Ralph Elizabeth, wife Benjamin, son		H		6	0	0	1
Chesworth, Thos. Hurt, Thos, lab Eaton, Mary, Mrs	£5	H		12	0	0	1
Deane, Thos, yeo Leicester, Eliz, sp *Leaseholder Richard Deane*	£30	H L	37	46 22	0 0	0 0	9
Dod, Wm, husb	£10	C		13	0	0	
Foxley, Edw Alice, wife Edw, lab		L	10	6	0	0	1
Frodsham, Peter, husb	£5	L	15	11	0	0	
Harper, John Joan, wife							
Heath, Eliz, wid Eaton, Mary, sp Hough, Thos, lab	£10	L	34	20	0	0	1
Higson, Randle Eliz, wife		L	7	4	0	0	1
Holford, Mathew *Leaseholder Mr Thomas Holford or Houlford*	£5	L	21	12	0	0	
Jackson, Peter, husb *Also had property in Allostock*	£5						

Kennardale, Thos		L	7	4	0	0	1
Margt, wife							
Wm, son							
Jane, dau							
Other spelling Kenworthley, Kennardy, Kenerley							
Kinsey, Ralph	£10	L	37	20	0	0	1
Kinsey, Peter, husb							1
Eliz, wife							
Kinsey, Peter, taylor							1
Eliz, wife							
Kinsey, John, elder, lab		L	17	10	0	0	
John, younger, lab							
Kinsey, Peter							
Jane, wife							
Barrow, Alice, sp							
Barrow, Wm, lab							
Resident in Allostock?							
Kirkham, Jane, wid							
Wm, son							
Ann, dau							
Leech, John		L	6	4	0	0	1
Ellin, wife							
Norton, Robt, sing							
Marsh, John							
Alice, wife							
John, son							
Alice, dau							
Mary, dau							
Mee, Hugh	£5	C		34	0	0	3
Dale, Roger, husb							
Jackson, Mat, lab							
Bennett, Marg, sp							
Mee, Thos		L	0.5	0	10	0	N.C.1
Ellinor, wife							
Mee, Hugh							
Hanna, wife							
Millington, Rich	£5	Freehold		4	0	0	
Pemberton, Mrs Ann, wid £15		L	61	32	0	0	
Pimlot, Thos		H		5	0	0	1
Issabell, wife							
Chesworth, Eliz, sp							

Taxpayer	Assessed income	Landlord	Statute acres	£	s	d	No. of hearths
Powdrell, John	£5	Freehold		12	0	0	1
Wm		L		0	5	0	
Ellen, wife							
Moores, Ellin, sp							
Ridgeway, Robt							1
Emma, wife							
Royle, Hugh		S		2	0	0	1
Eliz, wife							
Samuel, son							
Smith, Richard							
Ellin, wife							
Swinton, Thos	£10	L	23	14	0	0	2
Walker, Robt, husb	£5	C		17	0	0	
Williamson, Edw	£5	L	17	12	0	0	1
Worthington, John	£10						
(trust for infants)							
Wright, Geffrie	£7	L	15	11	8	0	3
Moores, Wm, lab							
Wright, Marg, sp							
Wright, Philip	£5	C		7	0	0	1
Peter, son							
Eliz, dau							
Kinsey, Emma, sp							
Leaseholder Peter Wright							

Note 1. If the taxpayer's income was assessed at less than £5, the taxpayer paid the minimum – 1s – and this column is blank

Table 2. *Not listed for Poll Tax but chargeable in Hearth Tax, 1664.*

Taxpayer	Assessed income	Landlord	Statute acres	Annual value £	s	d	No. of hearths
Borrow, Wm		H		17	0	0	2
Burrowes, John							1
Horton, Robt (see note)		C		10	0	0	1
Leadbeter, Thos							1
Lowton, Thos							1
Street, Wm							1
Swinlow, U							1

Note: Robt Horton was the collector of the Peover township Poll Tax. Did he leave himself out on purpose? Or did he pay in his property in Church Lawton for both?

Table 3. *List of people not chargeable to Hearth Tax, 1664.*

Barlow, Edward	Mee, Thomas (in Poll Tax)
Borrow, Margaret	Powdrell, Thomas
Bretton, John	Tomkinson, William
Bromall, Robert	Wilkinson, Elizabeth
Chesworth, Ann	Yate, Richard
Higson, Elin	

Table 4. *Properties listed in the estate surveys in which those in the three tables above who did not 'own' property are likely to have lived. For example Ellin Baguley, widow, assessed at £5 p.a. may have lived at Yarwoods.*

	Landlord	Statute acres	Annual value £ s d			Notes
Yarwoods	L	16	9	0	0	
Brettons Cottage	L	1	0	16	0	
Cowley's	L	1½	1	3	4	
Isabel Stretch (1666)	L	3	2	10	0	
Matthew Trevis	L	½	0	13	4	
Edward Steele	L					no rent paid
Edward Hall	L					no rent paid
John Finney (1676)	C		13	0	0	
George Strongitharme (1676) *see note*	H		12	0	0	

Note: A George Strongitharme paid tax in Allostock in 1660

Table 5. *People having cottages on Nether Peover Heath, which was jointly owned by the four landlords*

	If in Hearth Tax
Barlow, Edward	Non-chargeable
Chesworth, Thomas	Chargeable and also in Poll Tax
Egerton, Peter	
Hough, John	
Powdrell, Thomas	Non-chargeable
Sykes, John	
Tomkinson, William	Non-chargeable
Yates, Thomas	?Richard Yate – non-chargeable

C. Allostock

The Poll Tax payers in 1660, the Hearth Taxpayers in 1664 and the value of the property they owned.

1660 Poll Tax payer	Assessed income £ p.a. (Note 1)	Landlord	Statute acres	Annual value £ s d	No. of hearths taxed in 1664
Alcocke, Richard, husb	£16	L	41½	23 0 0	
Baker, Charles, husb Dale, Wm, lab Dale, Richard, lab	£10	M	23		1
Banister, Edward, yeo Norburie, John, husb Street, Peter, lab Banister, Sara, sp Banister, Margaret, sp	£7	Freehold	19		1
Bradshaw, Henrie, husb	£5	Freehold	8½		1
Bradshaw, Thomas, yeo Cooper, Eliz, wid Haywood, Ann, sp	£30	Freehold	72		3
Broome, Margaret, wid	£9	Freehold	21		1
Cragg, John, lab		L	3½	2 0 0	1 or 2
Deane, Marie, wid	£20	V	84½		2
Dykery, Francis, husb	£8	V	27½		1
Hale, George, husb Hale, George, Jnr, husb Hale, Marie, sp	£9 £9	L	149	50 0 0	
Higgenson, John, husb Higgenson, John, husb Higgenson, Rob, skinner	£14	W	27½	15 0 0	1
Houlford, Thos, gent Houlford, Mathew, son Houlford, Elizabeth, dau	£20	W	68	36 0 0	3
Houmfrey, Raph, husb Houmfrey, Raph, taylor Houmfrey, Ann, sp	£9	L	27	15 0 0	1
Jackson, Edward, carpenter Jackson, Edw, Jnr, carpenter Jackson, Ann, sp Jackson, Mary, sp	£8	L	35	20 0 0	1 1

Name	Value	Tenure	Acres	£	s	d	Hearths
Jackson, Peter, husb	£6	W	25	14	0	0	
Jackson, Edward, lab							
Boone, Hanna, sp							
Kennerley, Edward, husb	£7 13s 0d	L	49	25	13	4	1
Leech, Jane, wid	£10	M	25				1
Leech, Hugh, husb							
Maddocke, John, husb	£22 13s 4d	Freehold	23				2
Matley, Wm, husb	£9	L	19	12	0	0	2
Matley, Thos, painter							
Matley, Wm, husb							
Read, Wm, husb		L	4	2	10	0	
Alice, wife							1
Statham, Edward, husb	£11	W	34	16	0	0	1
Steele, John, husb	£7	L	20	11	0	0	1
Steele, Peter, husb	£12	L	33½	20	0	0	1
Hulse, Issabel, sp							
Stubbs, John, lab		L	33½ paying rack rent of £11 10s 0d p.a	20	0	0	NC 1
Stubbs, Priscilla, wid		L	30 paying rack rent of £12 p.a	17	0	0	1
Whishaw, Hugh, husb	£6	W	38	24	0	0	1
Whishaw, Joseph, husb							
Steene, John, lab							
Andrewes, Margaret, sp							

Notes

1. The Leicester tenants also included:
       Carter, widow with 62 acres worth £32.00, and
       Acson's Cottage with 9 acres worth £5 10s 0d.
   But neither of these names appear in the Poll Tax, except a Richard Ackson, blacksmith, was living in the household of John Forster, weaver, whose wife had inherited a cottage on the waste. Richard Axton paid on one hearth and Margaret Carter paid on two hearths in 1664.
2. Thomas Bradshaw is listed as having unnamed tenants.
3. Leicester gives a list of cottages in Allostock. Besides John Forster's mentioned above, these include:
       a) Chesworth, Rafe – not chargeable in Hearth Tax, 1664
       b) Dutton, Margaret – not chargeable in Hearth Tax, 1664
       c) Jackson, James – charged in Hearth Tax, 1664
       d) Stubs, Jane – not chargeable in Hearth Tax, 1664.

D. Sale of the five Warburton farms in Allostock, each with a fifth part of one-fifth of the manor, by Sir Peter Warburton, 11 April 1678.

Higgensons	1667	Robert Higgenson of Rudheath, skinner, bought a new lease for £155. The three lives were himself and his two children.
(Portford)	11 Apr 1678	Bought freehold for £107 all 3 lives in being.
	18 Apr 1678	Sold 2 mossfields for £75 to Thomas Amson.
	1685	Sold the remainder to James Amson for £255 (17 acres at £15 per acre).

Houlfords Unknown date. The Holfords sold the lease to Roger Barnes, who in 1678
(beside Peover   bought the freehold for £340 (2 lives in being in the lease).
Heath)

Jacksons	1673	Peter Jackson bought a new lease for £130. The three lives were himself, his wife, and his son.
	1678	Bought the freehold for £97, all 3 lives in being.
	1687	Sold to James Amson for £310 (£12.4 per acre).

Stathams &   1678   Freehold bought by Joseph Whishaw for £415 being £235 for
Whishaws   Stathams with 1 life in being, £180 for Whishaws with 3 lives in
                     being. (Stayed in Whishaw family till mid-18th century.)

Sources: DLT/D43, D379, D45, D238, D233, D370, D36, D368.

E. *A note on the use of the words 'gentleman', 'yeoman', and 'husbandman'.*

Attentive readers will have noticed that the words 'gentleman', 'yeoman', and 'husbandman' are almost entirely absent from this book. This is not by accident. The reason is that these words are more likely to mislead than inform the reader about the wealth and occupation of individuals. The history of these words in mid-north Cheshire seems to have been as follows:

Before 1500, the word 'gentleman' was more or less confined to members of the landed families listed in Appendix 3.5, Table A. Yeoman was the next status level below gentleman and was used for minor 'landed' families and large charterers or freeholders. The head of every other household was a husbandman. This was a pure status system and had no connection with occupations. In chartered towns with guilds, like Chester and London, all freemen were known by their company or occupation names – thus 'citizen and draper', and so on.

When country people applied to join City of London companies, the father's occupation was sometimes listed, though many rural residents were just given their status designations. For example, the Skinners enrolled James, son of John Bouer of Frodsham, shearman, in 1501. The revolution in land tenure and values in the sixteenth century threw the rural status system into confusion. After 1550, the descriptive value of these status words steadily diminishes. For example, a man like William Malbon of Budworth had started his adult life as a tenant at will of Norton Abbey. He was then definitely a husbandman. He described himself thus in his will, and was also listed as husbandman in the Parish Register in 1580. But his possession of a 90-acre freehold farm had, by 1578, carried him into a group who had to furnish a 'cote of plate' armour alongside such notables as Thomas Starkey of Higher Hall,

Stretton, and John Hayes of Litley, whose families are listed in Appendix 3.5, Table A.[6] In 1613, his grandson had his pedigree as a gentleman approved in the Visitation.

Not only did some individuals move from the bottom group to the top group in a few years, but the meaning of all the status words changed. The word husbandman fell slowly out of fashion. After 1650 it was used less often. Three-life leaseholders became known as yeomen. Most leases and wills adopted this practice after the Civil War. Anyone owning freehold land of more than four acres (worth over £2 p.a.) was sometimes called gentleman. Thomas Jackson, the Tabley manager, was sometimes referred to as gentleman. His freehold estate was small and it was subject to a three-life lease, so his rental income was negligible. His occupation as a lawyer seems to have had some influence in giving him gentleman status. So the category 'gentry' came to include people whose capital assets varied from a few hundred pounds to £50,000 or more and therefore diminished in meaning. In the seventeenth century, occupational descriptions slowly became more common in rural areas.

The 1660 Poll Tax return for Northwich Hundred is an old fashioned document. The returning Royalist government revived old practices. The quixotic way in which the old status designations were used illustrates the difficulty of attaching meaning to these words. For example in the above tables, Thomas Bradshaw and Thomas Deane were called yeomen and were assessed at £30 p.a. John Maddock was assessed at £22 13s 4d p.a., the next highest assessment. He owned a 23-acre freehold, but he was called a husbandman. Edward Banister, with a 19-acre freehold, was assessed at only £7 p.a., but was called yeoman. The description 'husbandman' was applied to only eight people in the 40 households in Nether Peover, but to 21 in 25 households in Allostock. It was used for George Hale, who owned a three-life leasehold of a 149-acre farm worth £50 p.a., and for John Norburie, who was living in the household of Edward Banister and may have been his servant.

Other examples of the bizarre use of these old status words in the 1660s occur in the return of 1661 for the Kinerton Hundred of Warwickshire. Two 'husbandmen' turn out to be a teacher and a physician, while the vicar was described as a yeoman and another clergyman as a gentleman.[7]

There is some evidence of another complicating factor. Puritans, Non-conformists and dissenters, as they were called after 1662, often believed strongly in social equality. They therefore disliked status gradations and some of them seem to have reacted by calling themselves by a lower title than they could have used. William Malbon above (whose grandson emigrated to America in 1637, see below pp. 180–1) may have been a man of this type. A second example is Benjamin Cooper, who described himself as husbandman in the passenger list of the *Mary Anne* before dying, worth £1,278, on the voyage to America in 1637.[8]

6 Irvine, 1901, p. 6.
7 Styles, 1978, p. 154.
8 Fischer, 1989, pp. 27–28.

Appendix 5.2. The 1666 survey and valuation of Nether Tabley combined with the Poll Tax return of 1667 and the Hearth Tax of 1664.

Leaseholder	Formerly	Statute acres	Annual value £ s d	Annual rent £ s d	Poll Tax residents (servants wages are given)	Number of hearths NC = not chargeable
Antrobus, Ann	Broomes	46.4	26 0 0	1 6 8	Ann Antrobus, widow Margaret Cragg, servant, £1 Andrew Pue Joanne Pue, his wife	3
Antrobus, Ann	Hales	8.6	6 10 0	0 6 8	Unknown, see below	
Beaumont, Katherine	Cottage	0.5	1 0 0	0 4 0	Unknown, see below	NC (1)
Beaumont, Thomas	–	6.3	4 10 0	0 4 0	Thomas Beaumont Ann, his wife Ann, his daughter	1
Birchenhough, James	Hunts	12.4	7 10 0	7 5 0	Ann Birchenhough	1 – James
Broome, Humphrey	–	39.7	24 0 0	1 5 0	Humphrey Broome Dorothy, his wife Peter, his son John, his son Humphrey, his son Elizabeth, his daughter Dorothy, his daughter	2
Carter, Margery	–	39.3	24 0 0	1 1 0	Margery Carter, widow Mary Wittar Anne Golden, servant, £1 Ralph Yannis, Margery's brother	2

Table 5.2 continued

	Property	Acres							Occupants	NC (2)	NC (1)
Cragg's cottage	Higginson's	0.3	1	0	0	0	4	0	Ann Cragg John Cragg Mary Cragg		
Eaton's cottage	Moores	2.1	1	6	8	0	13	4	Richard Eaton Henry Heyes, Jnr Mary Heyes, his wife		Peter
Faulkner, Hannah	–	30.8	18	0	0	1	2	4	Hannah Faulkner, widow John Chantler, her father William, her son Sarah, his wife Mrs Ellen Cotton Deborah Faulkner Hannah Faulkner	1	
Houghton, widow	–	20.4	13	6	8	0	14	0	Katherine Houghton Christopher Houghton Elizabeth, his wife	1	Raphe
Merriman, Robert	–	8.2	7	0	0	0	6	8	Robert Merriman, Jnr Elizabeth, his wife Mary Ward, servant, £1		
Merriman, Robert	Wilcoxens	11.8	7	0	0	0	8	0	Robert Merriman William Merriman Alice Broome, servant, £1	1	

Table 5.2 continued

										Peter Norbury	NC (1) Elizabeth
Norbury's	-	64.3	40	0	0	1	16	8		Thomas Pearson Anne, his wife Edward Allen Alice, his wife	2
Peacock, John	-	19.6	14	0	0	0	16	0		unknown	1
Ridgeway, widow	-	39.8	22	0	0	1	3	8		Elizabeth Ridgeway, widow Dorothy, her daughter Richard Rowlands Elizabeth, his wife	2 William
Stretch, Ann	Faircloughs	7.0	5	0	0	0	4	0		Ann Stretch Elizabeth Stretch Henry Smethley Katherine, his wife Christian, his daughter	
Wilkinson, Robert	-	30.0	16	10	0	1	0	0		Robert Wilkinson Anne, his wife Ellen, his daughter Margaret, his daughter Elizabeth, his daughter	2
TOTALS		387.5	238	13	4	20	1	0			

Table 5.2 continued

	Statute acres	Annual value £ s d			Poll Tax residents	Number of hearths
Sir Peter Leicester	719.3	376	4	4	*Family*	
					Sir Peter Leicester (£15 10s tax)	22
					his lady	
					Robert, his son	
					Thomas, his son	
					Ralph Leicester of Toft	
					Eleanor, his wife	
					(Sir Peter's daughter)	
					Byron, Sir Peter's daughter	
					Mrs Birch, (Sir Peter's daughter Elizabeth)	
					Servants	
					Thomas Jackson, £4	
					(wages and practice)	
					Thomas Matley, £3	
					John Pickering, £2	
					John Plum, cook, £4	
					John Asley, brewer, £5	
					John Cotton, £4	
					Thomas Warburton, £2	
					James Birchenhough, £4	
					William Norbury, groom, £3	
					Samuel Faulkner, coachman, £3	
					Ralph Sutton, £2	
					John Percival, £2	
					Henry Mason, £2	
					Mary Massey, £2	
					Sarah Buscowe, £2	
					Mary Jackson, £3	
					Elizabeth Beamond, £1	
					Priscilla Edwards, £1	
					Mary Shakerley, £2	
					John Harrison, £3	
					Others	
					Mr Charles Beverley	
					Mrs Byron Beverley	
					Jane Harrison	
					Margaret Bromhall	
					Margery Woolmer	
					Ephraim Meyre	
					John Faulkner	

GRAND TOTALS: Annual value 1,106.8
Annual rent   614 17 8
Ordnance Survey 1,110 (excluding roads and water)

Table 5.2 continued

These four households were presumably living in the three 'empty' properties. One of them might have been in part of Birchenhoughs.	Ralph Faulkner Elizabeth, his wife John, his son Mary, his daughter	1
	Henry Heyes senior Ann, his wife William, his son Robert, his son Ann, his daughter	1
	John Robinson Katherine, his wife Mary, his daughter William, his son Mary Beaumont Mary Wilcoxen	3
	Robert Wittar William, his son John, his son Edward, his son Roger NC (1) Katherine, his daughter	1

Sources: Survey DLT/D/44/6; Poll Tax DLT/F69

Notes:
1. Where Poll Tax payers had the same name(s) as the leaseholder, their households have been placed opposite. This process left four households to inhabit three 'empty' leaseholds, i.e., those of A. Antrobus, K. Beaumont and J. Peacock.
2. The spelling of names had been standardized everywhere.
3. The Leicester servants' occupations are not in the Poll Tax return, but have been derived from other sources. Compare with Foster, 2002, p. 85.
4. Every person listed paid one shilling poll tax. The servants paid an extra shilling on each pound of their wages.
5. The Christian name of the Hearth Tax payer is given where it is different from the poll taxpayer.

PART II
The emergence of a business society, 1650–1780

CHAPTER 6

The character of north-western society after 1650

The 130 years from 1650 to 1780 saw the development of an industrial-commercial complex in the north-west of England that was larger than anything of the kind that had appeared in the world before. It was more technically sophisticated and spread over a wider range of industries. The area had also become a trading hub that both depended upon and encouraged industries elsewhere, like the linen industry in Ireland and cotton growing in the West Indies and America. Some of its industries are well known from the mass of information available about them in the last quarter of the eighteenth century. Their growth in the previous century is much less well documented and the examples in the next three chapters will, I hope, make a contribution to closing this gap in our knowledge.

The problem, however, is not only to describe the growth of particular industries, but also to identify the reasons why the north-west of England achieved something that had eluded other societies. This book highlights three factors, of which two have not earlier been much noticed, while the third has attracted plenty of attention. The first was the wide distribution of wealth that enabled a great number of individuals to attempt to become entrepreneurs. I have described in Part I how this happened and here, in Part II, I follow some 40 or 50 families who lived on small farms early in the seventeenth century but who produced many successful businessmen – often several in one family – by 1770. The second reason was that the 'culture' of these north-western families was different to the 'culture' of the gentry and aristocrats who owned most of the wealth everywhere else in the world. The north-westerners had always worked for their living. Trading and other forms of business were highly regarded occupations that individuals and families were proud to pursue successfully, generation after generation. The third cause, both long and widely recognized, for the prosperity of north-western business was the huge growth of trade in the Atlantic region.[1]

The changes in property rights and land values in the study area, which I have described in detail in Part I, also occurred in the rest of England. The obverse of the increase in wealth of the customary tenants was the reduced position of the Crown, the Church and the major gentry. The Crown was probably the most damaged, if the examples given here were typical. The Duchy of Lancaster's behaviour in the Whitley Lordship, in the Honour of Clitheroe in Lancashire, and in Wensleydale in Yorkshire (see pp. 267–8), indicate that the Crown parted with

---

1 Hartwell, 1967, pp. 58–59.

possession of these great areas of land in the seventeenth century for between 2% and 15% of their full market value. These were lands belonging to the ancient royal estate, but similar events occurred on the land the Crown acquired at the Dissolution of the Monasteries. The large block of lands in north Lancashire, on which the Fells' estate lay in the seventeenth century, had come into the Crown's hands partly by forfeiture and partly through the dissolution of the monasteries. This all passed into other hands on equally favourable terms. The tenants, by asserting their 'tenant rights', got most of the value. The residual manorial rights, which were sold later, probably only represented around 5% of the full market value. The third way in which the Crown estate suffered was accidental. Many of the sales of old monastic lands seem to have been made in the 1540s and, as it turned out, this was before the big rise in the value of land. In the example in our area, the two families renting Norton Abbey's demesne land in Great Budworth bought their farms in 1544 for around £50 each. By the time of the Restoration, 120 years later, they were probably worth around £1,000 each.[2]

Church lands have been estimated at 20% to 25% of the total in England in 1436.[3] In addition the tithes represented 10% of the value of other owners' lands so, altogether, the Church perhaps controlled one third of the wealth in the country before 1530. The lands of the monasteries, chantries and chapels were a substantial part of this holding. They were also an important part of the patronage system operated by the Crown and the Church. The loss of these lands, first to the Crown and then often to the tenants, substantially reduced the Church's position in society. This was not the end of the Church's financial tribulations. Some monastic lands were transferred to colleges and schools – this study has provided an example in the Great Budworth tithes, which were given to Christ Church, Oxford. The college then leased them out for 91 years (pp. 24–5 above) at a small premium. We do not know the exact mixture of policy, stupidity and private avarice involved in this decision, but it cost the College many thousands of pounds in the lifetime of the lease and it seems to have been the middle of the eighteenth century before they were receiving the full annual value of the tithes each year.

Though there were no examples in the areas of this study, a similar pattern seems to have affected the rents of clerically-managed land. On the Merton College, Oxford, estate of Kibworth-Harcourt, 'old' rents continued until 1700 and beyond. Entry fines were first taken in 1594, apparently in response to the statutes of 1571 and 1576 regulating the leasing of ecclesiastical lands.[4] These fines were well below

2 In the 1720s these two farms were sold for around £1,500 each. WM Boxes 71, 72, 74.
3 Cooper, 1967, Table 1, p. 421.
4 13 Eliz c 10–11.

market level for a century or more. Nevertheless, the colleges did retain their lands and eventually they returned to market value.[5] The lands of bishoprics were also subject to attacks in the sixteenth century.[6] For example, the bishopric of Durham owned a large slice of the best coal-bearing lands near Newcastle upon Tyne. In 1577 the Crown gained a long lease of this land and by 1583 it was in private hands. Before the end of the century, the City of Newcastle had acquired the lease and they had given a monopoly of the trade to a small group of 'Hostmen' who became very rich.[7] In all these ways, by 1660, the property of the Church was but a shadow of what it had been in 1530.

Of the three large groups of property-owners, the landed gentry were the most successful at holding on to their landed wealth. The three-life leasehold system, installed on the great majority of gentry estates in Cheshire and Lancashire in the 1540s, allowed the gentry to share the increase in land values with their tenants.[8] Although the peers can be seen as just the richest members of the gentry, it seems that more of their tenants were declared by the judges to be copyholders, which adversely affected the revenue of their estates. Exactly why this happened is uncertain. Perhaps their greater distance from personal contact with their tenants and the history of their tenure played a part. Perhaps their managers, who may also have had tenanted land, deftly turned the legal details against the peers in some cases. Perhaps they were slower to put their tenants on leases. However, peers seem often to have had an opportunity to use their position as courtiers to enrich themselves so their economic position in relation to other major gentry does not seem to have altered greatly.[9]

The dramatic decline in the economic position of the Crown and the Church and the less marked reduction in the wealth of the major gentry and peerage brought corresponding changes in the social and economic structure of society. It strikingly altered the choices that 'ordinary' people could make about how they were to earn their living and fulfil their personalities. To illustrate these changes I offer two examples below on pp. 178–81.

The 'business' culture which grew up among the Cheshire and Lancashire families who benefited from the great redistribution of wealth, probably also existed in many areas of the south and east of England before 1660, but after the Restoration it appears, in those areas, to have been slowly overwhelmed by gentry culture for reasons briefly touched upon in this chapter and in Chapter 11 (pp. 317–28). The

5 Howell, 1983, pp. 52–53, 63.
6 Ives *et al.*, 1978, pp. 128–33.
7 Levine and Wrightson, 1991, pp. 21–22; Hatcher, 1993, p. 514.
8 As explained in Appendix 3.6.
9 Stone, 1965; Stone, 1973.

North-West resisted the charms of 'gentry' culture despite the fact that it was the 'high status' culture of England and indeed of the rest of Europe. One reason why it was able to do this may have been due to the gulf that existed in Cheshire in both 1545 and 1660 between the small number of major gentry and the great mass of ordinary families. Another reason why north-western culture was not swamped by the culture of the southern gentry related to religion. Cheshire and Lancashire became strongly Puritan or Presbyterian areas before the Civil War and these convictions were rooted both in the social structure and in the Church organization of the area. Unlike the south and east of England, where every village community on 1,000 acres had a parish church, the North had been so sparsely populated when parishes were laid out before the Norman Conquest, that many of them were extremely large. Great Budworth was one example, containing over 36,000 acres. As the population increased in the Middle Ages, chapels were built to provide for the outlying areas of these great parishes. These chapels had to be entirely supported by their congregations because the rectors of the old parish churches retained all the tithe income. So north-western people became accustomed to choosing and maintaining their own ministers.

The new north-western society, in which there were many people, each with a small amount of capital, seems to have given its members strong feelings of equality and independence, which were expressed in their religion. This was particularly noticeable in the commercial and industrial areas around the great centre of Manchester. In Puritan families, individuals emphasized their independence through their study of the Bible at home. It was common for prayers to be held within the family and sometimes more elaborate household devotions took place, at which psalms were sung and a chapter of the Bible was read.[10]

Following the Act of Uniformity of 1662, some 160 dissenting ministers in Cheshire and Lancashire were ejected from their parishes.[11] Many of their congregations remained loyal to these ministers and so became Nonconformist, especially in the industrial, commercial or business areas. As they were accustomed to financing their ministers and holding services in their own homes, it was easy for them to continue these practices and they had the wealth to do so. Conditions were different in the typical village in the south and east of England in the Restoration period, where there was often a squire, supported by less than half a dozen capital-owning yeoman farmers among a large number of poor families. The rector or vicar often lived beside his Church, financed by his income from the tithes and the glebe. The village of Chippenham, described on pages 324–5 below, fits this picture. In

10 Richardson, 1972, pp. 74–114.
11 Phillips and Smith, 1994, p. 119.

such villages, gentry culture supported by the Established Church, had little competition, whereas in the North-West, in both rural and urban communities, a more egalitarian, participative religion helped to create the culture that gave value and meaning to the business life by which so many people earned their livings.

Another important support for the business culture of the North-West was the similar culture that came to exist in the northern colonies of America. It is well known that New England was settled by the Puritans and it is often said that they emigrated to escape from religious persecution. We have just seen how Puritan ideas of equality and independence had great appeal to businessmen; many of the early settlers seem to have been business people who came from the textile areas in the eastern counties of England or in the West Country. About two thirds of them were townspeople who were mostly either in trade or were skilled craftsmen. They were well-off people and nearly three quarters of the adults paid their own passage across the Atlantic.[12] The two great periods of emigration to the northern colonies were 1620–40 and 1675–1715 – both times when many Englishmen thought that the Stuart kings were trying to re-establish absolute government in England. They were also periods when Catholic absolute monarchs were making war on Protestant business communities in northern Europe. The progress of the Thirty Years War (1618–48), the siege of La Rochelle in France (1627) and the flight of the Huguenots from France under Louis XIV (after 1685) must have made clear to English Puritan businessmen in the 1620s and 1630s and later that their property and way of life were not secure against Kings and Emperors. It could be that we should view the emigration to the northern colonies as the escape of a part of the business community from the threat of absolute government. Later in this chapter I give examples of two men from this area who were brought up in Puritan families and had successful business careers in London before emigrating to America in 1637 together with their minister and most of his congregation.

By the beginning of the eighteenth century the emigrants to the northern colonies of America had established a fairly equal, non-aristocratic, Nonconformist, business society. Its success in the next century was so great that de Tocqueville, writing between 1835 and 1840, could pronounce that 'No people on earth … has made as rapid progress as the Americans in commerce and industry'.[13] The tremendous growth and prosperity achieved by the business culture of the New World must have confirmed north-westerners in the home country in their view that their culture was at least as good as the gentry culture of southern England.

The great expansion of trading in the Atlantic region after 1650 has been widely

12 Fischer, 1989, pp. 28–30.
13 Mansfield and Winthrop, 2000, p. 528.

noticed. One important characteristic has been less often remarked: this trading created an unusual market for English goods. In Europe and much of the rest of the world the existing technology was widely disseminated. Every community provided itself with all the ordinary things of life and in order to sell to other nations, the exporting country had to offer something the importing country could not provide for itself. Thus, from the Middle Ages onwards, the English sold woollens abroad because few other countries grew enough grass to support sufficient sheep to make all their own (although, by the eighteenth century, English woollens were in demand because the quality of the both the wool and the workmanship was unequalled). In return England imported the produce of warmer climes – silks and spices.

The Atlantic markets were different because the importing countries could, in principle, have made many of the things which they imported. However, England was able to export to them all the common things of life – every kind of textile, all kinds of metalwork, nails, cooking pots, locks, tools, all types of leather goods – shoes, saddles, horse-harness – gunpowder to West Africa, fine furniture to West Indian planters – the list is endless. The reasons for this were varied: West Africa was technically primitive, Ireland had no coal and the domestic craft sector was unusually poorly developed except in the North, and the North American and West Indian colonists were too busy exploiting the special advantages of their new homelands to have time for traditional labour-intensive activities. The existence of these rapidly growing markets for such a wide range of goods was not only of great benefit to the manufacturing industries, but it also stimulated innovation in all the means of moving the goods – roads, rivers, canals, docks and shipping. North-western England was particularly well placed to exploit the new market in North America because a significant number of the emigrants came from the North-West and continued to have relations and friends there. There were also the religious affinities – already mentioned – with the Nonconformist groups remaining in the old country.

These three underlying causes of the great business expansion – the wider spread of wealth, the growth of a business culture and the opening up of Atlantic trade made entirely new opportunities for many people. I now discuss two examples that contrast the old world with the new.

A system of patronage is a characteristic feature of societies in which a few people have great power and riches and the rest of the population has little of either. A powerful individual can pick, out from the crowd below him, a servant whom he can reward with riches and influence. In return, the servant must give absolute obedience at every juncture. One mistake in crossing his master and he may be thrown back among the masses. For a man without position or money the best way to get on in such a society was to find a patron among the rich and powerful, and this practice of patronage was common in medieval society. The reduction in the wealth of the patrons – kings, bishops, noblemen and gentry – reduced the amount of patronage they were able to exercise. At the same time, the appearance of numbers of families with a small amount of wealth created a large group of independent people. Their money gave them the ability to do things without the help of a patron. In this way, seventeenth-century society was significantly different to the society that had existed before 1530. My research has provided examples of two young men, brought up on small farms in the North-West, who each created an important place for themselves in society: the first, living before 1530, raised his family to a higher rung in English society by finding good patrons; the second, living in the seventeenth century, carved an independent pathway for himself and thereby helped to establish a new society in America.

William Smith was born about 1460 into a family of small freeholders in Cuerdley in the parish of Prescot, Lancashire (see Map 8). The family was rich enough to educate William at Oxford. In 1485 he seems to have been part of the household at Lathom or Knowsley, attending on Margaret Beaufort, mother of Henry VII, and second wife of the 1st Earl of Derby. From her household he was taken into the royal service and became one of Henry VII's most trusted officials. In 1496 he was rewarded with the Bishopric of Lincoln, the most extensive bishopric in England, which probably provided him with an income of about £1,500 a year.[14] In addition, the Crown sometimes paid Bishop Smith a salary of as much as £20 a week.[15] His total income, therefore, may have exceeded £2,000 p.a., about four times that of the richest landowner in Bucklow Hundred.

Richard Winnington owned an estate centred on the township of the same name, which extended to about 3,000 acres (see Appendix 2.4). When he was looking for a wife, *c.* 1498, he fixed on a Jane or Joanne Smith. Major gentry did not normally marry the daughters of small freeholders so it seems likely that she became the wife of Richard Winnington because her uncle William was Bishop of Lincoln. The Bishop's wealth and influence made his niece an attractive marriage partner. Unfortunately, Richard Winnington died in 1503, so he did not profit from the connection. His widow Jane retained her attractions and made a second favourable marriage to Philip Egerton of Egerton and Oulton. The bishop used the majority of his great wealth to help found Brasenose College, Oxford, but there was enough left over to aid the preferment of a numerous clan of Smiths, many of whom obtained jobs in the Diocese of Lincoln. Thomas Smith, a merchant in Chester, and one of

14 Hoskins, 1976, p. 127; Dyer, 1980, for a detailed example.
15 For his attendance at Prince Arthur's court in Wales, see D.N.B.

the bishop's executors in 1514, became Mayor of Chester and was knighted. He established his family on a landed estate at Hough in Wybunbury.[16] The next Bishop of Lincoln, Thomas Wolsey, turned out to be even more powerful, becoming the King's principal minister and being created a cardinal in 1517.

There is a great contrast between this culture and the independent, self-reliant or 'do-it-yourself' culture that was common among the leaseholder/copyholder/ freeholder group. Between 1620 and 1640 many hundreds of English families transported themselves across the Atlantic and established new towns and villages along the coast of North America. The survey of occupations, in Ch. 4 above, describes two Cheshire families whose members did this. Theophilus Eaton was the eldest son of Richard Eaton, vicar of Great Budworth, 1604–16. The family were copyholders in Whitley Lordship until they bought their freehold in 1612 (see Appendix 3.4). Theophilus became a Freeman of the City of London in 1611, later becoming a merchant and deputy governor of the Eastland Company.[17] He lived in the parish of St Stephen's, Coleman Street, where his old friend John Davenport was minister.[18] The Davenports, a business family in Coventry, had been parishioners of his father, Richard, who had baptised John Davenport in 1597, while he was vicar of Holy Trinity Church, Coventry. Also living in John Davenport's parish in Coleman Street was Theophilus' old neighbour from Great Budworth, Richard Malbon, the second son of William Malbon of Brownslane Green Farm. The family had been tenants of Norton Abbey on this farm in the 1530s and had bought it in 1544 for about £50 (see Appendix 3.7). By the 1620s it will have had an annual value of about £50 p.a. Richard had been apprenticed to the Merchant Tailors' Company in London in 1604 (see Appendix 4.1). Theophilus and Richard will probably have been given portions of £100 or more when they became Freemen. By the 1630s they had probably increased their wealth, by successful trading, to several hundred pounds or more each.[19] In 1629 when the Charter of the Massachusetts Bay Company was granted, Theophilus subscribed £25 and was made one of the 18 assistants to the Governor. By 1636, Davenport and the Coleman Street congregation were being severely harassed by the Church under Archbishop Laud, no doubt for their Puritan, Nonconforming practices. Rather than endure the arbitrary rule of Charles I, they decided to emigrate as a group to Massachusetts. Theophilus led his whole family – his two brothers, Samuel and Nathaniel; his second wife, Anne

16 D.N.B; Churton, 1800; Armitage and Rylands, 1909, pp. 211–14; Ormerod, 1882, Vol. 2, pp. 199–205; Ormerod, 1882, Vol. 3, pp. 502–03.

17 Hinton, 1959, pp. 68, 219.

18 Moore, 1842.

19 New Haven records show Theophilus Eaton's estate was valued at £3,000 in 1643. Osterweis, 1953, p. 22.

(daughter of Thomas Morton, Bishop of Chester); his children by both his wives and Anne's three children by her first husband, David Yale.[20] The whole group of some 40 families from the Coleman Street parish chartered the *Hector of London* (250 tons) which arrived in Boston in June 1637. Later that summer they prospected the site of New Haven and in the spring of 1638 they settled there and started to build a town (see Pl. 15).[21] Theophilus was elected Governor in 1643 and was re-elected each year until his death in 1657. Richard Malbon became Captain of the Guard in 1640.[22]

There can hardly be a more striking example of self-reliance than is provided by this group of people. These were families who had lived all their lives in a comfort-ably-off, well-educated world, who decided in middle age to adventure themselves in a wild, uninhabited land. If the suggestions made above (p. 177) are right, they did it to protect their property and their way of life, as expressed in their Puritan religion, and they were able to do it because they had the money to hire shipping to transport them and to buy supplies to build their houses and lay in food for two years until they were able to provide their own. They furnished themselves with guns and swords for protection. Above all, they had the capacity to create a community which was able to work together to achieve a prosperous society in the New World. The organization of this community was similar to that of the townships they had known in Cheshire and Lancashire, where the Town Meeting was a gathering of the heads of all the property-owning households in the township. It was their experience of these democratic organizations that enabled the American colonists to create the democratic Constitution of the United States of America.[23] This was not the traditional culture of European states where government was firmly in the hands of the Crown, the Church and the major gentry.

The growth of the new industrial society, its markets and its culture, is a huge subject. All that is attempted in Part II is to illustrate the kind of things that happened, by providing three detailed examples of how the population of Cheshire and Lancashire created a business society between 1650 and 1780. Many aspects of the new society are well known. In 1650, Liverpool was a small port trading with Ireland with a population in 1662 of only about 1,000 inhabitants. By 1770 it had become a large town with a population of some 34,000,[24] trading with America, the West Indies, Europe and most of the rest of the world.[25] This great trading upsurge

20 Yale University was named after Elihu Yale, 1648–1721, grandson of David Yale.
21 Macbeath-Calder, 1934, pp. 28–31, 48–49; Rose-Troup, 1930, pp. 59–63.
22 Anderson, 1995, p. 1848.
23 Mansfield and Winthrop, Chicago, 2000, pp. 40–41 and 57–64.
24 Enfield, 1773, p. 28.
25 Ibid., p. 25.

was accompanied by the development of a wide range of manufacturing industries in the region. The manufacture of cheese and its despatch by sea to London was one of the first.[26] The manufacture of textiles in the line of 'textile towns' at the foot of the Pennines was another. Cotton was increasingly blended with the traditional linen, which enabled big improvements in the dyeing of fabrics. This paved the way for the development of the colour printing of textiles in the 'Indian' manner and by the middle of the eighteenth century, a great range of attractively coloured, new textiles was being exported to America and the West Indies.[27] In America, labour was more profitably employed cultivating the virgin lands and cutting down the ancient forests than in humble domestic crafts. Partly to provide for the American market, the coalfields of south Lancashire were much developed and, near the mines, numerous metalworking industries grew up, making such things as tools, watches, hinges and nails.

My first example is another industry that was important in the Mersey estuary in the early period – the salt industry. Chapter 7 describes this activity around Northwich and the people who owned and ran its businesses. It begins with a sketch of the history of the industry up to 1770. Many of the medieval practices remained until 1650 with insignificant quantities of salt being despatched by sea before that date. Then a revolution occurred and the technology was updated. By the 1690s, substantial tonnages of salt were being shipped around the coasts of Britain and exported to Ireland, the Baltic and America. By the 1760s, Northwich salt was the cheapest in the world and was driving other producers out of all but their local markets. With this history as the background, the rest of the section is devoted to an account of the families who were running the industry in the eighteenth century.

The second example, in Chapter 8, relates to a Quaker family group – the Hough family of Sutton Weaver. They were the leaseholders of one particular farm of 36 acres on the Warburton estate from 1539 to 1802. This fact may give a stay-at-home impression of the family. However, the stories which follow of nine of the descendants of Thomas Hough and Ellin Barnes, who married in 1676, show that members of the family group travelled widely and pursued a variety of careers. All the men whose careers are described had some connection with the Warrington area. All, like Thomas and Ellin, were Quakers. Their six relations, who stayed in the Warrington area, were in six different businesses.

My third example is provided by the sailcloth manufacturers of Warrington, 1740–71, described in Chapter 9. This was a new industry created by the Acts of Parliament passed between 1736 and 1746 to provide the Royal Navy with home-

26 Foster, 1998, p. 1–24.
27 Wadsworth and Mann, 1931; Montgomery, 1984; The Hyde Pattern Book, Styal Museum Library.

produced sails. The bulk of the chapter is devoted to an account of 13 families, each of whom owned capital assets of several thousand pounds, who all became manufacturers of sailcloth. Through this study we obtain a picture of a segment of Warrington society. The combination of the available information on the three groups – the people living in Warrington who were involved in the salt industry, the Quaker family group, and the sailcloth manufacturers – provides information on a wide range of Warrington inhabitants. In Chapter 10 an effort is made to create a profile of the whole of Warrington society.

This community, which may be typical of those in Cheshire and Lancashire, can be seen to be significantly different to most towns in Europe. Warrington in 1771 was a medium-sized town with about 1,800 houses containing 8,000 inhabitants. It was not a seat of Government or a centre for the Church or the Law. The surrounding agricultural land contributed only a minor part of its trade. It was primarily a business town which survived by trading and by manufacturing. Its inhabitants were almost all engaged in business, of which there was a great variety. There was much international trade and, while many ships were despatched to the Baltic and other parts of Europe, the main trading connections were with America and the West Indies. Several Warrington families had relations living and working across the Atlantic. There was frequent intercourse across the ocean so that these families were almost Anglo-Americans. Many of them shared the American taste for independence and self-reliance and they also shared, with the Americans, a substantial degree of self-government. Warrington had no charter or corporation so that the old Town Meeting still ran the town. In this respect it was like most towns in the North-West, even Manchester, although its population, including Salford, reached 27,000 by 1773.[28] An important group in Warrington, as in the American colonies, were the Nonconformists. Not all of these were Quakers – indeed the largest and richest group among the sailcloth manufacturers were the Unitarians.

Most of the more prosperous businessmen had come into Warrington from the country areas, where they owned property and were the descendants of the free-holders, copyholders or leaseholders of the 1660s. All the families making sailcloth appear to have arrived in Warrington after 1649. Successful business ventures in the late seventeenth and early eighteenth centuries had increased their capital considerably and, by the 1740s, this community seems to have built up a considerable zest for business. Each son seems to have entered the business of his choice – several of those who began sailcloth manufacture were in their early 20s. The sailcloth manufacturing businesses they created were unlike earlier businesses.

28 Aiken, 1795, p. 89.

They were not just merchants, importing and exporting, nor were they simply manufacturers making and then selling to merchants who exported or distributed the goods at home. They themselves bought the raw materials abroad; they manufactured and then exported the cloth themselves or they sold it in the home market from their own warehouses. They each had thousands of workers on their payrolls. Warrington manufacturers captured between a third and a half of all the sailcloth business in the country. This cloth could have been, and probably was, made in a large number of other areas, but for some reason manufacturers in other places were less successful. This may have been due to the extraordinary vigour of Warrington businessmen, or to their ability to provide the capital for the businesses and to manage these complex organizations. But probably the important consideration was that Liverpool had developed a particularly strong position in trading with the Baltic countries which provided the flax and the hemp for the cloth, because one of the few products the Baltic peoples wanted to buy was Cheshire salt.

CHAPTER 7

The salt industry around Northwich, 1536–1773

i) Introduction

The first part of this chapter is a brief account of the history of the industry up to 1773. Before the Norman Conquest kings and lords had discovered how to make money out of Cheshire salt. Their heavy regulatory system, based on antique and outmoded technology, survived to the Civil War period. The powerful political position of the landowners and their tenants, who were receiving the profits of the system, probably accounted for its longevity. In the 30 years from 1650 to 1680 the industry was modernized and became competitive with other salt producers in the country. The construction of the Weaver and Sankey Navigations (Section iii) between 1730 and 1760 enabled salt to be produced in Cheshire more cheaply than anywhere else in the world and the resulting expansion of the industry continued for more than a century. Cheshire salt was indeed a little-noticed part of the 'Industrial Revolution' in Britain.

My main interest is to examine the social and economic basis of this transformation. Who were the people who changed the industry? Where did they get their capital? In sections (iv) to (vii) of this chapter, the histories of some of the leading families are traced. It seems likely that much of the capital used to modernize the industry between 1650 and 1680 came from the major landowners, who had a long tradition of exploiting the minerals on their estates. However, over the next 50 years, most of them gradually ceased to be actively involved and their position was taken by families who had built up their capital through successful business operations over several generations. I have been able to trace the origins of some of these families back to the farms which they had in the sixteenth century. Many of these families were already engaged in other businesses when they saw the opportunity presented by the rapid expansion of demand for salt in the 1690s and invested their money and their energies in a salt-works.

For a few years rock-salt-mines and refineries were very profitable, allowing some families to amass capital in this period. Two of these families used their capital to help build the waterways that so dramatically improved the competitive position of Cheshire salt between 1730 and 1760. Other families entered the industry after the honeymoon period at the end of the seventeenth century. Some of them can only have had a small amount of capital when they began, but most seem to have done well from the industry. By the end of our period the major figures each owned capital measured in tens of thousands of pounds. The less rich families probably owned a few thousand pounds each. As it was the practice of most families who were not major gentry to divide their wealth equally among all their children, the capital saved in the salt industry was distributed among a large number of people. Many of these people then took up careers in other businesses.

ii) The history of the industry to 1730

At Domesday there were 1,195 manufacturers of salt on the coast of England between Lincolnshire and Cornwall.[1] These people were making salt from sea-water by the ancient Mediterranean technique of letting sea-water into a lagoon where the sun and wind evaporated the water. In the cold northern climate it was only possible to remove between half and two thirds of the water like this, so the remainder had to be boiled away. This was done in small lead pans with wood or peat as fuel. During the Middle Ages the number of these works slowly diminished as they ran out of local fuel.

Another cause of their decline was that from around 1200 onwards salt from the coasts of southern France and the Iberian Peninsula was regularly brought to England as ballast in ships bringing wine. This salt had been fully evaporated from sea-water by the sun, and so was cheap to produce. Its transport as ballast did not significantly raise its cost before it arrived at an English port. It was therefore normally the cheapest salt in England. However, the sun dries salt into large flat, hard crystals, whereas the salt obtained by boiling brine quickly was fine and powdery. So 'Bay' salt, as the salt brought by the ships was called, and 'white' salt obtained by boiling in England, were different products. Bay salt was preferred by fishermen because it did not dissolve easily in damp conditions, whereas white salt was chosen for the dining table.

The technical position in the Cheshire Salt 'wiches' – Northwich, Middlewich, and Nantwich – was different. Beds of rock-salt 30 feet and more deep (laid down in the ice age) originally lay as little as 30 feet below the ground near the rivers in the salt towns. The ancient brine pits had been dug down in places where little streams running on the top of the rock-salt had become fully saturated with salt (about 25.5% salt is full saturation) whereas sea-water contains only about 2.5% salt. Even after a half to two-thirds of the sea-water had been evaporated, the resulting brine still only contained between 5% and 8% salt. It therefore took much longer to boil the water away at seaside works than it did with Cheshire brine. Seaside works therefore used much more fuel and the resulting salt cost more, as fuel was the principal cost in English salt production. Salt-making in the Cheshire wiches was therefore very profitable. The Anglo-Saxon kings of England had learnt how to cream off this profit by charging tolls at the wiches; these are detailed in the

1   Bridbury, 1955, p. 19.

Domesday Book.[2] In the sixteenth century the profits of Northwich salt-making were being divided between the Earls of Derby, who had acquired the rights to the old royal tolls, and the local gentry, who owned the salt-houses where the salt was actually produced. Plate 16 shows the old town of Northwich where there were traditionally 113 salt-houses, each with four lead pans. The brine was brought up out of the pit in Seath Street in buckets and poured into wooden channels which carried it to the salt-houses. The whole operation was closely regulated by sundry officials who set the price at which the salt could be sold and controlled production, so there was always salt for sale at the fixed price, but never so much that there was pressure to lower the price. Only one account book of salt-making in this period appears to have survived. It was made by a member of the Wilbraham family, who owned five salt-houses in Nantwich, each with six lead pans. In the year beginning 12 May 1629 he produced a total of 1,238 barrows of salt worth £102 10s 4d. It has been calculated that a barrow probably weighed about 75 lbs,[3] in which case his total output would have been 41.5 tons. Each salt-house produced about 8.3 tons, worth £20 10s 0d, and Wilbraham's salt-houses were actually working on only 49 days that year.[4] The annual profit or rental value of each of his salt-houses seems to have been about £3 p.a. (see Appendix 7.3 for other salt-house values).

Technical development at the Cheshire wiches was completely blocked by their heavy regulatory system. Elsewhere in the country, the works which used sea-water improved their methods, led by the salt-works on Tyneside. As early as 1489 iron salt-pans were in use at South Shields,[5] a great improvement since the extra heat produced by coal melted the lead pans, but did not affect iron pans. This technical advance enabled a substantial salt-production industry to develop on Tyneside using local coal to boil partly evaporated sea-water in large iron pans. By the early seventeenth century, the area was the dominant supplier of white salt on the east coast of England.[6] On the south coast, the old Hampshire works at Lymington and Portsea had also by this time adopted iron pans, heated by coal brought by sea. Presumably the extra evaporation achieved in the sunnier south compensated for the costs of transporting the coal from a distance.[7]

In the North-West, there were some developments outside the wiches. (See Maps 4 and 8 for almost all the places mentioned in the text.) In Cheshire, before 1623, Sir Robert Needham and Sir Thomas Smith had built brine works with iron pans

2 Tait, 1916, pp. 39–43.
3 See Appendix 7.1.
4 See Appendix 7.2 for detailed accounts; Calvert, 1915, pp. 813–27.
5 Hawkins, 1844, p. 86.
6 Ellis, 1980, p. 58.
7 VCH Hants, Vol. 5, pp. 469–72.

Map 8. South Lancashire and Cheshire.

	Townships in Lancashire			Townships in Cheshire	
– – – – County boundary	1 RAINFORD	6 BEDFORD	12 CUERDLEY	17 OVER ALDERLEY	21 STANTHORNE
–––––––– Hundred boundary	2 WINDLE	7 ECCLESTON	13 PENKETH	18 LEFTWICH	22 ODD RODE
	3 ASHTON IN	8 RAINHILL	14 GREAT SANKEY	19 BOSTOCK	23 PULFORD
–––––––– Township boundary	MAKERFIELD	9 SPEKE	15 WOOLSTON	20 WHARTON	24 GRAFTON
	4 HAYDOCK	10 HALE	16 RIXTON		
	5 ATHERTON	11 WIDNES			

beside the River Weaver, near Nantwich.[8] In 1633 the Lowthers built salt-pans at Whitehaven in Cumbria, near their coal-mines. They copied the Newcastle iron pans, said to be made of tough iron one yard long, half an inch thick and nine inches broad. Their market was to be a short sea crossing away in Ireland.[9] The Booth family of Dunham Massey had installed similar iron pans before 1634.[10] How much

8   Webb, 1656, under Nantwich Hundred. Sir Robert Needham was created Viscount Kilmorey in
     1625; Sir Thomas Smith of Hough was Sheriff of Cheshire in 1623; see pp. 179–80 for his ancestor,
     Bishop of Lincoln.
9   Hainsworth, 1977, p. 33.
10 Hawkins, 1844, p. 87.

salt they produced at Dunham is not known, but it is possible that their business was very profitable. It was close to coal-mines in Lancashire, so its costs would have been low. It is likely that the supply of brine was not plentiful and so production, though cheap, may have been limited. In 1738 they bought rock-salt from the Rock Salt Co. of Northwich,[11] which appears to show that their own supply was not fully satisfactory. Nevertheless, the salt-works may have made a significant addition to the Booth family's income. In a survey made about 1620 the salt-works and three mills were together valued at £400 p.a., which suggests that the salt-works alone may have been worth £200–£300 p.a.[12] There are many references to new salt-works in Cheshire before the Civil War for example, in 1637, 'the many new salt-works lately found out and erected about us' were mentioned at a Northwich meeting.[13]

The impact of these new salt-making operations was reflected in a decline in the value of the old Northwich salt-houses, illustrated by some figures in Appendix 7.3. In 1536 a salt-house of four leads seems to have been worth less than £1 a year. Its value rose to a peak of £5 p.a. in 1589–93. From then until the early 1660s, £3 p.a. seems to have been more usual, except for a few years around 1648–51. Another example of the pressure which these new salt-works put on the old wiches is provided by the prices paid for the salt. Appendix 7.3 shows that in 1586–91 the Shuttleworths at Smithills paid two shillings a bushel for Northwich salt, which they collected themselves. From 1592 their salt was delivered to them at a total cost of 1s 8d a bushel including delivery, so there was a big drop in the price at that time. These falls in the price of salt and in the value of salt-houses around 1590 suggest that one or more substantial new salt-works started production at about that time. One of these may have been the Dunham works. The Wilbrahams of Nantwich received 1s 8d a barrow in 1629, 1s 6d in 1631 and only 1s 4d in 1638. These barrows were probably 'walmes'[14] weighing about 75 lbs, so the prices were the equivalent of 15d, 13.8d, and 12d a bushel. If this is correct, the price of salt at the wiches halved between 1591 and 1638.

The decisive change in the character of salt-working in the Northwich area appears to have come in the early 1650s, when it seems that Philip Pritchard established a new salt-works in Leftwich just across the Dane river from the ancient Northwich brine pit (see Pls. 16 and 18). This was probably a newly dug pit from which brine was pumped to iron pans heated by coal. The brine supply was adequate to maintain these pans in continuous operation so that a substantial supply of salt was produced. In the 1660 Poll Tax Philip Pritchard's income from this salt-works

11 Penrhyn Papers, see note 26 below.
12 EGR 11/1/5.
13 Calvert, 1915, p. 1057.
14 See Appendix 7.1, p. 221.

was assessed at £200 p.a., the highest assessment in Northwich Hundred. He was also assessed on lands worth £105 p.a. in Bostock and £6 15s 0d p.a. in Wharton.[15]

Pritchard's may have been the first salt-works in the Northwich area which continuously boiled fully-saturated brine in iron pans using coal as fuel (Pl. 17. Whether it was or not, several more were built in the next 20 years or so. When John Collins published his *Salt and Fishery* in 1682, he listed six pits in Northwich, seven in Middlewich and three in Nantwich. There were certainly others at Dirtwych, south of Malpas, and there may have been others near Wheelock. The best description we have of the operation of salt-works in this period is provided by the accounts of Earl Rivers' Leftwich Eyes works in 1671–75, which was probably the same salt-works that Pritchard had operated between 1650 and 1671 on a 21-year lease.[16]

Earl Rivers' works consisted of two salt-houses and an adjacent smithy. The buildings with four iron pans were partly of brick and slate and partly plastered and thatched. The brine was pumped up from their own pit which was cleaned out periodically. They produced salt continuously and in the three full years covered by the accounts the output was as follows:

	Output (tons)	Sales (£)
1672	685	833
1673	846	1,169
1674	875	1,305

The total direct cost of production in 1674 was £939. Of this, £782 was for coal and the balance of £157 was mostly wages but also included minor items like blood and eggs to clarify the boiling brine. These figures give a prime cost in 1674 of £1.07 per ton, or 6.4d a bushel. The coal was probably brought mostly from north Staffordshire pits, about 18 miles away to the south, rather than the Haydock pit, some 19–20 miles to the north in Lancashire. It came both by packhorse and by cart and the usual cost was between 14s and 15s a ton. Carts usually carried about 1,200 lbs while a horse carried between 150 and 180 lbs.[17] On at least one occasion, an attempt was made to bring a boatload up the River Weaver, but this failed and the coal had to be fetched overland from Pickerings.

Sales were made from the works every week all through the year. Two types of land-based customers are mentioned. 'Countrymen' were presumably people collecting salt for themselves or their employers. They usually paid slightly more than 'chapmen' whose trade it was to carry salt for resale. In the early months of

15 Lawton, 1979, pp. 155, 167, 172. See Appendix 7.4 for the evidence for this paragraph.
16 C.R.O. DCH/J/112–3.
17 These figures are calculated from the Leftwich Eyes Accounts using the measures in Appendix 7.1. Some carts brought barrels which enables a volume/price measurement to be made.

1673, the common price was 9.2d a bushel; it then fell to 7.5d in June but moved back to around 9d in September and in November some sales were made as high as 11d. These variations were probably due to the fact that the cost of transporting coal would have been higher in winter.

Sales were also made at Frodsham to people who were going to ship the salt around the coast or to Ireland. Some of these individual sales were for much larger quantities than the land-based customers ever took – a sale of £20 or £30 worth was not uncommon. The price of salt at Frodsham seems to have varied between 2s 6d and 3s 10d a barrel, a price which included the cost of transport, apparently by road, from Northwich to Frodsham. The transport cost only 9d a barrel in the summer when the roads were hard, but it could cost as much as 14d a barrel in January. If the carriage of a barrel of salt selling for 3s 10d had cost only 10d, the price the salt had fetched was 9d a bushel. However, a barrel selling at Frodsham for 2s 6d, when transport had cost 12d, had realized only 4½d a bushel for the salt. The low prices at which some consignments were sold may have been because of poor quality as we know that grey salt was much cheaper than white. In 1672, sales at Frodsham represented half of the total sales from the works and they rose to 56% in 1674.

The accounts do not provide much information about the stocks which existed at any period. Nor do they tell us about the costs of administration or the depreciation of the plant so we cannot obtain a realistic view of the profit of the business. In 1674 sales were £1,305, £366 more than the prime cost of production of £939. On average, the salt had cost 6.4d a bushel to produce and had sold for 8.9d a bushel. The existence of these figures seems likely to have had some influence in establishing the rent at which Lord Rivers let the works in 1675. William Hyde and John Broome paid £1,100 in rent between 5 November 1675 and Christmas 1678, about £360 a year.[18]

It is clear from these figures that the new salt-works were very profitable in the 1660s and 1670s. In Appendix 7.5, the rents of several salt-works in Cheshire are given from 1664 onwards, indicating similar profit levels However, there seems to have been something of a collapse in profitability in the 1680s and the dizzy profits and rents of the 1660s and 1670s were never seen again. The price of salt everywhere evidently came closer to the new costs of production, which were around 6d a bushel.

Against this background it is easier to understand why John Collins published his book, *Salt and Fishery* in 1682. It is mainly an extended plea for a duty to be put on imported salt, and was probably written at the request of one or more salt-works owners. He argued that the new Cheshire industry and the manufacturers in other

18 DCH/C/932–34, and DCH/J/72.

parts of the country could supply all the salt the nation used. However, his enthusiasm led him to exaggerate in his tables which appear to show the amount of salt
being produced by each works in Cheshire (see Appendix 7.6). To sweeten the
proposals for Government he suggested that, if a large duty were put on imports, a
smaller duty could be laid on English production, which would raise revenue for
the state. One can see that enlarging the market for English-made salt would seem
an attractive prospect to producers. Their profits had fallen dramatically because
they were now able to produce more than the market could absorb. Prices had thus
fallen to the level of costs and a larger market might allow both prices and profits
to rise a little.

The story so far has shown the destruction of the old regulated salt industry of
the Cheshire wiches by the 1680s. It seems to have happened in two phases. From
the 1580s to the early 1650s, the creation of many small works outside the wiches
forced prices down, from about two shillings a bushel in the 1580s to around one
shilling in 1638. There were probably a number of small brine springs in Cheshire
where the amount of brine varied greatly depending on the rainfall. The amount of
salt in the brine probably also fluctuated widely.[19] Works based on such brine
supplies could have produced small quantities economically in this period.
However, from the 1650s onwards, larger plants operating continuously, with good
supplies of fully-saturated brine, lowered the costs of production and the sale price
to around 6d a bushel. The reduction of the price to a quarter of what it had been
in the 1580s is the more remarkable, because most other prices – for example, wages,
food and rents – all continued to rise into the 1620s and 1630s. This price reduction
was achieved by modernizing the techniques of producing salt in the Cheshire
wiches. By contrast, the development of the industry from the 1680s onwards was
mainly due to improvements in transport technology.

With the flight of James II to France in 1688 and the accession of William and
Mary, a long, if intermittent, war with France began. French privateers appeared
in the Channel and off Ireland. French and Spanish salt came less often to England
so the demand for English-made salt increased all around the coasts and in Ireland.
In 1694, the Government gave in to the lobbying of salt producers and accepted
John Collins' advice. They imposed a tax of 2s a bushel on foreign salt and 1s a
bushel on English salt.[20] These duties were raised to 3s 4d and 1s 8d in 1697, and a
year later to 6s 8d and 3s 4d respectively, and they stayed around these levels for
most of the eighteenth century.

The accounts of the Salt Commissioners bring us an additional perspective on

19 A large number of passages in Calvert, 1915, illuminate the geology of Cheshire salt.
20 5 William and Mary c7.

the salt trade (see Appendix 7.9). Appendix 7.7 shows the salt shipped from Frodsham at the mouth of the River Weaver – one of the main quays of the port of Liverpool. No significant shipments were made before 1665, when about 80 tons went to Ireland. By the 1680s, shipments had increased to 1,500 tons a year, of which about 1,000 tons went to Ireland and 500 to other west coast ports. This was in line with what we saw earlier of the development of new works in Northwich. In 1689 the quantity of salt shipped along the coast began to rise. By 1693 shipments had leapt to over 5,000 tons p.a. and they remained at this level into the eighteenth century. Evidently Cheshire production had replaced imports from France and Spain in west coast ports. Along the east coast Tyneside had, in the 1680s, shipped between 5,000 and 8,500 tons a year, and between 1690 and 1704 their shipments increased to between 10,000 and 13,000 tons p.a.[21] The extra business on the home market for English salt-makers, resulting from the decline in imports, was shared equally between the two major centres of production.[22] In the case of exports, Cheshire did better than Tyneside, increasing exports to Ireland from the 1,000 tons a year of the 1680s to 5,000 to 6,000 tons a year in the 1690s. Exports were not subject to duty. Tyneside's exports continued at a few hundred tons a year until 1703 and, from then until 1730, they exported between 2,000 and 4,000 tons most years to northern Europe.

Cheshire sales in the 1690s included increasing amounts of rock-salt dug from mines (see p. 225). Although discovered by the Marbury family in 1670, rock-salt seems not to have been of commercial interest until the 1690s. What made it important then was a neat piece of political jiggery pokery. Someone succeeded in inserting in the Salt Tax Act a clause stating that 120 lbs of rock-salt should be deemed to be a bushel. In contrast, the Act fixed the weight of a bushel of white salt at 56 lbs. There was some dirt in rock-salt, but not as much as this. The effect was that the tax on rock-salt was only about 50% of the tax on white salt and, as the news spread, the demand for raw, unprocessed rock-salt knew no bounds. The process of converting it to white salt was simple. The rock-salt was dissolved in water, the mud settled out and the clear brine was then boiled so that white salt could be extracted. Refineries were set up around the Mersey Estuary: at least one was near Warrington, another at Liverpool, a third at Dungeon and a fourth on Hilbre Island off the Wirral Peninsula. The first shipments of unrefined rock-salt were to Bristol which was on a coalfield. During 1693 and 1694, it arrived at five other west coast ports, and ships carried it around Cornwall to Penzance and Plymouth, some even arriving in London in 1695. The anomaly in the tax law was only slowly corrected.

21 Ellis, 1980, pp. 57–58.
22 See Appendix 7.9 for approximate figures.

In 1699 the weight of a bushel of rock-salt was deemed to be only 75 lbs. In 1702 it was revised down again to 65 lbs, but in 1706 an allowance for waste on coastal trips was introduced.[23] The end result of it all was that the tax on rock-salt remained at a slightly lower level than that on white salt. It continued to be the case that most of the salt despatched coastwise from Frodsham was rock-salt. During the war, with the Royal Navy blockading southern European ports and shipping, Cheshire exports to northern Europe increased. With the coming of peace, some of these markets were lost (see Appendix 7.7).

iii) The Weaver and Sankey Navigations, 1730–73

The story of the development of the Weaver Navigation has already been told in great detail so I will just summarize the main events.[24] From 1665 onwards inter-mittent attempts were made to get an Act through Parliament allowing the development of the River Weaver. An Act was finally obtained in 1721 which appointed three Cheshire gentlemen to be 'undertakers' to build the waterway. One, John Egerton, was a member of the major gentry. Richard Vernon, the most active of the other two, was a lawyer who owned a salt-works at Winsford. These three did nothing so, at the end of 1729, Thomas Patten and his brother Jonathon, Thomas Eyre and John Dickenson offered to take over as 'undertakers' and build the navigation. They started work in 1730 and the first barges paid toll in January 1732 the construction having cost a total of about £20,000. This money seems to have been provided entirely by the Pattens and their partners without a public subscription or bankers' loans. Included in this total was a £1,800 fee to the under-takers for organizing the work and completing it during 1732 and interest at 6% on the capital they had advanced. The remainder was spent on materials, the contrac-tors who did the work and the legal expenses of obtaining the Acts. The barges, often known as flats, which normally carried between 25 and 40 tons each mostly plied from navigable water near Frodsham Bridge to Northwich, a distance of about 14 miles. It was possible to go on another six miles to Winsford, which was three miles from Middlewich, but in the 1740s, about three quarters of the traffic was to and from Northwich (see Pl. 19).

The great change brought about by the Navigation was in the cost of transport. The freight charge for carrying salt by barge from Northwich to Frodsham was about two shillings a ton.[25] The 'tonnage' toll for using the Navigation was 1s 3d a ton, so the total cost of carrying a ton of salt from Northwich to Frodsham was about

23 10 and 11 William III c22; 1 Anne c21; 5 Anne c29.
24 Willan, 1951.
25 See p. 197.

3s 3d. The lowest price for road freight paid by Lord Rivers in the 1670s in mid-summer was 9d a barrel or 7s 6d a ton. In the winter he sometimes paid as much as 14d a barrel or 11s 8d a ton.[26] So the main effect of the Navigation was to reduce significantly the cost of carrying Cheshire salt to the local ports and therefore to make it considerably more competitive in the export trade. The price of salt at Frodsham is likely to have fallen by at least 4s 3d a ton or about 1.3d a bushel.

Another big change made by the Navigation was its effect on the possible sources of coal for Northwich. Lancashire coal seems to have been only occasionally competitive at Northwich before the Navigation. In 1733, just after the Navigation opened, nearly 15,000 tons of salt was carried from Northwich down to Frodsham but only 2,600 tons of coal from Lancashire pits came up the river. Ten years later the salt moved had increased to over 19,000 tons, but the coal carried had grown to nearly 8,500 tons (see Appendix 7.7 for later figures). Lancashire coal had by then virtually replaced Staffordshire coal at Northwich, presumably because it was cheaper, so Northwich white salt producers were able to reduce the cost of the coal they used. Winsford and Middlewich producers, being closer to the Staffordshire pits than to the Lancashire ones, continued to buy from Staffordshire.

The best view of the economics of the white salt trade in the 1730s and 1740s is provided by the accounts of the works at Winsford started by Thomas Eyre and continued by Thomas Patten which are summarized in Appendix 7.10. In an average year between 1734 and 1744, this works produced nearly 2,000 tons of salt. 84% was exported and the remainder was divided approximately equally between coastal sales and those to local people in Cheshire. The price realized for export sales was 5.3d a bushel (17s 8d a ton), but the price obtained for sales in England was nearly 6d a bushel (£1 a ton). Thus the average price at which the whole 2,000 tons was sold was 5.4d a bushel. The total costs of the business worked out at 5d a bushel so the profit margin was a thin 0.4d a bushel, giving an annual profit on the business of only £129.[27] We do not know what the capital cost of the site, the buildings, the pans, and other equipment was, but it is evident that brine salt-production at this time was not a very profitable business. Annual sales fluctuated markedly, no doubt because wars and other political events affected export markets. Some years were probably very profitable, but others incurred losses. At the Winsford works in Patten's time, coal accounted for half the cost of production while wages for producing and loading the salt came to only 11%. Freight to Frodsham

26 B.L. Add Mss 36914 Aston correspondence gives various prices for carriage and coal around 1700. Hughes, 1934, gives more (e.g., p. 396). How accurate they were is uncertain.

27 The price for exports may have been the price paid by the Liverpool merchants. It is possible that Patten was in partnership with some of these merchants and was getting a share of their profit on salt exports.

was 24% and the remainder of the costs were expended on repairs and sundries.

Before the Navigation was opened, white salt will have been more expensive to produce in Northwich than in Middlewich, because the Staffordshire coal-mines were closer to Middlewich. After the Navigation opened, Northwich salt producers used coal from Lancashire. Appendix 7.11 lists the principal salt-works owners or operators using the Navigation between 1732 and 1741. This shows only five important people producing white salt from brine pits in the Northwich area. The economics of these works were improved by the fact that the Navigation provided cheaper transport of both coal and salt, which enabled them to increase their export sales.

In the Winsford-Middlewich area, there seem to have been about 13 brine pits. The works of Thomas Patten and Co., described above, was much the largest one to ship salt down the Weaver. This business, originally called Thomas Eyre and Co., changed its name after Eyre died in about 1735. Perhaps Patten and Eyre had originally been partners. Its works were evidently close to the wharves and ware-houses on the River Weaver, which formed part of the business. This made it cheap to load salt into the barges and explains why this works dominated the river trade at Winsford. Thomas Wrench was the only other white salt producer who shipped regularly down the Weaver from Winsford. His annual cargoes were usually only about one third the size of Patten's. The other eight or nine salt-works only shipped intermittently and many of their works were presumably on the east side of Middlewich so as to get the advantage of being closer to the Staffordshire coal pits. Together they will have had the lion's share of the sales to local customers. We have seen that these were at better prices than export sales, so these works will have made good profits on this part of their business. The export sales they made by shipping down the river can hardly have shown a profit after paying for three miles of carriage from Middlewich to Winsford. Perhaps they only exported the production they could not sell locally. In the following decades, this group further reduced their shipments down the Weaver.

Most of the brine works were leased from the freeholders (see Appendix 7.5 for typical rents). In contrast, some of the rock-salt-mines were operated by their free-holders. The typical procedure seems to have been for the owner or leaseholder to lay out the mine and its surface buildings employing contractors to sink the main shaft. Contractors were then employed to mine out each section, leaving pillars to support the roof. The operator sold the rock-salt from the surface warehouse. The costs and prices given in an old Warburton of Winnington account book may be typical.[28] In the four years 1737 to 1741:

---

28 Penrhyn Papers No. 1637, Book 1717–43.

	s	d	
Getting 19,363 tons of rock salt cost	2	4	per ton
'Tonnage' of 18,150 tons on Weaver cost	1	3	per ton
Freight of 18,150 tons on Weaver cost	2	0	per ton
Total cost at Frodsham	5	7	per ton

In 21 months from March 1737 to December 1738, the Rock Company, a cartel of rock-salt proprietors, sold 8,468 tons for £4,758, which works out at 11s 3d a ton.

These figures indicate that the profitability of rock-salt-mines was good in this period, presumably because of the cartel. As we have seen above, the opening of the Navigation reduced the cost of transporting rock-salt from Northwich to Frodsham by at least 4s 3d a ton. It would seem likely that the price of rock-salt at Frodsham had been at least 11s 3d a ton before 1732. The values of cargoes of rock-salt which were exported and appear in the 'overseas' Port Books, are often between 11s and 12s a ton, which may be the actual prices paid. The rock-salt-mine owners' ability to keep the price at this level may have been due to the formation of the Rock Company. It appears from entries in this old Warburton account book that all the mine operators listed in Appendix 7.11, except John Jeffreys, joined together in this cartel in 1732 (if not before) to divide production equally between them. The combined operation was called the Rock Company, and it made sales through a single agent. But in 1735 John Jeffreys began to ship down the Weaver. He must have undercut the Rock Company's price because the account book shows that in the four years between March 1737 and March 1741, the Company sold only 17,167 tons, while John Jeffreys sold 11,969 tons. Not too surprisingly, the Rock Company seems to have begun to split up after this. No doubt the price of rock-salt at Frodsham fell as the mine owners competed more amongst themselves. The eight members of the Company had had a good decade. In 1732, they seem likely to have each had sales of about 1,000 tons. This fetched about £550 and gave each member a profit of about £270. They had five years of similar profits until the end of 1736. In the next four years sales fell badly and profits seem to have declined to around £130 a year. Rock-salt was only obtainable from Frodsham at this period, whereas white salt and bay salt were widely available. It is likely, therefore, that the profit on rock-salt was always higher than on white salt.

The Winnington account book has a list of outstanding debts due to the Rock Company in 1737 and 1738. This suggests that most sales were made to the merchants who had obtained the coastal or export orders. Some 17 are listed, headed by Mr John Cunliffe, a member of the leading merchant family in Liverpool. Two customers were of a different kind – the refineries at Dungeon and Dunham owed £330 and £45 respectively at Christmas 1738.

In 1755, work began on building the Sankey Navigation (or Canal). This was designed to bring coal from the area now known as St Helens down to the Mersey. All the businessmen saw the desirability of widening and deepening the Weaver Navigation at the same time, so that the boats carrying coal down the Sankey Canal could go straight up the Weaver without unloading. This involved increasing the width of the Weaver locks to about 17 feet and improving the depth from four feet to a minimum of 4½ feet.[29]

An unusual feature of the Weaver Navigation Act of 1721 had been that control of the Navigation was vested in 112 Commissioners, who each had to have lands in the county worth more than £100 p.a. The county was also entitled to use any surplus arising from the tolls, after the initial capital had been repaid, for the repair of bridges and roads in the county. In the early eighteenth century these provisions had seemed sensible to people conscious of the great damage to unpaved roads and bridges caused by carting heavy minerals like coal and salt. They seemed less acceptable to later generations who thought that the County Rates should not be subsidised by the Weaver tolls. The existence of these powers seems to have been important in persuading a majority of the landowner Commissioners to act with vigour at this juncture in order to minimize the Rates levied on their land.

Under the leadership of Sir Peter Warburton and Sir Peter Leicester, the large landowners living nearest to the Navigation, the Commissioners entered into negotiations with the undertakers (the Pattens and their partners) which ended with the Commissioners taking control of the Navigation. They raised money through loans secured on the tolls, bought out the old undertakers and rebuilt the Navigation to the improved specifications so that it could be used by Sankey barges. To ensure that the Navigation under their control was in a sound legal position, they obtained an amending Act. This was drawn up by John Stafford of Macclesfield, Sir Peter Warburton's friend and attorney. Its passage through Parliament was guided by Sir Peter's brother-in-law, Lord Strange, MP for Preston and heir to the Earl of Derby. The rebuilt waterway established Northwich salt as the cheapest in the northern hemisphere. The cost of coal in Northwich was reduced to under ten shillings a ton compared to the 14s to 15s a ton that north Staffordshire coal had cost at Northwich in the 1670s. In the 20 years between 1752/3 and 1772/3 the amount of salt going down the River Weaver increased nearly threefold to almost 82,000 tons p.a. (see Appendix 7.7). Exports were made not only to Ireland and Belgium, but also to Dantzig and Riga on the Baltic and over the Atlantic to Philadelphia and Jamaica.[30] Northwich salt retained its dominant position for more than a century with over one million tons travelling down the Weaver in 1880.

29 Hadfield, 1970, pp. 45–48.
30 Complete list of export destinations in Enfield, reprinted in Calvert, 1915, pp. 283–84.

iv) Some people in the industry, 1530–1730

In the sixteenth century, most of the old salt-houses were owned by the local landed estates. They seem to have been leased either for lives or for years, just like other property. Taking a lease of a salt-house was evidently an activity which lesser members of landed gentry families could do without social disapproval, whereas other business activities, such as textile trading or tailoring, seem not to have been so acceptable. Richard and John Venables of Antrobus leased the Whitley and Cogshall salt-houses from the Duchy of Lancaster under Henry VIII.[31] John Warburton of Budworth, who died in 1580, leased two houses from Mr Brereton of Brereton. Two of the ten salt-houses owned by the Arley estate were leased in 1572 to Thomas Masterson who was also leasing Winnington Hall and some lands surrounding it.[32] The Mastersons were a Nantwich freeholder family with traditional interests in the salt industry there.[33] Thomas was related to the Warburtons in a number of ways. His wife was a Smith of Cuerdley – the family of the Bishop of Lincoln, whose niece had brought the Winnington estate into the Warburton family. Thomas Masterson's sister Ann was married to an illegitimate Thomas Warburton and their son Peter was the brilliant young lawyer who was Steward of the Warburtons' Manor Courts until about 1587. Peter was a Sergeant by 1580 and ended up as Chief Justice of the Common Pleas. He was a friend of Richard Shuttleworth and, like so many successful Elizabethan lawyers, made a fortune. He died in 1621, leaving an estate at Grafton in south Cheshire on which he had built a fine stone house (Pl. 20).[34] From these examples we can see that the traditional salt industry provided an income and a little occupation for a few members of the social group most closely allied to the major gentry.

In the 1570s and 1580s, salt-houses would have provided a growing income for their lessees. The main task of the manager of an old salt-house was acquiring a stock of wood to burn. As the landed estates owned most of the woods, good connections with estate owners were no doubt useful. The workers in the salt-houses – the men who split the wood and stoked the fires and the women who produced the salt – were probably contractors and, as work in any one salt-house was intermittent (see p. 187 above), they probably worked in several during the year. Their terms of service, like everything else in the old salt industry, were no doubt much influenced by custom.

We know very little about the new salt-works. Perhaps the Dunham works began as early as the 1590s; it was certainly built with landed estate money and was perhaps

31 P.R.O. Ind/1/17596, fol. 17.
32 WM Box 2 and at Arley Hall.
33 See Will of Henry Masterson, 1607, and Rylands, 1882, pp. 176–77.
34 Rylands, 1882; Armitage, 1909.

the source of the deliveries made by Mr Crofts to Smithills from 1592.[35] This salt probably did not come from Northwich because it was measured in bushels, not in walmes. This works had the merit of being closer to Lancashire coal than any other Cheshire salt-works. A salter in Budworth, Thomas Anderton, who went bankrupt about 1610, was perhaps trying to start another new works. We know a little more about Philip Pritchard. He and his father, John ap Richard (hence Pritchard), came from Flint and settled in Bostock in 1643. They were evidently of gentry stock, because Philip, born *c.* 1605, was commissioned in the Royalist army. His probable lack of business experience suggests that it was only his friendship with John, Earl Rivers (see Appendix 7.4) that induced him to invest his capital in the salt-works. Rivers had probably devised the project but was unable to carry it to fruition because of his debts and his imprisonment. This would be in line with what little we can glean about the other new salt-works in the area. The high rents listed in Appendix 7.5 suggest that the landowners had usually produced the capital to build these plants. Pritchard certainly made his fortune and his only daughter and heiress, Mary, married into the major gentry. Her husband Henry was a barrister and the second son of Sir Henry Brooke, Bt, of Norton Priory.[36]

If we are right in assuming that these works were largely erected by the landed gentry, it would be consistent with this group's traditional interest and involvement in mineral extraction. William Marbury of Marbury discovered rock-salt on his estate in 1670 while he was trying to find coal.[37] His wife, Katherine, was heiress to the Columbell estate, which included lead mines on its Darley manor in Derbyshire[38] and his sister, also Katherine, seems to have been active in developing a rock-salt-mine at Marbury in the 1690s.[39] At least two other landowners in the Northwich area sank rock-salt-mines at this period. Thomas Warburton, the owner of the manor of Winnington, made one, and another was opened by the Venables family, who owned the manor of Witton, which included most of the salt-bearing area.

35 See Appendix 7.3.
36 Adams, 1941, p. 93. Ormerod corrects the Visitation by stating that Henry Brooke was the second son. He may have continued the Pritchard interest in salt-works. He may have been the Mr Brook who had six pans in Northwich in 1680, according to John Collins (see Appendix 7.6). His wife or daughter may have been the Mary Brooke who was leasing a brine salt-pit to John Broome in 1733 (see Appendix 7.11).
37 Calvert, 1915, pp. 142–43.
38 P.R.O. C22/676/7.
39 Calendar State Papers Domestic, 1696, p. 124; and 1697, p. 123. William Marbury (1644–83) appears to have died with debts of £25,000. The estate was sold, under a decree in Chancery, for the benefit of his sisters. Ormerod, 1882, Vol. 1, pp. 635–37.

v) The rock-salt mine operators, 1730–70

The records of the Weaver Navigation, which opened in 1732, provide us for the first time with a complete list of the people who shipped salt down the river to Frodsham. In addition, a Salt Commissioner, James Cardonnel, visited the Cheshire salt producers the following year, and he has left us his Report. The combination of these two sources of information (see Appendix 7.11) enables us to identify the families involved in the business. The rock-salt-miners divide into two groups – five who belonged to major landed and business families in the area and five who were much less prominent. The second group are described at A below; the grander families at B.

A. The five less prominent families, in the order that they appear here, were: Antrobus, Claridge, Jeffreys, Vernon and Barrow. The Antrobus family seems to have been distantly related to the Knutsford woollen-drapers of the same name (see pp. 117–18) – there were many members of this family who had small properties in Cheshire at that period.[40] James Antrobus of Northwich, born in 1671, was originally a joiner, a description which seems to have been used sometimes for people we would now call building contractors. He married Mary Jeffries (Jeffreys) in 1695 and they had two sons, William and James. All three men were probably involved with the mine and owned the land on which they had sunk it. They may have already owned this small farm before the 1690s when the rage for rock-salt-mining developed, or they may have bought it specifically in order to open the mine – we do not know. We do know that the family shipped salt down the Weaver from 1732 to 1764.

Benjamin Claridge began his career in Dublin as a merchant. He probably had trading connections with people in the Frodsham-Warrington area, as they were the source, not only of salt, but also of many of the other manufactures which were imported into Ireland. He was a Quaker and so probably met his future wife at the Frandley Quaker Meeting on one of his visits. She was Hester Maddocks of 'Eaton Hall'[41] near Frandley (see Map 3). They were married in June 1702 and leased a salt-works from Ralph Broome before the latter went bankrupt in 1705. Claridge and his wife were living in Winnington when their first child was born in December 1706. In 1707 we see him owing tax on salt shipments and he eventually acquired leases of both a rock-salt-mine and a brine pit. He ceased trading in both businesses in 1735.[42]

---

40 Antrobus, 1929, p. 42.
41 No doubt one of the many Eaton properties in the old Whitley Lordship, see Appendix 3.4.
42 Hughes, 1934, p. 393; P.R.O. T1, Vol. cxii, folio 13.

It seems likely that John Jeffreys bought Claridge's rock-salt-mine in 1735. According to the Poll Tax of 1660 the Jeffreys (Gefferie) family dominated the butchery business in Northwich with seven out of the 12 butchers in the town having that surname. None of them had sufficient property to be assessed at £5 p.a.[43] John Jeffreys was described as an innkeeper in Northwich in a deed of 1728. He married Mary, sister of Thomas Eaton of Parkmoss, a 74-acre freehold farm in Crowley (see Maps 1 and 2). In another deed of that property, dated 1738, he is given the more prestigious title of 'merchant',[44] which seems to confirm our supposition that he made a lot of money in rock-salt between 1735 and 1740 (p. 197). His descendants probably continued the business, because Thomas, and Samuel Jeffreys shipped salt down the Weaver until 1767.

Jonadab Vernon was a younger son of Jonathon Vernon of Gravestones, a 48-acre freehold farm in Aston by Budworth.[45] He was born in the 1670s and trained in some occupation with a Richard Arderne in Stockport. He inherited from his father a small farm in Pickmere, subject to paying his mother an annuity of £2 p.a. and portions of £50 each to his two sisters. We do not know when he moved to Northwich and bought the mine. He died in 1752 without any children of his own, so he left some £2,500 to his nephews and nieces and their children. His mine was in Twambrooks, a part of Witton not owned by the Venables family, and he also owned a barge for carrying his salt down the river. He seems to have taken John Mort, the husband of his niece, Ann, into partnership with him in the salt business, and later made him one of his executors. Vernon's will reveals that he only owned one third of the mine and a quarter of the barge at his death, so the Mort family by then probably owned the other parts. John Mort and Co. began shipping salt down the Weaver in 1752 and continued to do so until 1800.[46]

Jonadab Vernon was a great friend of the Barrow family. The two brothers Ralph and Edward Barrow, who owned salt businesses in 1732, owed their positions to their uncle, John Hewitt, who was probably born in the 1670s and started his career as a mercer in Northwich. Hewitt owned at least two small properties in his 20s, because he settled them in 1699, probably on his marriage to Elizabeth Livesey. We know that he was already involved in the salt industry by 1707, because he owed tax

43 Lawton, 1979, pp. 144–48.
44 WM Box 48; Foster, 1992, pp. 21, 56, 76–77. In 1757 he owned a 38-acre leasehold in Witton but we don't know when he bought it. DLT/D445/21.
45 He is mentioned in my *Four Cheshire Townships*, 1992, pp. 22–23. From his appearance in a number of deeds I thought he must have been a lawyer. No occupation was mentioned in his long will and inventory. It was only when I studied the salt industry records that I discovered the real source of his wealth. This is a good example of the difficulty of discovering the occupations of rich (let alone poor) people in the mid-eighteenth century.
46 WM Box 70; Foster, 1992, pp. 22–23; will of Jonathon, his father, 1693; his will, 1752.

on salt shipments in that year.[47] In 1718 he acquired at least two salt-works – the 'Dunkirk works', which he bought from Cheney Bostock and the 'New Works' that Ralph Broome had established in 1694, partly in Witton and partly in Leftwich. Hewitt bought this from the heirs of Robert Fowle, a London goldsmith who had loaned money to Broome secured on the property. Fowle had acquired the works when Broome went bankrupt in 1705. John Hewitt's partner in this investment was his brother-in-law Ralph Livesey, who had a business manufacturing horse collars in Newton by Daresbury[48] – a manor on the Arley estate until 1743. Ralph Livesey had a small freehold there between 1717 and 1744, if not longer.[49]

John Hewitt had no children of his own. It seems likely that his three Barrow nephews went to work in his various salt-works and when they got married, he settled a salt-works and other property on each of them. Of his two Hewitt nephews, one became a mercer in Altrincham, and the other an ironmonger in Knutsford. They too received properties from him either in settlements or in his will. In addition, by his will of 1736, he disposed of some £1,800 in cash, so it is clear that the salt industry had made him a rich man. However, these families had evidently had some capital earlier, because Ralph Barrow's eldest son, Hewitt Barrow, was left portraits of his Livesey great-grandfather, his grandfather Ralph Barrow, and his aunt Lydia Barrow. A Hewitt great-nephew was left portraits of John Hewitt's father as well as of John Hewitt and his wife, Elizabeth.

The wills of all three Barrow nephews have been preserved. John died in 1726 leaving only a daughter. Edward died in 1746 and settled his property on his only son, still a child. The third brother, Ralph, died in 1754. When he married in about 1725 he had settled the lands in Wincham and Pickmere, that he then owned, on his wife and their future children. By 1754 Ralph owned four salt-works: 1) in Leftwich, leased from George Venables-Vernon; 2) in Anderton, leased from Sir Edward Stanley; 3) in Newton by Middlewich; and 4) a rock-salt-pit in Twambrooks. He also had lands in Hale, Lancashire, and a house and gardens in Northwich, leased from George Venables-Vernon. Ralph had five sons and two daughters. The Leftwich works and the rock-salt-pit were left to his eldest son, John, who continued in the business and shipped salt down the Weaver until 1767. Ralph left a salt-works each to two younger sons and divided the rest of his lands between his four older sons. He also left £1,200 to each of his daughters and £800 to his youngest son, Jonadab.

---

47 P.R.O. T1 vi 12, f13.
48 Hughes, 1934, pp. 391–94. The Exchequer case on which Hughes based his account is now missing from the P.R.O. It should be in CHES 15/132, but has probably been misplaced. There may have been other works included in the purchase from the Fowle family.
49 WM Box 2, Appleton and Newton rentals.

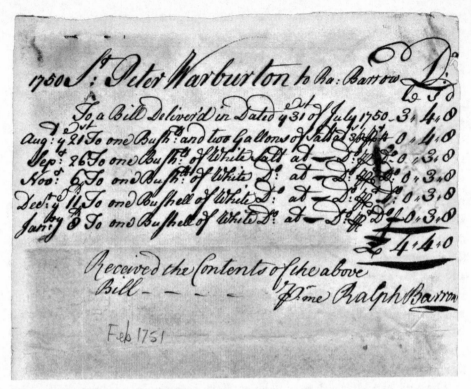

Figure 2. Ralph Barrow's invoice for salt supplied to Arley in 1750. We have seen that salt cost about 5d a bushel to produce and sold wholesale for 6d a bushel. This invoice shows that the Salt Tax raised the price to the retail consumer to 3s 8d a bushel.

We know that two of these five families who owned rock-salt-mines – Vernon and Hewitt – had owned small landed properties before they entered the salt trade. It is likely that the other three also had capital assets including a landed component – freehold, leasehold or mortgage. Claridge and Jeffreys married women from families with small freeholds, who would not normally have agreed to a wedding unless the wife was provided with a settlement secured on land. Antrobus came from a family with many small landed properties. The five men who acquired these rock-salt-mines had all started their careers in other businesses, which demonstrates that by the start of the eighteenth century there were a number of entrepreneurs among the new business community with sufficient capital to embark on substantial new enterprises when opportunity offered. All seem to have made substantial fortunes out of salt, so that, if they all divided their wealth as widely among their families as those whose wills have survived, there would have been a larger number of potential entrepreneurs in the next generation. At the same time, it seems that in four of these families a descendant continued in the business.

B) The five more prominent rock-salt-mine operators in the order in which they are described were: Venables-Vernon, Barons of Kinderton, Warburton of Winnington, Lyon of Warrington, Blackburne of Orford Hall, Warrington, and Patten of Bank Hall, Warrington. Two of these families were old landed gentry who had sunk mines in the 1690s and continued to operate them until 1748. The Venables part of the Venables-Vernon family had owned the manor of Witton for centuries. This included most of the area now known as the town of Northwich, as well as a large part of the salt-bearing land in the area. This manor was sold to the Leicesters of Tabley in 1758 see Pl. 18. The Warburtons of Winnington were descended from the Warburtons of Arley. In 1673 Sir George Warburton of Arley gave the manor of Winnington to Thomas, his eldest son by his second wife. The Warburtons of Winnington were active developers of their salt-bearing lands from the 1680s onwards.

The other three mines were owned by families who had already created important positions in the world by their success in business. Matthew Lyon acquired his rock-salt-mine from his uncle, Matthew Page, who died in 1727. In the sixteenth century the Page family had been tenants of the Warburton estate in Warrington, and in 1545 Christopher Page was assessed on £6 worth of goods.[50] In 1572 Geoffrey Page and his mother were paying £1 19s 3d p.a. rent for what was presumably a three-life leasehold of about 60 acres. As only the principal manors of the estate were included in the settlement made by Peter Warburton before his death in 1626 (see p. 26), his daughters were able to sell the outlying lands. The Page family probably bought their farm at this period in the same way that Thomas Patten III bought the lime-kiln fields in Warrington (see below, p. 209). William Page was one of the more affluent citizens in Warrington and paid 2s 6d tax in 1649 when Thomas Patten III paid three shillings (see Appendix 10.1). Matthew Page was post-master of Warrington from 1676 to 1695. This business was probably conducted from the Eagle and Child, described as his house in a legal dispute in 1696.[51] The parish registers of Warrington do not tell us how these people were related, but it seems likely they were all in one family. The 60-acre farm would have been worth over £600 by 1649 and so would have been likely to attract a tax charge in that year. The Matthew Page who entered the rock-salt trade in the 1690s was probably the son of the postmaster. In 1701 the Earl of Warrington's survey and rental of his 217

50 P.R.O. E179 130/132.
51 P.R.O. E134/8 Wm 3/East 35.

three-life leasehold tenants in Warrington shows Matthew Page, Jnr, at the Eagle and Child (see Pl. 40), which was valued at £30 p.a. while another Matthew Page, presumably senior, was in Sankey Street at the George, worth £60 p.a.[52] The rock-salt producer established a wharf on the Mersey to receive the rock-salt, nearly adjoining Bank Quay (see Pl. 21 and Map 9). He built a 'commodious salt-works' behind it to refine it with local coal which was a most profitable business until 1702. In 1704 he requested Customs' authorization to use the wharf for trade. This was not given because Thomas Patten's wharf at Bank Quay was regarded as 'large enough for the trade'. Page petitioned again, several times over the next ten years, but was always unsuccessful. After being accused of smuggling cargoes to Ireland and the Isle of Man he finally obtained Customs consent in 1716, because the trade had increased. Patten's wharf was then described as 'not sufficient for the trade' and was liable to flooding.[53] In Page's will his nephews, John and Matthew Lyon, were named as his residual legatees and executors and were therefore evidently his favourite relations. As well as the legacies to them, he left about a dozen pieces of property and more than £800 in cash which was distributed among nearly 20 relations.

Matthew Lyon inherited both the mine and the wharf, two investments which probably made him a rich man. The will suggests that the mine may have been bought from the Wilbraham family, because Matthew Lyon had to pay Ralph Wilbraham of London £100 p.a. for his life. In 1736 Matthew Lyon entered into an agreement with Thomas Patten and the undertakers of the Mersey and Irwell Navigation to manage the three quays at Warrington as one and to share the profits, as described more fully in the section on the Pattens below. The Lyon family's ancestral freeholds seem to have been in the parish of Prescot. Two of them paid tax there in 1525/6[54] and by 1573/4 there were well-off family members at Rainford and Eccleston in that parish.[55] Family members were no doubt in a wide range of occupations all over the world by the seventeenth century. For example, we earlier met William Lyon, Bishop of Cork and Ross, as a copyholder in Whitley in 1612.[56] Matthew Lyon died in 1760 and his property passed to his son, John, whom we will meet again on p. 257 as the purchaser, in 1772, of the Partington mills and Millbank House, which became his home.[57]

John Blackburne, 1693–1786, was brought up at Orford Hall (see Pl. 25), just

52 EGR 11/1/6.
53 Cal. of Treasury Books, Vol. xxx, part 2, pp. 482–83.
54 P.R.O E179/130/84.
55 P.R.O E179/131/258.
56 See Appendix 3.4.
57 Foster, 1992, pp. 11, 19, 20, etc. See also above p. 33.

14. *Packhorse Bridge.*
One of the surviving packhorse bridges over the Gowy at Hockenhull Platts near Tarvin.

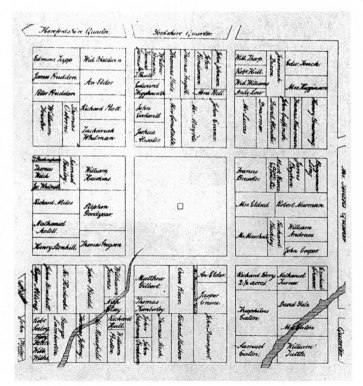

15. *New Haven.*
The map, made in 1641, shows the church in the centre of the town. The families from Cheshire were clustered together in the bottom right-hand corner round John Davenport, the minister, who was given a special passage to get to the church, Theophilus Eaton who had the largest plot in the town, David Yale, two other Eatons and Richard Malbon.

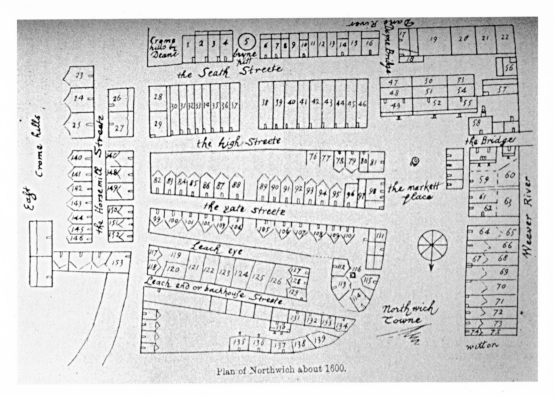

Plan of Northwich about 1600.

16. *Northwich town c. 1600.*

Notice the bridge over the River Weaver to the right and that over the Dane at the top. The whole town was very small and occupied only 13 acres. This map is upside down with south at the top.

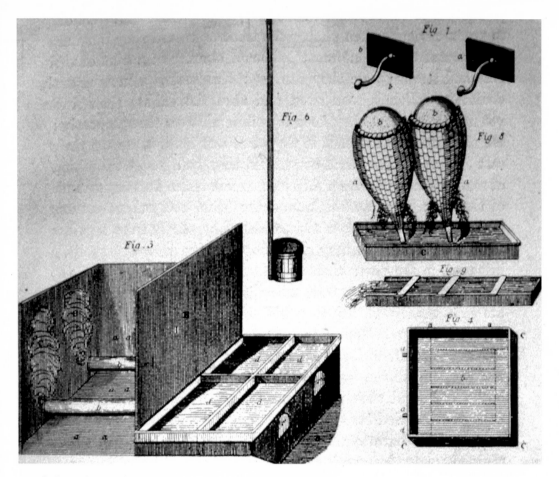

17. *Salt-making, 1669.*

William Jackson's engraving shows four iron pans each about four feet square on a brick hearth heated with coal. In the hot-room behind, the barrows, which had been filled with newly crystallized salt, dripped into a pan until the salt was hard and dry. There was little change before 1780 except that the pans grew larger. In the engraving:

Fig. 4 is a typical pan 6 inches deep.

Fig. 5 is the general layout with two tunnels *bb* carrying the smoke from the fires through the hot room to the flues, *cc*, in the rear wall.

Fig. 6 is the bucket with its long handle used to raise the brine from the tank or 'ship' below to fill the pans.

Fig. 7 are the 'loots' used to scrape the crystallizing salt together in the pans.

Fig. 8 are two barrows or baskets newly filled with salt *bb* dripping into a trough.

Fig. 9 is a gutter which they laid over from one pan to another to run the brine into the furthest pan.

18. *Witton in 1721.*

This detail from the Venables estate map shows the main salt-producing area. Observe the two bridges in the bottom left-hand corner leading into the open space which was the old town of Northwich. The map (Pl. 16), when turned upside down, will fit into this area with the old Northwich market leading into Witton Street, the main road of the town which is now all known as Northwich. The church, which still stands, is in the bottom right-hand corner. Philip Pritchard's salt-works was in Leftwich, probably just south of Barrons Croft, close to Seath Street in old Northwich. Just to the north are shown 'Mr Hewits Land', probably the site of the salt-works he bought in 1718 (see p. 203). In 1758, when a survey of the Venables-Vernon estate was made before the sale to Leicester, there were three salt-works. Mr Bridge was leasing one at Broynshaw at the junction of the River Weaver and Witton Brook. Mr Brassey apparently had two in the Meadows beside the Weaver, at the end of Witton Street, but one and perhaps both had recently fallen in. According to a map in Calvert, p. 203, Mr Blackburne's rock pit was in Marbury, west of Witton Brook and Mr Jeffreys' was north of the brook near Heywood.

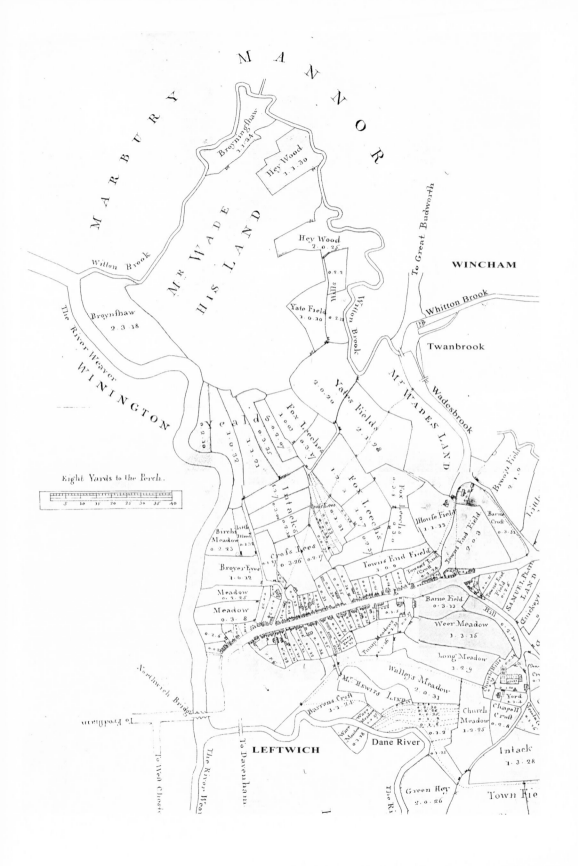

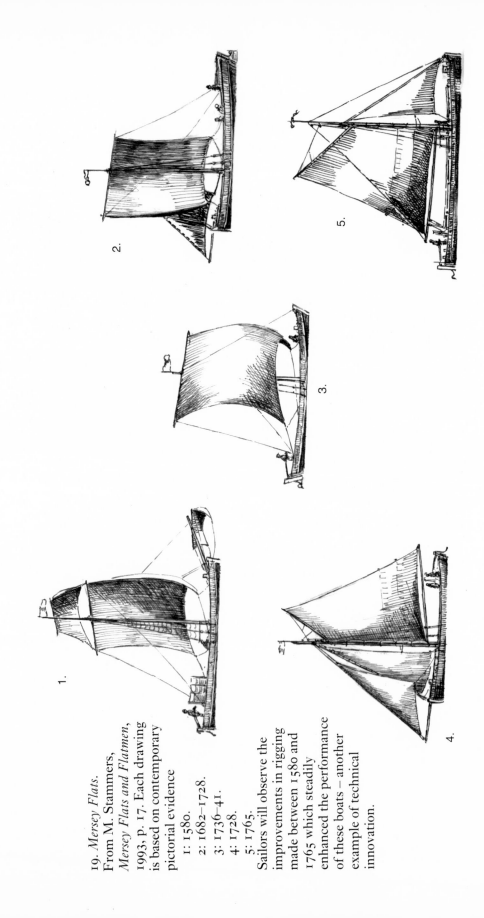

19. *Mersey Flats.*
From M. Stammers,
Mersey Flats and Flatmen,
1993, p. 17. Each drawing
is based on contemporary
pictorial evidence

   1: 1580.
   2: 1682–1728.
   3: 1736–41.
   4: 1728.
   5: 1765.

Sailors will observe the
improvements in rigging
made between 1580 and
1765 which steadily
enhanced the performance
of these boats – another
example of technical
innovation.

20. *Grafton Hall.*
Demolished in 1963, it had
much in common with
Gawthorpe Hall, Lancashire,
perhaps because both were
built by successful
Elizabethan lawyers. Grafton
was erected a few years later
than Gawthorpe, in 1613, for
an even more senior judge,
which perhaps explains why
it was a little larger. Sir Peter
Warburton's only daughter
and heiress married a Stanley
of Alderley and the house
remained with that family
into the twentieth century.

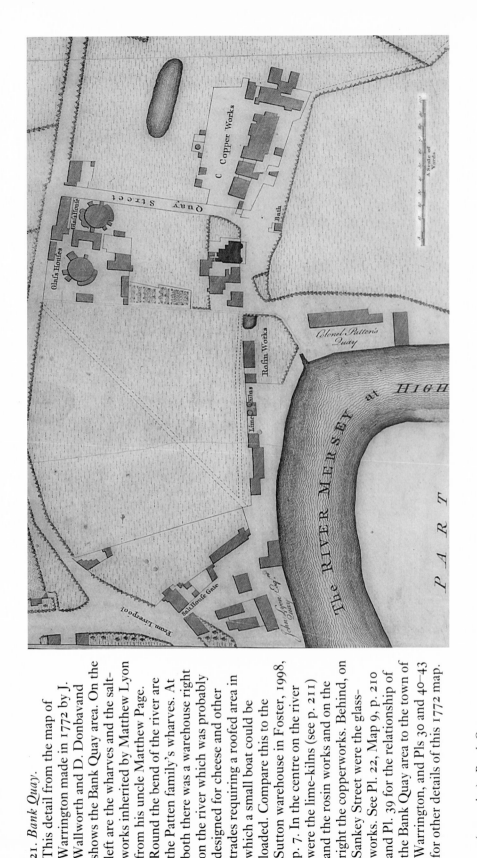

21. *Bank Quay.*
This detail from the map of Warrington made in 1772 by J. Wallworth and D. Donbavand shows the Bank Quay area. On the left are the wharves and the salt-works inherited by Matthew Lyon from his uncle Matthew Page. Round the bend of the river are the Patten family's wharves. At both there was a warehouse right on the river which was probably designed for cheese and other trades requiring a roofed area in which a small boat could be loaded. Compare this to the Sutton warehouse in Foster, 1998, p. 7. In the centre on the river were the lime-kilns (see p. 211) and the rosin works and on the right the copperworks. Behind, on Sankey Street were the glass-works. See Pl. 22, Map 9, p. 210 and Pl. 39 for the relationship of the Bank Quay area to the town of Warrington, and Pls 30 and 40–43 for other details of this 1772 map.

22 (opposite). *Bank Quay.*
This view, engraved from Donbavand's painting, shows on the left four 'flats' moored at Lyon's Quay and behind it the cone-shaped roofs of the glasshouses. Just to the right can be seen Bank Hall, home of the Pattens, with its colonnaded entrance and double staircase (see Pl. 29) and the town extending up the hill to the tower of Trinity Chapel at the top. On the right are seven flats moored at Patten's Quay with the copper works behind and to the left.

23. *Newton Hall (demolished 1967).*

A watercolour done by P. Egerton-Warburton in 1870. When Richard Blackburne bought the Hall from the Fairclough family in 1586 it may not have consisted of more than a single-storey, timbered hall similar to that shown in Pl. 11, as the Faircloughs' estate was probably not very different to that at Cogshall. Did Richard Blackburne decide to live on the coalfield at Newton because he had grown used to the luxury of coal fires and chimneys in London? Or did he invest in the rapidly growing coalfield? Whatever the reason there is no doubt that brick building seems to have expanded greatly in this area in the 1580s and 1590s. Coal-fired kilns burnt the bricks and the lime for mortar and the new multi-storey brickwork houses included hearths and chimneys suitable for coal fires (see Foster, 2002, pp. 45–48 for these changes at Smithills). So the Blackburnes seem to have kept the old Hall as the centre of their house, inserted a new first floor in it and built the two brick wings, and they may well have done it all before 1600. After their purchase of Orford Hall in 1638, this house became of less importance. Did they move to Orford because of its larger size or because of its proximity to the mercantile centre of Warrington?

Note: Rimmer (1852) has a drawing and a description of the house. He refers to an Ireland family diary of 1634 which is probably not relevant as the Blackburne and Ireland families only became connected in 1752. The windows and the diaper work shown here on the north wing, and described as plastered brickwork in the VCH, were probably a post-1852 restoration as they are different to Rimmer's drawing.

24. *Liverpool in 1725.*

This is the southern end of J. Chadwick's map. Blackburne's salt-house is number 52 with a narrow channel into the sea. The 'Pool' of 1705 (a marshy area fed by a small stream) was transformed into the Wet Dock (50) with the Customs House (55) at its head. At the entrance to the Wet Dock there was a small Dry Dock (49). See also pp. 327–28 for the building of this Dock and Pl. 49 for the 1728 Buck view of the area.

26 (opposite below). *John Blackburne (1693–1786) in 1743.*

Originally he had in his left hand a pineapple which he had grown (a rare feat at this time) but it was painted out and replaced by a sketch of the greenhouse which he had built. This seems to have had a sloping glass roof which would have been an innovation for horticulture at this time, as well as a triumph for the local glass industry.

25 (above). *Orford Hall c. 1820.*
This print shows the south
front as it was reconstructed in
1716 by Jonathon Blackburne.
The house remained substantially the same until it was
demolished in 1935. When
Jonathon's father Thomas
bought the house in 1638 it
was known as Tildesley Hall,
after the family who had built
it about 20 years earlier. It was
a large, three-storey, brick
building with its entrance in
the middle of a west front nine
bays wide. It was a gentry-style
house on its own in the
country and was a much larger
place than Newton Hall, so the
Blackburne family evidently
became richer at the beginning
as well as at the end of the
seventeenth century. (Wells,
1996.)

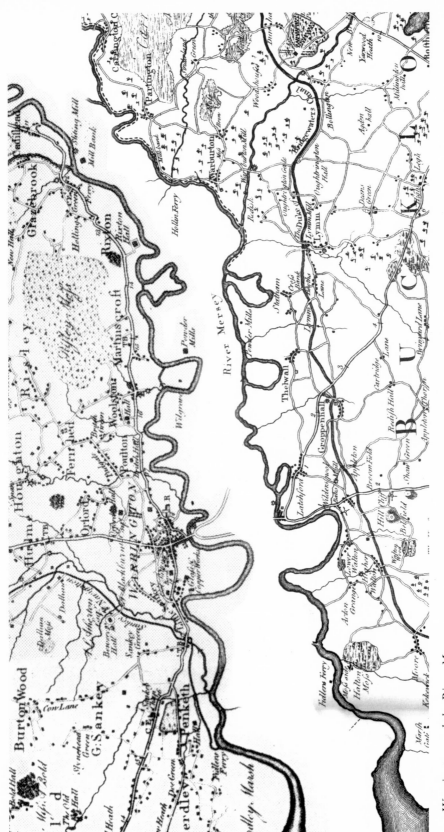

27. *Warrington and the River Mersey.*

Peter Burdett's map of Cheshire 1777 and William Yates' map of Lancashire 1786 were both drawn to a scale of one inch to the mile, but the surveys were not quite accurate enough for the maps to fit together – hence the gap. They show many places mentioned in the text, of which the most notable are perhaps the junctions of the Sankey Brook and the Navigation with the River Mersey, the gentlemen's seats, the industrial sites and the Bridgewater Canal.

29 (above). *Bank Hall.*
Now Warrington Town Hall, it was built by Thomas Patten in 1750 to the designs of James Gibbs, and described by Pevsner as 'the finest house of its date in South Lancashire'. Compare it with Tabley House, Pl. 3.

28 (left). *Thomas Patten VI of Bank Hall (1690–1772).*
A portrait by Hamlet Winstanley, 1737, of Patten as a typical English gentleman with grand furniture and a coat of arms. Compare the plain dark clothes in which the businessmen had themselves painted (here and Pl. 26) with the brilliance of the major gentry's outfits (Pls. 1, 4, 5 and 6).

30. *Bank Hall.*
This plan from the 1772 map shows that the house was set in extensive and fashionably designed gardens similar to those created at Arley Hall in the 1750s and 1760s (Foster, 1996, p. 261). Patten built a house and garden rivalling that of any old major gentry family, except it did not stand alone in the country: it was only 400 yards from Pattens Lane off Bridge Street where his family had lived for more that a century (see Pl. 40). Unlike many successful businessmen in London he did not leave town to become a country gentleman but stayed with his family and friends in Warrington. A number of successful Manchester businessmen built similar houses in Manchester in the eighteenth century (see Casson & Berry's map of 1741).

north of the old town of Warrington. He was descended from William, the elder of two brothers, who had made money in the Russian trade in Elizabethan times.[58] Both brothers had acquired 'estates' in Lancashire[59] – William lived at Thistleton in the Fylde and, in 1586, Richard, the younger brother, bought the property later known as Newton Hall (Pl. 23).[60] Thomas, William's grandson (1604–63), inherited from both brothers, bought the Orford estate and came to live with his family in Warrington. His second son, Jonathan (1646–1725), probably entered the salt business during the boom of the 1690s. He was a friend of Sir Thomas Johnson, Mayor of Liverpool in1695 and MP from 1700 to 1723. In 1701 Blackburne and Johnson together petitioned the Treasury about Customs' duties on salt. Jonathan Blackburne does not seem to have lived in Liverpool, although in 1705 he owned a salt refinery 'over the Pool' in that town. For the Land Tax of 1705 the buildings were valued at £95 2s 9d a year and the business profits at £150 p.a., making a total of £245 2s 9d p.a. In 1708 the valuation seems to have been raised to about £360 p.a.[61] This works had been built on agricultural land, presumably in the early 1690s, and both salt and coal could be brought in and out of the works by water (see Pl. 24). The tax assessments illustrate the great profitability of rock-salt refineries in their early years.[62] In 1702 Blackburne seems also to have been involved in refining rock-salt in Flintshire.[63] In 1709 he invested part of the profits of his business activities in the purchase of Grimsditch Hall in Lower Whitley[64] (see Map 3). It would seem that his elder brother Thomas had been destined to inherit the estate and become a landed gentleman. However Thomas died without issue, so Jonathan inherited Orford. Like his father, he seems to have hoped that his eldest son would inherit Orford, while the salt business would pass to his third son, John.

So John Blackburne (1693–1786), younger son of Jonathan, owned the refinery in Liverpool when the Salt Commissioner James Cardonnel inspected it in 1733. He also owned the rock-salt-mine that was a member of the cartel known as the Rock Company in the 1730s. For a second time in this family, the elder sons died without heirs, so that this John also inherited Orford (see Pls. 25 and 26). He had a large family including six sons, of whom the eldest married into the old major gentry. The management of the salt business again passed to the second son, known

58 Foster (1873) is the source of all the genealogy.
59 The word 'estate' described any size of landed property in the seventeenth and eighteenth centuries.
60 VCH, Lancs. Vol. 4, p. 134, note 27.
61 Peet, 1907, pp. 37, 95.
62 See Foster, 1992, pp. 50–55 for Land Tax and annual values.
63 Hughes, 1934, p. 237.
64 C.R.O., D5494, Box 15.

as John Blackburne, Jnr, who played a key role in the development of the salt trade in the middle of the eighteenth century. He and John Ashton, the owner of the Dungeon refinery, promoted the Sankey Navigation – the first canal built in England. They quickly provided much of the capital required for this large project in 1754, subscribing for most of the shares. This decisive act illustrates the important part played in technological developments by businessmen who were actually engaged in production. It was because they knew about the market for coal in the Mersey estuary that they had the courage to invest. They knew that coal would be brought into the estuary so cheaply by the canal that it would sell in a sufficient volume to make the canal profitable. They also had the vigour and technical competence to ensure that the canal was built quickly (see Maps 8 and 9 and Pl. 27).

Blackburne and Ashton were also the main enthusiasts for improving the Weaver to enable a fully-laden coal barge to sail all the way from St Helens to Northwich. They attended meetings with the Weaver Commissioners to press the case for improvement upon them. Much of the credit for making Cheshire salt the cheapest in the world is due to them.[65] Helped by the improvements to the Weaver Navigation the Sankey Canal soon became a profitable business. By 1772 the shareholders were said to be making 'near twenty percent' on their money.[66] John Blackburne, Jnr's important contribution to business in the area was recognized when he became Mayor of Liverpool in 1760. Meanwhile his elder brother, Thomas, had been fully accepted into major gentry circles and became High Sheriff of Lancashire in 1763. The Blackburne family, and the Pattens, the last family to be described here, are interesting examples of businessmen who also became landowners. I have not found, in my research, an example of a younger son of an old major gentry family establishing a successful business. However, these two families, and others who made money in business, were able to combine business careers and landowning in one family.

The Thomas Patten family[67] of Bank Hall and Bank Quay, Warrington, included some of the most active entrepreneurs in the area in the seventeenth and eighteenth centuries. An astonishing six generations built up the family fortune by running successful businesses, all of them living on the west side of Warrington. The family seems to have come originally from the township of Cuerdley, about four miles to the west. Four Pattens paid tax there in 1545.[68] Humphrey Patten paid 1d in Warrington in that year. The existence of a deed of 1653 in the Patten archives about

65 Hadfield, 1970, Vol. 1, pp. 43, 47
66 Ibid., p. 50.
67 Many families liked to keep their property in the possession of a son with the same Christian name as his father.
68 P.R.O. E179/130/132. Two paid 2d each on land, the other two paid 4d and 1d on goods.

the sale of a farm in Cuerdley 'lately in the occupation of Jane Patten, widow' strengthens this hypothesis.[69] Thomas Patten I is a shadowy figure, about whom we know only that he was the father of seven children in Warrington, the eldest being Thomas Patten II (1561–1639), who lived in Pattens Lane on the west side of Bridge Street, where he owned a three-life leasehold (see Pl. 40).[70]

The family fortune seems to have increased under his son, Thomas III (1595–1663) who was an important merchant in the town by 1652.[71] The main foundation of the family's future wealth seems also to have been acquired in this period. In 1653, Thomas bought from some of the daughters of Peter Warburton of Arley 2½ acres of land called Limekiln Fields which had originally been part of Warrington Heath. In 1659 he bought Bankfields and Dagger Acre from John Edgeworth for £500. These lands and Limekiln Fields appear to have been the site of what later came to be known as Bank Quay.[72] In a letter written in 1697 to Richard Norris,[73] Thomas Patten V (1662–1726) described how he cleared the Mersey estuary of fish weirs and made it navigable up to Bank Quay. This passage is well known,[74] but less famous is the Customs' Report which tells us that from '1678 port tidesmen [customs men] of Liverpool were sent daily to Bankfields to see the landing of coast goods as an experiment whether it was a convenient place for the despatch of the coasting trade'.[75] These tidesmen will have come from Sankey Bridge which was the 'Legal Quay' serving Warrington at this time (see Map 9). This appears to show that the Bank Quay (see Pl. 21) was beginning to take shape in the 1670s under Thomas IV (1634–84). A cheese warehouse was probably built at this Quay to facilitate the shipping of cheese to London (see Pl. 22).[76] In 1696 the Liverpool Surveyor of Customs reported that 'Mr. Patten has, at his own great charge, by clearing the river, paving the highway and building warehouses, made the Bank Key proper and large enough for the trade of the place'.[77]

In the letter to Richard Norris of 1697, quoted above, Thomas Patten also set out

69 W.P.L. MS 1259/1.
70 Foster, 1873, Vol. 1. The connection between the illustrious figures in the early part of this pedigree and the Pattens in Warrington is suspect. Humphrey Patten, the 1545 tax-payer, is said to have been the father of Thomas I.
71 P.R.O. E134/1652/3/HIL 14 lawsuit about a cargo of grain. See also a tax return in Appendix 10.1.
72 MS 1296/1–12. See pp. 26 and 205 above for Peter Warburton's daughters.
73 Liverpool merchant. Mayor 1700, MP 1708–10. Younger brother of Thomas of Speke, MP 1688–95. Heywood, 1846, p. xi–xx.
74 Liverpool R.O. 920 NOR 1/37, and printed in Hughes, 1934, pp. 254–55.
75 Cal Treas Books, Vol. x, Pt III, p. 1140.
76 Foster, 1998, p. 8.
77 Treasury Out Letters (Customs) XVI pp. 380–82.

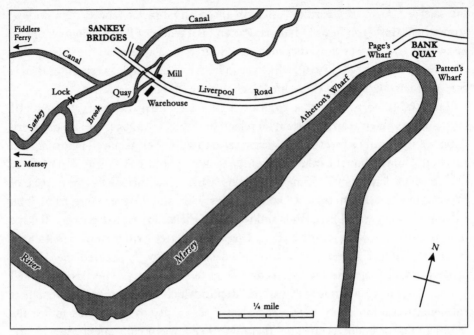

Map 9. Sankey Bridges and Bank Quay.

In the sixteenth and seventeenth centuries Sankey Bridge was the port of Warrington. Ships came up the Sankey Brook from the Mersey on the rising tide (see Pl. 27) to a wharf beside the bridge. The Customs man resident there had less than a mile to walk to get to Bank Quay in the 1670s and he would have walked past the Page's saltworks and wharf. This suggests that there was a political element in the refusal of the Customs authorities to make Page's wharf a 'legal quay'. After 1736, when the three wharfs in the Bank Quay area were managed as one wharf, they were no doubt able to exploit their monopoly position to raise prices. Other Warrington businessmen, like Bent and Woodcock (see p. 284–5), reacted to this by refurbishing the Sankey Bridge area for their own use. In 1754 the Sankey Navigation Act prevented the canal company making wharves in the Bridge area (see Geo II cap. 8 XLVII). When the Fiddlers Ferry extension (built in 1762) proved successful at avoiding delays caused by waiting for the tides, the canal seems to have been extended backwards to the Sankey Quay as shown in Yates' map of 1786 (Pl. 39).

his conviction that the Mersey was 'very capable of being made navigable' up to Manchester. An Act of 1721 (7 Geo I c15) established the Mersey and Irwell Navigation Company, but it took a long time to do anything. Locks and weirs enabling boats to reach Manchester were not built until the 1730–36 period and the Company was not profitable until the late 1740s. One reason for this was that there was not a sufficient depth of water in the river in summer. To try to improve the position, they raised the Woolston Lock (see Map 8 or Pl. 27) 10 or 11 inches in 1744. Even this was not enough to provide an adequate depth over the Hollin ferry/ford between Rixton and Warburton. They had to narrow the river with piles so as to allow the winter flood waters slowly to scour out the ford.[78] Administration of this Navigation was in the hands of a large group of Manchester businessmen determined to keep control of 'their' waterway.[79]

Thomas Patten VI (1690–1772) was probably displeased at his family's exclusion from this company and scornful of their incompetence in not creating a good waterway more quickly. This may have been one of the reasons why he was determined to control the Weaver Navigation himself. In the 1730s, there were three quays on the Mersey near Warrington – Patten's, Lyon's and Atherton's (see Map 9).[80] The Mersey and Irwell Navigation Company bought Atherton's quay and then in 1736 an arrangement was made that the Navigation would own half of each of the three quays and the Patten and Lyon families would own the other half. They would manage them jointly, sharing the profits, and would also be equal partners in the important business of burning limestone on the quays to make lime.[81]

Long before the Patten family had established their strong and profitable business in the docks and warehouses of Warrington, they had cemented their improved social position in the area. In December 1660, Thomas Patten IV married Mary, the daughter of John Leigh of Oughtrington in Lymm. The Leighs were old freeholders of about 450 acres.[82] The connections between this old landed family and the new businessmen were strengthened when Mary's niece, Elizabeth Leigh, married William Clayton, who became mayor of Liverpool in 1689 and one of its MPs. In 1686 Thomas Patten V married Margaret, the daughter of Jonathan Blackburne of Orford. So three of the leading families on the Mersey estuary were all closely related in marriages with each other and with older landed families. Despite this connection with landed estates, the 'new' families continued to divide their wealth among their children and launch their younger sons into their own occupations.

Thomas Patten VI, the builder of the Weaver Navigation, was one of the most dynamic businessmen of his family. Although his father was still alive, it was probably his idea to enter the copper and brass industry in about 1719, when he was 29 years old. There were two parts to this enterprise. He entered into a partnership

---

78 WM Box 23, folder 5, particularly item 9. See Foster, 2002, p. 219, for a fuller account.
79 See the Act for a list of them and Willan, 1933, pp. 59–61 for information about some of them.
80 Sir Richard Atherton of Atherton (d. 1696) inherited the Bewsey estate via Eleanor, heiress of Sir T. Ireland. See Pls. 27 and 39.
81 W.P.L. MS 1256.
82 They do not appear in the 1545 tax return because Lymm is one of the missing townships. They appear in the 1578 list of freeholders just after the major landowners. Irvine, 1901, p. 5; WM Box 27, Folder 2, item 3.

with William Wood to erect and operate a works to smelt copper at Bank Quay. William Wood, although infamous to Jonathan Swift for his copper halfpenny scheme, had extensive knowledge and investments in the copper industry. The works they built was to refine copper ore in order to produce copper and brass.[83] The second leg of the project was the founding of the Cheadle Brass Wire Company, also in 1719. Patten was an original shareholder and the company established a brass works at Cheadle, Staffordshire.[84] The copper and brass industry was to be an important area of the family's business for the rest of the eighteenth century.[85]

We do not know when the Pattens acquired their rock-salt-mine, but it was probably the work of Thomas Patten V in the 1690s. So when Thomas VI and his partners were engaged in trying to be appointed as undertakers of the Weaver Navigation in 1727–29, he and his brother were experienced businessmen with interests in wharves and warehouses, copper and brass manufacture, and general trade and transport as well as in the salt industry.

Thomas Eyre, another of the partners, does not seem to have been so experienced in salt and transport. However, he does seem to have been a major figure in the business world in the Stockport-Macclesfield area. His original business was in the linen trade (see Chapter 9 (iv) for a general description) but, by the mid–1720s, he was extending his interests more widely. In December 1726, he and Thomas Foxley of Manchester contracted with Peter Legh of Lyme to buy £2,400 worth of trees from Legh's estate in Dalton, Lancashire.[86] Whether through this or because they were both Governors of the King's School Macclesfield, he seems to have become friends with Peter Legh. After a meeting of the Governors in December 1727 when it had snowed heavily, Eyre offered Legh a bed for the night.[87] Earlier, in March 1727, Eyre had sought Peter Legh's help and advice about advancing his and Thomas Patten's scheme to build the Weaver Navigation.[88] Not content with his new investments in building the Weaver Navigation and setting up a new brine salt business with wharves, warehouses and barges beside the Navigation at Winsford, he also launched into the silk industry. The Lombe patent for 'throwing' organzine silk expired in 1732. In June of that year Eyre headed a partnership to build a new silk throwing mill in Stockport. Copied by one of Lombe's Italian managers from the works at Derby, this new plant was the first water-driven textile mill in the

83 W.P.L. MS 1258, D.N.B. for Wood.
84 Plant, 1881, p. 36; and Hamilton, 1926, p. 111 and later.
85 See also Harris, 1964, p. 13, etc; Barker, 1954, p. 75.
86 Greater Manchester R.O. E17/10/2.
87 C.R.O. DLT/C35 P. Legh's letter to Sir Francis Leicester.
88 DLT/C35.

Cheshire/Lancashire area.[89] Eyre's death in 1735 cut short a promising entrepreneurial career.

Whether Eyre and Patten were always partners in the Winsford works we do not know. Possibly they bought the existing Vernon/Vaudrey salt-works at Winsford in 1727–29 to minimize opposition to their proposals to build the Weaver Navigation,[90] as we can see (Appendix 7.10) that this works was not very profitable. Patten and Eyre may have been sufficiently far-sighted to see that the white salt trade was not the only business open to wharves and warehouses on the Navigation at Winsford. By 1730 the pottery industry had been developing in Burslem and neighbouring villages (now all part of Stoke-on-Trent) for nearly a century.[91] Coal came from north Staffordshire to boil the brine in Middlewich and Winsford and salt to glaze the pots would make a small part of the possible return loads. The pottery industry was experimenting with new materials which all had to be imported into Staffordshire. In the 1730s they were bringing white pipe clay (ball clay) from Teigmouth and Bideford in Devon and flintstones from the beaches of Sussex and Kent. The potters were also discovering that there were growing markets for their ceramics in London and other ports. It must have seemed likely to a good entrepreneur that the Weaver Navigation between Winsford and Frodsham would be the cheapest way to move these goods. The carriage of raw materials up the river and of finished goods downstream would enable barges to travel loaded in both directions. Warehouses at Winsford quay would be kept busy receiving and despatching goods. Perhaps Patten and Eyre had discovered all this in the late 1720s and it was one of the reasons why they became undertakers of the Navigation and bought land at Winsford. Perhaps they did not know and were just lucky. Anyway, these two parts of Patten's business at Winsford proved much the most profitable. From the figures in Appendix 7.10, we can extract the following:

	Average annual profit over 19 years *(1734–52) £ p.a.*
Saltworks	129
Barges	218
Wharves and warehouses	85
	432 p.a.

There were six barges in 1744 and eight in 1752. There was effectively no capital involved in the barge business, as the building of the barges and their repair was

89 Heginbotham, 1882, Vol. 2, p. 318; Lysons, 1806, p. 778; Arrowsmith, 1997, p. 98.
90 Willan, 1951, p. 27 and above, p. 194.
91 Shaw, 1829; Weatherill, 1971.

regarded as a running expense of the business. We do not know how much capital was invested in the other businesses, but if it was around £4,000 the investment had been yielding more than 10%. In 1744 Patten let it all to Isaac Wood for £200 p.a. Wood seems to have been living in Winsford in 1736 and to have been a close associate of Patten's at that time, so he may have been the manager of the Winsford operation all along.[92]

Developments in the Potteries were also important for another part of Patten's business. The largest importers of clay and flints were the firm of J. Watkins and W. Dumbell, both Warrington businessmen. John Watkins was probably the man of that name who was managing the copper works. William Dumbell was also a partner or manager in the copper company and in the company selling lime from the lime kilns on the Warrington wharves.[93] In 1745, the Warrington firm went into partnership with Weatherby and Crowther, who also brought clay from Devon. They were not Warrington people but were possibly based in Devon. Isaac Wood of Winsford also joined the partnership[94] and this three-way partnership seems to have dominated the growing trade for the next 30 years.[95]

Thomas Patten VI was the most vigorous entrepreneur of his remarkable family. His businesses were so successful that his family's wealth was greatly increased. He built Bank Hall, now Warrington Town Hall, in 1750 and bought the Winmarleigh estate in the Fylde, Lancashire, which provided the name of the barony to which his great-grandson was elevated in 1874. See Pls. 28, 29 and 30.

vi) The white salt producers of Northwich and the organization of the salt industry in the eighteenth century

The making of white salt from brine was carried on by people who were, in general, less wealthy than the rock-salt-mine owners. This may have been because it was more competitive and so less profitable. Nevertheless, the white salt-works owners were still substantial people. In the 1730s, only the Barrow family were involved in both parts of the industry. Benjamin Claridge, who also owned both types of salt-works, retired in 1735. The names of the other four families operating in Northwich were Bridge, Broome, Ford and Marshall. The Bridge family were leasing salt-

---

92 W.P.L. MS 1256/3.
93 Arley invoices 1750–68.
94 At the time of the merger in 1745, Watkins and Dumbell had 214.5 tons of Teignmouth clay at Winsford and 37.5 tons from Bideford. Weatherby and Crowther only had 48.5 tons from Teignmouth. The clay cost 8s 6d a ton in Devon, 12s to 14s a ton to transport to Warrington or Liverpool, and 5s 3d a ton to send on up to Winsford. It was probably often the return cargo of ships delivering salt to the fishing industry in Devon and Cornwall.
95 Willan, 1951, pp. 45–46.

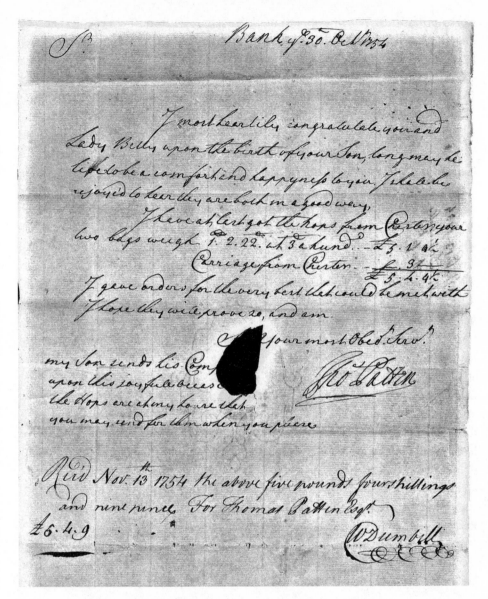

Figure 3. Thomas Patten writes from Bank Hall to congratulate Sir Peter and Lady Betty Warburton on the birth of their son in 1754. The letter ends with an invoice for hops. It illustrates the friendly relations that existed between the old and the new major gentry in Cheshire. It is worth noting that a letter blending social and business like this would have been most unusual a century later, when these major gentry families had no involvement with 'trade'.

works in both the Northwich and Middlewich areas from the Venables-Vernon estate. They were also renting Baron's Croft Pit jointly with the Barrow family (see Pl. 18 and Appendix 7.5). The 1736 lease to this property states that, as they were spending £1,000 on the quay and the buildings, their lease should run for 21 years after the death of the last of their three lives.[96] The family continued in the business until the nineteenth century, but their money was not all invested in the salt industry. Ralph Bridge briefly owned the Brownslane (Belmont) estate in Great Budworth, because he had to foreclose on the mortgage. He sold the estate to Sir George Warburton in 1739 for £2,120.[97]

The Broome family had a long history in the salt industry. In 1609, Joan Broome of Witton owned a 'piecing'[98] of an old salt-house, worth £3 5s 0d, together with wichwood valued at £4, and barrows worth 5s. John Broome was one of the partners who took over the Leftwich Eyes works in 1675 (see p. 191 above). Ralph Broome, who was running this works in 1692, seems for a while to have been one of the most active developers of the Northwich salt industry in the 1690s. Before 1695 he bought land on the borders of Witton and Leftwich and established the successful 'New Works' there. He also invested in another new works called 'Andertons' but unfortunately went bankrupt in 1705.[99] Ottiwell Broome was one of those who tried to resuscitate the Northwich Town Pit in 1691–93. He too failed in about 1705. John and Isaac Broome, who were operating salt-works in the 1730s, do not seem to have had descendants in the business. Thomas Marshall, whose descendants were to be one of the most successful dynasties of Northwich salt entrepreneurs in the nineteenth century, also had ancestors in the business as early as 1707.[100] Stephen Ford lived in old Northwich at Neilds Fold near the Crumhill. When he died in 1746 he divided his wealth between his three sons and one daughter. As well as his house and salt-works, he estimated that he had some £1,700. This was probably a typical amount of capital for a white salt manufacturing family to possess. His eldest son Richard seems to have closed the salt-works in about 1748.[101]

The workers in the 'new' salt industry that emerged in the middle of the seventeenth century fall into two groups – 'servants' and 'contractors'. The people who boiled the brine in the salt-works were servants – employees – earning a wage, but

96 C.R.O. DLT/D445.
97 WM Box 72.
98 A 'piecing' was the right to brine and days of salt-making as permitted by the Rulers for a period. This was probably about one year if £3 p.a. was the rent of a salt-house. See above p. 187. Will, 1609.
99 Hughes, 1934, pp. 391–93. DCH/J/112–3 for a 1690 letter from him to Bretland, the plaintiff in the 1733 lawsuit.
100 Iredale, 1965, pp. 59–82.
101 Calvert, 1915, p. 685.

most other workers were contractors. The people who brought coal to Leftwich Eyes were probably mostly small farmers using their own horses. They seem to have bought coal in Staffordshire and carried it to the works, where they were paid for it. The price paid seems to have been on the basis of quality and volume as no weights were recorded. So these men were trading in coal as well as providing transport services. The same system was in use at Arley Hall from 1749 to 1759.[102]

The chapmen who bought salt at Leftwich Eyes were contractors who were trading in salt as well as in transport services, selling the salt to customers at a higher price than they had paid for it. The farmers/carriers who carted the salt from Northwich to Frodsham were also contractors, asking a different price each time, depending on the state of the roads and how busy they were. According to the Arley papers, Peter Clare, the tenant of Burleyheyes Farm in Appleton, discovered sometime in the 1690s that a high price was being paid for carrying coal from Frodsham to Northwich and for returning with rock-salt. He therefore opened a new short-cut road from his farm so that he could take his two teams to Northwich.[103]

The development of the industry after 1660 clearly involved much construction work. Buildings, chimneys and ovens were erected. Brine pits and rock mine shafts were sunk. Quays, locks, bridges and roads were required. Such evidence as we have suggests that most of this work was done on contract, not by servants who were paid wages. On the Navigation, the masters of the barges seem to have been contractors. Out of their share of the freight charges they paid the crew and provided their food and many other minor items required to keep the boats in service (see Appendix 7.10).

This system of business organization operated as a nursery for businessmen. Large numbers of men learnt to work 'for their own account' – to make savings, to look for improved methods, to co-operate with others in order to achieve results and to make the best of their capital, however small. The transformation of the Northwich salt industry from an antiquated relic in the 1640s to the cheapest supplier in the world after 1760 was only achieved through the well directed and vigorous work of a large number of people. The style of organization adopted, which reflected the wide distribution of wealth, may have made a significant contribution.

The story of the transformation of the Northwich salt industry into the most competitive producer in the world is one example of the sort of developments that

102 See Foster, 2002, p. 211.
103 WM Box 23, folder 7. Savage and Knowles' evidence. See Foster, 1998, pp. 15, 46 for Peter Clare and Burley Heyes.

occurred in the area in the century before 1770. Other local industries achieved the same status. The watch, clock and tool industry on the south Lancashire coalfield north of Warrington was one; the cotton textile industry of Manchester was another. This chapter has also illustrated how the new business families took over from the old major gentry, first as the managers and then as the providers of capital. The major gentry were willing to invest in exploiting the minerals on their own estates but the capital for innovations in the technology was all found by businessmen. These businessmen built the rock-salt refineries, they owned the barges, they financed and built the canals. It was also important for the North-West that the major gentry and the businessmen were able to work together to get legislation passed for the canal and river improvements and that they were able to agree that the businessmen should finance and build them.

The waterways the saltworks owners built and helped to manage were, as a group, an important innovation in the North-West, and demonstrated that an interlocking network could join together an international port, coal-mines, salt-works, glass-works, sugar refineries, metal, ceramic and textile manufacturing businesses and make important economies for all of them. These waterways were the pioneers, and to some extent the models, for the much more famous canals built in the following 50 years, linked to the names of men like Brindley, Bridgewater and Wedgwood. A key feature of the business culture greatly assisted their construction – a reluctance to resort to the law-courts. The archives of both the Warburtons and the Leicesters show that disputes about property rights and customs of every kind were common, but they were virtually all resolved outside the legal system. Sometimes the parties met in the presence of an independent conciliator, sometimes inquiries were set up which collected and recorded evidence, thus clarifying the position and leading to agreement. On other occasions three independent gentlemen met for a day or two, listened to evidence and arguments and then pronounced a judgment. The lawsuit about the Hollin Ferry described in *Seven Households*[104] was almost the only court case in which Sir Peter Warburton (1708–74) was involved and it followed 29 years of negotiations. This conciliatory, non-legal feature of the business culture must have greatly speeded the invasion of the peaceful countryside by the ribbons of water with their tow-paths and strange, tough, boat people. The tendency to avoid the legal system also had an effect in speeding the innovative process. Before 1770, north-western manufacturers seem not to have bothered much with patents, so development proceeded without any documentation, a habit which perhaps explains, for example, why Samuel Crompton never thought of patenting his 'mule' spinning machine (see Appemdix 11.1 on p. 340 below).

104 Foster, 2002, p. 219.

The stories of the 13 families who operated salt-works in Northwich in the 1730s (excluding the two old major gentry families) have shown the slow build-up of capital in these families. I have been able to trace – more or less plausibly – the origins of two of them back to the 1545 Tax records. The ancestors of the Page family seem to have been on their 60-acre farm in Warrington at that time. Similarly, Thomas Patten I was either the son of Humphrey Patten of Warrington or a member of one of the four Patten families in nearby Cuerdley. In 1545 neither family probably owned wealth exceeding £20 or £30. The Blackburnes may well have been similarly placed at that period. The two brothers who made money in the Russian trade are likely to have been apprenticed to a City of London company, as were so many young northern men.[105] Their surname suggests that they came from a farm in the Ribble valley. While in London they participated in the Russian voyages that were organized there and then retired with their profits to the area in which they had been brought up. When their descendants came to live in Warrington they may have been richer than the Pages and Pattens who probably didn't have more than £1,000 each in the 1650s. However, from the facts recorded in this chapter it would seem likely that, by the 1730s, the main descendants of all three of these families had nearly £10,000 each, and perhaps a lot more.

Several examples have been given which show how the business families normally divided their wealth among all their children. It is important to ask how they did this while still increasing the capital in the possession of the eldest son of the family. The answer seems to lie in the high level of savings practised in these families. We have seen in my *Seven Households* how Thomas Jackson saved hundreds of pounds to provide portions for his sons and gave a £200 dowry with his daughter. Both the Shuttleworth and the Fell families had clearly saved in order to invest in land to build up their estates. In the same way we have seen in this chapter that Jonadab Vernon, John Hewitt and Ralph Barrow saved their profits from the salt trade so that they had a considerable amount of wealth to dispose of in their wills. A successful man seems to have been able to save enough to set up each of his younger sons in their careers and to pass the ancestral property or business to a selected son together with additional capital. The evidence from these salt families shows that one generation often succeeded another in the family business while other family members entered other enterprises, so that the business community and its capital resources were always expanding. This habit of saving seems to have been a major difference between the business families and the old major gentry who frequently spent all their incomes, and sometimes more than their incomes, so that they built up debts. They felt they had an important position in society which required them

---

105 See pp. 121–2 above.

to maintain a great house, wear grand clothes and travel about in an elaborately appointed coach drawn by fine horses.

Only two of the 13 families discussed in this chapter seem to have been non-conforming in religion – the Quaker, Benjamin Claridge and Jonadab Vernon, whose parents had themselves buried on the farm, apparently in order to avoid having a Church of England burial. However, these religious differences do not seem to have caused these two families to behave very differently to the other 11. Most of the young men born into the families seem to have become businessmen, although Thomas Patten III did have a younger brother who became a successful lawyer in Preston. However, towards the end of the eighteenth century, the richer families were being converted to gentry culture, and in this way they seem to differ from the Quaker family described in the next chapter.

Appendix 7.1. *Salt measures*

This is a difficult and uncertain area. To enable a cogent account of the trade to be presented this chapter is based on the following interpretations:

A *walme* was the volume contained in a *barrow*, which was the wicker basket in which salt was dried.[1] A barrow (or walme) contained approximately six pecks, as stated by John Ray in 1674. Four pecks made a bushel.

The *bushel* was an old Winchester bushel (of eight gallons containing 268 cubic inches).[2] A bushel of salt was normally thought to weigh 56 lbs. The statute of 1694, which first imposed a duty on salt, laid down that a Winchester bushel of eight gallons was to be the measure used, and the weight of white salt in a bushel was deemed to be 56 lbs.[3]

A walme theoretically weighed 1½ times this, or 84 lbs. In practice, salt was not densely packed in barrows, so they probably usually weighed about 75 lbs.

A *barrel* was 32 gallons or four bushels in the Irish Sea trade in the 1630s.[4] In the Leftwich Eyes salt-works accounts, 1671–75, three walmes normally made one barrel. At 56 lbs to a bushel, a barrel contained 224 lbs so that the three walmes that filled it each weighed 75 lbs or approximately one and a third bushels. In this section, walmes have been converted to bushels on the basis that a walme weighed 75 lbs and therefore contained 1.34 bushels. The reason that a barrow and a walme were made this size may have been that one loaded on each side of a horse made a convenient load. The carrier's normal horse load was 160 lbs.[5]

The Shuttleworths of Smithills[6] bought salt in Northwich in *crannocks* and walmes. A crannock was a 'quarter' or eight bushels,[7] and so contained six walmes. A Northwich salt 'law' forbade the sale of salt except by crannocks or walmes.[8] Salt delivered to Smithills in the 1590s was measured in *mettes* or Winchester bushels.[9]

1   Plot, 1682, p. 94.
2   John Ray in Calvert, 1915, p. 81.
3   5 William and Mary c7.
4   Hainsworth, 1977, p. 33.
5   See Foster, 2002, pp. 50–51.
6   See Foster, 2002, Ch. 1.
7   Rogers, 1882, Vol. 2, pp. 165–66.
8   DLT/A2/60/36.
9   See Foster, 2002, Appendix 1.3, Table F, p. 63.

Appendix 7.2. *The accounts of Mr Wilbraham's five salt-houses in Nantwich, 1629–30.*[1]

Reconstruction of the accounts for the period 12 May 1629 to 28 April 1630

	£	s	d	£	s	d
Sales				102	8	4
Costs:						
Wood for fuel	72	15	8			
Two women to 'wall' (i.e., produce) salt in 16 three-day 'kindlings' at 10s each, plus one extra day = 49 days	8	3	4			

Men to cleave the wood and make the furnace under the
leads 16 × 5s 6d + 1 day   4   9 10
Sundries (approximately)   12   3

           86   1   1

Gross Profits   16   17   3

Notes:
1 Nantwich salt-houses each had six leads. Calvert, 1915, pp. 813–27.
2 The five salt-houses, with a total of 30 leads, appear to have been entitled to make salt for 49 days. All the work appears to have been done in one building. There were 16 'kindlings', which each lasted three days, except one which lasted four days.
3 There is no allowance for depreciation of lead pans or buildings.
4 In 1630, he states that his wood only cost £60.

Appendix 7.3 *The prices paid for salt by the Shuttleworths at Smithills and the value of Northwich salt-houses from the Tabley papers.*

Year	Price per bushel	Annual value of one salt-house of four leads	Evidence	Reference DLT
1536		under £1	5 salt-houses and other property let for 22 years at £4 p.a.	A2/36, A2/26
1553		just over £1	3 salt-houses sold for £35	A2/25
1559		£1 10 0	2 salt-houses leased for one life at £3 p.a.	
1586–87	2s[1]	£3 6 8	Rental	5524/2/2
1588	2s	£4 10 0	Rental	5524/2/2
1589–91	2s	£5	Rental	5524/2/2
1592–93	1s 8d[2]	£5	Rental	5524/2/2
1596–99	1s 8d	£2 to £3	Rental	5524/2/2
1600		£3 10 0	Rental	5524/2/2
1607–11		£3 to £3 10 0	Rental	5524/2/2
1641		£2 16 8	Rental	B/84
1646		£2 8 10	Rental	5524/2/2
1648		£4 8 0	Rental	B/98
1651		£10 13 4	Iron pans at the cost of P. Leicester. The rent of £32 seems to have been for 12 leads, but might have been for 24.	B/98
1663–66		£3 to £4	£9 corrected to £12 for 12 leads	D44/6

Notes:
1. From 1586 to 1591, the Shuttleworths collected their salt in Northwich with their own packhorses

so there was no charge for transport.
2. From 1592 their salt was delivered by Mr Crofts and the price included the cost of delivery.
3. Salt apparently sold for 2s a bushel in Newcastle-upon-Tyne in 1635. Sir William Brereton reported that a chaldron of coal was three wainloads. A Newcastle chaldron was 53 cwt so a wainload was 17 2/3 cwt. He tells us a wainload of salt was worth £3 10s od. From this by calculation a bushel of salt was worth 2s. Hawkins, 1844, pp. 88–89.

Appendix 7.4. *The evidence for Philip Pritchard's saltworks in Leftwich*

In C.R.O. DCH/J/112-3 are the 1671–75 accounts of a saltworks at Leftwich Eyes owned by Thomas, Earl Rivers. Included with these papers is a document dated 22 February 1653, in which John, Earl Rivers (father of Thomas) and Philip Pritchard sell lands in Leftwich. This seems to link Pritchard to the Leftwich Eyes site in 1653. In a letter of 1692, Ralph Broome, who was by that time tenant of Rivers' Leftwich salt-works, stated that his brine supply was failing because of the rebuilding of the old Town Brine Pit. (We know from Tabley papers DLT/A2/53 and 58 that this happened in 1692.) This seems to place the Leftwich Eyes works near the old Northwich brine pit, and suggests that the sinking of a new pit in this area in 1651–53 could well have robbed the old Town Pit of much of its brine. The continuous operation of the Leftwich works would have produced salt much more cheaply than the intermittent working, characteristic of the old town salt-houses, and probably fatally undermined their profitability. The Town Pit had evidently been disused for a number of years when the scheme to rebuild it was floated in 1691 (DLT/A2/58). John, Earl Rivers, died in his Frodsham Castle in October 1654. His probate papers, taken out by a creditor, describe him as 'late a prisoner in the upper bench prison in Southwark'.[10] This suggests that the sale of a 20–21-year lease of his saltworks site in Leftwich to Philip Pritchard may have made an important contribution to his release from the debtors' jail. Philip Pritchard was a Captain in the army of Charles I,[11] and so may have served under John, Earl Rivers.

Appendix 7.5. *Some rents of Cheshire salt-works, 1664–1757.*

1. 26 Jan. 1664/5. C.J. and Robert Wright of Wich Malbank, (Nantwich), gents, took a 3 year lease of the great brine pit in Upper Dirtwich at £380 p.a. (DCH/C/932-34.)
2. 20 Jan. 1667/8. Robert Roe, gent, took a 3 year lease of the brine pit in Lower Dirtwich in Iscoyd (Flint) late in the tenure of Robt Wright at £220 p.a. (DCH/J/72.)
3. The same day he leased the Great Pit as in (1) above for 3 years @ £380.
4. 2 Nov. 1671. Richard Eddowes leased the Great Brine Pit in Upper Dirtwich late in the holding of Robt Roe for £310.
5. 8 May 1676. Robt Roe leased one moiety of the great brine pit in Upper Dirtwich for 4 years @ £100 for 1 year and £120 p.a. thereafter. (3,4,5 – DCH/J/72.)
6. In his Marriage Settlement of 17 June 1671 Peter Venables, Baron of Kinderton, put in Trust his saltworks in Kinderton (Middlewich) and Witton (Northwich), and on 1 Jan. 1674 he charged them with paying:

10 G.E.C. Peerage.
11 Adams, 191, p. 93.

a) £200 a year to his mother
b) a portion of £4,000 to his sister
c) his own debts, not exceeding £4,000 (DLT/D241/43).
But rents did not stay at these fancy levels.

1. From 1680–88 Robt Roe paid £35 p.a. for the Cholmondeleys' Dirtwich salt-works.
2. From 1688–94 Wm. Eddowes paid the same, £35 p.a. (DCH/1/57.)

After the excitements of the 1690s, rents declined again in the first half of the eighteenth century. The Cholmondeley half of Dirtwich let for £52 in 1706, £40 in 1716, £32 in 1727, and £22 in 1730 (DCH/J/72). In 1734, George Venables-Vernon let the Barons Croft pit in Witton to R. Bridge and R. and E. Barrow at £20 p.a. In 1757 the two other salt-pits in Witton, on the Venables-Vernon estate, were valued at £50 p.a. and £40 p.a., including their meadows (DLT/D445).

Appendix 7.6. *John Collins and Northwich salt producers, c. 1680.*

Collins' tables, which are represented by Calvert, 1915, p. 282, show Northwich producers as:

Salt-works owners	Pans	Bushels of salt made weekly
Earl Rivers (Thomas)	4	2,400
Baron of Kinderton (Venables)	4	2,400
Mr Brook (Henry)	6	3,342
Mr Marbury (William)	2	1,300
Town Works	7	2,772
Totals	23	12,214

Calvert adds the following table (using 56 lbs as 1 bushel):

	Weekly output
Northwich	305 tons
Middlewich	107 tons
Nantwich	105 tons
	517 tons

Annual Output: 26,927 tons

Collins was inaccurate. For example, we have seen reasons for believing the Town Pit in Northwich was disused in the 1680s. He was also overly optimistic. For example, at Lord Rivers' works the best production from one pan in a week was 386 bushels in March 1673. The best four weeks' production from four pans was 5,542 bushels in August 1674. The best annual production was 875 tons in 1674. See also Appendix 7.8 for later production figures for Northwich.

Appendix 7.7. *Salt shipments from Frodsham (Port of Liverpool), 1641–1773.*

I. Sample years, 1641–1716

Year (Christmas to Christmas)	Coastal White tons	Coastal Rock tons	Overseas White tons	Overseas Rock tons	Total tons
1641	1.5		10		11
1661	10				
1665	–		80 (approx.)		
1669	151		335		486
1673	308				
1674	261				
1678	179				
1679	296		400 (approx.)		696
1681	474		952		1,426
1686	460		1,093		1,553
1689	1,593		307		1,900
1693	4,643	498			5,141
1694	3,422	1,065	5,621	60	10,168
1695	2,880	1,992	6,518	122	11,512
1696 (to 28 May)	1,809	1,940	1,635		5,384
1704	176	3,906	6,496	2,126	12,704
1716	623	3,346	8,769	6,454	19,192

Source: P.R.O. Port Books E190.

II. Salt going down the Weaver to Frodsham, 1732–73

Year	White (tons)	Rock (tons)	Total (tons)
Sept. 1732–33	6,989	7,954	14,943
Sept. 1742–43	10,803	8,239	19,042
Sept. 1752–53	13,640	14,360	28,000
Apr. 1762–63	23,353	30,391	53,744
Apr. 1772–73	43,317	38,585	81,902

Source: Willan, 1951, pp. 39–40 and Appendix 5.

Notes on rock-salt:
1. In 1702 (1 Anne c21) rock-salt was not allowed to be refined except within 10 miles of the pit or at established works. This appears to have limited the spread of refineries up the east coast of England. Great Yarmouth appears to have been the most northerly.
2. Some rock-salt contained very little except salt. The Cardonnel survey, 1733, (P.R.O. T64/232) says that the refinery in Liverpool melted 1,120 bushels of rock-salt per month and produced 1,300 bushels of white salt. The weight of 1,120 bushels of rock at 65 lbs is exactly the same as 1,300 bushels of white salt at 56 lbs each.
1. A letter from the Salt Commissioners to the Treasury (P.R.O. T1/112 item 13) says that 12,971 bushels of rock salt despatched to Ireland in the year ending 1 September 1707 were only diminished to 12,899 bushels on receipt in Ireland. So the waste in transit was only 0.6%, not the 3.75% allowed in 5 Ann c29.

Appendix 7.8. *Production of salt in the Cheshire Wiches, 1630–96.*

1. *c.* 1630   We have seen above that the Wilbraham salt-houses in Nantwich produced about 8.3 tons each year in 1629–30. The old salt-houses numbered:

Nantwich	216
Middlewich	107
Northwich	113
Total	436

If 8.3 tons per year was an average of the output of these salt-houses, the total in 1630 may have been of the order of 3,600 tons.

2. 1694–96   The accounts of the Salt Commissioners allow one to break down the production as follows:[12]

Production and export of salt in the Cheshire wiches, 1694–96

	Production (tons p.a.)	Exports (tons p.a.)
Middlewich	5,402	1,978
Nantwich	1,232	–
Northwich	7,759	4,788
Wheelock	3,174	–
	17,567	6,766

The overseas Port Books of Liverpool provide a similar figure of 6,162 tons as an annual average of the exports in the 26 months of the Salt Commissioners' accounts (P.R.O. E190). Virtually all this was white salt and was shipped to Ireland. These figures show that over 60% of Northwich salt was exported and about 37% of Middlewich's. This is exactly what one would expect because Northwich was only eight or nine miles from the shipping at Frodsham, whereas Middlewich was four or five miles further away. Nantwich and Wheelock were still further away and so exported nothing. However, Wheelock was about four miles nearer the coal-pits and so probably had lower costs than Nantwich.

3. The coastal Port Books of Liverpool tell us:

Salt shipped coastwise 26 March 1694 – 17 May 1696

	Tons	
White	6,198	
Rock	4,804	
Total	11,002	divided by 26 × 12, to give annual average of 5,078 tons

It must be likely that all this salt was also made in Northwich and Middlewich, so it seems that out of the total annual production in these two towns of 13,161 tons (7,759 plus 5,402), 11,844 tons (6,766 plus 5,078) was shipped from Frodsham. So we can calculate:

12 P.R.O. E351/2866.

4. Cheshire salt distributed locally by road 1694–96

	Tons
Northwich and Middlewich (13,161 – 11,844)	1,317
Wheelock	3,174
Nantwich	1,232
Total	5,723

Due to the many distortions in the figures in these first two years of the salt tax, it may be wise to think of these local sales as being approximately 5,000 to 6,000 tons p.a.

Appendix 7.9. *Salt production in the major English centres, 1694–1730.*

	1694–96 tons p.a.	1704–05 tons p.a.	1714–15 tons p.a.	1729–30 tons p.a.
Cheshire	17,567	20,862	22,448	22,407
Tyneside	17,161	17,353	23,345	14,045
Lymington/Portsea	3,682	2,609	7,080	5,683
Droitwich	2,278	7,494	10,216	11,657

Source: P.R.O. E351 2866–2888.

Notes:
1. Production in the minor places is difficult to assess. It is unclear how the Salt Commissioners dealt with remelting of rock-salt, damaged salt, or foreign salt, for example. Production in the major centres was normally 85% to 90% of total national production.
2. These figures are calculated from the tax collected using a bushel as 56 lbs. As noted above on p. 193 a bushel of rock salt was originally deemed to be 120 lbs. This and various other distortions make these figures only approximately true.

Appendix 7.10. *Accounts of Thomas Patten and Company – Winsford, 1734–52.*

A. Account of Thomas Patten and Co.'s saltworks at Winsford for an average year in the eleven years 1734–44.

Sales	Tons	(£)	%	Price per bushel (d)
Exports	1,696	1,503	84	5.3
Coastal	136	134	7.5	5.9
Local land	150	150	8.5	6.0
Total sales	1,982	1,787	100	5.4

Costs				Cost per bushel (d)
Coal[13]		841	50	
Freight –				
Navigation tonnage @ 1s 3d/ton = 115				
Freight of boats @ 3s/ton = 275		390	24	
Wages–				
Making salt = 168				
Loading salt = 8		176	11	
Sundries and repairs		251	15	
Total costs		1,658	100	5.0
Gross Profit		129		

B. Thomas Patten and Co.'s accounts for operation of barges 1734–1752 (19 years)

	£
Gross freights received	19,977
less Master's share of freights £10,193	
Building and repair of barges £6,445 =	16,638
Gross operating profit	3,339
Value of eight barges in 1752	800
Gross profit of barge business	4,139
Average annual profit over 19 years	218

C. Thomas Patten and Co. accounts of wharf and warehouse

	Sales £	Cost £	Profit £
1734–44	612	15	597
1744–52	1,182	155	1,027
	1,794	170	1,624

Average annual profit over 19 years = £85

Source: J.R.U.M.L. Deansgate. Arley MSS Weaver Navigation.
Note. The business was Thomas Eyre and Co. till his death in 1735.

13 From Staffordshire. The price would have been about 12s a ton.

Appendix 7.11. *Principal owners and operators of salt-works who shipped salt down the Weaver Navigation, 1732–41*

A. Northwich area

White salt producers	Pans in 1733	Remarks
Barrow, Edward	3	1 rented of Mr Vernon of Witton
Barrow, Ralph	6	2 rented of Mr Vernon of Witton
(some Hewitt, John in 1734)		2 in lawsuit with Mr Bretland
		2 his own
Bridge, Ralph		Began in 1737, rented of Mr Vernon of Witton
Broome, John	2	Rented of Mary Brooke
Claridge, Benjamin	2	Rented from Mr Livesey (in lawsuit
(ended 1735)		with Mr Bretland)
Ford, Stephen	4	Rented of General Hugh Warburton, owner of Winnington Manor
Marshall, Thomas		began in 1735

Rock-salt mines		
Antrobus, James		his own
Barrow, Ralph		rented of Mr Blackburne
Blackburne, John		rented of Charles Leigh of Wincham
Claridge, Benjamin		rented of Hugh Wade – a new pit with 3 eyes (ended 1735)
Jeffreys, John		probably Claridge's pit (started 1735)
Lyon, Matthew		his own
Patten, Thomas		rented of Charles Leigh of Wincham
Venables-Vernon, George		owner of Witton manor
Vernon, Jonadab		rented of Walter Warburton, younger brother of General Hugh
Warburton, Mrs Anne		widowed mother of General Hugh

B. Winsford and Middlewich

White salt producers	Pans in 1733	Brine pits in 1733	Remarks
Boden, E	2	1	Leased from Mr Parker
Bridge, Ralph and Charles	2	1	Leased from G. Venables-Vernon
Ellison, Richard	2	1	Leased from brother
Kenyon, George	2	1	His own
Lowndes, Richard			

Parrott, James	3	1	Leased
Patten, Thomas			
(1732–35 Eyre &			
Company)	6	1	Their own
Puleston, Thomas			
and Ann	2	1	Their own
Seaman, William			
Walker, George			
Wilkinson, George			
and Peter	4	1	leased from G. Cholmondeley
Wrench, Thomas			
and ...?	3	2	Their own
Younge, Robert			

Notes:
1. The information on pans and brine pits and the ownership of salt-works comes from the 1733 Cardonnel Survey P.R.O. T64/232 and 233, reprinted in Hughes, 1934, p. 390.
2. This survey is combined with Weaver Navigation Papers in Cheshire R.O. and materials from LNW/1, LNW9/1, LNW9/2, LNW 17 to produce the list of owners and operators. See also Calvert, 1915, pp. 684–85.
3. Jonathon Blinston appears to have been connected with the Rock Co. in which many of the Rock proprietors were involved. Richard Brassey seems to have been connected with the Bridge family works. In 1758 he was leasing 83 acres and a brine salt-pit in Witton from Venables-Vernon, but on what terms is unknown. The brine pit sheath had recently fallen in. DLT/D445/2. Other people operated plants for short periods.

CHAPTER 8

A Quaker family group, 1650–1815: the Hough family and their connections in the Warrington area

i) Introduction

This chapter illustrates a different aspect of the emerging business community and, by focusing on a single family, it seeks to examine the culture of these business people more closely. The family chosen were Quakers – this is partly due to the excellence of this sect's records, but also because the Quakers were an important group among the Dissenters in the North-West – a fact that is demonstrated by their members' participation in both the salt and the sailcloth manufacturing industries.

Traditional European society was hierarchical, with kings, nobles and the gentry standing above the rest of society. Information derived from the 1545 tax return demonstrates that this dominance was originally economic as well as social. However, the 1660s tax returns show that, by this later period, there were many families with incomes as large as those of minor members of the old gentry. With this narrowing of the gap between the wealth of the major gentry and that of other members of society, it is not surprising that by the 1640s and 1650s groups had appeared in the business community who wished to see the old hierarchical society replaced by one in which all men treated each other as equals. The traditional hierarchical secular society had always been supported by a Church with a similar structure in which bishops dominated the lowly parish priests. However, in the 80 years from 1560 to 1640, the growing numbers of small businessmen, who were becoming freeholders in villages like those in the Whitley Lordship, developed a new spirit of independence. The new-found ability of young people to pursue a wide range of careers and the fact that many left the area to do so, increased their habits of self-reliance. These new ways of thinking were also imbibed by the people who became priests, like the members of the Eaton family who were vicars and rectors of parishes in our area.

Independent religious groups, like John Davenport's congregation in London, existed widely in England before the Civil War. They remained, however, within the framework of the Established Church. The War seems to have loosened these conventions encouraging new sects to grow up. Perhaps those who most challenged the existing way of life were the Quakers – the Society of Friends. Embedded in the

heart of their practices were forms of passive disobedience to the traditional hierarchical customs and structures of society. The major gentry like the Warburtons
and the Leicesters spent a high proportion of their income on display. Sir Peter
Leicester and his wife spent large sums in London on their clothes in the 1650s and
1660s and they had a coach, always a very expensive item. They rebuilt the façade
of their house and erected an elegant chapel beside it. Lady Betty Warburton went
shopping in Knutsford in her coach and walked the streets accompanied by her
liveried footman, complete with powdered wig and gold hat. It had been the custom
for a long time for other people to doff their hats when meeting these grandees and
to address the men as 'Your Honour'. Four practices of the Quakers were clear
affronts to these customs. They normally wore very plain clothing in sober hues, in
contrast to the glorious colours frequently adorning the gentry. They never wore
swords or carried any weapon, because they were a peaceful people opposed to
violence. They kept their hats on in every situation, refusing to doff them to
grandees, and they addressed everyone as 'thou'. Samuel Pepys described 'a pretty
Quaker woman' delivering a petition to the king. When he argued with her she
replied 'with these words "O King!" and thou'd him all along'.[1] It is not surprising
that many gentry saw Quakers as a threat to the established social order and that the
Cavalier Parliament quickly passed an Act against 'persons called Quakers'.[2]

  This behaviour may have been socially offensive, but it was not actionable at law.
However, the Quakers followed two other practices which did bring them into the
courts. One was directed against the Church and the other against the Law itself.
The doctrine that every person had within them an 'inner light', that allowed them
to commune directly with God, destroyed the role of priests as intermediaries
between God and man. Quakers referred to priests contemptuously as 'hirelings' –
no member of the Society of Friends was paid. If priests were unnecessary, it was
wrong to support them, so Quakers refused to pay tithes. For this they could be
imprisoned for debt and their goods distrained. Quakers suspected that courts, with
their elaborate procedures and fine distinctions, were places of deception. In particular, they felt an honest man could tell the truth without the need to swear an oath
that he was doing so. Swearing was condemned in the Bible, so they would not swear
oaths. Therefore, they could not swear an oath of allegiance which exposed them to
severe penalties for treason. In response to these attitudes towards the gentry, the
Church and the Law, several Acts of Parliament were passed which further
penalized Quakers and other Dissenters. With all these disadvantages and dangers,
it was surprising that so many people joined the Society of Friends. Many members

1   Latham, 1971, 11 January 1664.
2   13 Charles II c1.

were well-off people with freehold lands, for example, nine Quakers are listed in Appendix 3.4, Table B, as freeholders in the Whitley Lordship in 1662.

The persecution of the Quakers was hottest between 1660 and 1688. On Midsummer's Day 1677 Sir Peter Leicester, in his role as a Magistrate, enforced the Conventicle Act against a Quaker Meeting of about 200 people at William Gandy's house in Frandley. Margaret Fell was fined £20 for preaching at this meeting. Her fine was paid by the Meeting and they refused her offer to reimburse them.[3] After 1689 the Toleration Act and the Affirmation Act, permitting Quakers to affirm instead of swearing oaths, made life easier for them.[4] However, it was still an uncomfortable business being a young Quaker. Samuel Fothergill told Mary Chorley that 'Joshua Toft, being on a journey of Business when very young, soon after his convincement, was accosted by a person with much bad language and rough treatment for wearing his hat on and speaking in the singular Number which was matter of great trial to him'.[5] Such verbal abuse was not as bad as being incarcerated in a cold, damp castle with holes in the roof, the fate of a number of Quaker prisoners in the seventeenth century, who complained that their bedding was soaked every time it rained.

Among the Acts against non-conformity, the Test Act of 1673[6] barred Dissenters from entry to the occupations which employed many educated people, such as the civil service, the Church, the Law and the armed forces. Business and medicine were therefore the main careers open to young Quaker men. This led to the development of different attitudes towards business. Members of the Established Church who made a fortune in business often educated their children to enter the Church or the Law because these occupations had high social status. Dissenters were more inclined to build up their businesses so that their sons or other relations could follow them in an interesting and profitable career.

As Dissenters were unable to participate in important parts of life in this country, many chose to emigrate to the New World. There were no restrictions on that side of the Atlantic. The opportunity to establish a society in which all men and women were equal appealed strongly to many. In Pennsylvania and some other states they could practise their different styles of religion freely, although some congregations were hostile to members of other denominations. They could participate in government and help to administer the law. In this way, large parts of American society were created by Dissenters, who shaped the structure of these societies to conform

---

3 Penney, 1920, p. 461, n. 1.
4 Toleration Act 1689, 1 William and Mary c18; Affirmation Act 1697, 7, 8 W3 c34.
5 Friends Library, Toft MSS, Vol. 3, No. 5, letter 3.a. 1770.
6 25 Charles II c2.

with their image of a 'good' society. Quaker practices tended to improve and expedite trading by making it easier, quicker and safer. George Fox urged his supporters 'to deal justly, to speak the truth, and to owe no man anything but love'. If men followed these three precepts, it made trading over distances, between people who never met face to face, much easier. A Quaker in Warrington could rely on another Quaker merchant in London to send him good quality merchandise at a fair price. The London trader could trust that he would get paid. To go bankrupt was to risk being ejected from the Society of Friends.

These two strands of Quakerism made a powerful cocktail in the second half of the seventeenth century. The ability to trade confidently with other members of the Society because you knew that they would deal with you fairly and justly was reinforced by the feeling that members were all fighting to establish a more just, fairer and more equal world and equal for women as well as men. For those with the fortitude to withstand the derision of their neighbours at their unconventional behaviour and the physical and mental strength to resist the rigours of imprisonment, the excitement and the determination to persist and to win must have been stimulating. The Quakers of this time were a self-selected body of zealots who banded together to succeed in business so as to gain a way to a better world.

By the beginning of the eighteenth century, some part of this better world had been won. The only legal disadvantage to being a Friend was the regular distraint of small sums for non-payment of tithes. The Quaker style of honesty and integrity in business dealings was creating efficient enterprises that flourished and grew. This led to a steady increase in the size of the Quaker business network. Since they believed in the importance of business, they passed their businesses down in the family, if possible, or to other members of the Society. The close social group formed by members of a Meeting and their dedication to assisting each other was psychologically supportive for all members. The practice of discouraging young members from marrying outside the Society also created many family links between members. Moreover for outsiders who were pursuing trading occupations, there were advantages in becoming members of the Society. New members were recruited, like William Stout of Lancaster[7] and Thomas Watt, who will be described later. As the number and size of their enterprises increased and their capital grew, the Quakers became a powerful force in British and American business in the eighteenth century.[8]

---

7 Marshall, 1967. This has been known as a classic work for a long time. Many features of his career – the small family farm, the dedication to business, honesty and hard work, the build-up of his capital to £5,000 – are paralleled in the lives of Dissenters given in this book.

8 For a full account of Quakers, see Braithwaite, 1955 and 1961. Also Raistrick, 1950.

The Quakers were particularly important in the iron industry, as names that will appear in this chapter and in my *Seven Households* remind us. They operated in all parts of the industry, as primary producers in blast-furnaces and forges – the Fells of Swarthmoor, Abraham Darby, the Rawlinsons of Lancaster and Thomas Titley, in slitting mills – the Titley family and Alexander Chorley, to finished product manufacture and distribution – Joseph and Henry Fothergill, Alexander Chorley and Joseph and Benjamin Titley. The importance of business, and in particular metal-working, to the Quakers is illustrated by the fact that their principal Meeting in the Mersey basin was at Hardshaw on the St Helens coalfield. At the end of this chapter, there is a brief description of an Anglican kinsman of one of the Quakers, Richard Watt. In his working life, between 1751 and 1796, as a trader in the West Indies, he amassed a fortune as large as any commoner in England. Almost nothing is now known about him, but he is included as an example of how huge capital sums came into the hands of a few 'ordinary' people in the last half of the eighteenth century.

The relationship of the people described in this chapter is set out in three genealogical tables that follow this Introduction, detailing the Hough, Fothergill, and Chorley families. The men whose careers are described are in bold type in these tables. With the exception of one Quaker minister and one doctor of medicine, they were all businessmen. With one exception, one member of each of the married couples described was a descendant of Thomas and Ellin Hough of Sutton Weaver, Cheshire. Thomas Hough and Susanna Chorley had three sons and two daughters, but none of them had any children, so the Hough fortune was divided among many Fothergills and Chorleys. Mary Chorley, married to Thomas Watt, was one of these legatees. They are the only couple in which neither person was descended from Thomas and Ellin Hough. So all the people described form a family group. Moreover I have included in the analysis only those family members who had a connection with the Warrington area. Other members of the family group, like the four daughters of Joseph Fothergill who married men living elsewhere, have not been followed.

A feature of the social group to which all these people belonged was that they were geographically mobile. Whereas the families who lived in rural Cheshire before the Civil War often married into other neighbouring families, this pattern does not seem to have remained true after 1650. Margaret Hough married John Fothergill from Wensleydale, while the Woolrich family came from Staffordshire. Thomas Woolrich personified another typical characteristic: he crossed the Atlantic several times and worked for 20 years in the West Indies. Two of the other men also visited the New World: John and Samuel Fothergill went to preach there and spread the Quaker message; Dr. John Fothergill never crossed the ocean, but he had a large number of American friends and played an important part in the start of the Philadelphia Hospital. As a family group, it might be said that they were Anglo-Americans.

I have tried to trace the origins of the families in this group. The Houghs had been on a 36-acre farm in Sutton since 1539 and probably earlier. The Fothergills are traced to an even smaller holding in Wensleydale in 1605 (Appendix 8.1). The Barnes family had a 50-acre freehold in 1613. However, I have not succeeded in tracing the other families back beyond the middle of the seventeenth century. None of them appears to have been descended from old major gentry families, so it seems likely from the earlier analysis of the 1545 tax returns that they came from similar small farms.

This chapter, then, is about a family group who were mostly businessmen, traders and Dissenters, coming from small farms in the country, and having strong connections with the New World. Between 1773 and 1802 the capital accumulated by the Hough family, Dr John and Samuel Fothergill, and Thomas Woolrich was distributed to their Fothergill, Chorley and Woolrich nephews, nieces, and remoter relations. Over 60 young people entered on their adult lives with sums ranging from a few hundred to as much as £2,000. As individuals they had been brought up to rely on their own initiative in order to establish their way of life. As we shall see in the next chapter, there were plenty of other families like them in Warrington. There is a striking contrast between this society and that revealed by the tax return of 1545, when the community's wealth was concentrated in the hands of a few families. By 1800, the wealth of this society was fairly widely distributed. The late-eighteenth-century Dissenter families did not have enough capital to live simply on their rents and interest; they expected to use their money to help them make a living in business because, as Dissenters, most other careers were closed to them.

ii) Thomas Hough and Ellin Barnes
The Hough family had lived in the Warburtons' manor of Sutton Weaver from early in the sixteenth century. Appendix 3.1 shows them in 1539 paying a rent of £1 1s 8d p.a. as customary tenants for their farm of 36 acres. We have seen that such customary tenants later became three-life leaseholders. Like many of the families in Sutton, the Houghs stayed on their farm. Thomas Hough died in 1642, leaving four underage children. His friend and executor, John Hale, entered into a bond for £80 to administer the will truly, so we can estimate that the value of the chattels in the inventory was about £40, as these bonds were usually taken out for double the real debt. Thomas Hough had not been a rich man. His assets were similar to those of many of the leaseholders described in Chapter 4. The lease of the farm was probably worth about £100, so with his chattels of £40, his total wealth was around

Figure 4. The Hough family tree

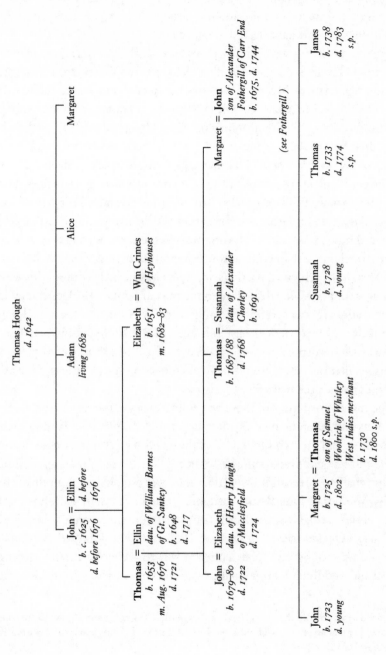

Sources: Quaker registers, wills. Lease in WM Box 4.

£140. In 1648, his eldest son, John, renewed the lease making his wife Ellin one of the 'lives'. John and Ellin probably became Quakers soon afterwards.[9] The births of their children, Elizabeth in 1651 and Thomas in 1653, were registered by the Quakers, but this may not have been done until later.

In 1676 John and Ellin's son Thomas Hough married Ellin Barnes, daughter of William Barnes of Great Sankey, the leading Quaker in the Warrington area, whose house was the place where Meetings were normally held and where the wedding took place. The Quaker marriage certificate survives, complete with a list of those attending the wedding.[10] Neither John nor Ellin Hough attended, so they had presumably died before then. Thomas's sister, Elizabeth, seems to have been the only member of his family present. This marriage seems to have established Thomas Hough in the centre of a prosperous business community which is worth examination. His father-in-law, William Barnes, had inherited freehold property of about 50 acres in Sankey from his father or grandfather.[11] By the time of his death in 1681, he had acquired much more land. The original freehold was left to his second son, and property worth more than twice as much was left to his elder son, William. His three daughters were each given portions of £200. How he had acquired this wealth we do not know, but as he lived so close to the port at Sankey Bridges it may well have been in trade. He was certainly farming, because his inventory includes £57 worth of grain and £35 worth of cheese. It is quite likely that he was involved in the cheese trade or the return cargoes of the cheese ships.[12] Eight other people at the wedding, also called Barnes, were probably members of one of at least four other Barnes families in the area who were Quakers.

One of the more prosperous of these was John Barnes, a mercer in Warrington. He had no sons and when he died in 1698, he left several pieces of land to each of his four daughters and their children. One of the daughters, Ann Davies of 'Rudlth' in Denbigh, and her children, had as a trustee Thomas Hough, an appointment which implies that, 20 years after his wedding, he was established as a reliable man in this circle. Another of John Barnes' daughters, Ellen, had married John Chorley (see Chorley family tree). He was a distiller in Warrington and a son of John Chorley of Rainhill, also a Quaker (see p. 243 below). Both Ellen and John were at Thomas Hough's wedding amongst a total gathering of 30. Almost all the surnames mentioned at the wedding recur in Quaker records. One curiosity in the document

9 There seems to be an error in the transcribing of these early Quaker registers where the parents of Elizabeth and Thomas are given as Thomas and Ellin of Sutton. The original lease in Sutton gives John and Ellin. WM Box 4.
10 Friends History Society, Vol. 4, 1907, pp. 38–39.
11 Rylands, 1880; I.P.M. Ralph Barnes 1613, pp. 267–68.
12 See below pp. 239–40.

is that Ellin, the bride, only 'marked' and did not sign. Apparently, even quite rich Quakers were not able to find anyone to teach their daughters in this period. When Ellin's future brother-in-law, Gilbert Thompson, set up his well-known school in Penketh, the position changed. He had been educated at Sedbergh School and his Penketh School drew Quaker pupils from a considerable distance and may even have become the most renowned Quaker school in England. Abraham Darby I, the famous iron-master of Coalbrookdale, Shropshire, the first person to use coke as fuel for blast furnaces, sent his three sons and daughter, Sarah, to the school in the 1720s. Springett Penn[13] was there in 1749–50 when Gilbert Thompson II was head-master. J. C. Lettsom, later the famous doctor (see p. 249 below), came to the school from the island of Tortola in the West Indies and left an account of school life there.[14]

How had Thomas Hough obtained acceptance in this circle, which seems consid-erably richer than the one his grandfather had belonged to in 1642? We don't know the answer, but it seems likely that Thomas or his father John had become more involved in trade. It is not easy to find evidence about occupations in this period and for many people, our only evidence is their will, if it survives, and yet we have seen that wills and inventories seldom provide information about occupations or trading. A cargo of grain might be bought, shipped and sold in a month. Even if a man died in the full tide of business, such transactions might only appear as debts owed or owing.

However, occasionally other records provide a glimpse of trading. One such example involves William Gandy of Frandley in Sevenoaks, Over Whitley. He was a similar figure to Thomas Hough's father-in-law, William Barnes, of Great Sankey; Quaker meetings were also held in his house. His family had had freehold property since 1612, when they had bought the Crown's rights in their 23-acre farm (see Appendix 4.4, Tables A and B). The William Gandy who died in 1624 had been quite a rich man. He had ready money of £107 as well as over £300 owing to him and another £300 in chattels. He had divided his property among his large family. His grandson, also William Gandy, no doubt inherited some capital as well as the enlarged ancestral farm in Frandley. He is likely to have been the William Gandy who shipped a cargo of 30 tons of cheese to London in the *Ann of Brighton* on 10 October 1670. This was the first year that cheese ships departed from the new warehouse in Sutton Weaver beside Frodsham.[15] Gandy does not seem to have sent another cargo in his own name, but he may have been one of the partners in 'Thomas

13 Great-grandson of the founder of Pennsylvania.
14 Raistrick, 1953, pp. 48–49; Shrewsbury R.O. MSS 6001/329; *The Pennsylvania Magazine* (1915), Vol. 39, pp. 247–48; Abraham, 1933, pp. 18–19. The cost of schooling and boarding was about £15 p.a. See also D.N.B. for Darby and Lettsom.
15 P.R.O. E190/1338/15; Foster, 1998, pp. 7–8.

Hall and Partners' who shipped cheese to London from Sutton throughout the 1670s.[16] Thomas Hall of Brownslane Farm in Great Budworth[17] was a relation as well as a neighbour. Gandy's mother, Mary, was a daughter of a Thomas Hall of Brownslane. In Gandy's will of 1684, Thomas Hall was described as his friend and he was appointed as executor and one of the trustees for Gandy's grandchildren.

Thomas Hall did not die until early 1689. His inventory showed that he was a substantial dairy farmer with 22 cows, together valued at £59, and 1.85 tons of cheese worth £37. His whole inventory totalled £493. Unusually, included in it was his 'one sixth part of a vessel called *Elizabeth and Judith* with one sixth part of the stock in her'. This ship appears in my *Cheshire Cheese*.[18] This evidence supports the view that the shipper of cheese up to 1680 was indeed Thomas Hall of Brownslane and that he maintained his interest in the trade until he died. It also shows that substantial freeholders, living up to 10 miles from the Mersey estuary, were among those engaged in the cheese trade to London in the 1670s and 1680s.

Many business people engaged in this trade. William, George and Thomas Patten all sent cargoes, and so did Thomas Lyon of Windle – to name some people from trading families whom we have examined. Indeed, coastal trading became part of the business of quite a large number of people in the North-West in the second half of the seventeenth century. In my *Seven Households*, Sarah Fell and Thomas Lower were described despatching ships loaded with grain in 1674 to Liverpool and Bristol, (Ch. 4, p. 134). The Port Books show that, in the first six months of 1681, 43 different people despatched coastal cargoes from the Port of Liverpool, not including the 12 merchants who sent cheese to London.[19] The difficulty is to identify who they were. The Port of Liverpool had three 'legal quays', where customs officers attended – Frodsham/Sutton, Sankey Bridges for Warrington and Liverpool itself. The first two could only accommodate ships of up to about 80 tons (probably less in 1680). All coastal trading seems to have been carried out in smaller vessels than this in the seventeenth century. Liverpool had deeper water that could be used by ocean-going ships, which were sometimes between 200 and 300 tons. The traders who despatched cargoes may have lived anywhere within, say, 15 miles of one of these quays. The squire of Crosby Hall, eight miles north of Liverpool, took an eighth share in a voyage to Barbados in 1666.[20]

Against this background, it seems quite likely that both John Hough and his son,

16 P.R.O. E190/1339/21, 1674 – 226 tons; E190/1340/2, 1675 – 70 tons; E190/1341/2, 1677 – 28 tons; E190/1341/14, 1679 – 212 tons; E190/1342/12, 1680 – 52 tons.
17 See pp. 79–80 and 125 for his ancestors.
18 Foster, 1998, p. 94.
19 P.R.O. E 190/1343/11.
20 Wadsworth, 1931, pp. 45–46.

Thomas, engaged in some trading. From their strategic location in Sutton beside the Frodsham Bridge, they could easily have been involved in conveying cheese from their area to the ships leaving the Port of Chester for London in the period 1652 to 1669. Sir George Warburton's decision in 1669–70 to build a cheese warehouse and a quay in Sutton is likely to have been based on detailed information about the cheese trade, provided by his tenants. The Houghs could have been among those providing it. Another possibility is that they were involved in the activities of Richard Hough and Company, whose ship the *Ann of London*, in November 1682, brought to Liverpool a mixed cargo, including copperas, redwood, fustic and other dyestuffs, groceries, paper and cotton.[21] A third possibility is that they might have been involved in the salt trade. Bringing salt from Northwich, warehousing it in Sutton or Frodsham, and despatching it by sea were all new activities in the 1660s and 1670s. A fourth possibility was that they may have built and operated the first lime kiln on the quay at Sutton, built in 1670 by Sir George Warburton. Whatever the truth, there is no doubt Thomas Hough accumulated wealth. By 1694 he owned two more leaseholds in Sutton, bringing his farm up to 73 acres.[22] When he died in 1721, he had the three leaseholds in Sutton, 15 acres of freehold in Newton-by-Daresbury and two parcels of land in Runcorn. As well as the contents of his house and farm, he was owed at least £1,400, lent on mortgages and bonds. With these material possessions, he was certainly the equal of many of his Quaker friends and relations.

Thomas's eldest son, John, inherited the ancestral farm and the seven acres known as 'Muskets', together with the freehold land which was probably let. His younger son, also Thomas, got the other farm (Wrights) and all the horses and cattle. They each got £600 of the money owed to their father. John must already have been in poor health, because all the land was put in trust for Thomas or grandchildren. Indeed John survived his father by only nine months. He left his wife Elizabeth £200 in cash and the leasehold farm in Sutton called Higginsons for her life.[23] She was the daughter of Henry Hough of Macclesfield who was probably a cousin. They had no children and she died in 1724, so the three farms in Sutton[24] and the freeholds all reverted to the younger brother, Thomas, who therefore inherited from his father and brother capital assets worth at least £2,000.

21 Copperas is a sulphate of copper, iron or zinc. Jeremy Hough brought a similar cargo in October 1683.
22 WM Boxes 4 and 5. The 1694 rental is the first to survive after one of 1628. 'Muskets', 7 acres was acquired before 1685. 'Wrights', 30-acre farm might have been bought by the Houghs any time after 1657, when there is a lease to the Wrights.
23 John's father had bought this farm of 28 acres for him in 1712.
24 The ancestral farm, Muskets and Higginsons.

iii) John Fothergill and Margaret Hough

As well as their two sons, Thomas and Ellin Hough had a daughter called Margaret. In 1709 she married John Fothergill, the owner of Carr End (Pl. 31), a 200-acre farm overlooking Semerwater near Bainbridge in Wensleydale, North Yorkshire (see Map 4). His grandfather had built the house there in 1667. Like the Shuttleworths of Gawthorpe and the farmers in Over Whitley, most of the inhabitants of Wensleydale, on the south side of the river Ure, had been customary tenants of the Crown. A detailed survey of 1605 shows 753 families of them occupying 11,256 acres of enclosed land and having rights to 5,884 'pasture gates', which probably gave access to at least another 11,000 acres of hill country.[25] In 1663 these customary tenants confirmed their title as freeholders. In 1605 the Fothergill family's farm had been only 10 acres and one pasture gate,[26] but they had acquired more land before 1663. As the eldest son, John, inherited the Carr End farm on the death of his father, Alexander, in 1695. The annual market value of the land would have been of the order of £50 to £100 p.a., so the Fothergill family, including widows and younger children, would have had a significant unearned income and the property would have been worth £1,000 to £2,000.[27]

George Fox, the founder of the Society of Friends, had visited Wensleydale in 1652. As it was an area with many small copyhold/freehold farms, his message had been enthusiastically received. The Fothergills had evidently been among those who joined the Society. Less than a mile from Carr End, at the north end of Semerwater in Countersett was the house belonging to Richard Robinson where the local Quaker Meetings were held.[28] John Fothergill's grandfather, who died in 1684, had been an active Friend and the early death of John's father, Alexander, had been brought about by his imprisonment in York for not paying tithes. John was to follow in the tradition which they had established. The Quakers had a system of travelling preachers whose appearances gave heart and new vigour to the members of local meetings. It also kept the people in the movement in touch with each other. It spread information around the country, not only about the faith, but also about business. Aged 21, John Fothergill became one of these preachers or ministers and made several tours in England, Scotland and Ireland. In 1706, he went to America to visit Friends in Maryland and other colonies on the mainland, before going on to Barbados, Antigua and Jamaica.[29] He must have met Margaret Hough on one of

25 Willan, 1941, pp. 82–150.
26 See Appendix 8.1 for a fuller discussion of this Wensleydale example.
27 A surveyor commenting on the 1605 survey (above) probably in the 1630s estimated the value of the best meadow at 16s an acre and the 'pasture gates' at 6s 8d each (Willan, 1941, p. 149).
28 Hall, 1989.
29 Crosfield, 1843, p. 9. This in turn was based on 'An Account of the Life and Travels of John Fothergill', London, 1753.

Figure 5. The Fothergill family tree

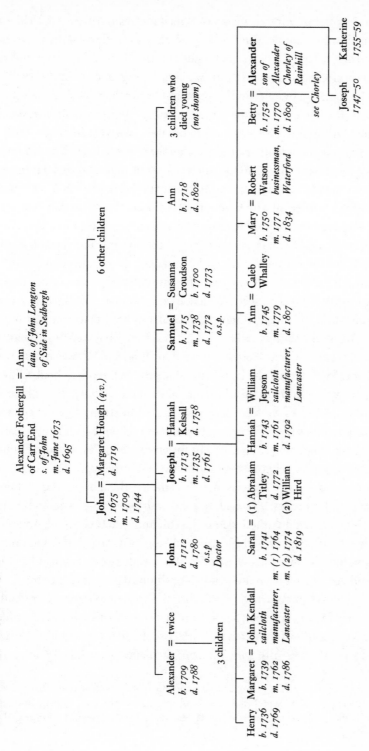

Source: Abbreviated from Fothergill genealogy in *Corner & Booth*, 1971, p. 508.

his visits to Cheshire before 1706, as he wrote her a letter from America in February 1707. He returned to England in March 1708 and they were married the next year. They lived together at Carr End and had eight children before Margaret and the last baby died soon after each other in 1719, her eighth pregnancy in ten years. This was unusual. The common practice in Cheshire and Lancashire seems to have been for mothers to feed their children for a year or more. This normally prevented pregnancy so that children were born at approximately two-year intervals. Only if a child died very young did a mother produce another within a year. The old major gentry families were the exception to this rule as they put their children out to wet-nurses. Had these 'gentry' customs spread to the small freeholders in Yorkshire?

Margaret left John Fothergill with seven small children. After less than two years on his own, he was overcome with the desire to return to his vocation of preaching and travelling. He decided to make another tour of the Friends in America. Before he left for Virginia in the spring of 1721, John arranged for other members of the family to look after his children. He was away for more than three years and during this time at least three of his sons seem to have lived mainly at Marshgate Farm in Sutton with their uncle, Thomas Hough, who seems to have taken on part of the role abandoned by their natural father.[30] The children first went to school in Frodsham, then in 1724 Thomas Hough arranged for John and Samuel to stay with a Quaker family in Brigflatts so John could attend nearby Sedbergh School. Gilbert Thompson, their cousin and the headmaster of Penketh School, had probably recommended this move. As we have seen Sedbergh had strong Quaker connections and was only 20 miles from Carr End. It was also a school which taught Latin, a good knowledge of which was a requirement for entrance to a university. Samuel probably attended a Quaker school where Latin was less important. The children's education was assisted by the legacies which came to them from their Hough relations. Their grandfather left £60 each to John and Joseph, and £20 each to the other children. Their uncle John left £20 to Joseph and £10 each to the others. It seems likely that their uncle Thomas provided not only board and lodging at Marshgate Farm, but also anything else he felt they needed as if they had been his own children and, as we have seen, he was in a position to provide for them.

Alexander, the eldest son, returned to look after the house and farm at Carr End.[31] His father remarried in 1727 and soon handed the farm over to his son and continued his work as a travelling minister. When in Yorkshire, he lived in Nidderdale, near his second wife's family. His fifth son, William, died aged 12, while Thomas, the

---

30 Ibid., p. 12; Corner, 1971, p. 5. These two books contain much of the information presented here about Margaret Hough's children and their descendants. Marshgate Farm was originally 'Wrights'.

31 See his diary and other documents transcribed by M. Hartley and others, North Yorkshire C.R.O. Pub. No. 37, 1985.

second son, only survived to the age of 22, but the other three sons all lived full lives.

iv) Dr. John Fothergill

John left Sedbergh in 1728 to be apprenticed to an apothecary in Bradford. From there he went to Edinburgh's medical school in 1734, gaining his degree in 1736. From Edinburgh he went up to London to get clinical experience in St Thomas's Hospital, and in 1740 he set up in practice on his own. By the late 1750s, he had become one of the most distinguished physicians of his day. It has been suggested that his earnings in his busiest years reached between £7,000 and £10,000 p.a. In 1774 Lord North, the Prime Minister, suggested that he should be one of George III's doctors, but the King thought that his membership of the Society of Friends made that inappropriate.[32] In 1743 he was appointed by the Friends' Yearly London Meeting to be their correspondent with the Philadelphia Yearly Meeting and from this developed friendships with many American Quakers. He played an important role in the foundation of the Philadelphia Hospital and its School of Medicine. Amongst his patients was Benjamin Franklin who later became a friend.

At this period plants were the source of most medicines, so John Fothergill carried his scientific approach into horticulture. He created a great garden on 30 acres at Upton in Essex, including a 260-foot long hothouse and his American friends sent him many plants. His name is remembered by gardeners today in the genus, *fothergilla*, a small American shrub introduced into England at this time. The stream of distinguished people who visited his house in Harpur Street, near the British Museum, astonished his niece Betty when she stayed with him from October 1769 to May 1770.[33] John Fothergill never married and in his mature years, his unmarried sister Ann came to live with him. Two years before he died, as an act of remembrance for his own education, he helped to found Ackworth School in Yorkshire for Quakers 'not in affluence'. In his will in 1780 he left further money to the school as well as more than £9,000 to his various nephews and nieces and their children. In short, John became and has remained a famous figure. His two brothers lived rather humbler lives in Warrington.

v) Joseph Fothergill and Hannah Kelsall

Joseph became an ironmonger in Warrington with a shop in Horsemarket Street in 1745; by 1762 he had moved to Sankey Street (see Pls. 40 and 41). His shops seem to have sold the usual items, such as iron, tools, locks, hinges, screws, sash cord and

---

32 Corner, 1971, pp. 16–17.
33 Betty Fothergill's Diary 1769-, Friends Library, MS Box 4/8, p. 65.

pitch, (see Fig. 6). Many of these things will have been made in workshops on the coalfield to the north. He described the business in a letter of 1748 as 'finding work and wages for 140 families'.[34] If workmen in manufacturing workshops normally earned about £15 p.a., this implies that the sales of his shop were around £2,000 a year. In 1745 he insured his household goods and stock for £500.[35] In 1735, aged 22, Joseph married Hannah Kelsall, daughter of another Warrington Quaker businessman, and produced a large family. Their nine children were born between 1736 and 1755 at approximately two-year intervals. Joseph died in 1761 aged 48, his will showing that he had been a reasonably successful businessman. He estimated his total assets at £1,800. He left £200 to each of his six daughters and another £200 was to be used to repay a loan from Thomas Hough. It is possible that it was this loan which had helped him to set up in business a quarter of a century earlier. Only one of his two sons survived to adult life. Henry, the eldest child, worked in the business which he continued to run after his father's death. He was left £400 in his father's will but must have been given part of the business earlier, because he insured his stock for £1,000 in 1762.[36] Sadly, he died, unmarried, in 1769, aged only 33.

vi) Samuel Fothergill and Susanna Crewdson

Samuel also became a businessman. He trained with Henry Arderne, a Quaker shopkeeper in Stockport. After a time he rebelled against the strict discipline of apprenticeship and got into trouble with his Quaker friends and relations for drinking and keeping bad company. He returned to Sutton to be with Thomas Hough and his brother Joseph. There he met Susanna, the daughter of another Warrington businessman, William Crewdson (Croudson). She was a Quaker minister and under her influence he too became a minister. They set up a shop together in Warrington and they married in 1738 when he was 23 and she was 38. They had no children but they shared both the ministry and the shop, which seems to have started as a linen-draper. In 1748 Samuel insured his goods and stock for £200 so his was a smaller business than that of his brother. He also insured his house in Horsemarket for £100 and a house opposite, which he had just built, was insured for another £100.[37]

Samuel travelled as a Minister in the 1730s and 1740s.[38] In 1754 he made a tour of the Friends in America which seems to have widened the scope of his business.

34 Corner, 1971, p. 8.
35 Guildhall Library, London, MS 11936; Sun Policy 104650.
36 Guildhall. Sun policy 189340.
37 Guildhall. Sun policy 111107.
38 Friends Library, John Kelsall. Account of Friends who visited Dolobran. MSS S185. Crosfield, 1843, pp. 31–34, 72, 86, 115.

Figure 6. Joseph Fothergill's invoice to Sir Peter Warburton for 1754. These invoices tell us a lot about the way of life as well as about the goods on sale and their prices. Seven different Arley people had collected goods – the steward, the groom and the cooper, and three men known by name in the shop as well as one who was just a man. This bill was paid 15 months after the end of 1754 as the prices included the provision of credit (like modern credit cards). The bill was paid by Wm Sumner, the tenant of Cowhouse Farm, on one of his carting trips for the estate.

While he was in America in 1755, Susanna supplied the Pembertons of Philadelphia with linens.[39] The Pembertons, originally from Wigan, were one of the leading Quaker business families in Philadelphia and they had been Samuel's hosts when he arrived in 1754. In 1757, Samuel imported 'a large cargo of wheat and flour from Maryland'.[40] In 1758 he supplied tea to Arley Hall (see Fig. 7). After this period, his business was described as a grocer while his fame as a preacher seems to have grown greatly. The records he left of his ministry provided the materials for George Crosfield's biography of him.

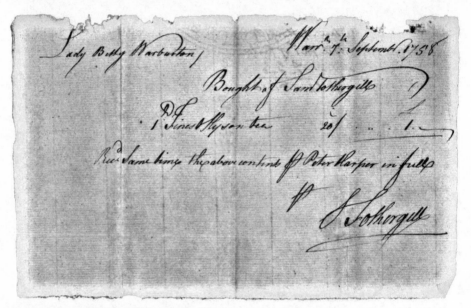

Figure 7. Samuel Fothergill's invoice for tea at £1 per lb in 1758.

Among the duties this fame brought Samuel was the guardianship of various children. In about 1758, Abraham and Thomas Hutton Rawlinson of Lancaster asked him to become one of the guardians of John Coakley Lettsom. This boy had been born in 1744 on a tiny island near Tortola in the Virgin Islands. His Quaker parents had sent him to the Rawlinson family in Lancaster to be educated when he was only six years old. Aged 14 he was transferred to Gilbert Thompson's school at Penketh. After being apprenticed to an apothecary in Settle for five years, he went down to St Thomas's Hospital in London where he met Dr John Fothergill. He later became the doctor's biographer and was his successor in his London practice.[41] In the 1760s, two other children from Tortola, Isaac and Josiah Pickering, came to

39 Friends Library, Portfolio 21, letter 146.
40 Friends Library, Portfolio 22/17.
41 See D.N.B. for his many activities.

Warrington to live with Samuel and Susanna and to be educated at Penketh. Their father John Pickering was a friend and partner of Thomas Woolrich, whom we will meet shortly. Samuel Fothergill died in 1772 and, after providing generously for the poor of Warrington and for his widow, he left everything to his nieces – Joseph's children although he seems to have been rather less well off than his eldest brother. His 'good friend' and executor was Thomas Woolrich, the husband of Thomas Hough's only daughter, Margaret.

vii) Thomas Hough and Susannah Chorley

Before describing Margaret Hough's marriage to John Fothergill and their children we had left Thomas Hough in 1722 having just inherited all the families' property in the Sutton area from his father and brother. Thomas continued in the prosperity that his father had enjoyed, but unfortunately we know almost nothing of his trading activities. It could be that his loan to Joseph Fothergill and another to James Maddocks (below pp. 258–9) indicate that one of his activities was providing seed capital to new or expanding Quaker-run businesses. He steadily acquired more freehold property and when he died in 1768 he owned three freehold farms containing a total of at least 270 acres, as well as his 100 acres of leasehold in Sutton. Their capital value will have been more than £6,000 and his rental income will have exceeded £200 p.a.

In the 1750s Thomas Hough became a friend of Sir Peter Warburton, 4th Baronet, of Arley. In 1752 they co-operated together in a series of property transactions in Crowley. The purpose of these deals was to allow each of them to create dairy farms out of smaller holdings. They each then let the farms that they had acquired to tenants.[42] Thomas became a commissioner of the Weaver Navigation and a member of the management committee. He assisted this committee by making regular inspections and reports on the progress of the works from 1758 to 1760. Thomas Gorst, a well-known lawyer in the area, objected to Thomas Hough's appointment because he was one of Sir Peter's tenants. Sir Peter successfully defended Hough on the grounds that he was a gentleman with freehold property worth £400 p.a.[43]

In 1720 Thomas, aged 32, had married Susannah, daughter of Alexander Chorley of Rainhill. Before 1651, an earlier Alexander Chorley had inherited, through his mother Elizabeth Ley, half the manor of Rainhill,[44] a township on the road from Widnes to Prescot. The family had become Quakers in the 1650s. Alexander's brother John was a distiller who married Ellen Barnes. John and Ellen were present

---

42 WM Boxes 56 and 58.
43 Willan, 1951, pp. 58, 68, 72, 171–72. My figures above may be too conservative.
44 VCH Lancashire, 1907, Vol. 3, p. 369.

Figure 8. The Chorley family tree.

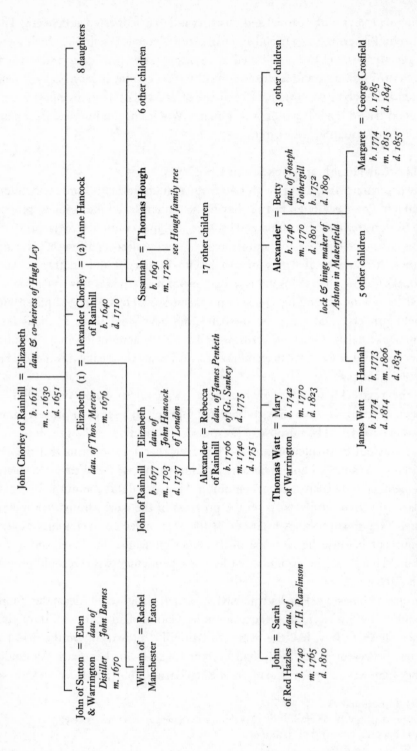

Sources: abreviated from Chorley genealogy in J. Foster, 1873. Additional material from Quaker Registers.

at the wedding in 1675 of Thomas Hough and Ellin Barnes. There was nothing surprising, therefore, in Susannah deciding to marry Thomas Hough in 1720. The Rainhill estate seems to have had gross rents of about £375 p.a. in 1710 when Susannah's father Alexander died.[45] The main estate was left to John, the eldest son, but complex provisions in the will seem to have been designed to provide £200 each for younger children. In this way the Chorley children were in a similar financial position to the children of other leading Quaker families. Thomas and Susannah had five children, of whom two died young. The two surviving sons died in their early 40s, apparently without marrying. The third child, Margaret, the wife of Thomas Woolrich, survived her brothers, dying at the age of 77 in 1802.

viii) Thomas Woolrich and Margaret Hough

The Woolrich family came from Staffordshire, a county with large numbers of small businessmen in the seventeenth century. Humphrey Woolrich was an early Quaker enthusiast who was persecuted for preaching in Stafford in 1656.[46] There were coal- and iron-mines in the north of the county as well as the growing pottery industry while, in the south, the Black Country was one of the principal iron-working areas in England. These industries created a substantial amount of trading and the Woolrich family was probably involved in this trade. Thomas Woolrich, who died in Congleton in 1719, had a number of properties in the Stone area on the main road from Warrington to London via Birmingham or Coventry. Thomas Woolrich of Shallowford, near Stone, and Sarah Cossinett of Pardshaw in Cumberland were both Quakers when they married in 1682. They lived in or near Leek in Staffordshire while they brought up their family of seven children. Two of their sons were probably trading into the Mersey estuary area when they met their future wives. John Woolrich married Elizabeth Wallsworth of Norley in 1722 and in 1724 Samuel married Elizabeth Towers, a member of the Frandley Meeting in Whitley. Both the ladies seem to have been heiresses, because the two Woolrich brothers went to live on their wives' farms.

Thomas Woolrich, the subject of this section, was born in 1730 on the Towers family farm in Over Whitley, the second son of Samuel and Elizabeth.[47] In March 1753 he obtained a Certificate from the Frandley Meeting held in Newton-by-Daresbury that he was 'a young man of orderly conversation intending to settle in

---

45 Will filed under 1734 lists Candlemas rents at £187. If rents were paid twice a year, £375 would have been the annual figure.
46 VCH Staffordshire, Vol. 6, p. 251.
47 He was probably born on one of the two large farms he owned there when he died in 1800. C.R.O. Will of T. Woolrich; D5494 Land Tax Return of Whitley in 1785.

Tortola', and departed for that small Virgin island in the West Indies.[48] We do not know why he chose Tortola although several Quakers traded with the Virgin Islands. Thomas Woolrich may have been apprenticed to one of them since he intended to be a trader not a planter. This business involved buying the sugar and cotton grown on the island and despatching it to England or North America. The return cargoes were goods required by the islanders, bought in England or America and retailed in Tortola. For this last operation, Thomas formed a partnership with James Rawleigh and John Pickering, the leading Quaker businessman on the island.[49] Thomas Woolrich spent 20 years in the West Indies, during this time making two trips to America and three to England. He also visited Barbados, Antigua and St Kitts.[50] From 1761 he was part-owner of several ships trading between Tortola, America and Liverpool. These ships were owned by groups of Quakers who probably also provided some of the cargo.[51]

A short digression on the trading position may be helpful. The West Indies were in a pivotal position in the eighteenth-century Atlantic trading system. Their principal product was sugar for which the demand in England was continually increasing. Imports of sugar into England were worth £667,000 in 1700. By 1770 they were nearly four times larger at over £2.4 million. Sugar was the largest category of imports into England, in 1770 representing nearly 20%.[52] At the prices the English were willing to pay, growing sugar in the British West Indian islands was extremely profitable especially since they were the only suppliers of sugar to Great Britain. The incentive for the British settlers to try and grow more sugar was so large that it drove the whole trading system in the Atlantic area.

The greatest problem for the settlers was obtaining a supply of workers, since growing and harvesting sugar cane was unpleasant, labour-intensive work which Europeans were not willing to do in the tropical climate of the Caribbean. The English adopted the practice of their predecessors, the Spanish and Portuguese, and bought workers, as slaves, in West Africa. The goods most sought after by the African chiefs who sold the slaves were textiles, and providing suitable cloth for these customers had a major impact on the English textile industry.[53] The slave

---

48 Jenkins, 1923, p. 81.
49 Ibid., p. 83.
50 Ibid., p. 79.
51 Liverpool Plantation Registers 1744–73. The ships were: *Planter* 1761, *Hillary* 1762, *Isaac* 1763, *Peggy and Ann* 1773. His partners included Thomas Cragg (not a Quaker), William Fish, Richard Hillary, George Nibbs, John Pickering of Tortola, Abraham and Henry Rawlinson, John Scott and Abraham Zeugers (see note 14, p. 269).
52 Schumpeter, 1960, Tables IV, VI.
53 See pp. 276–8 below.

trade developed into a large business. Jamaica was the largest of the British islands, its area greater than that of all the other islands put together. When it was captured from the Spaniards in 1655, it had a total population of about 3,000 people.[54] By 1728 the population had grown to 7,600 Europeans and 74,000 slaves and by 1767 the numbers had increased yet again to 17,000 Europeans and 167,000 slaves.[55] In 1787 there were estimated to be about half a million people in the British West Indies – 64,000 Europeans and 437,000 slaves.[56]

In the seventeenth century, the West Indian planters grew most of their own food and built their houses with wood from their own forests. However, when they discovered that sugar production was so profitable, they tried to concentrate all their labour on this. Consequently, they began to buy more and more of their food from Maryland and Pennsylvania, and from the colonies further north they bought the timber for their houses and the staves to make their sugar and rum barrels.[57] The West Indies became the main market for the exports of these colonies in North America. With the money earned by these exports, the colonies were able to increase greatly their purchases of British manufactures. British exports to countries on the Atlantic – Ireland, West Africa, the West Indies and North America – increased 6.4 times between 1700 and 1770. This was in striking contrast to the position in Europe where exports to Spain and Portugal only approximately doubled in this period, while exports to Holland and Germany increased by only 6%.[58]

Thomas Woolrich evidently acquired a reputation as a wise and reliable merchant, because in 1767 it was proposed to appoint him a member of the Council for East Florida.[59] He seems to have continued in the same business when he returned to Warrington. In 1778, he petitioned to export military stores to Canada.[60] In 1790–91, he was thought sufficiently distinguished to be asked to give evidence to the House of Commons about the abolition of the slave trade.[61] We do not know the place or the date of Thomas's marriage to Margaret Hough and, sadly, they had no children. Part of the Hough fortune had been left to Fothergill and Chorley

---

54 Bridges, 1828, Vol. 1, pp. 179–80 (reprinted 1968).
55 Ibid., Vol. 2, p. 14.
56 B.L. Add MSS 12435.
57 Renny, 1807, pp. 236–38 for some statistics.
58 Schumpeter, 1960, Table V. The figures are:

	1701–05 (£,000)	1766–70 (£,000)
Atlantic	918	5,906
Spain and Portugal	730	1,599
Holland and Germany	2,956	3,148

59 J.C.T.P., Vol. 12, p. 345.
60 Ibid., Vol. 14, p. 177.
61 Jenkins, 1923, p. 79.

descendants by Margaret's brother, James, in 1783. The remainder followed the same path in 1802 when she died. Her husband had died two years earlier and his considerable fortune was distributed in the conventional way among his Woolrich relations.[62]

ix) Alexander Chorley and Betty Fothergill

The Hough, Fothergill and Chorley families, all closely related, were among the leading Quakers in the Warrington area in the 1750s and 60s. Their children will have gone to school together and encountered each other at Meetings. It may well have been that young Alexander Chorley was already courting Betty, one of Joseph Fothergill's daughters, when her brother Henry died in 1769. Alexander was probably an apprentice in the Fothergills' ironmongery shop and seems to have taken over the business in the crisis created by Henry's untimely death[63] the year before he married Betty.[64]

Alexander Chorley seems to have had a bold entrepreneurial spirit. The original business he bought from the Fothergill daughters was just the ironmongery stock in the ground floor and basement of the house in Sankey Street while the Fothergill family continued to live above (Pl. 41). This stock was assessed for Poor Rate in 1771 at £7.50 p.a., which implied a probably conservative valuation of £150. By 1777 he seems to have moved to Ashton-in-Makerfield. This was the centre of the area making things like locks, hinges, nails, etc. He appears to have been a partner there in two businesses, one called Chorley and Peet, manufacturing hinges, locks, etc., the other a distribution business which bought all types of ironmongery from manufacturers and sold it on to retailers and users. Chorley and Leech of Ashton was one of the two wholesalers who bought quantities of files from young Peter Stubs in 1777, soon after he started the file-manufacturing business that was to make him a rich man. Stubs allowed Chorley and William Barrow of Prescot discounts of 20% and 25%, respectively, off the retail price. Later that year Stubs supplied files to Chorley and Watson – presumably a partnership between Alexander Chorley and Robert Watson. The latter had married Mary Fothergill, Betty's sister, in 1771 and was in business in Waterford, Ireland. In 1781 Stubs sold files to Chorley and Harrison, who became the rated occupiers of the Sankey Street shop at that period. Alexander had evidently taken a partner called Harrison to run the original shop and was presumably trying to create a network of distributors to sell the output of

---

62 Will, 1800.
63 Arley invoice 15 November 1769 from executors of Henry Fothergill receipted by Alexander Chorley. Arley accounts July 1770 invoice from Mr Chorley for ironmongery.
64 C.R.O. Minutes Penketh Prep. Meeting.

the numerous little factories on the coalfield of south Lancashire.[65]

Unfortunately, Alexander seems to have been distracted from this business in the early 1780s. He became a partner in a new iron-slitting mill set up on the Blackbrook at Stanley near St Helens, beside the copper smelting works established by Thomas Patten. This slitting mill was not a success; it was offered for sale in 1784 and in 1785 Alexander Chorley was made bankrupt. He must have been able to satisfy most of his creditors since he was not expelled from the Society of Friends. He became the salaried manager of the Stanley (Copper) Smelting Company, who bought up and refurbished the old Patten works at Stanley in 1785. With his capital gone he was unable to invest in new enterprises. His children seem to have retained an interest in the wholesalers Chorley and Leech and in Chorley and Peet, the hinge-manufacturer in the Ashton area.[66] The money they inherited would have been protected by trusts from the bankruptcy.[67]

Betty Fothergill was the youngest of the six daughters of Joseph who survived to adult life. As mentioned earlier, the fifth daughter, Mary, married Robert Watson of Waterford. Two other daughters, Margaret and Hannah, married respectively John Kendal and William Jepson, both of whom were sailcloth makers in Lancaster. The sailcloth industry in Warrington is the subject of the next section, so their careers are not described here.

x) Abraham Titley and Sarah Fothergill

Sarah, the second daughter of Joseph Fothergill, married Abraham Titley in 1764. The Titleys were a Cheshire family who, in the middle of the seventeenth century had a farm in Helsby, a village on the Chester road three miles west of Frodsham. Abraham's great-grandparents, Thomas and Mary Titley, were already Quakers when their son Joseph was born in February 1677. Joseph became a grocer in Warrington, married Esther Squire of Great Sankey in 1700 and had three sons and four daughters. Joseph was a successful businessman who expanded his operations into a number of separate businesses. At his death in 1731, he left to his eldest son Thomas, born in 1703, the three-life lease of an iron-slitting mill in Great Sankey, and a farm in Acton Grange. When he became 21, the second son, John, was to receive £100 cash, £8 p.a. from his brother Thomas's lands and all the tools of the trade of confectioner. He was probably already working in the business, which had a shop beside the George Inn in Bridge Street, Warrington[68] (see Pl. 40). It seems

---

65 Manchester Central Library Stubs Papers L24/1, Boxes 7, 22, 24; Ashton, 1939, pp. 6–7.
66 Peter Stubs had a letter from Chorley and Peet of Ashton in 1789. Box 24.
67 Awty, 1957, p. 107; Barker, 1954, pp. 77, 87–88, 126.
68 W.P.L. MS 1162, LW 15, Sale of 1733.

that this speciality had developed alongside the original grocery business and that the shop dealt in both confectionery and grocery. The third son, Benjamin, received a farm in Atherton, subject to a £20 p.a. annuity to his mother. There was a nail-making shop on this farm which was to be kept going by the executors until he was 21. The four daughters were to share the original Helsby property.

In 1733 Thomas Titley, the eldest son, married Esther, a sister of Abraham and Thomas Hutton Rawlinson of Lancaster, a family who has already appeared as friends of Samuel Fothergill and Thomas Woolrich. The Rawlinsons were interested in iron manufacture as well as in the West Indian trade, and one of their investments was the Caton Forge, near Lancaster. In 1747 Thomas Titley bought the lease of another forge and slitting mill near Wigan.[69] The following year he bought the freehold of a site and erected a third slitting mill opposite Partington Lock on the Mersey and Irwell Navigation (described below), which enjoyed the rights to use the water of the Mersey.[70] The Partington mill will have enjoyed much greater and more consistent water power than the old mill on the Sankey,[71] so the family is likely to have sold their rights in the latter and concentrated on their new Partington works. Thomas Titley died at Bath in 1753 leaving his 17-year-old son, Abraham, as his heir.

The lease on the Wigan mill had ended by 1761. From the profits of the Partington mill, Abraham probably acquired the money to buy out Ellis Crompton's interest in a new paper mill that had been erected beside the Partington slitting mill. These mills were ideally placed to supply the growing industrial markets. The Navigation provided cheap water transport to Manchester, ten miles away to the east, and to Warrington and the Mersey estuary, seven miles off in the other direction. Abraham was closely involved in the management of both these enterprises. He built a house beside them and would have anticipated a happy and prosperous life there with his wife, Sarah. Unfortunately, they had no children and, in 1772, Abraham died in Buxton at the early age of 37. His will directed that his whole estate at Partington be sold. The advertisement described:

> a convenient mill for slitting and rolling iron with wheels, rollers, and cutters...and a dwelling house and warehouses thereto belonging ... a large new built paper mill with a drying bay ... dwelling houses and appurtenances ... a fishpond and two gardens

69 The Titley interest in iron manufacture is discussed in the context of competing works in Awty, 1957, pp. 106–07.

70 W.P.L. MS 1162, LW 15, John Lyon's mortgage of the property in 1779.

71 This is likely to have been the mill at Sankey Bridges (Map 9) which would have been ideal for processing iron bars imported from Spain or elsewhere to the Sankey Quay and would have been an important innovation.

and

> a new capital messuage called Millbank House pleasantly situated beside the river with a good garden walled round and well stocked with fruit trees; a summer house, convenient offices ...

and nine and a half acres of land.[72] (See Pl. 27).

The whole property was acquired at auction by John, son of Matthew Lyon. Sarah, a young widow aged only 31, received more than £2,000. The rest of Titley's fortune – probably at least another £2,000 – was distributed among a dozen other relations. Two years later, in 1774, Sarah married William Hird, a physician in Leeds. It would appear likely that Mrs Hird invested her £2,000 in a partnership with Messrs Empson and Horner when, in 1778, they sank a new pit at their colliery in Wakefield Outwood, south of Leeds.[73]

xi) Thomas Watt and Mary Chorley

The last couple in this Quaker family group to be described is the only one in which neither party was a descendant of Thomas Hough and Ellin Barnes. However, as they had so many connections with the group and so much of interest has survived about them, I thought they should be included. Mary Chorley's younger brother was Alexander, described earlier, and her elder brother was John Chorley, married to Sarah, daughter of Thomas Hutton Rawlinson. It was Rawlinson's sister, Esther, who married Thomas Titley in 1733 (see p. 256 above). The three Chorley siblings were great-nephews and niece of Susannah, wife of Thomas Hough, and were among the many heirs and heiresses of the Houghs' fortune (see p. 254 above).

The link between the Chorley and the Watt families may have come about because of the fact that Mary's elder brother John Chorley started his career as a West Indian merchant in Liverpool in the late 1760s, thereby meeting Thomas. Or Mary may have met Thomas through her younger brother, Alexander, who lived in Warrington. It may well have been because of Mary that Thomas began attending Quaker Meetings in 1768. He became a member of the Society in 1769 and married Mary in 1770.[74] They had two daughters and a son, James, born in 1774.

The origins of the Watt family are mysterious. Our Thomas was born in 1730 in Newton-in-Makerfield, the son of James and Elizabeth.[75] According to Quaker records, his parents were still living there in 1770, when Thomas married although

---

72 Adams Courant 15 September 1772. Some of the farm building are still standing and the site of the mill can be identified.
73 Miles, 1981, p. 134. John Eagle of Bradford was the attorney who introduced them.
74 C.R.O. Minutes Penketh Prep. Meeting.
75 Winwick P.R.

they do not seem to have owned any property there.[76] The only other thing we know about his Watt relations is that he was described as 'kinsman' by a very rich man, Richard Watt, in his will. Thomas Watt and his son, James, were appointed executors and trustees of Richard's estate in this will.[77]

Richard Watt had spent his working life from 1751 to 1782 in Kingston, Jamaica, where he made a fortune approaching half a million pounds through trading. Richard Watt thought of himself as being from Shevington, a township in the Lancashire parish of Standish. He died aged 72 and was buried in Standish Parish Church, where there is a large, handsome marble memorial to him.[78] The most likely hypothesis for Richard's background and the origin of his wealth, discussed in Appendix 8.2. (which sets out the details of my search for Richard Watt), seems to be that he had relations living in Barbados, Virginia and Lancashire, some of whom were traders rather than planters. Thomas Watts' father, James, may have been a buyer of Lancashire metal manufactures for this trade. It seems that Richard was sent from the West Indies to school in Liverpool. There is another tiny bit of information which possibly supports the suggestion that the Watts were a kind of mid-Atlantic family. A Thomas Watt, possibly the grandfather of our Thomas, or of Richard, was living in Haydock Lodge when he died and was buried in Standish parish churchyard, ten miles away to the north, in April 1726. Haydock Lodge was the mansion of the Legh of Lyme family on their manor of Haydock. Peter Legh, 1674 – 1743, normally lived at Lyme Park, Cheshire, but he evidently kept a suite of rooms at the Lodge for his own use, as some of his letters were addressed from Haydock. Apparently other parts of the big house were let out. This Thomas Watt must have been a reasonably well-off man to rent part of such a property. Perhaps he had returned to Lancashire from the West Indies to restore his health.

Our Thomas possibly started work in his father's business in Newton-in-Makerfield. His parents or other relations presumably then supplied him with the substantial capital required for the large investment he made in 1759. Aged about 29, he acquired the business of a 'tallow chandler and soap boiler' in Fryars Gate, Warrington (see Pl. 40). We have some information about this business which had been owned since at least 1749 by a Quaker called James Maddocks. In 1749 Maddocks borrowed £200 from Thomas Hough of Frodsham,[79] secured on:

    2 large sisterns lined with lead
    2 large tubs or kneaves

76 J.R.U.M.L. Legh of Lyme Rentals and lists of freeholders, G.M.R.O. E17/12/1; E17/13/1; E17/30/2.
77 Canterbury 382, Exeter 1797, copy in L.R.O.
78 See Appendix 8.2 for my search for Richard Watt.
79 Correctly Sutton Weaver. (Our Thomas, 1687–1768)

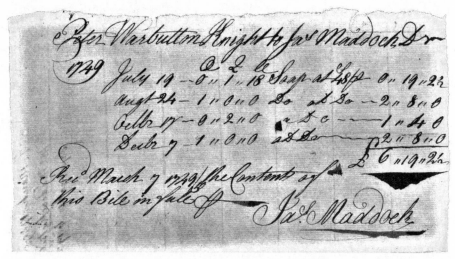

Figure 9. James Maddock's invoice for soap in 1749. The three weight measures are: Cwts (hundredweights = 112lbs), Quarters = 28lbs, and lbs (pounds).

3 lead pumps

3 furnace pans

16 dozen moulds and all other materials, implements and utensils in buildings on the south side of Fryars Gate.

The rate of interest on the loan was 4½%.[80] In 1750 he insured two buildings at £50 each and utensils and stock at £200 in each, making a total sum insured of £500.[81] Between July and December 1749, Maddocks supplied Arley Hall with soap at £2 8s od a hundred weight (see Fig. 9). In December 1752, Maddocks borrowed £600 from Ann Walmsley of Wigan, secured on shops, warehouses and other buildings in Fryars Gate that he was engaged in building (Pl. 44).[82] In December 1753 he revised the insurance valuations, recording the new total value of the business and its factory at £1,000. He also insured at this time his house and contents for £500 and two houses and a stable, 'not quite finished', for a further £300. The business evidently continued to grow rapidly and in January 1757 the insurance valuations were revised again. The utensils and stock in one building were now worth £500 and in the other £1,000 and the total value of the business and factory was raised to £1,700. The building development was complete by this period, including four houses, of which the Maddocks family lived in one. This house was

80 WPL MS 1254, Box 2.
81 Guildhall, Sun Insurance Registers, MS 11936, Policy 124674.
82 WPL, MS 1254.

valued at £230 and the contents at a further £200. The largest of the other houses was lived in by Dr Chorley and was said to be worth £350. The other two houses and two stables were in at £420, so the total housing complex was valued at £1,200.

James Maddocks had invested a total of £2,900 in the whole site. £800 worth of this may still have been mortgaged to Thomas Hough and Ann Walmsley, but his net equity investment was at least £2,100. In 1757 James Maddocks must have regarded his business life with some satisfaction. He had built up a good firm and his son, William, aged 24, had joined him in the enterprise. The outlook was fair. Alas, in June 1758 William died and with his own health probably beginning to fail, the whole picture had changed. Within the next 12 months, he sold the business to Thomas Watt.

It is interesting and significant that there was a young man with the training, the courage and the money to buy a business of this size in Warrington in the mid-eighteenth century. However, it is not clear exactly what Thomas Watt did buy. Ann Walmsley converted her mortgage into the freehold of some of the property because in 1763 she was renting to Thomas Watt two factory buildings, valued at £150, and a house, valued at another £150, where he presumably lived.[83] Whether Watt bought all the utensils and stock from Maddocks, at their 1757 value of £1,550, we don't know, but it seems likely. In addition he may have had to provide working capital. Watt seems to have continued the business with vigour. Whereas Maddocks had lost much of the Arley business in the 1750s, Thomas Watt regained it in 1759 and continued to supply the Warburtons for the next 40 years (see Fig. 10). He also obtained the business of the Leghs of Lyme Park, nearly 30 miles from Warrington. This suggests that his business acquired the reputation of being the best in a large area.[84] It seems also to have been profitable. In 1767 he bought £400 worth of property on the site from Ann Walmsley and another £280 worth from Gilbert Thompson.[85] In 1772 when he insured the site there were two factory/warehouse buildings valued at £200 and £300 respectively. The stock and equipment in the first building were valued at £1,000, and in the second building at £500. Thomas Watt presumably himself lived in the house, which was valued at £500 with its contents at a further £300. His total investment in the site was therefore £2,800.

It is likely that a growing part of Thomas Watt's business was the export of candles to the West Indies. In 1770 the British West Indian islands imported about 1.9 million pounds of candles, worth around £23,300. Liverpool exported 39% of them – £9,068 worth[86] – and it is likely that Thomas Watt's business in Warrington

83 Sun Policy 198923.
84 J.R.U.M.L. Legh of Lyme letters, T. Watt to P. Orford, Steward, 1771–89, 17 letters.
85 W.P.L., MS 1254, Box 3.
86 Total exports P.R.O. Cust 3. For Liverpool exports see Enfield, 1773, p. 87.

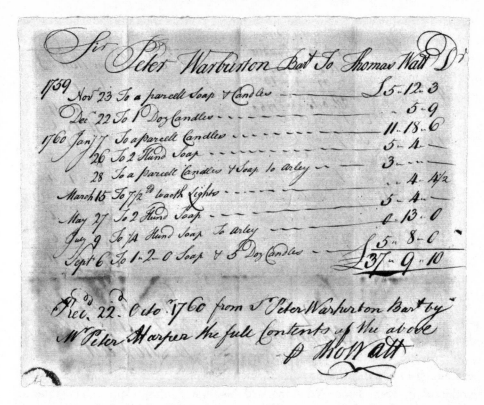

Figure 10. Thomas Watt's invoice for soap and candles in 1760. The price of soap had risen to £2 12s 0d per hundredweight and candles were 5s 9d per dozen.

supplied a significant proportion of these candles because three quarters of Liverpool's exports went to the two islands of Jamaica and Barbados, and Richard Watt was in Jamaica. The competitive position of Warrington soap and candle makers improved in the 1750s and 1760s partly due to the development of the sailcloth manufacturing industry which greatly increased Liverpool's trade with the Baltic (see Chapter 9 below). In the 1750s, the alkali used both for bleaching sailcloth and for making soap was supplied by ashes imported from that area. In the 1760s, alkali was increasingly produced from kelp (seaweed), which came from the coasts of Scotland and Ireland, and so was also delivered cheaply to Liverpool.

By the 1790s the domestic sales of the soap and candle business were probably about £15,000, and exports may have totalled another £5,000 or more.[87] By 1800 Thomas Watt was pretty rich, probably helped by sharing in some of his cousin

---

87 The annual payment of Excise duty was £5,000 to £6,000 in Parr, Lyon and Kerfoot's Bank Ledgers. WPL microfilm.

Richard's trading with Jamaica. In the Income Tax years 1800 and 1801, he returned a net taxable income of £1,485.[88] He bought Morris Brook House, a small estate in Grappenhall, and also bought farms in the country and property in Warrington.[89] Although his son, James, was working with him in the soap business,[90] they decided to sell it. The purchaser, in September 1802, was William Eyres, a well-known stationer and publisher of Warrington, who paid £2,800 for the house, the workshops and the warehouses. Eyres bought it for his son, who wrote 'William Eyres, junior, successor to Thomas Watt' at the head of his invoices in 1803[91] and continued to run the business for nearly 20 years.

Thomas Watt was living close to Thomas Woolrich in Stanley Street in Warrington when he died in 1803 (see Pl. 33). He left his wife the house there and an income for life of £600 p.a., secured on gilt-edged securities and property. His kinsman, Richard Watt, had returned from Jamaica in 1782, and in 1784 had bought an estate of several thousand acres at Bishop Burton, Yorkshire. In 1795 Richard Watt also bought Speke Hall near Liverpool but died in November 1796. His will divided his fortune between his two nephews, Richard Watt and Richard Walker[92] and his executors were his two nephews, 'his kinsmen', Thomas Watt and his son James, and the Liverpool merchant, Thomas Leyland. By 1807 both the two nephews and Thomas Watt were all dead and James Watt and Thomas Leyland thereupon found themselves trustees for much of the Watt fortune on behalf of children. In 1806 James Watt married his first cousin, Hannah, daughter of Alexander Chorley and Betty, née Fothergill, and they apparently lived at Speke Hall until he died in 1814.[93]

xii) Epilogue

Samuel Fothergill died in 1772. His business was continued by his executor Thomas Woolrich although the day-to-day management was probably done by Samuel's old employees. In 1777 Woolrich secured the services in some capacity of George Crosfield, a young man of 23 who had just completed his apprenticeship to a grocer in Kendal. George was the third son in an old Quaker family who had a 78-acre farm near Kendal.[94] By 1781 he was running the grocer's shop[95] which was not a large

---

88 WPL MS 201, 202.
89 Firtree farm, Crowley (WM Box 56); Questy Birch, Hatton (Ormerod, 1882, Vol. 1, p. 744. He was Peter Stubs, landlord at the White Bear in Bridge Street; Ashton, 1939, p. 71.
90 Arley invoice 18 March 1800 signed James Watt for father.
91 Arley invoice 2 February 1803. WPL MS 1254, Box 3.
92 Canterbury 382, Exeter 1797, copy in L.R.O.
93 Foster, 1873.
94 *The British Archivist*, 1913; for genealogy see Musson, 1965, pp. 4–21.

business. In 1790 he insured his household goods, utensils and stock in Sankey Street for £400.[96] He became a close friend of the family group described in this section, and along with Thomas Watt became one of Thomas Woolrich's executors.

In 1799 George Crosfield was invited to go and run a sugar refinery in Lancaster, as one of the three partners who bought the business. He probably contributed little of the capital, but got a good share of the profits. The refinery had been owned by the two Quaker families of Lawson and Rawlinson.[97] We have seen that Samuel Fothergill was a friend of Abraham and Hutton Rawlinson (p. 248 above). Hutton's sons, Abraham and John, had continued their business in the town and it was probably their retirement and John's death, in 1799, that brought the need for new management in the sugar refinery. John Chorley, elder brother of Alexander, and an important merchant in the West Indian trade in Liverpool, was married to Sarah, a sister of Abraham and John Rawlinson. It is probable that Chorley assembled the partnership which bought the sugar refinery in Lancaster, as the other two partners were Liverpool merchants. George Crosfield owned two thirds of a new partnership, made in 1809, and his assets were about £14,000 when he died in 1820.

George Crosfield kept on the grocery business in Warrington with the help of his assistant aged 20 and his son, George, aged 14. He had altogether six sons, some of whom developed the sugar refinery and the grocery business into Harrison and Crosfield Ltd. One son, Joseph, was apprenticed to a soap manufacturer in Newcastle-upon-Tyne in 1807 and in 1814, set up his own soap business at Bank Quay, Warrington in Rogerson's old rosin factory (see Pls. 21 and 34). It is possible that this enterprise might have been aided by knowledge from the old Watt soap business, but we do now know. Joseph Crosfield's business became one of the largest in the town in the nineteenth century and remains so today as part of Lever Faberge. George Crosfield became a brother-in-law of James Watt when he married Margaret Chorley in 1815. When young Joseph Crosfield was threatened with bankruptcy in 1820, Hannah Watt, James's widow, came to his rescue with a loan of £4,500.[98]

Part of Richard Watt's West Indian fortune was soon dissipated. Richard Walker, one of the two nephews who divided the inheritance on Richard Watt's death in 1796, died in 1801. He left a young widow, Alethea, who acquired a taste for grand London parties and 'distinguished herself by her great routs in London. They were given at vast expense – £5,000 or £6,000 a night. The Prince of Wales has had

---

95 Bailey's Directory, 1781.
96 Sun policy 566171.
97 Bailey's Directory, 1784; Foster, 1873 for Rawlinson genealogy.
98 Musson, 1965, p. 18.

twenty tickets sent to him.'[99] She didn't survive this way of life for long, dying in 1805, aged only 35. The West Indian riches disappeared in other ways. In 1808 John Chorley went bankrupt. Like many others he was brought down by the difficulties the West Indian economy suffered during the Napoleonic Wars, especially in the severe depression which lasted from 1803 to 1810.[100] He died two years later.[101]

This story of an extended Quaker family has illustrated the important role of Quakers in the build-up of business in the 120 years 1650–1780 despite the fact that they were never a large group in English society. It has been estimated that, in 1660, there were 30,000 to 40,000 members of the Society, including women and children, and that at its maximum size, in the 1680s, membership may have been only double this.[102] The other Nonconformists or Dissenters were a much larger group, who had come into existence in 1660–62, when some 2,000 ministers refused to accept the Act of Uniformity.[103] While many people in their congregations remained loyal to these ejected ministers, they did not form separate chapelries until after 1689. The national organization created by the Quakers during Charles II's reign, with its regular meetings and separate registers of births, marriages and deaths, was unusual.

Quakers also had exceptionally good links with America. In 1676 the Quaker, William Penn, acquired the western part of New Jersey and established a Quaker colony there. In 1681 he acquired from Charles II a large tract of adjoining land which he called Pennsylvania. With excellent access up the Delaware estuary to this great area, a large Quaker settlement soon arose there with its capital at Philadelphia, on the banks of the Delaware. Quakers existed in many parts of England, but the largest concentration seems always to have been in the five northern counties of Cheshire, Lancashire, Yorkshire, Cumberland and Westmorland. This was partly because George Fox and Margaret Fell were based in the centre of this area at Swarthmoor in the Furness peninsula (then Lancashire) and partly because these counties included large numbers of small farms owned by freeholders, copyholders and three-life leaseholders as described in Chapter 3 above. These people, known as 'statesmen' in Cumberland and Westmorland, were particularly attracted to the religious independence offered by the Society of Friends. It was therefore from these five counties that the greatest number of the new settlers on the Delaware

99 Greig, 1923, pp. 267–68 and notes, 11 July 1804.
100 See Ragatz, 1928, Ch. ix, pp. 286–330 for the complex chain of events that deprived the planters of a profitable market for their produce in this period and Morgan, 2000, pp. 50–53 for a more modern view.
101 VCH, Lancs., Vol. 3, p. 369.
102 Braithwaite, 1955, p. 512.
103 Gow, 1928, p. 25.

were drawn.[104] For the Quakers who remained in England, the new settlers were both a market for their manufactures and suppliers of new American raw materials. They opened up new investment opportunities and they required the religious and moral support provided by visiting preachers like John and Samuel Fothergill. All these connections between the five northern counties and the colonies on the Delaware greatly stimulated the economy of north-western England. The English Quakers were a small, highly organized group of businessmen, whose effect on British industry and commerce in the seventeenth and eighteenth centuries was out of all proportion to their numbers.

This story has shown how the Quakers were groups of families drawn together to establish and maintain a strong moral code about how the whole of life including business should be conducted. Great stress was laid on two qualities which have been widely recognized as vital to successful business – honesty and integrity. Similar emphasis was placed on the idea that all people had equal status. Both these principles had wide implications for the behaviour of group members. One aspect of these principles was that it was wrong to treat gentry – or even kings – in a different way to other people. The same principle applied to the poor who had to be helped, and to women. This equal status enabled Quaker women to be both ministers and independent property-owning business managers, like Susanna Crewdson, who married Samuel Fothergill, or Sarah Fell, described in my *Seven Households*.[105] From the 1760s, when they realized what they had been doing in the West Indies, slaves were also seen as equal people. Quaker owners freed their slaves, as J.C. Lettson did when he visited Tortola in 1767, though the act left him 'five hundred pounds worse than nothing'.[106]

Another area of life about which Quakers felt deeply and acted decisively was education. We have noticed that Dr John Fothergill gave the bulk of his fortune to found Ackworth School and also that the two Gilbert Thompsons – father and son – ran a high-quality school in Penketh near Warrington. This involved a considerable belief in the value of what they were doing, as not only were they fined for being unlicensed teachers, but as capable property owners, they were foregoing the much greater financial rewards they could have gained by engaging in business.

These philanthropic and socially responsible attitudes may have been particularly widespread among Quakers, but their dedication to their business affairs seems to have been shared with other Anglicans and Dissenters in the North-West. The

---

104 Fischer, 1989, pp. 419 – 603 (Map p. 440) where this migration is described as one of the Four British Folkways in America.
105 Foster, 2002, Ch. 4.
106 Jenkins, 1923, p. 48.

Pattens, Blackburnes and Lyons seem to have been just as active in business as any of the Quakers. What may have distinguished the latter was not their earning but their spending habits. We find no mention of the grand houses they built, the parks they laid out or the great entertainments they provided. They invested spare capital in income-producing farms and probably saved large sums annually for reinvestment. It is possible that the Hough fortune was built up gradually during the eighteenth century, principally by accumulated annual savings. Even as 'a gentleman with freehold lands of £400 p.a.' Thomas lived in an ordinary farmhouse while the Pattens and the Blackburnes built large mansions and Mrs Alethea Walker – a non-Quaker heiress to a West Indian fortune – splashed £5,000 a night on parties for royalty and their friends.

Another important difference between both Quaker and Anglican north-western businessmen and many of those who made their business fortunes in London was their involvement in manufacturing. Much London business was either in financial operations or in foreign trade. The north-western businessmen included merchants like Thomas Woolrich or John Chorley in the West Indian trade, but many of them were also engaged in manufacturing such as Titley's slitting mills, Watts' soap and candles and the salt-works operators. Manufacturing businesses necessarily involved an engagement with technology, and therefore with technical innovation. We do not know exactly what improvements these people made in their businesses, nor what suggestions Joseph Fothergill and Alexander Chorley may have made to their metal-working craftsmen on the coalfield. However there is no doubt that the Quakers made a large contribution to the technical innovation in manufacturing which was at the heart of the Industrial Revolution.[107]

107 Raistrick, 1950.

Appendix 8.1. *The tenants of the Crown in Wensleydale*

Soon after Domesday, the land to the north of the River Ure was given to the Abbey of Jervaulx. The Crown continued to own the land on the south side of the river. At the beginning of the sixteenth century it was called the Lordship of Middleham. The 1605 survey[1] shows that there were three types of land in the Lordship. The demesne lands contained 2,840 acres and included Middleham Castle and other parks. There were 68 freehold tenants, some of whom were occupying the demesne lands. Thirdly, there were 753 customary tenants. They paid a total annual rent of £597 9s 6¾d for 11,256 acres of enclosed meadows, pasture and arable land and 5,884 pasture or beast gates, the latter being the right to use the hilly country beyond the enclosures for pasture. It can be seen from these figures that the average tenant had some 15 acres of enclosed land and he was paying a rent of about one shilling an acre for it.

The rents of these tenants were not raised in line with rising market rents in the 1530s, 1540s or 1550s. In the early 1560s, as Elizabeth consolidated her position, inquiries were made about the position of tenants and rents on the manor.[2] The tenants claimed 'a customary estate in the nature of copiehold to them and their heyres', although 'they cannot or will not shew any deed, graunt or copie'.[3] In 1571–72, the tenants and the Crown agreed that the tenants would pay a fine of two years' rent and each receive a 40-year lease of their holdings on the old terms, with a right to renew their leases on the same terms. This arrangement extracted some £1,200 extra from the tenants, but otherwise seemed to secure them as effectively freeholders.

In 1605 further inquiries were made by James I's officials and the survey was carried out. In 1608–9 an attempt was made to have 'a composition to remedy their defective titles'. Some tenants paid six years' old rent to renew their leases for a further 40 years with the right to renew again at the end of their new leases. No general settlement was made. In 1628 Charles I sold the Manor, less the rents being paid, to the City of London as part of the Royal Contract. The manuscript of the 1605 survey includes 'Observations' made by a surveyor, probably in the 1630s, saying that these tenants are likely to have been old 'tenants at will' and noting various defects in their legal position – for example, they could not claim to hold both by custom and by lease.[4]

The City of London seems to have taken up the surveyor's suggestions. In their files are the records of a number of lawsuits in the 1650s,[5] but they were not successful. In 1663 they sold the manorial rights to groups of tenants. The tenants of ten hamlets near Bainbridge, which included Carr End, bought the rights in their area (now named the Manor of Bainbridge) for £214 11s 11d. So these 175 old customary tenants acquired the freeholds of their ancient holdings at a total cost of 2 years' old rent in 1572, and just over one pound each in 1663. Of course, they still had to pay their medieval rents until they bought out the people to whom the Crown had sold them. The acquisition of the manorial rights in 1663 allowed the inhabitants to enclose and reorganise the land as they could agree amongst themselves.

Carr End is an isolated farmhouse, not in one of the old hamlets. It seems possible that it was built, in the 1660s, on newly enclosed land. The only Fothergill family in Wensleydale

1 Willan, 1941.
2 Ibid., pp. xxvii–xxx.
3 Ibid., pp. 147–48.
4 Ibid., p. 148.
5 Corporation of London R.O. Manor of Middleham, Suit cards.

in 1605 lived in West Witton on 10 acres and one pasture gate. It seems likely that John of Carr End and Anthony of Brough Hill, who was one of the trustees for the 1663 purchase of the manorial rights, were descended from the West Witton family. They had improved the family's fortune.

The different fates that could befall the customary tenants of the Crown are illustrated by events in Wensleydale to the north of the River Ure. The Abbey of Jervaulx came into royal hands at the dissolution of the monasteries. Henry VIII gave the Abbey's Wensleydale lands – known as Abbotside – to the Earl and Countess of Lennox in 1544, the Countess being his niece. The manor returned to the Crown in the person of James I, their grandson. He gave it in 1603 to Ludovic Stuart, Duke of Lennox. The tenants had paid fines of ten times their old rents for leases of 21 years in the 1580s. Some of them paid fines of 30 times their old rents to the Duke of Lennox and he conducted a successful court action against those who refused to pay. He then sold the manor for £10,000. There were about 105 tenants paying a total old medieval rent of £102 p.a. The true annual value of the land in 1614 was estimated at just under £1,300 by a surveyor. So the Duke sold for 7.7 times the annual value. If the tenants had actually been paying the £1,300 a year rent, he might have got nearly double the price. The discount represented the problems the new owners would have in getting the tenants to pay. After nearly 20 years of lawsuits, the tenants settled for keeping one third of their holdings at one third of the old medieval rents and giving up or paying a full market rent for the remainder. When, in 1663, the tenants on the south side of the valley won their long struggle to hold on to their farms at the old medieval rents, those on the north side must have been jealous. The law was very uncertain in these affairs.[6]

Appendix 8.2. *The search for Richard Watt and his family.*

1. The name Watt does not occur in Standish Parish Registers before 1652–56.[7]
2. There were Watts in Shevington at the end of the seventeenth century and in the early eighteenth century. The last baptism entry in the Parish Register is 28 May 1718, when Ralph, son of Robert and Margaret, was baptised. Robert Watt, a 'gardener', died in 1758 leaving lands in Heskin, Standish, Wrightington and Shevington. These may have been all the family's lands. I have found nothing more about his only son Ralph.
3. Ten people named Watt had their wills admitted to probate in Barbados between 1684 and 1788.[8] From 1745 onwards a considerable number of Watt children were born in Barbados.[9]
4. In a list of all the landowners in Jamaica *c.* 1750, only a single acre in Vere parish was owned by a Watt.[10]
5. A number of people called Watt emigrated to Virginia. In the 1750s and 1760s a number of people called Watt were connected with ships in the West Indies-America-United Kingdom trades (see footnote to (7) below). It seems likely that the American Watts owned some of the Barbados properties. Watt family members may have been in Lancashire, Barbados and America.

6 Willan, 1941, pp. vii–xxv and 1–80.
7 L.P.R.S., Vol. 46.
8 Oliver, 1919, Vol. 5, pp. 272, 275, 294–96.
9 Index of Parish Registers of Barbados.
10 B.L. Add MSS 12,436.

6. Richard Watt, who made the half million-pound fortune, was born about 1724. He was probably apprenticed to a merchant in Liverpool, and was probably a bit too old to have been the boy who drove the only hackney carriage in Liverpool in about 1750.[11] The Watt family archives[12] show that he bought two slaves in Kingston, Jamaica, in October 1751 and in this document he is described as 'merchant'. We have seen that Thomas Woolrich arrived in Tortola aged 20 in 1753 to begin a career trading between the islands and England and America. It seems likely that Richard Watt arrived in Kingston in 1751 with the same intention.

7. In the Liverpool Plantation Registers, Richard Watt appears as one of the owners of 17 ships registered between 1755 and 1769 (see list at the end of this Appendix). In the first six, between 1755 and 1758, he was in partnership with Richard Savage of Liverpool and George Nelson of Manchester. In five more, later on, he was a joint-owner with Richard Savage, and in four the joint-owner was John Walker. The latter may have been related to Richard Walker, the husband of Richard Watt's sister, to whose son he left part of his fortune. In many cases we know that the part-owners of ships were also the owners of cargo that travelled in them, so it is reasonable to infer from this long list of ships that he was a substantial trader. In the period 1786 to 1788, the firm of Watt and Walker were the owners of several ships.[13] It seems likely that our Richard Watt and his two nephews, Richard Watt and Richard Walker, were all partners in Watt and Walker. Others, including Thomas and James Watt, may also have had an interest.[14]

8. The Watt family archives show he first bought land in Westmorland parish, Jamaica, in 1767. In the next 11 years, he bought four more blocks of land so that by 1778 he owned 1,335 acres. By Jamaica standards this was a good estate, but not a great one. The largest estates were more than 10,000 acres. It is likely, therefore, that these plantations were bought as a secure investment for his surplus capital and were not the original source of his wealth.

9. Richard Savage and George Nelson presumably provided a large part of the cargoes of English manufactures carried on the voyages to the West Indies and America. On page 261 above, evidence is set out to show that Thomas Watt probably sent a significant volume of candles. It is possible that his father James' business was to supply locks, hinges and other ironmongery made in the Newton-in-Makerfield area.

Conclusion
Richard Watt was probably the son of parents who were rich enough to educate him and give him sufficient capital to start his business. He may well have begun trading with the advantage of having relations and contacts in the West Indies, England and America.

---

11 Brooke, 1853, pp. 177–78.
12 Brynmor Jones Library, University of Hull, DDGE2 9/4.
13 Craig, 1967 pp. 33–34, 45, 70, 108 and 123.
14 Liverpool Plantation Registers are on microfilm at Liverpool Maritime Museum. M. Schofield's working papers and indexes are in Sidney Jones Library, Liverpool University, D.514. His computer discs are in ESRC Data Archive 2923, Essex University, as 'Liverpool Trade and Shipping 1744–1786'.

Richard Watt's ships 1755 to 1769

Date	Name	Partners/other owners
Apr 1755	*Betty*	Richard Savage, George Nelson
Mar 1756	*Nancy*	Richard Savage, George Nelson
Jan 1757	*Ellis*	Richard Savage, George Nelson
Jan 1758	*Ellis*	Richard Savage, George Nelson
May 1758	*Rose*	Richard Savage, George Nelson
Aug 1758	*Adventure*	Richard Savage, George Nelson
Mar 1760	*Adventure*	Richard Savage, George Nelson
Oct 1758	*Martha*	Richard Savage, George Nelson
Oct 1760	*Martha*	Richard Savage, George Nelson
Feb 1759	*Beckford*	Richard Savage, George Nelson
May 1761	*Prince Ferdinand*	John Walker
May 1762	*Prince Ferdinand*	John Walker
Aug 1762	*Beaver*	John Walker
Oct 1762	*Pitt*	John Walker
Nov 1762	*Betty*	Richard Savage, George Nelson
Apr 1763	*Betsey*	John Walker
May 1763	*George*	Richard Savage, George Nelson
Oct 1765	*Sally*	Others
Nov 1768	*Susannah*	Others
Nov 1769	*Martha*	Richard Savage, George Nelson
Nov 1769	*Betty*	Richard Savage, George Nelson

Note:

The snow *Ellis* (60 tons) is listed in Wardle, 1941.

CHAPTER 9

The sailcloth manufacturers of Warrington, 1741–70

i) Introduction

This third example of north-western business in the period 1650–1780 is about top-quality sailcloth manufacture, a new industry in England at the beginning of the eighteenth century. Why did a third to a half of all the sailcloth made in Britain in the period 1750–1780 come from the Warrington area? How did the Warrington manufacturers achieve so large an output? Why did businessmen in other parts of the country not seize a greater share of the market? We will not find the answers to all these questions, but this chapter does show that north-western businessmen were able to respond quickly to change and to organize large firms efficiently. These were both skills that they demonstrated again when mechanical cotton-spinning became possible in the 1780s.

The Royal Navy's efforts to establish and nurture a home-produced supply of this essential component of their ships is described at the beginning of this chapter. Linen manufacture was well understood in many parts of Britain. It was a declining industry in the South-East, because wages in and near London had risen so much that it had become uneconomic,[1] but in the West and the North linen was still manufactured in many places. We do not know exactly where the early sailcloth was made. It seems that none was made in Lancashire before 1740, perhaps because the business was on too small a scale to be of interest to Warrington businessmen. This changed when the build-up to the War of the Austrian Succession (1740–48) spurred the Navy into frenetic activity. The Sailcloth Acts of 1736 and 1746 created a large market for British-made sailcloth which triggered the Warrington men into action.

The linen industry in the Mersey estuary had seen many changes in the first 40 years of the century. Irish and Scottish cloth came flooding in. Raw flax from Danzig and Riga as well as coarse cloth from northern Germany was imported. A rapidly growing export market developed to America and the West Indies. These changes had brought into existence a group of linen-trading businessmen, and the first Warrington sailcloth manufacturers came from this background.

After a description of the operations of a typical manufacturer, the bulk of the chapter describes the histories and businesses of the families who entered the sailcloth industry and obtained Navy contracts in 1756–57. An unusually precise impression of the progress of these businesses is available because of a happy

---

1 Gilboy, 1934, Chart 39, p. 220.

accident. The hemp and flax, of which the sailcloth was made, was highly flammable so all the manufacturers insured their stocks with the Sun Fire Office, whose Registers have luckily survived. Some of the families can be traced back into the seventeenth century. All of them seem to have arrived in Warrington after the Civil War, as their surnames do not occur in the 1649 tax return for the town.[2] Before launching into sailcloth manufacture, they had previously been involved in a wide range of business activities, and several of them continued to have business interests other than sailcloth. They were businessmen first and textile manufacturers second. Sailcloth manufacture was not technically complex, with success depending on commercial rather than technical competence. By following this group of families in some detail it is hoped to paint a portrait of Warrington's business society. More than half the families were Nonconformist: five of the richest ones were Unitarians, who were all related to each other and all belonged to the same congregation, while two families were Quakers. The other six seem to have remained with the Established Church, but these religious differences do not seem to have affected the business behaviour of members of the group.

ii) The creation of the British sailcloth manufacturing industry

Before the Glorious Revolution of 1689, the best grades of sailcloth used by the Royal Navy were not made in England. They were imported from France under such names as Poldavy and Vitry, names which derived from two towns in Brittany, probably Pontivy and Vitré, which had specialized in this manufacture. Lower grades may have come from Holland or Germany. When Britain, under William III, came to be at war with France, this supply of high-quality cloth was cut off. In 1693 the Navy was buying 'Best Holland Duck Canvas' at 1s 9d a yard as its top grade.[3] The Admiralty was unhappy with this dependence on foreign supplies. In 1694 they bought the best that England could supply – 'Double Suffolk Canvas' – at 1s 5¼d a yard. This was said to be fit for the same uses as third grade Holland Duck.

In 1696 an Act was passed allowing the Navy to pay 2d more per yard for English than for foreign-made sailcloth.[4] With this power in their hands, the Navy, in September 1696, ordered 'English canvas to be equal to Holland duck' at 2s 2½d a yard. The price of best Holland duck was then 2s 0½d. However, the cloth that was supplied was apparently not as good as hoped for. In October 1698 orders were placed for English Duck, which was required to be equal in quality to a sample which

2 W.P.L. MS 734.
3 P.R.O. ADM/3583 for 1693–98 purchases.
4 7 and 8 Wm 3 c10, p14.

had been submitted and which was 'reported to be superior' to Holland. This may or may not have been the same sailcloth that the Mediterranean squadron reported to be inferior to Holland in October 1699. Other reports reaching the Admiralty were conflicting. Portsmouth thought their supply of English Duck was superior to Holland, but Sheerness judged their supply inferior.[5] The battle to make the best quality sailcloth in England was not won until April 1703, when an order was placed with a contractor called Sir Owen Buckingham for cloth made 'in imitation of the French taken at Vigo'.[6] This seems to have become the standard cloth that other manufacturers also learnt to supply. By 1707 the price of No. 1 grade English was 1s 7d a yard compared with 1s 9d a yard for Holland Duck.

In 1713, with the end of the war in sight, there was anxiety in the Admiralty about what would happen to the sailcloth manufacturers whom they had encouraged into existence. German sailcloth was cheaper, at least in the lower grades, and it seems to have been adequate for the merchant marine. An Act was obtained that laid a duty of 1d per ell on foreign sailcloth and also provided for 1d drawback (subsidy) on exports of British-made sailcloth.[7] This was apparently not very effective in encouraging British manufacture, because, in 1731, the drawback on exported cloth was increased to 2d a yard. At the same time the duty on imported flax was removed, so that imported flax became cheaper than that grown in England. This change, it was hoped, would lower the cost of British manufacture.[8]

British production may have become cheaper but it was still not competitive. In 1736 a new Act was passed that set out a detailed specification for the manufacture of British sailcloth.[9] This appears to be the first detailed, published, textile specification. The number of threads in the warp and the weft were described and the weight of a bolt (38 yards long) of each grade was set out. There were eight grades: No. 1 was the heaviest at 44 lbs per bolt; No. 8 had to weigh only 15 lbs. The cloth was to be 24 inches wide. Every new British and colonial-built ship was to have British sails, but despite all these excellent innovations the Act seems to have been less than fully effective. It was not until a new Act was passed in 1746 that British sailcloth gained a guaranteed market in British ships. This Act forbade Customs to unload any British ship until they had inspected its sails to check that they were all British-made.[10]

5 P.R.O. ADM 106/525.
6 P.R.O. ADM/3584, 3585 for purchases 1699–1707. Vigo Bay in Spain was the site of a famous naval victory in 1702, when the British and Dutch defeated the French and Spanish fleets.
7 12 Anne c16.
8 4 George II c27.
9 9 George II c37.
10 19 George II c27.

How large was the market these Acts created? There are no simple statistics. One approach that provides clues is to examine the exports from Britain which were almost entirely to America, the West Indies and other colonies. Before 1736 the value of exports only amounted to just over £3,000 p.a. The requirement to fit British sails on all *new* British and colonial-built ships raised the figure to between £5,000 and £9,000 p.a. in the years 1737 to 1745. The 1746 Act caused the annual figures to increase to more than double to £21,000 p.a. By the 1760s these exports to the colonies expanded further to over £40,000 p.a. (see Appendix 9.1, Tables A and B).

We can use these figures for sailcloth exports to arrive at an approximate idea of the size of the total market. Around 1760, the population of the American colonies and the West Indies was probably about 3 million. The population of Great Britain (including Ireland) was perhaps 12 million. So, if £40,000 worth of sailcloth went across the Atlantic every year, four times as much – say £160,000 – was probably required in the British Isles. So the merchant fleet may have bought some £200,000 worth a year. When British ships were first registered in 1786 there were 7,926 English-owned ships with a total tonnage of 751,626 tons. In 1760 the Navy had 325 ships rated at a total of 321,000 tons and in 1756 they ordered about £85,000 worth of sailcloth. In peacetime, Navy orders averaged less than one tenth of that, so their requirements were volatile. We can perhaps tentatively estimate that the total market for sailcloth was worth between £200,000 and £300,000 a year in the 1760s.

iii) The structure of the British linen industry in the first half of the eighteenth century

To understand who might have manufactured the sailcloth the British Navy wished to have made at home, it is necessary to make a brief review of linen manufacture in Britain.[11] I have already described the linen industry that existed in the plains of Cheshire and Lancashire in the sixteenth century (see pp. 112–16 above). Until the end of the seventeenth century, this area supplied its own linen requirements and also those of the people living on the western side of the Pennines. It also sent supplies into North Wales and the centre of England down to north Buckinghamshire. A similar industry in Yorkshire, centred at Knaresborough, Pontefract and Darlington, met the needs of its own area and those of other people living on the east side of the Pennines.

---

11 The word 'linen' will be used here to describe textiles made from both hemp and flax or mixtures of the two. Hemp, when heckled fine, was similar to coarsely heckled flax. Flax replaced hemp in clothing as living standards rose. Some sailcloth included hemp. Aikin, 1795, p. 302.

In the South and West there was a good industry in Worcestershire and Warwickshire, and in Somerset and Dorset. London and the east and south coasts were principally supplied from France, Germany and the Low Countries, where wages were often lower than in England. There were pockets of good hemp and flax lands on rivers in the south and east of England; the largest area was probably the Fenland of south Lincolnshire and Norfolk. All these places supplied their local areas with everyday cloths. Top-quality cambrics, lawns, Hollands and lace, which were the types of linen used by the gentry, were almost all imported.[12] In the eighteenth century most traditional English linen manufacture was declining as better-paid occupations appeared. Ireland and Scotland, where labour was cheaper, began to produce much more and to export it to England. In the 1730s and 1740s the British Parliament called into existence a second type of linen manufacture in Britain, when it became aware that slaves in America and the West Indies were normally clothed in a type of cheap brown linen called Osnaburgh. As its name implies, this cloth was usually imported from northern Germany and then exported to the colonies. Parliament discovered that it could be made in Britain and thought its manufacture would be a good employment for the poor, one of whose principal occupations everywhere was processing and spinning linen. The laws were changed to allow the import of flax and hemp, free of duty, and a bounty (or subsidy) was provided to encourage the export of cheap British-made linen cloth.[13] Like the creation of the sailcloth industry, this was a successful piece of Government intervention and large quantities of 'British' linen were exported to the West Indies and the southern states of America. Much of it appears to have been made in Scotland.[14]

Most of the British sailcloth bought by the Navy before 1741 was supplied by a few London merchants, but there is no record of where it was made. Some probably came from Suffolk, while that supplied by Sir Owen Buckingham was made in Dover.[15] There are no names among the contractors to the Admiralty that suggest a Lancashire or Warrington origin for any sailcloth. In 1741, early in the War of the Austrian Succession, the Navy bought sailcloth from 19 contractors, only one of whom, John Robinson, came from Warrington. Three years later, as Naval operations became more extensive, there were 48 British contractors, of whom five or six came from Warrington. The big orders placed in 1756, at the start of the Seven Years War, were divided between 61 contractors, of whom 18 came from Warrington (see Appendix 9.2, Table A for a list of their names). I have been unable to find out where most of the others came from. At least 13 were merchants with

12 Harte, 1973, pp. 102–03; House of Commons Reports, Vol. 2, pp. 65–72, 11 March 1744.
13 J.H.C. Vol. xxiii, pp. 76–82; Harte, 1973, pp. 74–112 for a good summary of the laws.
14 Durie, 1996 (see Index 'linen' – Osnaburgh); Durie, 1979, pp. 25–28, etc.
15 ADM 106/525, letter 13 December 1699.

warehouses in London, while the rest probably came from all over England and Scotland. There was also certainly a sailcloth factory in Ireland near Cork.[16]

From this it appears that Warrington businessmen entered the industry when the market became substantial, several of the major firms only setting up large facilities after 1746. The Warrington businessmen who became sailcloth manufacturers were not interested in small market areas, but when the opportunity to make large sales appeared, they moved quickly. We shall see why this was. Many of them were men owning a significant amount of capital. In 1756 18 Warrington contractors obtained nearly one third of the Navy's orders but Appendix 9.2, Table A, shows that there were in fact only nine manufacturers in Warrington. Nevertheless these nine firms are likely to have made at least one third and possibly one half of all the sailcloth manufactured in Britain.[17]

iv) The linen industry in the Warrington area

Before we examine the Warrington manufacturers it is desirable to focus more closely on the position of the linen business in Cheshire and Lancashire, and particularly on the situation in Liverpool and Manchester. Since before 1600, Manchester textile traders had been as active in the woollen cloth industry as in linen. Large quantities of cheap woollen cloth, which had been made in the hills around the town, were sent up to London. It was probably because of these trading activities that, around 1600, they began bringing cotton, imported into London from the eastern Mediterranean, to Manchester. With the cotton they began to make fustian – a cloth with a linen warp and a cotton weft.[18] One variant of fustian was jeans – dyed a 'sad' colour for working clothes. Others were dense cloths used for pockets or to enclose feathers for pillows – similar cloths woven for bed ticking may have had stripes for ornament. Fustians of these and other kinds were made throughout the seventeenth century in the area north of Manchester[19] and, whereas all the cotton was spun locally, it is likely that increasing quantities of the linen yarn were spun in Ireland. The production of linen yarn is extremely labour-intensive, requiring huge numbers of men- and women-hours, and there simply were not enough people in the Lancashire area to supply the increasing demand for linen yarn.

In the 1670s an entirely new kind of textile appeared in England – an all cotton cloth from India, named calico. Some was white, some dyed, painted or printed in new ways, and it was all brought by the East India Company to London, where it

16 Stephenson, 1757, p. 180; See Appendix 9.2, Table B for the London merchants and Table C for the possible location of other contractors.
17 See Appendix 9.3, Note 2 for calculations based on the numbers of spinners employed.
18 Wadsworth and Mann, 1931, pp. 15–23.
19 Ibid., pp. 79, 113–14.

quickly became fashionable. People who had learnt the dyeing techniques from India set up factories around London to print European designs on white calico. These cloths became so popular that the woollen industry, fearing for its market, started a campaign against them. In 1721 Parliament passed an Act which prohibited the wearing of any printed or dyed calico or other cotton cloth.[20] Two established activities were exempted – fustians could still be produced and sold in Britain and the printing firms could still print calico for export. This latter activity was important because coloured Indian cottons, and the imitations of them printed in England, were the type of goods which sold best to the West African chiefs who traded in slaves.

It was probably around 1720 that the Lancashire fustian manufacturers realized that they might be able to sell cloth with a linen warp and a cotton weft in West Africa, if they learnt how to dye cloth with stripes and checks in the bright, strong colours the Africans admired. By 1731, if not before, they started exporting such cloths.[21] In 1736 they obtained an Act[22] which made it clear that linen warp, cotton weft cloths could be dyed and printed and sold in England. Free of legal entanglements, the production of cotton and linen checks and stripes grew briskly. By the early 1750s annual exports were over £50,000; they rose to three times that figure in the 1760s, and approximately half of all these exports were sold in West Africa. This was the big new market which Manchester had gained. Other places – the West Indies, the American colonies and Ireland – only took small quantities. A range of less vivid furniture checks was fashionable in England in the 1750s,[23] but the market for printed cloths of this kind was much slower to develop. The export figures show only a modest growth in the late 1750s. At this period undyed fustian cloth known as 'grey' from the Blackburn area began to supplant imported calico with the London printers. Around 1760 the cloth-printing industry started moving to Lancashire and exports of printed cloth soared.[24] A third new type of cloth appeared

20 7 George I c7.
21 Wadsworth and Mann, 1931, pp. 152–53; Schumpeter, 1960, Table X.
22 9 George II c4.
23 The Holker manuscript *c*. 1750 reproduced in Montgomery, 1984, Plates D22–23, 28, 29.
24 The figures from Schumpeter, 1960, are as follows:
   Cotton and linen cloth exported. Annual averages.

	Checks (£)	Printed (£)
1750–54	53,326	2,349
1755–59	83,153	3,233
1760–64	160,646	34,528
1765–69	147,715	57,920

   See for further discussion: Wadsworth and Mann, 1931, pp. 145–73; Chapman, 1981, pp. 287–316, House of Commons Reports, Vol. 2, pp. 287–316. Checked and striped linens 26 April 1751.

in the Manchester area in the 1750s – cotton velvet – which started slowly, but developed large markets in England and Europe in the 1760s and 1770s.[25]

These three new Lancashire industries must have put a great strain on the spinning capacity of the area. The linen yarn required seems to have been obtained entirely from imports. In the 1740s it came from Ireland, but the extra demand raised the price, so additional supplies were brought in from North Germany. In 1756 the duty on foreign imports was abolished, and after that Germany shared the Lancashire market for linen yarn with Ireland while small amounts came from Scotland.[26]

Merchants like the Nicholson family of Liverpool visited Ireland regularly. They would order the quantities and grades of yarn that they required from traders in the spinning areas. Months later, when these men had accumulated enough yarn, it was shipped to Liverpool. The Nicholsons had regular customers in all the textile producing towns from Preston to Stockport.[27] The cotton was all spun in Britain, and the increasing volume is likely to have greatly enlarged the area in which cotton-spinning was carried out. For example, in the 1740s the Latham daughters took up cotton-spinning in Scarisbrick (see my *Seven Households*, pp. 161–62), which was a long way west of the traditional fustian area. The fact that Blackburn 'greys' sold strongly to the cotton printers is an indication that cotton-spinning was also spreading further north. In the 1760s, the need to mechanize cotton-spinning must have been very great.

Almost all this growing trade went through the Port of Liverpool, which handled exports of Lancashire textiles to Ireland, Africa and America, also sending them round the coast to London. Linen cloth and yarn came in from Ireland, Scotland, Germany and the Baltic countries, while flax came from Dantzig and Riga.[28] In Liverpool town and in Warrington (also part of the Port of Liverpool) there were large warehouses in which all these products were stored, where the exporters selected their goods and from where the merchants despatched their parcels around Britain. These were the premises of the new 'linen drapers'.

The traditional Warrington 'linen drapers' had organized the production of linen in south Lancashire and had directed its marketing to the South from their strategic location beside the principal bridge over the Mersey. In the first half of the eighteenth century they had to adapt to all these new conditions. The innovators among

25 Montgomery, 1984, pp. 287–88.
26 House of Commons Reports 1751, Vol. 2, pp. 287–316.
27 Liverpool R.O., Nicholson papers 920 NIC 5/5/17–93.
28 Mrs Latham bought flax in Kirkham in the 1730s that had come from Riga. It had probably been imported by John Langton. See Appendix 9.2, Table C. Also see Singleton, 1977, pp. 73–108; Wilkinson, 1994.

them will have started to buy the competing products available from Ireland, Scotland and north Europe and will have used their old distribution channels to sell them in England. As Russian and north-German flax became competitive with locally-grown supplies, they began to import it and organize its dressing (heckling) and distribution to local spinners. Through the connections established by the timber and salt merchants, who had been sending ships into northern waters since the 1680s, they will have appointed agents to buy flax and yarn of the right quality.[29]

Not only did Warrington linen drapers have to adapt to a tide of imports, they also had to learn to provide the exports that were demanded in ever-growing volumes by English colonists across the Atlantic. Many of the imports were in fact quickly exported, for example, Irish linens went to America from Liverpool with other cargo. Before the 1740s, German Osnaburghs were imported and then exported for use by the slaves and, as Scottish production built up with the help of bounties, it came to Liverpool to replace the German imports.

v) The operation of a typical Warrington sailcloth manufacturer

The nine firms that were established in Warrington to manufacture sailcloth between 1741 and 1756 were not all based on old linen draper businesses. I examine the history of the families that started them in section (vi) below. All these firms had much in common, so I will begin by looking at one firm in detail, as an example of much that was also true of the others. The firm we know the most about was started in 1747 by members of three families – Hart, Turner and Woodcock. All three families were members of the Unitarian Chapel in Cairo Street, Warrington, and they all lived adjacent to one another in the Friars Gate area – possibly in Stanley Street or Chancel Street, also known as Friars Green (see Pls. 35 and 40).[30] The partnership was created by a deed dated 1 November 1747, in which the five men agreed to be sail canvas makers together for five years, and it was renewed for a further seven years in January 1752.[31] The oldest of the five was William Woodcock, aged 38. Thomas Turner was also in his 30s and was in the linen business. John and Thomas Hart were two brothers, aged about 26 and 23. Their father had been a linen draper in Warrington who had died in 1728, but it is unclear whether his business had been kept going. The fifth partner was Jeffrey Hart, their first cousin, also about 23.

The firm began in a warehouse adjacent to William Woodcock's house. In 1747,

29 Clemens, 1976, Table 6, p. 225 shows between 20 and 30 ships a year in northern waters between 1713 and 1723.
30 Rate book, 1771,
31 Liverpool R.O., Coleman deeds, Lancashire 107.

they insured their hemp and flax and their 'utensils' there and in a range of buildings in the yard for £300. In 1747 and 1750 William Woodcock insured his own house and its contents for £130 and the warehouse for £20. He also insured other tenanted property he owned in the vicinity for £430.[32] By 1750 the value of the firm's stock had risen to £1,000 and by 1753 they had had to build a new warehouse in Friars Green, which they insured for £100. The stock it housed was insured for £1,000, so by this time they had £2,000 worth of stock.

In the early years of these firms, it is likely that their principal activities were buying the flax and hemp in the Baltic and dressing or heckling it when it arrived on their premises. In many of the early insurance documents, these firms were called 'flax dressers'. Heckling was important as flax had to be heckled differently for each grade of yarn. Correct heckling helped to control the quality of the finished cloth. After heckling the flax was sent out for spinning to women working in their homes.[33]

In early March 1756, John Hart appeared before the House of Commons to give evidence on the Linen Bill. His evidence, described in a letter from John Seddon[34] to Robert Nicholson, his cousin and a Liverpool merchant, tells us more about how these firms conducted their business. The Hart firm employed about 8,000 spinners in and near Warrington. He also employed 30 persons 'to put out flax in various parts of the country'. Very few of his spinners were full-time workers – they did spinning 'when they had no other employment … At some seasons of the year the number of spinners was greatly reduced when the Dairy or the Harvest or other country business called them off.' Although a full-time spinner could make between 4d and 6d a day, the firm only paid out a total of about £60 per week for spinning.[35] Just how far afield the sailcloth makers had to go to get spinning done and how ingenious they had to be in organizing it is shown by the following example. In 1794, Samuel Gaskell (whom we shall soon meet) instructed Peter Stubs (see p. 254 above) to send a few files to Samuel Barrett in Woore, Shropshire. He explained to Stubs that Barrett put out spinning for him and that he paid him by sending files.[36]

Samuel Barrett may have been one of the nearest of the people who 'put out' flax for the Harts and other firms in Warrington. The ability to get spinning done controlled the amount of cloth a firm could produce. The British Linen Company organized spinning in Caithness and Orkney to supply their Edinburgh weavers.[37] The Nicholsons in Liverpool sent heckled flax to their cousins in Dumfries for

---

32 London Guildhall MS 11936, Sun policies 110913, 124272.
33 For illustration of heckling, spinning and winding, see Foster, 2002, pp. 33 and 34.
34 The minister of the Unitarian chapel in Warrington 1762–67.
35 Liverpool R.O., Nic 920/5/34/12.
36 Ashton, 1939, p. 63, Note 2.
37 Durie, 1996, pp. 27, 65.

spinning.[38] It is likely that Warrington manufacturers put out flax for spinning all the way up the coast to the North, even as far as Scotland, and they probably found pockets of inland spinners as well. They were also in the market for spun yarn, the British Linen Company hoping to secure them as a customer in 1758.[39]

After the flax was spun into yarn, the yarn had to be bleached or whitened. As early as 1749 the Hart firm had its own yarn crofts (see Pl. 36). These yards were broken into on the night of 19 July and the firm advertised in the *Manchester Magazine* on 20 July to warn that 'destructive engines had been set to wound any who enter at unreasonable hours'. In these bleach yards the yarn was boiled in an alkaline solution in 'bowking' cauldrons. It was then exposed outside to the sun and the rain. In Warrington most firms seem to have had their yards on Mersey Street, also known as the 'Bongs', with land running down to the banks of the Mersey. The source of the alkaline solution used for bleaching in the 1750s was wood ashes imported from the Baltic,[40] but in the 1760s they started to replace the ashes with kelp (seaweed) from Scotland and Ireland.[41]

After bleaching, the yarn had to be checked, then some of it was warped (see Pl. 37), probably always done in one of the rooms beside the warehouse, and it was then ready for weaving. Originally this will have been done by weavers in their own homes. Slowly the practice of having a few weavers and looms in a weaving shop developed. This change was probably introduced to control quality and to allow for the making up of urgent orders. When a sailcloth factory was advertised for sale in 1765, it contained eight looms. The firm had also had 40 looms working on sailcloth and other linens in weavers' own homes.[42] The partnership between the Harts and Turner and Woodcock was dissolved in about 1766 when John Hart went bankrupt. In 1771 Turner and Woodcock, who had continued the business, had 'weaving and warping shops adjoining 10 houses under one roof'. They were small houses, insured for only £15 each, where presumably the weaver lived (see Pl. 38).

This picture of the operations of a typical firm can be amplified by the detailed cost figures for sailcloth manufacture presented to the House of Commons by Josiah Wallis in 1749 and reprinted here in Appendix 9.3, Table A. Table B in this Appendix has some information on prices. It would seem likely that there were two main influences on the profitability of these firms. There seem to have been considerable fluctuations in the price of flax in the Baltic, when some growing seasons produced much larger crops than others, and demand in western Europe also varied

38 Liverpool R.O., Nic 920 5/5/29.
39 Durie, 1996, p. 103.
40 Ibid., pp. 48–49, 83.
41 Ibid., p. 207; L.R.O. Nicholson Nic 920 5/5/74.
42 Wadsworth and Mann, 1931, pp. 302–03.

greatly as wars and the threat of wars altered the amount required by Navies. The problem for managers was to buy cheap in advance of a growing demand and not to buy dear before a slump. The other task that seems to have plagued some firms was the failure to maintain quality, causing the Navy's inspectors to reject significant quantities of sailcloth. There was a substantial working capital employed in these businesses. The raw materials had to be paid for in Riga, where little credit was extended, then there was the voyage back to England, and some months, perhaps, of spinning, bleaching and weaving before the cloth was finished. Stocks of finished cloth then had to be kept in the warehouse and credit extended on sales. This was clearly a trade in which only the well-capitalised could participate.

vi) The sailcloth manufacturers of Warrington

The families who took up sailcloth manufacture can be divided into three groups. As well as the Harts, Turners and Woodcocks, two other Unitarian families started firms, making five Unitarian families in the industry, all related to each other and clearly forming a well-integrated social group. The other main Nonconformist group in Warrington – the Quakers – was represented by two families. The remaining six families in the industry, who seem to have supported the Established Church, created four firms.

By trying to trace the earlier history of these families, where they came from, what other occupations and investments they had, and what their brothers, sisters and children did, I hope to create a picture of the social and economic life of this group of entrepreneurs, who had a major influence on the culture and way of life in Warrington. In the course of these enquiries, I have also found a few snippets of information about the buildings they erected, which helped to determine the physical shape of the town. To add to this picture Plates 40–43 are details taken from the fine map of the town drawn in 1772 by D. Donbavand and J. Wallworth. Our understanding of these is further expanded by 2 samples from the more detailed surveys made *c.* 1740 of some of the Booth Family's properties in Plate 44. The shape of the town as a crossroads, where the north-south road from London to Scotland was crossed by the east-west road from Liverpool to Manchester, can be seen clearly in the Yates map, Plate 39.

In the early eighteenth century, there were three Hart brothers in Warrington, Thomas, Jeffrey and Joseph. The family property, including a mill, was in the township of Bedford near Leigh, about eight miles north of Warrington. Between 1710 and 1720 Thomas Hart, a 'linen draper', married Hannah, daughter of John Bent, an apothecary in the town, whose male descendants also entered the sailcloth business. When, in 1728, Thomas died the family property was left in trust, with the stipulation that the younger children were to receive £200 each, suggesting that his total assets were probably £600 to £800. He left three sons. John and Thomas, the two elder, went into partnership with Turner and Woodcock in sailcloth. The youngest, Cheney, born in 1726, studied medicine at Edinburgh University and became a doctor in Shrewsbury.[43] I have not discovered the occupation of old Thomas Hart's brother Jeffrey, but his son, also Jeffrey, joined his cousins, John and Thomas, in the sailcloth partnership. The other brother Joseph, a maltster in Warrington, married Elizabeth Dannet, whose family were also in the sailcloth business and whom we will meet later. They had no children so his property eventually passed to his nephews, Jeffrey and John.[44]

The Hart family had other property and other businesses. For example, in 1753 Jeffrey insured his own house in the Friars Gate district and other tenanted property there for £500.[45] In 1770 he insured goods (unspecified) in a warehouse at Rudge (or Ruds?) Fold for £700. In October 1761 the three Hart men bought the Arley estate's three-life lease of the Saracen's Head public house at Wilderspool from the executors of the Reverend Thomas Moss. The property came complete with malt-kiln, brewhouse, warehouses and stables,[46] and in 1763 the pub and three or four houses were insured by the firm of Hart and Company for £800.[47]

In 1766 John Hart went bankrupt[48] and I have found no record of his death. Thomas died in 1767 and Jeffrey in 1780. In 1786 Thomas Turner, as an executor, sold the brewery to Orrett, Lyon and Greenall and it remained Greenalls' brewery until the 1990s. From about 1775 onwards, Theophilus Hart, presumably named after his great-uncle Theophilus Bent, and evidently a young man of energy, owned a sailcloth business in Warrington, and before 1791 he had started a cotton-spinning factory in the town.

I have found much less information about the families of Thomas Turner and the William Woodcock. They were both the children of successful Warrington businessmen. Thomas Turner's father was William, a tanner who died in 1736 and who had been part of the congregation that became the Unitarians of Cairo Street. The trustees of the settlement created by his will were Charles Owen, Doctor of Divinity and minister of the congregation, and Ellis and Theophilus Bent. Thomas

43 See below p. 284 for bequest from Theophilus Bent.
44 Lancs. R.O. WCN, 1763.
45 Sun policy 134274.
46 Arley Rentals WM, Box 17; Slater, 1980, p. 24.
47 Sun policy 203543. The Hart family owned property in the area in 1744. Some of the insured property may have been theirs before they bought the Saracen's Head. See Foster, 1992, p. 69.
48 W.P.L. MS 1268/1,2. He and John Bent (see below, p. 285) may have been brought down by the disruption to West Indian trade caused by the new regulations imposed by Britain in 1763 on trade with the Spanish colonies in the Caribbean.

had a son, also Thomas, born about 1732, who joined his father in the sailcloth partnership. William Woodcock's father John, who died in 1751, was a merchant in the tobacco trade in Warrington.

Much more information survives about the Bent family. John Bent, an apothecary in Warrington from the late 1670s to his death in 1721, left four sons and a daughter who all led full lives. The eldest son, John, became a Dissenting Minister in Lancaster while the daughter, Hannah, married Thomas Hart, as we have just seen. The three other sons all went into business. Jonathon (1684–1762) and Theophilus were cornfactors and maltsters, important occupations in Warrington in this period. Barley does not grow well in this region, despite being its traditional bread grain. From the mid-seventeenth century onwards, an increasing number of ships carrying cheese and salt sailed from the Mersey estuary to destinations around the coasts of Britain,[49] and one of the common returning cargoes was grain, particularly barley. Coke was made on the coalfield and was available cheaply in Warrington. An important seventeenth-century innovation in the area was its use in malt-kilns, causing a considerable number of these kilns to be set up in the town. The malt was not only sold for conversion to beer in the large number of inns with brewing facilities in Warrington, but was probably also carried up to Manchester and other inland towns.[50]

Jonathon had a malt-kiln in Friars Gate, beside the house he lived in. He let three other houses on the site as well as a number of other pieces of land around the town.[51] Theophilus seems to have been at least as successful and purchased the freehold of the 48-acre farm at Shaw Green, Appleton, which he left to his nephew, Dr Cheney Hart of Shrewsbury.[52] In 1751 Theophilus rented the newly rebuilt Warburton corn mills from Sir Peter Warburton for £80 p.a. In 1757 he insured his own house, including the malt-kiln and slaughterhouse beside it for £150 and nine other properties for a further £650. Neither he nor Jonathon seem to have had any children of their own, so their fortunes were distributed among their Bent and Hart nephews and nieces.

Ellis Bent (1690–1749), the youngest of the apothecary's sons, became a 'linen draper' and was certainly successful. When he died, leaving two sons and four daughters, three of them under 21, he was able to leave them all handsomely

49 See above, Chapter 7, for salt; Foster, 1998, for cheese.
50 Marshall, 1967, p. 110 for this use of coke. At Arley Hall from the 1750s, malt was normally carried from the Derby area, but Arley was six miles further from the coke and the shipping. See Ashton, 1939, pp. 72–75 for Stubs' barley purchases.
51 His will in WPL MS 1286/1 and MS 1266/2 and 1266/3.
52 See Foster, 1992, pp. 19, 67, where the doctor is called Bent instead of Hart. The farm became the site of Appleton Hall.

provided for. His wife got property in Sankey Street and a £100 annuity. His elder son John received £1,000 in cash and some 16 pieces of property around the town, as well as his father's share in 'the navigation at Sankey Bridges'.[53] The second son, Ellis like his father, inherited all the rest of his father's properties, which included 26 tenants in freehold property and nine in leaseholds. All this land seems to have been within about 20 miles of Warrington. The four daughters divided the remainder of his goods and fortune. If he followed the usual convention and provided similar portions for all his younger children, he must have had substantial wealth.[54]

John, the elder son, seems to have continued in his father's linen business, which probably included other trading activities. In 1755 he insured a new warehouse and the stock in it for £850, and the Red Lion Inn in Bridge Street for £600 in 1757. He married Elizabeth, a daughter of Matthew Lyon, so he was evidently at that time regarded as a substantial merchant. Unfortunately, something went wrong in 1766 and in February 1767 John had to assign all his property, provisionally valued at £6,000, to trustees whose job was to make a settlement with his creditors. The trustees were his wife's brother, John Lyon, Dr Edward Pemberton, married to John's niece, Ellen, and William Turner. The disgrace was evidently too much for John Bent and he died just under a year later.[55]

His younger brother Ellis, born in 1732, was under 21 when his father died in 1749. He must have decided to become a sailcloth manufacturer soon after he took possession of the property his father had left him, as he obtained his first Navy contract in 1755 and was also involved with shipping early in his career. He explained to John Seddon on 12 September 1754 that he had 'been the week past in Liverpool discharging the ship *Warrington*'s cargoes which is at last arrived safe'.[56] He continued successfully in the sailcloth business without partners. His cousin, Robert, and one John Hart (probably a son of Thomas or Jeffrey) set up in the sailcloth business in 1771. Their main warehouse was in Friars Gate and had probably been used by the old Hart partnership. They also had a bowkhouse at Wilderspool,[57] but this partnership did not last long. Ellis and Robert Bent were partners in the business in the late 1770s. In the 1780s Robert started trading with the West Indies and, with his cousin's help, owned at least eight ships between 1784 and 1794. In 1802 he became MP for Aylesbury but went bankrupt in 1806. Along

---

53 This refers to improvements in the quay and warehousing (and perhaps the brook itself) below
   Sankey Bridges, see Map 9.
54 W.P.L. MS 1263/2.
55 W.P.L. MS 1263/3 and 1263/4. See note 48 on p. 283 above
56 W.P.L. MF4.
57 Sun policy 299656.

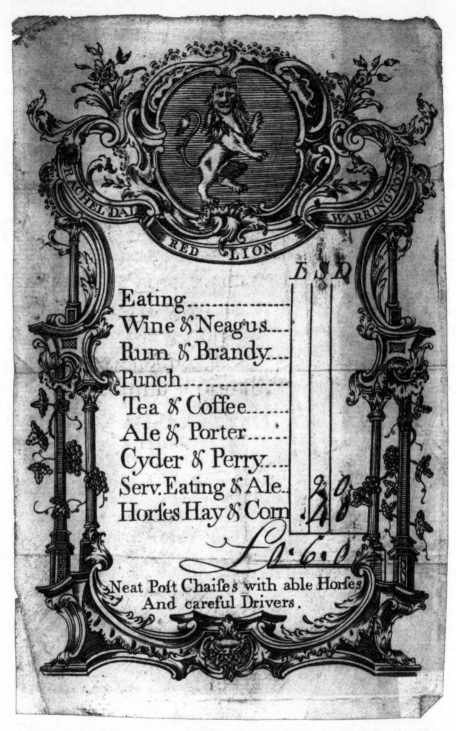

Figure 11. An invoice from the Red Lion when Rachel Dale was running this inn. Compare with invoices on pp. 189 and 193 of *Seven Households*.

with John Chorley and many others, he was brought down by the severe depression in the Jamaican economy between 1803 and 1810.[58]

To people who have lived since 1850, the most famous name in the Cairo Street congregation was Gaskell. William Gaskell, husband of Elizabeth the novelist, was descended from this Warrington family.[59] He was the minister at the Unitarian Chapel in Cross Street, Manchester, when his wife was writing her novels. In about 1760 two Gaskell brothers – Samuel and Roger – had married the two daughters of William Woodcock. Woodcock was then in partnership with the Harts and Turner in sailcloth manufacturing, as we have seen. Samuel Gaskell and Ann Woodcock were the grand-parents of William, the novelist's husband. Roger Gaskell, father of Samuel and Roger, was probably born in the last years of the seventeenth century. His original business seems to have been that of maltster, like many others in Warrington. In 1736 he bought part of the Limekiln Field near the Bank Quay site, and later in the year sold some of it on to Thomas Patten.[60] He evidently retained enough to continue in the business of burning limestone and selling lime, because between 1759 and 1761 he sold 2,990 measures at 6d each to Arley Hall. In 1753 he insured his house in Cornmarket and his household goods for £140, while a warehouse there and its stock were worth another £60. The stables and three other houses on the site were included at £200 and the malt-kiln, in Old Buttermarket, with its stock was valued at £370.[61] This dry catalogue illustrates how mid eighteenth-century Warrington was a mixture of residential and business premises, seemingly jumbled together as business convenience and residential needs had dictated.

When he died in 1770, Roger divided his remaining property (which he valued at £1,140) almost equally between his three sons and his daughter.[62] He had evidently given them each a large portion many years earlier, because they were all married with families and running substantial businesses at the time he died. John, the eldest son, followed his father into the malt business. He was nine years older than his next brother Samuel, who was only 20 when he first insured his 'utensils' and flax for £500 in 1753, and John seems to have helped young Samuel get started. He obtained one of their Navy contracts in 1756. When the third brother, Roger, joined Samuel in the sailcloth business, John seems to have left them to it. The two

58 Craig, 1967, pp. 4, 10, 23, 43, 60, 111, 130, 140; Thorne, 1986, p. 184. See p. 264, Note 100.
59 Bulmer, 1980.
60 W.P.L. MS 1262/1 and 1262/2.
61 Sun policy 138262.
62 W.P.L. MS 1262/3 will.

brothers continued in sailcloth all their working lives and it was probably Samuel's son, Samuel, who started the cotton side before 1791.

As well as the five Unitarian families just described, there was a group of Quaker families in the sailcloth business. John Johnson described himself as a wool-comber in the Quaker record of his marriage to Ellen Kendall in 1723. In 1747, when he insured his house in Bridge Street beside the Rose and Crown (see Pl. 40), the Sun agent described him as a shopkeeper. With the other buildings on the site and his household goods and stock worth £300, the total sum he insured was £500. His eldest son John, aged 22, was by then already launched into the sailcloth business, and insured his stock of flax, stored in his father's outbuildings, for £200.

The elder John Johnson died in 1752. Of his ten children, four had died in childhood, but some of the other six were probably still at home then, the youngest, Thomas, being only 12. In 1755 when John, the eldest, married Mary Wilkinson, he took another house in Bridge Street with warehouse attached and in 1757 insured this for £200. The business was still in the old house beside the Rose and Crown where it was insured for £400. A year earlier, John's sister, Mary, had married Samuel Eaton, who was in the linen business in Warrington but was not a sailcloth manufacturer. Nathaniel, the second son, born in 1728, was probably already an apprentice. He became first a draper and then a pawnbroker in the town. Benjamin, the third son, went out to Tortola and was already there in 1757, aged only 21.[63] He may have gone to work with a fellow Quaker, Thomas Woolrich, and seems to have spent about 20 years in the West Indies as a trader and shipowner. He and his elder brother John were joint-owners with Samuel Eaton in a number of ships trading to Tortola in the 1760s and 1770s. The *Prince George* made voyages between 1762–71; the *Johnson* 1766–72; the *Ellen* 1766–71; and the *Ann* 1771–80.[64] John Johnson and Samuel Eaton may have only been investors in these ships or they may have been exporting sailcloth, cheap brown linen for the slaves, and other British manufactures which Benjamin sold in the islands. Thomas, the youngest son, probably went to be apprenticed in the middle 1750s and he may have been the Thomas Johnson who was a distiller and a dealer in brandy in Warrington in the 1780s.

Having got almost all her children out of the house, Ellen seems to have had time on her hands, so she set up as a shopkeeper again. In 1765 when she reinsured the old house, she had £390 worth of household goods and stock for the shop. She died in 1776, aged 75. Ann, her younger daughter, never married and died a few months before her mother. Perhaps the shop was really Ann's career.

John Johnson seems to have continued in the sailcloth business all his working

63 Jenkins, 1923, p. 77.
64 See Liverpool Plantation Registers, note 14 p. 269.

life. By 1772 his family and the business were in no less than five different rented buildings. He and his brother, Nathaniel, and their families were in a big house in Old Buttermarket, which their landlord James Percival was insuring for £400. He was also insuring for £100 the adjacent warehouse which was let to the sailcloth business. John Johnson was insuring stock in this warehouse for £840. There was a warping room nearby and a flax-dressing shop in Percival's Brow. John Johnson had built two weaver's houses in Factory Lane, which were insured for £20 each, and there was still a weaving shop in his mother's yard in Bridge Street, another one in Factory Lane, and a third one in an old thatched building in Cockhedge. The total value of the business assets insured was £1,700.

John's wife, Mary, gave birth to eight children between 1755 and 1770, but, before she died in 1771, they were all dead, Benjamin surviving the longest, to the age of only eight. Whether conditions in central Warrington had deteriorated so much by this period that such mortality was common, we don't know. The death of so many children in one family certainly did not happen in Great Budworth at this period. An important factor may have been smallpox, which anecdotal evidence suggests was rife in late eighteenth-century towns. There is a striking contrast between the mortality of John Johnson's children and the good health of Joseph Fothergill's family, which just might have been because Joseph Fothergill had his children inoculated. We know that Dr John Fothergill advised his eldest brother, Alexander, to inoculate all his children and gave him a detailed description of how to do it, so he may well have done the same for his other brother, Joseph.[65]

The other Quaker who started a sailcloth business in Warrington was John Titley. He was the second son of Joseph Titley, the grocer and charcoal ironmaster, whom we met earlier, p. 255. John inherited the grocery and confectionery shop beside the George in Bridge Street (see Pl. 40), where he continued to trade into the 1740s. In March 1746, when he was 35 years old, he insured a stock of £400 worth of flax. He was living in a house, with warehouse attached, in Old Buttermarket, which his landlord James Percival insured for £340.[66] By December 1753 the value of his stock had increased to £750. In 1756 and 1757 he must have been quite desperate for Navy orders because he not only applied for and received contracts in his own name, but he also got his younger brother, Benjamin, and his eldest son, John, aged 20, to apply. They also both received contracts. Then, in early 1757, John decided for some reason to move half his business to Liverpool. Even the large Navy orders could not save him in this crisis and he went bankrupt in 1758.[67] The premises which

65 Corner, 1971, pp. 140–41, letter of 5 January 1751.
66 Titley was still referred to as grocer when he increased the value of his stock to £600 in 1748.
67 *Manchester Magazine*, 28 November 1758.

he had rented in Warrington were advertised for sale in 1759. They contained 19 looms, a thread mill and a hemp mill, as well as items needed for sailcloth manufacture, so Titley had evidently had a more diversified business.[68] He died in 1762, leaving a wife and several children without support. The main reason for his failure may have been that he appears (from the insurance valuations) to have had a smaller amount of capital than any of the other manufacturers.

Four more sailcloth firms contracted with the Navy in 1756/7. These firms were run by six families who seem to have stayed within the Established Church. One firm was started by John Robinson, who seems to have been the first man ever to make sailcloth in Warrington. He originally contracted with the Navy in 1741, but seems to have been involved in linen manufacture for at least 20 years before then. In 1722 he was described as 'weaver' when his daughter's death was recorded. It seems likely that he may have largely given up direct manufacture in favour of wholesaling both home-produced and imported linens, before he went into sailcloth manufacture. He probably dealt mainly in Irish and Scottish linen. In 1746 when he first insured his property and stock of hemp and flax in Bridge Street, he was described by the Sun Insurance agent as 'chapman'. The description of his business is typical of this early period. He insured his dwelling house and his household goods for £150 and also a brick-built warehouse, cellars and ancillary buildings in the yard.

John Robinson was part owner of the sloop *Dispatch*.[69] This may have been used to carry linens from Ireland and Scotland to Liverpool and London, or it may have made voyages to the Baltic for hemp and flax. In March 1749/50 Robinson told the House of Commons that he had employed about 5,000 persons during the war (1740–48, the War of the Austrian Succession). Two thirds of these were now laid off and he would be glad to sell his stock at prime cost. He also said that several British manufacturers of sailcloth had gone bankrupt in 1748 and 1749.[70] He died about 1750, but the business was continued by his widow, Ellen, with his two daughters and their husbands. The eldest daughter Jane had married John Nangreave. When the latter became a trustee of the marriage settlement of Matthew Lyon and Ellen Fairclough in 1754, his address was given as Cotton Wharf,

---

68 Wadsworth and Mann, 1931, p. 203. It was apparently a factory like this that Arthur Young saw in 1769. When he saw men spinning thread and twine on the mills, he thought it was for sailcloth. Women spun the yarn of which cloth was made. The thread which the men were spinning (which was used for sewing sails, shoes, etc.) was several strands of yarn spun together. Young, 1770–71, Vol. III, p. 211–12.

69 Wardle, 1941, p. 88.

70 House of Commons Journal, XXV, p. 1027. The contrast between John Robinson as a shipowner and employer of 5,000 people and the earlier one word descriptions of him as weaver and chapman highlights the dangers of one-word descriptions discussed earlier in Appendix 5.1.E.

Southwark, Surrey. In the same year he and his partner Joseph Baker, describing themselves as 'wharfingers', insured their Chambers warehouse on the wharf for £800 and their stocks there for £1,000, making a total insured of £1,800.[71] The younger daughter, Mary, married Henry Dannett who also seems to have been a London merchant. He gave evidence to the House of Commons in March 1749 that the Bounty Fund for the export of linens was defective.

Both Nangreave and Dannett seem to have come from Warrington families. In 1771 both these families had property in Buttermarket Street. The Dannetts were related to the Hart family.[72] It may have been these good connections in London that gave John Robinson the information about the Navy's contracts for sailcloth in 1740. The existence of the two Warrington families of Nangreave and Dannett in London, engaged in businesses that included a warehouse and a knowledge of the linen industry, suggests that they were the London end of businesses that organized the production of linen in Lancashire, Ireland, Scotland or the Baltic. A London sales organization with a warehouse was vital if orders were to be obtained from London merchants exporting to America and the West Indies. The British Linen Company in Edinburgh sold much of its output through its London agent.[73] John Robinson was presumably an important customer of, or supplier to, the Nangreave and Dannett businesses. Sailcloth manufacture was evidently a successful venture for these two families as they kept it going. In 1775/6, John Robinson's two grandsons, John and Richard Nangreave, contracted to supply sailcloth to the Navy.[74]

I have not found much information about the other three families. Edward Dainteth was in partnership with his brother, Josiah, when they insured their warehouse, workshop and stock for £1,200 in 1765. Edward died in 1772. He left £40 to Trinity Chapel School, (also known as the Bluecoat School) in central Warrington, which was an Anglican estalishment of the kind common in the North-West where the chapel, and the school attached to it were entirely financed by its congregation, without support from the Parish Church (see Pl. 40). His brother, Josiah, continued the business. John Tunstall occupied a house and outbuildings in Bridge Street, which were insured by his landlord, a maltster named Peter Winstanley, for £200 in 1746. Tunstall at the same time insured other buildings on the site and his stock for £350. By 1755 the value of his stock had risen to £1,000. This was in line with other sailcloth makers and presumably reflects the growth of the industry in the town. The Tunstall business continued into the 1780s.

71 Sun policy 141193.
72 W.P.L. MS 132, will of Joseph Hart, 1763.
73 Durie, 1996, p. 85, 102–04.
74 W.P.L. 1230 for the family relationship.

Thomas Lee lived in a house in Bridge Street, insured by its owner John Haywood for £200 in 1753. In 1746 he first insured his goods and stock for £300 and the value of the stock was increased both in 1750 and in 1754. By 1763 he appears to have bought the house, as he insured the buildings, his goods and his stock for £1,400. This steady increase in the values insured again indicates that his business was keeping pace with the others.

In the introduction to this chapter, I asked why Warrington was so successful in the new sailcloth industry. Although there were many places in England with the technical skills required to make sailcloth, Warrington had several advantages. We have seen that it possessed enough businessmen to start nine well-capitalized firms to enter the trade. The large export of Cheshire salt to the Baltic fishing fleets gave the merchants of Liverpool good connections in Danzig and Riga, where flax and hemp had to be bought. However we have identified one serious disadvantage; the Mersey basin area was short of spinners because of the rapidly increasing volume of cotton goods being produced in the textile areas around Manchester and Preston. Indeed from the 1770s onwards the sailcloth trade drifted north of Warrington to Lancaster and Whitehaven.[75] It is surprising that Hull, the gateway to the flax-working areas of west Yorkshire, or Newcastle upon Tyne, which produced salt, did not offer stiffer competition. Both ports had long connections with Baltic trade. Did they not have a sufficient number of businessmen with the capital required to enter the industry? Did their businessmen feel unable to organize the shipping and the purchase of flax, hemp and ashes, although the British Linen Company in Edinburgh managed to buy their supplies in Riga at this period?[76] Was there a special entrepreneurial flair in Warrington?

75 Robinson, 1998, pp. 44–65.
76 Durie, 1996.

Appendix 9.1. *The size of the overseas market for British manufactured sailcloth, 1731–70*

Table A. The average annual value of exports of British sailcloth

Five-year periods	£
1731–1735	3,211
1736–1740	8,989
1741–1745	5,529
1746–1750	21,794
1751–1755	21,931
1756–1760	29,520
1761–1765	41,211
1766–1770	45,090

Source: Schumpeter, 1960, pp. 29–30.

Table B. Destinations of sailcloth exports in 1770

	%
Colonies about to become USA	53
West Indies	18
India	8
Ireland	6
Newfoundland	5
Others	10
	100

Source: P.R.O. Cust. 3.

Approximately 50% of these exports were made from London, and 28% were made from Liverpool.

Appendix 9.2. *Sailcloth contractors to the Admiralty, 1756–57.*

Table A. Warrington-based contractors

Contractor's name	Partner	Insurance Year	Property	Stock	Address	Sun policy number
Bent, Ellis	none	1757	–	1,400	North	158,636
		1761	–	1,500	Warrington	178,619
Dainteth, Edward	Josiah, brother	1765	300	900	Old Buttermarket, Church St	215,674
Dannett, Mary	Robinson and Nangreave					
Gaskell, John	John, Samuel,	1753	–	500		138,923
Gaskell, Samuel	Roger were three brothers	1761	–	1,500	Cornmarket, New St	185,701
Hart, John	Turner and Woodcock					
Johnson, John	none	1748	–	200	Bridge St	111,113
		1753	–	300	Bridge St	134,258
		1757	200	400	Bridge St	158,640
		1760	–	700	Old Buttermarket	178,655
		1772	–	1,700	see text	316,425
Lee, Thomas, Snr	Father and son	1746	–	300	Bridge St	106,855
Lee, Thomas, Jnr		1750	–	600	Bridge St	124,269
		1754	–	800	Bridge St	144,016
		1763	400	1,000	Bridge St	195,109
Nangreave, John	Robinson and Dannett					
Robinson, Ellen	Nangreave and Dannett	1746	230	570	Bridge St	107,705
		1748	–	500	Sankey St	114,234
		1752	–	500	Bank Quay	133,351
Titley, John	Probably all John's	1746	–	400	Buttermarket	104,651
Titley, John, Jnr	business	1748	–	600	Buttermarket	111,069
Titley, Benjamin		1753	–	750	Buttermarket	138,928
		1757	–	900	Liverpool and Warrington	155,523
Tunstall, John	none	1746	150	350	Bridge St	104,647
		1747	150	500	Bridge St	110,058
		1755	150	1,000	Bridge St	144,728
Turner, Thomas	1747	1747	–	300	Friars Gate	110,911
Turner, Thomas, Jnr	partnership:	1750	–	1,000	Friars Gate	124,271
	John, Thomas	1753	–	1,000	Friars Gate	138,924
	and Jeffrey Hart,	1753	100	1,000	Friars Green	138,927
Woodcock,	Thomas Turner	1756	–	700	Friars Gate	152,225
William	and William Woodcock	1771	500	–	Stanley St	302,664

Sources: P.R.O. ADM 106/3604, 3605; London Guildhall, Sun Fire Register, MS 11936.

Notes:
1. Sometimes household goods and stock are valued together.
2. It is not always clear whether the warehouse is included with the flax stored in it, so stock may sometimes include household goods and the buildings in which the flax is stored.

Table B. Contractors who were probably London merchants

Name	*Probable address*
Bond, John	Crutched Friars
Dodding, William and Lovell, William	St Mary's Hill
Gower, Sir Sam	Goodmans Field
Haydon, Humphrey	Whitechapel Road
Higgs, Benjamin	Harp Lane
Irish, John	Old St
Mackintosh, John	Milk St
Ouchterlony, George	Angel Court
Prestwick, Aphen	Bell Dock, Wapping
Prestwick, John	Bell Dock, Wapping
Prestwick, Oliver	Bell Dock, Wapping
Robinson, Robert	Globe Yard, Wapping
Wallis, Josiah	Hermitage, Wapping

Table C. Possible locations of other contractors

a) Other places in Lancashire

Langton, John	Kirkham	*definite*
Chorley, John	Prescot	*likely*
Rawlinson, William	Manchester area	*likely*

b) Other places (*all only possible*)

Crow, George and Watson, John	Stockton-on-Tees
Finch, John	Dudley
Kidd, William	Newcastle-upon-Tyne
Pyall, Robert	Dover

Yorkshire, Lincolnshire and Dorset all had well-known flax working communities.

Table D. Notes on other Warrington sailcloth/linen manufacturers

To complete the picture of the Warrington industry up to 1770, a few additions should be made to the list of Navy contractors in 1756/7 in Table A:

1. John Kelsall was a Quaker linen draper who had stocks of hemp and flax in a warehouse. He insured them for £400 in 1745, £600 in 1747 and £500 in 1750 and 1755 (Sun policies 104,652, 111,068, 122,428 and 150,057). Sailcloth is not mentioned in these policies. Was

he just producing yarn and selling it to the sailcloth makers? Was he making sailcloth and not supplying the Navy for religious reasons? Was he only making other linen products? His country house was robbed on Saturday night, 17 May 1760 (*Manchester Magazine*, 19 May 1760).

2. Richard Higginson was a sailcloth maker who insured his goods and stock for £300 in 1760 and 1763 (Sun policies 177,650 and 203,544). Mary Higginson got a Navy contract in 1775.

3. John Howard got a Navy contract in 1775 and insured in 1782.

4. Thomas Topping was a seedsman in Warrington from 1751 to 1765.[1] He then changed to sailcloth manufacture. He insured his stock for £600 in 1765 (Sun policy 215,672) and got a Navy contract in 1775/6.

Appendix 9.3. *The costs of manufacture and the prices of sailcloth*

A. Costs

Josiah Wallis, one of the London merchants supplying the Navy, told the House of Commons on 2 March 1749 that the typical costs of 144 bolts of sailcloth (each 38 yards long and two feet wide) were:

	£	s	d	%
72 cwts flax at 28s	100	16	0	33.5
540 doz. flax dressing	15	15	0	5.2
396 doz. spin warp	59	8	0 ⎫	23.9
144 doz. spin shoot	12	12	0 ⎭	
540 doz. whitening	22	10	0	7.5
144 bolts weaving	64	16	0	21.5
Foreman, winding, warping	25	4	0	8.4
	301	1	0	100.0

Source: House of Commons Journal, *XXV, p. 1025.*

Notes:

1) If this statement was approximately correct, it allows one to calculate the cost of any operation when the information in the table is combined with the detailed specification of the cloth in 9 George II c 38. For example, the weaver was paid 2.8d a yard. He had to do three yards per day to earn 8.4d a day.

If the annual output of sailcloth was worth about £200,000 (see p. 274 of text) we can calculate: the value of spinning annually was £47,800; the value of weaving annually was £43,000. If weaving cost 8d a day (which is a likely average from figures given elsewhere in the Arley Archive Series) then about 4,300 full-time weavers had to work for a year to provide the cloth required. If the average spinner earned only 4d a day, the production of the yarn would have required 9,560 full-time spinners to work for a year. As we have seen on p. 280 of the text, spinners were actually usually part-time. For Mr Hart they worked only 22½ full days a year on average. At that rate, about 127,000 part-time spinners were needed for the sailcloth industry.

If the sailcloth produced in a year was worth £300,000, it would have required about 190,000 spinners to provide the yarn. John Hart's firm was employing 8,000 spinners directly. The 30 people who were 'putting out' flax for his firm are likely to have reached at least 2,000 more. So

---

1 Foster, 1996, p. 269.

his business was probably consuming the yarn spun by at least 10,000 women. It was the largest of the nine firms in Warrington, if the insurance figures in Appendix 9.2, Table A, are a good guide. From this, one may calculate that the Warrington firms could have been employing at least 60,000 spinners. This could have been between one third and one half of the total employed in the industry in the country. Aikin's suggestion that half the nation's sailcloth was made in Warrington may not have been a bad estimate.[2]

2) Josiah Wallis could be confident of the costs of manufacture because the work was normally all done on piecework rates. For example, the typical price for spinning these grades was 10d to 12d a spindle. The price of yarn was 2s 1d to 2s 7d a spindle.[3]

B. Prices paid by the Navy in October 1756

Grade	Price per yard (s d)
1	1 3¼
2	1 2¾
3	1 2¼
4	1 1¾
5	1 1
6	1 0¼
7	11
8	10¼

Notes
1. The prices the Navy paid were always graduated in this way. They varied considerably – from 1s 7d a yard in 1742 to 1s 0¾d a yard in 1753 for Grade No. 1.
2. The price was probably most influenced by the cost of flax in the Baltic.

2 Aikin, 1795, p. 302.
3 Durie, 1996, p. 107; Liverpool R.O. 920 Nic 5/5.

CHAPTER 10

The wealth and occupations of the inhabitants of Warrington in 1771

This short chapter sketches the structure of Warrington society in 1771 as an example of a north-western business town on the eve of the Industrial Revolution. In 1781 there were 1,941 houses in Warrington, containing 8,791 inhabitants.[1] In 1771 there would have been a slightly smaller number of houses – perhaps around 1,800. The earliest rate-book of the town to survive is for 1771, listing 411 ratepayers. Most of these ratepayers were owners of residential or business property, and most of it was freehold. In 1628 Sir George Booth of Dunham Massey had bought the tenanted properties of the old Botelor of Bewsey estate from the Ireland family. Around 1700 his great, great grandson, the Earl of Warrington, had some 216 properties there, let on three life leases, but from about 1725 he sold the freehold of individual properties, often to the three life leaseholder, so that there were probably only ten or twenty leaseholds remaining when the manor was sold to John Blackburne in 1762. The Legh of Lyme family, who were the other major landlords in the town, behaved in a similar fashion.[2] A few occupiers paid rates on their business assets. Thus Alexander Chorley, who had just taken over the Fothergill ironmongery shop in Sankey Street, had his stock there assessed as worth £7 10s 0d per annum.[3] Rates on this property, where the shop occupied the ground floor on the street and the Fothergill daughters were living above or behind, were probably charged on Samuel Fothergill as Executor of his brother's and nephew's wills.

In Appendix 10.1, Table A, is a list of the fourteen highest assessments. The three top ratepaying families were John Blackburne of Orford, assessed as the owner of property worth £1,292 per annum, Thomas Patten of Bank Hall assessed at £1,041 p.a., and John Lyon assessed at £578 p.a. We have already met all three of these families as leading investors in the salt industry. The other 11 were all assessed as having incomes between £132 p.a. and £330 p.a. Four of them were sailcloth manufacturers – Bent, Hart, Lee and Woodcock. We have also met Thomas Lyon who was descended from the other favourite nephew of Matthew Page. His side of the family was to make an exceptional contribution to the business of the area as sugar

---

1 Aikin, 1795, p304.
2 EGR 11/1/6, 11/1/8 & WPL MS 851 Legh Survey & MS 1073 Booth Survey.
3 The assessors probably used 4% or 5% as the 'going' interest rate. If so, they had estimated the value of the goods in the shop at below £200. This was probably a conservative estimate so as to avoid arguments.

refiners, brewers, cotton merchants and bankers, before building Appleton Hall in the nineteenth century. Samuel Fothergill was equal lowest on £132 p.a. It was probably his role as Executor to his brother that had raised him so high (see above). The other five were property owners, innkeepers, brewers and mercers.

Table B lists the assessments of most of the other Warrington people we have met in the previous three chapters and a few others whom I will describe. These rating assessments are not a perfect indicator of wealth. Of the other sailcloth manufacturers, the Turners had property rated at a total of £223, but it was divided between five different ownerships. The Gaskells' property was worth £120 p.a. Other evidence suggests that some of them may have lived in the Wilderspool area, outside the town. A Mr Nangreave and two Dainteths owned properties. Ellen Johnson owned the house beside the Rose and Crown in Bridge Street where she had her shop, valued at £35.10s p.a. Her son, John, operated his sailcloth business from rented property as described earlier. The ships, in which he and his brother-in-law Sam Eaton owned a share, were not rated, nor were their cargoes. There must have been substantial wealth tied up in their trading activities, but John Johnson was only rated at £16.10s p.a. and Sam Eaton at £7.10s p.a. John Tunstall was assessed at £77 and Mr. Dainteth at only £45.5s. These sums may reflect the reality that these last three were less rich than the other manufacturers.

This brief analysis shows that the sailcloth manufacturers all belonged to a group below the three richest families. We have seen that the Blackburnes, Lyons and Pattens all had large investments outside Warrington – salt mines, copper works, quays and navigations, as well as agricultural land. Their wealth was on a different scale to that of the sailcloth manufacturers and each of these three families may have had assets worth more than £50,000. The wealth of the manufacturers was probably in a range from £1,000 to £10,000 each.[4]

Some of the other people in this group with the sailcloth manufacturers were junior members of the three big families. The Pattens, for example, were represented by six ratepayers, including Robert Patten's sugar refinery (Pl. 41). In 1768 he and his partners, George Robinson and John Atherton, had insured the buildings, utensils and stock of this business for £5,600.[5] The £60 p.a. rating was evidently highly conservative. The other large capital intensive manufacturing facility in the town was the glassworks known as Seaman and Company, which was also rated at £60 p.a. (Pls. 21 and 22). This had been erected soon after 1758 by a partnership in which Peter Seaman owned one-third, Robert Patten owned another third and two

4 The capital value of the rated assets is likely to have been at least twenty times the assessments. So the value of Ellis Bent's Warrington property will have been at least £4,000. We know he had other lands in south Lancashire as well as capital in trading goods.
5 Sun policy 252833.

Sir Peter Warburton Bar.t _____

1757 Bought of Rob.t Patten & Co _____

Jan.y 26	4 Lumps Qty — "3" 9½	. . .	at 75/	0" 2" 7¾
	4 D.Ref.d Lo.t Qty 1" 3	. . .	at 10¾/	1" 10" 4½
			£	4" 12" 11¾

April 20.th	4 Lumps Qty — 3" 6	. .	at 74/	2" 19" 5
	4 D.R. Lo.t Qty 1" 2½	. .	at 11¾/	1" 9" 10
			£	4" 9" 3

June 17	4 Lumps Qty 2" 26½	. . .	at 74/	2" 14" 6
	4 D.Ref.d Lo.t Qty 1" 4½	. . .	at 11½/	1" 11" 1
			£	4" 5" 7

Sir   Warrington Feb.y 15.th 1760

above are Invoices of Three parcels of Sug.r Sent
you; which I imagine, had slip'd your
memory, therefore, I make bold to put you in
mind of them, & if it be agreeable, to order
me payment in a week or ten days, it will
be of Service, & Oblige me. I am for Self & Co.

Sir Your most humble Serv.t _____

                              Rob.t Patten

3 parcels as above . . . .   13" 7" 9¾

Liverpool businessmen had the remainder. The partners had provided £3,000 between them to establish the business.[6] Peter Seaman was the tenant of the *Eagle and Child* in Bridge Street, inherited by Matthew Lyon from Matthew Page and owned by his son John Lyon in 1771. The Inn seems to have operated as the sales office of the glassworks.

The town had the normal range of occupations that one would expect in a place of this size. As well as Dr. Dainteth, there was Dr. Pemberton, the doctor who attended the Warburtons at Arley, brother-in-law to Thomas Lyon,. There may have been an unusually large number of grocers. Much of their stock – tea, coffee, spices, dried fruits, etc – will have come from London in the returning cheese ships. One of the grocers, William Hesketh, was a ship owner and brought raisins, figs and lemons direct from Malaga and Valencia.[7] His family was assessed at £99.10s p.a. for three properties in Sankey Street. Richard Travers, rated at £43 p.a., owned the grocer usually patronised by Arley. William Turner and Walter Kerfoot, the most respected lawyers in the town, handled the affairs of Lord Derby's unmarried daughters – Ladies Isabella, Jane and Mary Stanley – from 1777 to 1803.[8] Kerfoot married the widow of John Bent, who had started life as Elizabeth Lyon. His partner, William Turner, was assessed at £84.15s p.a. Abraham Titley, whom we have seen was a rich man, had a small house in Warrington, worth £16 p.a. Mr. Watkins, a colleague of Thomas Patten's in the copper business, and in the wholesale trade of materials for the potteries in Stoke-on-Trent, had significant Warrington property worth £118.15s p.a. Thomas Watt, who was to become a considerably richer man by 1800, was still at an early stage in his career. He had only been in his soap and candles business twelve years. He was assessed at £50.10s p.a., although he was to insure his assets in Fryars Gate for £2,800 in 1772. His soap manufacture may have consumed a little of the rosin (resin) made in a new factory built at Bank Quay in 1768, by an iron-monger called Roger Rogerson who was assessed at £83.15s p.a.[9] Robert Gwyllym's wife had inherited Bewsey Hall from her father,

Figure 12 (opposite). Robert Patten's invoice for sugar, February 1760. The first item in January 1757 was '4 lumps of sugar weighing a total of 3 quarters 9 pounds (i.e. $3 \times 28 + 9$ = 93lbs) at 75 shillings a hundredweight (or 8.0357d per lb.) cost £3 2s. 7d. The second item was 4 Double Refined lumps weighing 1 quarter and 3 pounds (i.e. 31 lbs) at $11\frac{3}{4}$d lb cost £1 10s $4\frac{1}{2}$d. These prices show that one pound of ordinary sugar cost the same as a labourer's daily wage and a pound of double refined sugar cost the same as a craftsman's wage.

6   Cheshire R.O. DMD L/6/1.
7   Gore's Liverpool Advertiser 22.12.1769 lists their arrival in the 'Ellin.' Liverpool Plantation Registers show him as the part owner of the 'William' and 'Salesbury' in 1771.
8   WM Boxes 29 & 30.

Richard Atherton. This house was rated at £108 p.a. and returned to the ownership of people called Atherton when her children reverted to that name.

Finally, I have included in this group, as an unusual figure, Benjamin Yoxall, who, in 1757, was insuring property in Buttermarket Street for £200, and who was described as a schoolmaster in a deed of 1761. In 1765 he surveyed and drew a large map of the Warburtons' Appleton manor, and in 1772 he was the tenant of a house, shop, two warehouses and associated buildings, also in Buttermarket Street, insured for £150. His business there was described as hair-cloth maker.[10] Was this all the work of one man? Or did he have a son of the same name? The ratebook mentions only one man, assessed at £85 p.a. Only one educational establishment was rated – The Academy (Pl. 43). It had been set up by the Dissenters, among whom the Unitarians were strongly represented, and was designed to provide a higher education for their sons and to train their Ministers. Jeffrey Hart was Treasurer, 1764–1780 and it was assessed at £70 p.a.[11] At the end of the ratebook are notes of newly erected buildings that might have given rise to increased rateable values since the rating list was made. The vigour of the expansion in sailcloth manufacturing at that time is apparent in these entries. Of the 21 names listed, five are new factories built by these firms – Bent and Hart, Gaskell, Johnson, Nangreave, and Turner and Woodcock.

Two earlier comprehensive tax returns for the town survive. In 1545 there were 124 tax-payers which suggests it was then more than twice the size of Knutsford but about half the size of Manchester,[12] see p. 52 above. The second tax return was made in 1649 and lists 184 people. We may surmise from this that the number of property owners in the town had only just over doubled in the 122 years 1649 to 1771. It also suggests that Warrington may have been a town with 3,000 inhabitants in 1649 – perhaps three times the size of Liverpool. The leading 17 taxpayers are listed in Appendix 10.1, Table C. Four of them are from families with whom we are familiar – Ashton, Blackburne, Page and Patten. Three others were major gentry families, one of whom – Gilbert Ireland of Hale – owned Bewsey Hall, while Edward Bridgeman, his wife and her son, Peter Brook, were probably renting Sankey Hall. It is interesting to note that in 1649 the assessment of Bewsey Hall was similar to that of the three business families of Blackburne, Patten and Page, but by 1771 the latter's descendants were each assessed at many times more than the Hall; business fortunes had by then overtaken landed wealth. With the exception of the

9 Musson, 1965, p 15.
10 W.P.L. MS 1288/2; Arley invoice 23 December 1765; Sun policies 156024 and 316424. Haircloth was used to support the grain over the coke fire in malt kilns.
11 McLachlan, 1943. Turner, 1813. The Grammar School, as a charity, was excempted from rates.
12 PRO E179/130/132.

31. *Carr End, near Bainbridge, Wensleydale, Yorkshire.*
The original house, with six windows looking towards the lake, has been extended at both ends, but it was always a substantial house and so provides clear evidence of the wealth of the copyholders by the 1660s.

32. *Carr End.*
The datestone recording the year the house was built was placed by John Fothergill over the principal fireplace.

33. *Stanley Street, Warrington.*
These three eighteenth-century houses are the only survivors in what was, in 1772, perhaps the best street in the town. In the eighteenth century they enjoyed open views over the fields to the north and south. (These three houses, at the end of the street, are just off the bottom left-hand corner of Pl. 40.)

34. *Crosfields – now Lever Faberge.*
The front entrance was built in 1905/6 when the family still owned and managed the business. This building is on old Sankey Street, north of the rosin works shown in Pl. 21, and the firm now occupies several acres behind it.

35. *Unitarian Chapel in Cairo Street.*
The south, entrance, front, built in 1745 which is shown in the top left corner of Pl. 40, marked Dissenters Chapel.

36. *Yarn Crofts.*
Five men are hanging skeins of yarn in the open so that they would be exposed to the sun and the rain (from a nineteenth-century stained glass window at Bridport, Dorset)

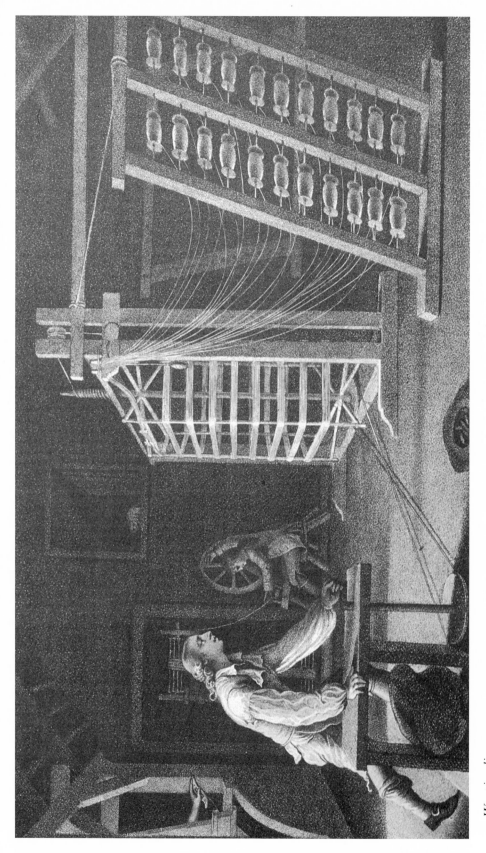

37. *Warping linen yarn.*
An engraving by William Hincks, 1783.

38. *Weaving linen.*
An engraving by William Hincks. Since sailcloth was always only two feet wide, the weaver would not have had to stretch as much as this one was doing.

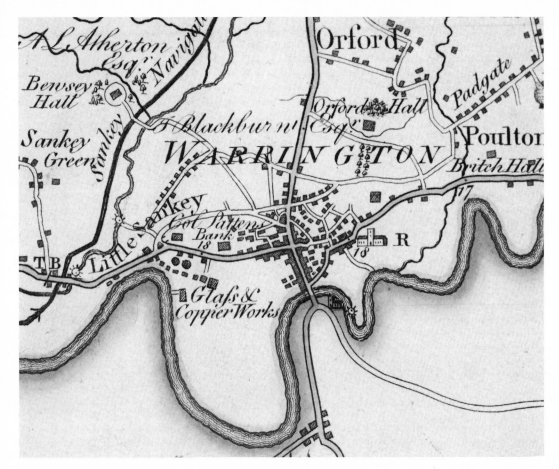

39. *The Warrington area.*

This map, made by Yates in 1786, shows the bridge over the Mersey, the main crossroads and Sankey Street running west past Patten's Bank Hall to the Bank Quay area and on to Sankey Bridge and Liverpool. The parish church can be seen at the extreme east end. This had been the centre of the town in the early Middle Ages, before the bridge was built, when the river was crossed at the Lach Ford. The two gentry houses – Bewsey and Orford Halls – complete the picture.

40. This is the first of five detailed excerpts of the map, which together show most of the buildings in the town. Bridge Street ran north from the bridge over the Mersey to the crossroads in the centre of the town called Market Gate. Half-way up on the west was Friars Gate leading to Chancel Street, alias Friars Green. The Augustinian Friars Church had once stood to the south of Friars Gate and this was the area where Thomas Watt lived and had his soap and candle business, and also where the Unitarian sailcloth makers, Hart, Turner and Woodcock, had houses.

Further north still on the west side was the Eagle and Child, where the Matthew Page family had a three-life leasehold in the seventeenth and early eighteenth centuries. Immediately to the north of this inn was Patten Lane where Thomas, George and Mary Patten still held three-life leaseholds in 1701. Thomas Patten II (1561–1639) had lived in Patten Lane, presumably in one of these leaseholds, and it is thought that Thomas VI may have lived in the large house immediately above the word Eagle before he built Bank Hall. Further north still was the George Inn which was Matthew Page senior's three-life lease in 1701, the freehold of which was bought by his nephew Matthew Lyon in 1733 (EGR 11/1/6). The Titley family's grocery business was in a shop beside this inn

Immediately to the north of the George on Sankey Street was Trinity Chapel whose tower dominates the town in the engraving (Pl. 22). Originally built in 1708, it had been rebuilt and enlarged in 1758 and was the place of worship of the top families of Warrington who belonged to the Established Church – Patten, Blackburne, Page, Lyon, Pemberton, Watkins, Hesketh and others. It had been erected by these families and was largely maintained at their expense. Beside it was the Bluecoat School, a charity also maintained by them, which provided a free education for some 12–20 Warrington boys before they were apprenticed at the age of 14.

On the east side of Bridge Street, the Red Lion Inn, at one time owned by John Bent, is marked as a large establishment but there were many more pubs in the street, for example the Legh survey of 1775 shows the Ram's Head and the Rose and Crown beside each other opposite Friars Gate. The Johnson family (p. 288) had a three-life lease of land along the lane behind the Rose and Crown.

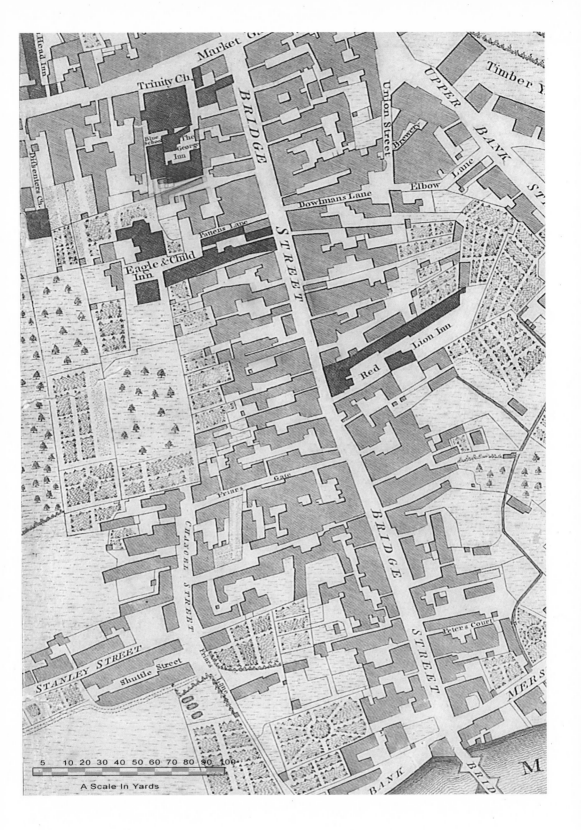

Market G...

Trinity Ch.

Timber Y...

UPPER

BANK

Union Street

Brewery

Elbow

Lane

Blue
...choo...
The
George
Inn

BRIDGE

Dowlmans Lane

Pattens Lane

STREET

Eagle & Child
Inn

...Head Inn

Dissenters Ch.

Red

Lion Inn

Friars

Gate

Peters Court

CHAPEL

STREET

BRIDGE

STREET

BANK

MERS...

BRID...

STANLEY STREET

Shuttle Street

Friars

Lane

M

5   10 20 30 40 50 60 70 80 90 100

A Scale In Yards

41. This is the western part of the centre of the town. The main road continuing north was called Horsemarket. Sankey Street went west and passed in front of Bank Hall, just beyond the left-hand edge of the map. The quarter between Horsemarket and Sankey Street was the market area with the Cornmarket, Golden Square, the little Cornmarket and the Town House. There were three large inns, the Talbot, the Nag's Head and the White Bull, and many smaller ones. It can be clearly seen in this map that there were gardens and orchards immediately behind the houses, and beyond was still agricultural land. North of the market area was another section of town where the Patten family were important. The Sugar House belonged to Robert Patten and his partners, and he probably lived in one of the large houses on Patten Lane, beside some of the other four Patten families who lived in the town (see p. 299). On the east side of Horsemarket, marked 'Machine', was the weighing machine beside a coal-yard belonging to the Legh of Lyme family. Carters going north to Haydock to fetch coal would have their carts weighed empty and then weighed again on returning to the town when they would receive a ticket. There are a number of these tickets in the Arley archives just giving the date and the weight of the coal. The machine was quite a sophisticated piece of technology.

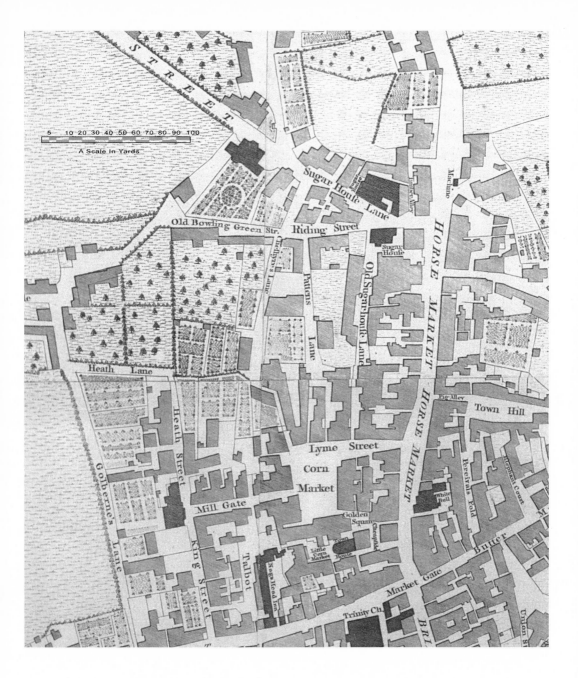

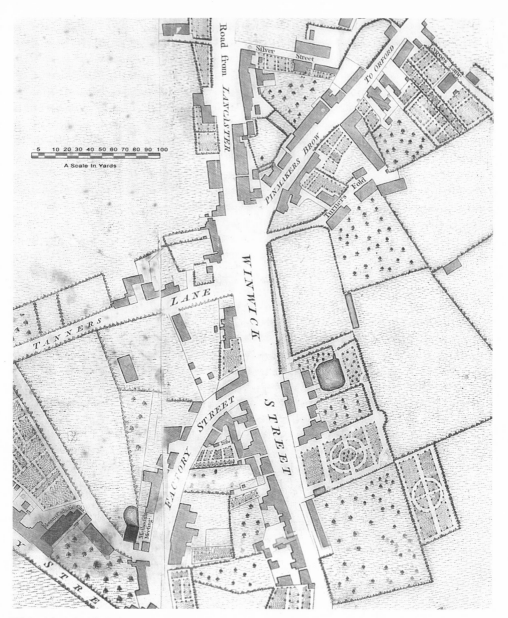

42. This third detail follows the road north through the outskirts of the town where there were fewer buildings and larger gardens. On Factory Street, notice the Methodist Meeting House and further west the Roman Catholic Chapel. At the north end of the town was Pin-makers Brow (see p. 304).

43b (opposite, lower illustration). Further to the east on the edge of the town and shown in this fifth detail was the Parish Church and the Free School. This Grammar School had been founded with an endowment by Sir Thomas Botelor of Bewsey in 1526 and had been re-established in 1608 by Sir Peter Warburton, the judge, and Thomas Tildesley of Orford after the endowment had been stolen. The schoolmaster from 1757 to 1807 was the Rev. Edward Owen, M.A., a distinguished classical scholar, who published a new Latin Grammar in 1770. In 1767 he was presented by the patron, Mr. Gwyllim, as rector of the Church, thus combining the two offices. The rector had been a less important person in the town than he might have been for the previous two centuries because his tithe income had been leased in 1542/3 for the small rent of £20 p.a.

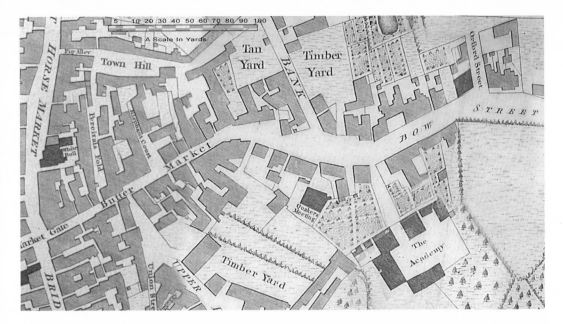

43a. This fourth detail shows the eastern part of the centre of Warrington. South of the main Buttermarket Road, going towards Manchester, was the Quaker Meeting House, the home of the fifth congregation financed entirely by its members in the town (see p. 176). Nearby were the impressive buildings of the Academy (founded in 1757) which moved to this larger site in 1762 (see p. 302).

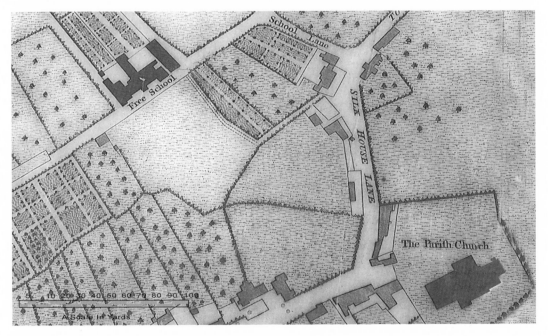

for two hundred years – a transaction similar to the lease of Budworth tithes acquired by Peter Warburton in 1575 (see Ch. 2). The teaching in Grammar Schools at this period was mostly about writing and speaking Latin, so the entry requirements and the cost of 'incidentals' probably restricted the pupils to those seeking a career in the Church or the Law, despite the title, 'Free School'. Mr Owen, who lived in the school, had added boarding accomodation to increase its attractions (HSL & C, vol. 8, 1856).

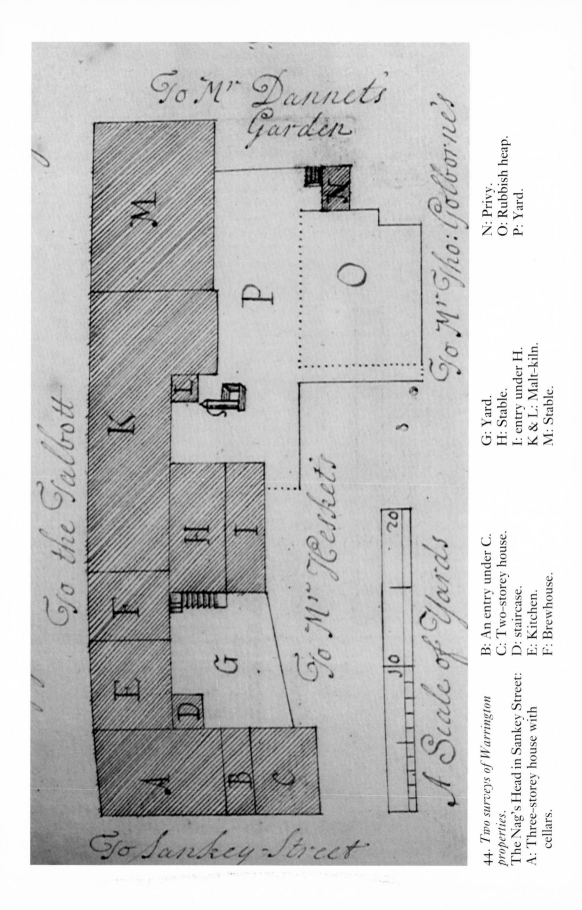

To Mr Dannet's Garden

To the Talbott

To Mr Tho: Golborne's

To Mr Hesketh's

To Sankey-Street

A Scale of Yards

44. *Two surveys of Warrington properties.*
The Nag's Head in Sankey Street:
A: Three-storey house with cellars.
B: An entry under C.
C: Two-storey house.
D: staircase.
E: Kitchen.
F: Brewhouse.
G: Yard.
H: Stable.
I: entry under H.
K & L: Malt-kiln.
M: Stable.
N: Privy.
O: Rubbish heap.
P: Yard.

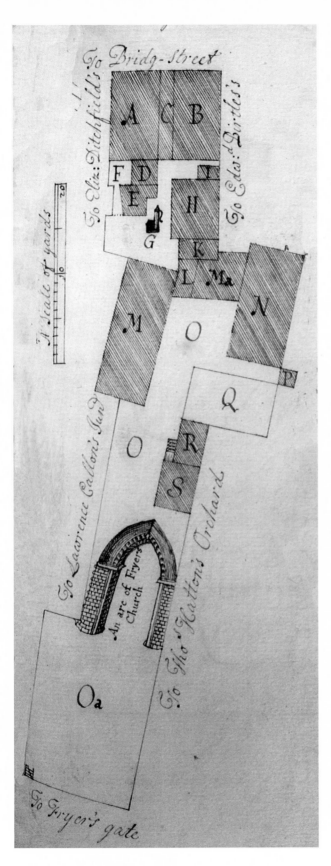

These two detailed surveys of properties belonging to the Earl of Warrington were probably made *c.* 1740 (WPL MS 1073). They provide a good idea of the buildings that existed on the three-life leaseholds at this period when the Booth estate was selling the freeholds. By modern standards these were large properties; the Nag's Head had a 45ft frontage on to Sankey Street and was about 52 yards deep. The other had a 37ft frontage to Bridge Street and was 85 yards deep, stretching back to Chancel Street (Friars Green). All the houses were brick with slate roofs – three storeys high at the front but sometimes only two storeys behind. Old stables, barns and malt-kilns were still thatched. Both properties had large malt-kilns and brewhouses. A significant part of the Bridge Street property, called Rud's Fold, was undeveloped and was apparently grazing land, so that the animals had to be kept out of the garden with a fence. It is evident that several of our business families had properties like this on which additional warehouses, work rooms and dwellings could be erected.

Bridge Street property (south of Friars Gate):
A & B with C & D: Two three-storey houses with an entry between and staircase to A.
E: Kitchen and brewhouse to A.
H with I & K: Two-storey house.
G: Yard.
M & Ma: Malt-kiln with L, an entry under.
N: Barn.
O & Oa: Rud's Fold.
Q: Garden.
R: Workhouse.
S: Warehouse

45. *John Wyke's centre lathe.*
An example of the huge range of tools he sold from premises in Prescot and Liverpool
from about 1740 and illustrated in his catalogue from the 1750s. About 500 tools were
eventually shown there and, since many were available in other sizes and types, a total
of over 1500 different tools were offered.

46. John Caldwell's clock.

This beautiful, long-case, three-train clock with quarter chiming on eight bells and a spherical moon, was made for Sir Peter Warburton by John just before he died. His widow presented the invoice for £17 in January 1751. John was the three-life leaseholder of the 67-acre farm and alehouse in Appleton, now the Thorn Inn, which his family had owned since at least 1693 (see also Appendix 3.3 for the family in 1545). The buildings and some of the land are shown in the map on p. xviii of *Seven Households*, edged red and tinted brick. Appleton was near the southern edge of the clock- and tool-making district centred on Prescot and St Helens, but there were two clock-makers even further south in Aston-by-Budworth (see Ch. 5, n. 30 for Key, and Foster, 1992, p. 60 for Richardson). All three clock-makers were men of substantial wealth; Caldwell's leasehold was worth around £500 and he will have had other assets in his clock, farming and alehouse businesses, as well as household possessions. We don't know how many people he employed.

47. *McConnell and Kennedy's cotton-spinning mill in 1800.*
The building towered above the neighbouring housing. The chimney for the steam engine was not yet finished when this engraving was made and only appears as a stump. In the foreground the Rochdale Canal had arrived in Ancoats, but had not yet been completed by joining the canal basin at Piccadilly (just to the left in the picture) which was to be the hub of Manchester's waterway system. These canals would bring the coal for the steam engine and the cotton from America and distribute the finished yarn to weavers all over the North-West.

48 (opposite). *Elijah Boardman (1760–1823).*
A dry goods merchant of New Milford, Connecticut, USA, painted by Ralph Earl in 1789, standing at his desk beside a display of the textiles he was selling (from the collection of the Boardman Tyler family). The National Portrait Gallery in London tell me that they know of no similar portrait of an Englishman painted in his place of business. Compare it with Pls 26 and 28 which show two of the most successful businessmen in the North-West as traditional English gentry in their drawing rooms – one with his coat of arms. This suggests that north-western businessmen, despite their many cultural differences from the southern English gentry, did not have quite the same full-hearted confidence in their business culture as their American cousins.

49. *View of Liverpool.*

S. and N. Buck's engraving of the southern half of Liverpool in 1728 shows the Wet Dock crowded with shipping and its jetty projecting out into the estuary. Blackburne's salt-house was to the right, as shown in the map of 1725, Pl. 24. Liverpool was still a small place, with boats being built along the shore. The Copperas House on the hill (13) and the Glass House (14) were early industries to arrive.

Boardmans, the remainder seem to have left the town before the 1720s, because they are not included in the levy raised to maintain the parish Church at that time.[13]

This Church levy provides a list of the 247 people who owned land in the 1720s. The Blackburne, Page and Patten families continued to be important but they had been joined by the Bent, Lyon and Turner families. All the other sailcloth manu-facturing families had arrived in the town by then except Nangreave, Titley and Tunstall. The continual division of property among all the children in each gener-ation is reflected in the number of individuals from the leading families who owned land – 6 Pages and 6 Pattens, three Bents and 3 Blackburnes. These three tax returns also show that the number of property-owners in the town increased much more rapidly in the 45 years before 1771 than it had in the 75 years from 1650 to 1725.

The notes that follow Table B in Appendix 10.1 attempt to estimate the capital owned by ratepayers. If these estimates do not err too greatly, there may have been about 150 families in the town with capital of £1,000 or more. The 52 ratepayers in Tables A and B were mostly the more prosperous of these families. Virtually all the rest of the ratepayers constituted a second group whose wealth exceeded £100 per family. This group included about 250 families, so there were probably a total of around 400 families in Warrington, each with capital of more than £100, repre-senting about 22% of the population. There is likely to have been at least as large a group whose capital was less than £100. This group will have included the skilled men and women working in the town. Capital of £15 or £30, equivalent to one or two years' expenditure in a thrifty family, was an important possession. In 1771 the total raised in Poor Rates in Warrington was nearly £600 which I estimate could probably have supported about 200 families.[14] This leaves about 800 families without significant capital, dependent on their earnings each week to survive

Table 9. *Estimated distribution of wealth in Warrington, 1771.*

Number of families	%	Approximate capital (£)
3	0	more than 50,000
0	0	10,000 to 50,000
150	8.0	1,000 to 10,000
250	14.0	100 to 1,000
400	22.0	5 to 100
800	45.0	nil to 5
200	11.0	Poor and receiving alms
1,803	100.0	

13 W.P.L. MF35 Reel 23 St. Elphin's Parish Church 1700–1781. The basis was an old 'mize' or medieval land assessment so the valuations are not a reliable estimate of wealth in the 1720s.

14 J.R.U.M.L. *Account book of Newton-by-Daresbury Poor Rates 1710–46.* This shows that annual payments of £2 or £3 per person assisted were common in the 1730s and '40s. See also Boyd, 1928.

without recourse to charity as Table 9 shows.

The only other labour-intensive mass-production industry in Warrington, besides sailcloth and linen manufacture, was pin-making. This business had been in the town since the second half of the seventeenth century.[15] The names of the ten pin-makers I have found to be active between 1750 and 1771 are listed in Appendix 10.2. As capitalists, they were a markedly different group to the sailcloth manufacturers. Only Richard Owen had substantial capital. He was rated at £42 p.a. and owned 18 houses when he died in 1775. The rest of them had a few hundred pounds each. It was not necessary to have much capital to make pins. These firms were mostly clustered together in a part of Horsemarket Street known as Pinners Brow (Pl. 42). The town owed the existence of this industry partly to the watch and clock makers, whose centre was at Prescot on the coal-field, 15 km away to the north-west. Technically, pin-making depended on the wire-drawing technology, developed by the watchmakers.[16] Commercial success was related to the ingenuity with which toolmakers had contrived the 'jigs and fixtures' that allowed children to form the point and fix the head on hundreds of pins a day. The second reason for Warrington to be a centre for pinmaking was its location, as carriers passing through the town carried its pins all over the country.

Warrington and the coal field to the north had large numbers of these toolmakers. In the town itself they may have formed a significant group among the less well-off households. Sadly, they have left almost no documents for historians to study. However, in the 1590s, watch-making was going on in a little Puritan community in Toxteth Park, Liverpool, and the area had a reputation for watch, clock and tool-making in the seventeenth century.[17] By the 1680s they had made a 'curious engine for cutting the teeth of a wheel [as used in watch and clockwork] whereby that part of the work is done with an exactness which far exceeds what can be performed by hand'. Eighteenth-century catalogues demonstrate the enormous variety of tools that were available (see Pl. 45).[18] Unusual information about a Warrington toolmaker called James Foster is contained in an advertisement of 1745, in which he offered – glaziers' vices, heckles for flax dressers, screws and boxes (bushes) for presses, and all sorts of pin-making tools.[19] Two more famous tool/instrument makers in the town were Peter Atherton and John Kay, who appear to have done

15 P. Goulden, pinmaker, buried December 1677; Edward Bird, pinmaker, buried April 1683.
16 Bailey, 1967, p8.
17 Bailey, 1967, p7.
18 For example, John Wyke's catalogue 1758–1782. Wyke of Prescot and Liverpool sold tools to both Watt and Boulton. Dickinson, 1936, p108; Ford, 1777, was among the archives of Peter Stubs.
19 Manchester Magazine 23 July 1745.
20 Fitton, 1989, p14.

the main development work on Arkwright's roller-spinning machine in 1767.[20] Peter Atherton was to become a successful mechanical cotton spinner with the third largest firm in 1795.[21] What we know of the organisation of the watch, clock and tool trades in this area suggests that the work was done in hundreds, or perhaps thousands, of little workshops attached to craftsmen's houses. Many of them specialised in one or two tools or watch parts. This physical dispersion seems to have grown up from the system of property owning in the area. Each family owned their own holding, either on a three life lease, freehold or copyhold. The family erected the buildings on the site and so were able to create a workshop when they wanted to. As a community, these independent, property-owning craftsmen exchanged ideas and stimulated each other, while as individuals they competed . They usually sold their tools and watch and clock parts through factors in the main manufacturing areas. In the fifty years from 1770 to 1820, the importance, for the economic development of the north-west, of this large community of tool and clock-makers can hardly be overestimated. The great store of knowledge and skill they had built up over more than a century and the wide range of materials and accurate tools and instruments available to them allowed these people to transform the crude prototypes and sketches of the famous inventors into working, commercial machines which they then improved nearly every year. See Pl. 46.

One example of a Warrington craftsman's accounts has come down to us. In the earliest of four little booklets, Peter Stubs listed his sales from December 1776. In the year 1777, Stubs and his apprentice made and sold files to only two large customers who bought files in bulk for resale – William Barrow of Prescot and Alexander Chorley, operating as Chorley and Leech in Ashton-in-Makerfield. In 1778 he added a third large customer, John Wyke of Wyke and Green in Liverpool. From then on he began to get new customers regularly. He was not well off and his wife seems to have taken in washing. A note in the book tells us that Edward Nangreave came to the house 'to nurse', which probably means that his wife began 'wet nursing' the child of the sailcloth manufacturing family, described on pp. 290–1 above. Yet he had a little capital and he was able to extend a short credit to the factors, and to pay other file makers for their work before he sold it.[22] Stubs' business was transformed from an old-style 'craftsman supplying factor' operation to a new-style 'manufacturer supplying the nation' by a happy idea. He took the lease of the *White Bear* in Bridge Street, Warrington,[23] from where he persuaded passing carriers to take samples of his files around the country. He was a capable man who

21 Chapman, 1970, p. 256.
22 Manchester City Library. Stubs Papers L 24/1, Box 7 and Box 22. Ashton, 1939, pp 6–8.
23 Owned by Thomas Watt.

made good files and in a few years he had a large business.

Warrington was a business town. Apart from a few professionals – doctors and lawyers – and perhaps a few pure rentiers, every family was in business. No branch of Government was established in the town and there were no law courts. There was no cathedral or abbey and no large charitable foundations or colleges. There were no Navy dockyards or soldiers' barracks, nor did a great landowner's mansion nearby spread its influence over the town. The town depended entirely on business. The business ethos was so widespread that Walter Kerfoot, the solicitor, held onto the Titleys' Partington mills when he inherited them on the death of his wife. She, the widow of John Bent, had inherited them from her brother, John Lyon, who had bought them at an auction after Titley's death. Kerfoot was persuaded by his relations, the Lyons and the Parrs, to join them in founding the bank – Lyon, Parr and Kerfoot – which was later to be known as Parr's Bank.[24] The town was given its character by the four hundred families who had capital and were employing it in manufacturing and trading businesses. Warrington was probably a different type of town to most towns in the south and east of England, and was possibly even more unusual when compared to most towns in continental Europe. It was, however, not so dissimilar to Manchester, Liverpool and other growing towns in the north-west. Towns of this type were to demonstrate great innovative prowess in the following decades, as their citizens accumulated capital and invested it in new technology and other business assets.

24 Now National Westminster Bank, Warrington regional headquarters.

Appendix 10.1. *The structure of Warrington society. 1649–1771.*

Table A. *1771 Rating List 411 taxpayers*

> Rateable value of the whole town – £14,350.5 per annum
> Average rateable value – £35 p.a. approximately
> Lowest rateable value – £1.75 p.a.

Top 14 annual values

	£ p.a.	Notes
Bent, Ellis	192	Sailcloth manufacturer
Blackburne, John	1,292	Of Orford. See pp. 207–8.
Borron, Mr	200	Property owner
Crosley, John	233	Innholder of White Bull
Fothergill, Samuel	132	Grocer, see pp. 246–50.
Hart, Thomas and Jeffrey	157	Sailcloth manufacturers
Lee, Mr	132	Sailcloth manufacturer
Lyon, John	578	See pp. 205–6.
Lyon, Thomas	255	See pp. 298–9.
Patten, Thomas	1,041	Of Bank. See pp. 208–14.
Peacock, John	157	Mercer and draper
Percival, Messrs	330	Property owners
Rimmer, Edward	182	Brewer
Woodcock, William	173	Sailcloth manufacturer

There were 40 assessments between £120 and £60 p.a. and 89 assessments between £59 and £24 p.a.

Source: W.P.L. MS 132.

Note:

1. The rate-book shows the value of 1d in the £ rate against each name. This is easily converted into the assessment in £ by changing the pennies into £s. Thus a 2s rate equals a £24 p.a. assessment. The actual Poor Rate in 1771 was 10d in the £, i.e., ten times the rate shown in the book.

Table B. *Rateable values of 39 others mentioned in the text*

	£ p.a.		£ p.a.
Academy	70	Patten, the Misses	90
Bent, John	19.5	Patten, Mr	106.5
Bent, Mrs	20	Patten, Mr and sisters	95
Blackburne, Jos	45	Patten, Robert, Jnr	12
Chorley, Alexander	7.5	Patten – sugar house	60
Dainteth, Mr	45.25	Pemberton, Dr	58
Dannett, Thomas	49.25	Rogerson, Roger	83.75
Dannett, Dr Joseph	83.75	Seaman and Company	60
Eaton, Sam (stk)	7.5	Titley, Abraham	16
Gaskell, Mr	86.5	Topping, Mr	31.75
Gaskell, S and R (new factory)	34	Travers, Richard	43
Gwyllym, Robt, Esq	108	Tunstall, John	77
Hart, John	12	Turner and Company	26
Hesketh, Mr execs, Mr W	99.5	Turner, Mr W.	47.75
Johnson, Ellen	35.5	Turner and Woodcock	43
Johnson, John	16.5	Turner, Thomas	94
Kerfoot, Mr	84.75	Turner, Thomas, Jnr	12.5
Lyon, Mr M	47.25	Watkins, Mr	118.75
Nangreave, Mr	30.75	Watt, Thomas	50.5
Patten, Dr	39	Yoxall, Ben	85

Notes:

1. Some of the ratepayers were much richer than the assessments in Table B suggest. We know that Abraham Titley and Samuel Eaton, for example, had major capital assets outside the township of Warrington. We also know that some of the rating assessments were highly conservative.
2. A £24 p.a. assessment probably implied property with a capital value of around £500 (21 times the annual value).
3. If we allow for these outside assets and for conservative valuations, it could be that an assessment of £24 p.a. or more would correspond, on average, to a family wealth of £1,000 or more.
4. On this basis there may have been around 150 families in the town with capital of £1,000 or more.
5. The smallest rating assessment was £1.5, which implied capital of £31.5. After adjusting this figure for conservative valuations and outside assets, it seems likely that no ratepayers owned less than £50. As there were only 13 assessments under £3, we can say that around 400 ratepayers owned £100 or more.

Table C. List of 184 taxpayers, 1649

        Average payment – 1s od approximately

        Highest payment – 5s 6d

        Lowest payment – 2d (see notes below)

Top 17 taxpayers	s	d		s	d
Ashton, widow	2	9	Gillman, Henry	2	6
Blackborne, Thomas	3	6	Ireland, Mr Esq	3	0
Bordman, Peter	2	6	Marsh, William and son	2	6
Bridgeman, Mr	3	4	Mascey, Robert	2	4
Broocke, William and son	2	6	Pedge (Page), William	2	6
Brooke, Peter, Esq	2	6	Patten, Thomas	3	0
Bullinge, Thomas	2	6	Sorrocold, William	5	6
Corllas, Henry	2	6	Woolley, William	5	0
Everett, Nicholas and son	2	6			

Source: Kuerden MSS, copy in W.P.L. MS 734.

Notes:

1. Christian name spelling modernized. Surnames as original.
2. £9 13s 6d was assessed on the town. The rate of tax is unknown.
3. Mr Bridgeman was Edward, younger brother of John, who became Bishop of Chester in 1619. The brothers came from Exeter and Edward probably helped manage his brother's property which included the rich rectory of Wigan, an estate in Great Lever, Lancs., and a salt-works at Dirtwych, Cheshire. He was MP for Liverpool in 1625 and married the widow of Thomas Brooke of Norton. Peter Brooke Esq. was her son who bought the Mere estate in Cheshire in 1652. Mr Ireland was Gilbert of Hale and Bewsey. His family had sold the tenanted properties in Warrington to Sir George Booth of Dunham Massey in 1628.

Appendix 10.2. *Warrington pin-makers, 1750–71.*

Name	Address and rateable value p.a., 1771	Other information
Callon, Gilbert		W.P.L. MS 1254, Box 2
Cotton, John	Horsemarket, £5	Keele University, M. Lyon Cashbook No. 1, Box 158. Wills 1738 and 1756
Croughton, Richard	Horsemarket, £20.75	Sun policy 316234
Galbreath, William	Horsemarket, £8	*Gore's Liverpool Advertiser*, 23 February 1770
Gaskell, William	Heathside, £7.5	Will 1773; likely value of chattels £100
Johnson, Thomas	Horsemarket, £10	E. Surrey Dane; *P. Stubs*, p. 195
Owen, Richard	Horsemarket, £42	Will 1775; Methodist, owned 18 houses
Rylands, Thomas	Sankey St, tenant	Sun policy to J. and T. Percival 316237; W.P.L. MS 1288/2
Thirlwind, John		Will 1777; W.P.L. MS 1270/3 and 1270/7; likely value of chattels £100
The Cooper family business may have been continued by others		Patten deeds MS 1269

PART III
Comparisons

CHAPTER 11

The business society of Cheshire and Lancashire compared with other societies

i) Introduction

The aim of this book has been to provide a detailed description of the social and economic development of the study area in the hope that it may throw light on events leading to the Industrial Revolution. Part I described the changes in property rights around 1540 and showed how rising property values caused wealth to be more widely distributed. This new wealth both created markets for new products and allowed investment in business assets. Part II has provided three detailed examples of the build-up of the business society in the 130 years from 1650 to 1780 and a picture of Warrington society in 1771. This concluding chapter sketches briefly and broadly the place of these detailed studies in the wider world of the business society of the North-West and the societies of England, Europe and the rest of the world.

ii) The number, the capital and the achievements of the manufacturing entrepreneurs in the 1770s

We have just seen that in 1771 there were about 150 business families with assets of over £1,000 in Warrington, out of a total population of something over 8,000. The two largest towns in the North-West at that time were Liverpool and Manchester. By 1770 Liverpool had a population of 34,000 and its economy was based on its port facility. The population of Manchester was then about 27,000 and its main business was textile manufacture and trading.[1] If Manchester had a similar social structure to Warrington, there will have been 400 to 600 business families there, worth more than £1,000 each. Mrs Raffald's *Manchester Directory* of 1773 lists over 500 people engaged in various aspects of textile manufacture.[2] There were probably another 500 in the manufacturing areas on the south Lancashire coalfield, such as Prescot, Wigan and Atherton, and a further 500 in the textile towns between Preston and Blackburn in the north and Macclesfield in the south. As we shall see in (iii) below, the Staffordshire area and the West Riding of Yorkshire (see Map 4) were also part of the heartland of the business society, and they will have had at least as many well-off families as Cheshire and Lancashire. There may therefore have been around 5,000 business families with assets of more than £1,000 in the four

---

1 Enfield, 1773, p. 25 and advertisement facing p. 1.
2 Analysed in Wadsworth and Mann, 1931, pp. 254–60.

counties and probably a majority of them were engaged in manufacturing. With the much larger number of families possessing a smaller amount of capital the business society was a major social phenomenon. This study ends in 1780 because in the 1770s this society made the great technical innovations that created the modern world.

The two revolutionary innovations of the 1770s were spinning machinery and a much more efficient steam engine. Before 1780, half the human race – virtually every female over 10 years old – had always spent every spare minute of the day spinning. By 1900, all over the world, it was being done by machines, and women were free to get on with other things. Steam engines not only drove machinery, they also revolutionized transport through their use in railway trains and ships. This study aspires to contribute to a greater understanding of why these technical advances occurred in the 1770s. Trying to make significant technical innovations has always been one of the most risky investments available. Developing a machine that would successfully spin cotton, setting up a factory equipped with water power to drive a group of the machines and nursing the business through to profitable operation were formidable and expensive challenges. The role of the entrepreneur was vital. He had to have not only the capital but also enough knowledge of the business and its technology to be willing to invest on the scale required. We have seen that from the 1740s onwards there was a great need for such machinery in Lancashire (p. 278 above). Lewis Paul and John Wyatt attempted to set up mechanical cotton-spinning factories between 1738 and 1756[3] but they never found adequate support. When Matthew Boulton visited one of their old factories years later he remarked that their machinery had failed because it had not been 'in good hands'. By this he seems to have meant the hands of a rich, technically competent entrepreneur like himself.[4]

One reason for this was that such entrepreneurs were still scarce in 1740. We have seen families like the Pattens, the Eyres, the Blackburnes and the Ashtons, among the richest entrepreneurs in the North-West, investing large sums in river improvements and canals in the period 1730 to 1760. However, these schemes used relatively well-known technology and Thomas Eyre was the only one who may have been at all familiar with textile manufacturing. In the 1740s the sailcloth making families were nothing like so rich as these four. The figures given earlier about members of Quaker families and the sailcloth makers suggest that £2,000–£3,000 was their average wealth in the 1740s. Ellis Bent, who died in 1749, worth perhaps £5,000, may have been the richest of them. The wealth of the fustian and check

3   Wadsworth and Mann, 1931, pp. 419–48.
4   Fitton, 1989, p. 12.

manufacturers of Manchester was probably on a similar scale. The new technology for printing on cotton, which was developed in Lancashire and which caused the industry to migrate north around 1760, and the other textile innovations mentioned earlier (see p. 277) created a new group of richer entrepreneurs, who were willing to risk their capital on experiments in mechanical cotton spinning.

The people who invested successfully in the development of cotton spinning and the steam engine were all manufacturers. We have seen how a number of manufacturers in the Warrington area built up their capital in the 30 years between 1740 and 1770. The families of the entrepreneurs who supported mechanical cotton spinning and the steam engine in the 1770s appear to have done the same. Robert Peel[5] (1723–95), who played a major part in bringing mechanical spinning into profitable commercial use, acquired his main capital when he inherited a farm, worth around £2,000 in the 1750s. Before that, in the 1740s and early 1750s, he and his partners produced fustian in the Blackburn area for the cotton printers, an expanding and profitable business. In 1764 they were just starting to do their own printing when James Hargreaves invented his spinning jenny. Peel immediately offered him a partnership as a result of which Hargreaves went to work in Peel's factory to make more jennies. A few years later, Peel also installed Arkwright's roller spinning machinery under license and he is thought to have improved it. Peel was one of the people who, in 1780, paid to look at Samuel Crompton's 'Mule', after which he offered Crompton a partnership, but was refused. Peel was then among the half-dozen businessmen who adopted and improved Crompton's ideas in their own factories[6] and got the first mule spinning machines into production.

Samuel Need and Jedediah Strutt (1726–97), who supported Arkwright's successful roller spinning machinery, were prosperous Nottingham hosiers (see Map 4). Strutt had earlier made technical improvements to the framework knitting machine. They paid £500 for a share of the patent rights in 1770 and provided Arkwright with both money and technical and commercial advice. Strutt told the House of Commons in 1774 that the partners had 'expended upwards of £13,000 in [developing] the manufacture'.[7]

Matthew Boulton (1728–1809) worked for ten years in his father's successful silver stamping business at Snow Hill, Birmingham, before he inherited it in 1759. He married a rich wife in 1760 and their combined capital was used to build his new factory in Soho, Birmingham, which opened in 1762. It cost £20,000, was capable of employing 1,000 men, and established Matthew as the greatest manufacturer in

---

5 Grandfather of the Prime Minister.
6 Chapman, 1981, pp. 34–40, 68; Chapman, 1969, pp. 61–89; French, 1859, pp. iv, vii, 79–82.
7 Fitton, 1989, pp. 27, 35.

Birmingham.[8] The water-mill at his Soho works was sometimes not able to provide enough power for his machinery, and it was his desire to obtain a steam engine to improve the power supply that brought him into partnership with James Watt in 1772.

John Wilkinson (1728–1808), whose boring machinery made Watt's steam engine possible, was the son of a successful iron founder of Backbarrow in Furness, Lancashire. He and his father had built up a large business at Bersham, near Wrexham, before he patented his new boring equipment in 1774. This machine tool, largely designed and made by the sophisticated toolmakers of south Lancashire, bored all the early separate condensers for Boulton and Watt.

From these four mini-biographies, it can be seen that these great technical developments were brought into practical, commercial, use by rich businessmen in the prime of life, among the greatest and richest manufacturers of their day. Such men had hardly existed 30 years earlier. Without such people to support them the technically skilled people, who might have been able to get these new machines into production in earlier decades, were not given the chance to try (see App. 11.1, *The cult of the inventor*). The successful introduction of these technical improvements was due to the appearance of richer manufacturers in the 1760s and 1770s. For those looking for the trigger that started the Industrial Revolution, I suggest that a key factor was the emergence of this large group of fairly rich manufacturers, some of whom decided to have a go at solving the pressing technical problems of the day – the need for a quicker method of spinning and a better power source. Much of this book has aimed to show that such people were a natural part of the evolution of the business community, a society that had been growing steadily larger, richer and more sophisticated for more than 200 years before 1770. These innovations were not just the brainchildren of the inventors who happened to live in the 1770s; they were the progeny of this whole earlier north-western society. Before the end of the eighteenth century these innovations had brought about the following great changes:

1. Cotton cloth manufactured with mechanically spun yarn was being distributed all over the world at prices lower than anyone else could make it. It was the first international mass-production product.

2. By 1795, around £2 million had been invested in fixed capital equipment for cotton manufacture by at least 150 different firms, the largest of which was Robert

8 Rolt, 1962, pp. 44–45.

Peel, Sons & Partners with an investment worth £192,000.[9] By 1789, it was computed that there were about 2.4 million mechanically driven spindles in use.[10] Much of this machinery had been made by the tool- and clockmakers on the south Lancashire coalfield. Together with the dozens of small improvements they had made to the original inventions, this demonstrates that these 'engineers', as they came to be called, must have already been a large and highly skilled group in 1770.

3. By 1797 two of these young engineers, James McConnell and John Kennedy, were building one of the first great eight-storey mills containing 'mules' driven by steam, which were to be the visible symbols of Lancashire's cotton-spinning mastery.[11] (See Pl. 47.)

The speed with which these things were done confirms the previous existence of a large number of manufacturing entrepreneurs in north-western society. Such a group had never existed in the world before.

iii) Gentry culture and business culture contrasted
The success of societies in generating the technical and commercial innovations that increase the wealth of their peoples may be based on four features of social organization: a wide distribution of wealth; an appropriate business culture; pluralist political arrangements; and a legal system that protects individuals and property. The importance of the last two have been noticed by many historians.[12] The first two have attracted much less attention. The distribution of wealth has been a major topic in Parts I and II, so here we concentrate on cultures.

The two cultures can be briefly contrasted. Traditional English gentry culture placed central Government firmly in the hands of the Crown and the nobles, while local government was controlled by the gentry. Their position was based on their ownership of most of the land. Entry to this group was only open to those who acquired a large landed estate, so obtaining such an estate therefore became the much desired objective of all successful men. The purpose of making money was to buy an estate, and the size and grandeur of the house at the centre told every visitor something about its extent.

This group both controlled and was supported by institutions: the Church, the Law, the civil and military services and city corporations. Senior positions in these institutions gave individuals wealth, power and status. People entered and rose up

9 Chapman, 1970, pp. 235–66.
10 Lee, 1972, p. 4.
11 Ibid., p. 101.
12 Hill, 1967, pp. 3–5.

the hierarchy of these bodies by the favour of those already occupying the top jobs
– in other words, it was a patronage system. A man wishing to rise had to obtain the
support of one or more people, already in high office, to help him to progress up
the ladder.

Samuel Pepys, the seventeenth-century Englishman about whom we know the
most, may serve as an example. The son of a younger son, he began his working life
with nothing but his university education and family connections with an uncle,
who had about £80 a year from land, and cousins with considerably larger estates.
We first meet him, in the great *Diary*, living in London in the company of many
other young men, all trying to ingratiate themselves with possible patrons. Edward
Montagu, Pepys' cousin and leading patron, rose high and carried Pepys with him,
so that he in turn was soon acting as patron to younger men. In his Navy office
employment, Pepys acquired a lot of money (much of it through taking bribes) and
was soon living in the style of the major gentry with a coach and a bevy of servants.
His other patron was James II and, by the time of James' departure in 1688, Pepys
had managed to save at least £30,000 to £40,000, although he had loyally lent
£28,000 of this to James, a loan which was never repaid. Pepys had thus amassed a
much larger fortune than that possessed by any north-western businessman in 1688.
Although he amused himself with science in the Royal Society there is no evidence
that any part of his capital was ever invested in technical or commercial development.

Besides such aspiring gentry there were a large number of lesser positions. These
were usually supported either by taxes, tolls or restrictive practices. For example,
tithes and Church rates financed the lesser clergy and their helpers. Tolls provided
the salaries of those who regulated the markets in many towns. In Corporate towns
only Freemen were allowed to trade and licences issued by Corporations and other
institutions protected many traders from the rigours of competition.

The business culture that developed in north-west England was different. A large
number of families owned small farms on a secure tenure – freehold, copyhold or
three-life leasehold. These farms were income-producing capital investments that
gave the families economic independence. The farms also provided a site from
which trading activities could be conducted: for example, workshops could be built
on them for tool- or watchmaking. These independent families formed egalitarian
religious congregations who were naturally out of sympathy with the hierarchical
style of the traditional Church. Before the Civil War some of these families had
emigrated to America and established the settlements that became the northern
colonies. After the Restoration, independent congregations were declared to be
'Non-conforming'. Their members were barred from careers in government
service, law, education and the Church, so the only occupations left to them were

in business and medicine. A well-conducted business career was regarded by this group as a valuable life's work (see Pl. 48). The egalitarian nature of this society encouraged the equal division of the property of parents among all their children, so the business society had few great men with large fortunes wielding massive economic power. Instead, there were a large and steadily growing number of families with a small amount of capital.

This business society and culture was, of course, dependent on pluralist political arrangements and an independent legal system that would protect the land tenure of the small proprietors. In England, the same happy accident that created the business culture and society also provided the means for preserving it. Traditional culture had, in the Middle Ages, established parliaments composed of knights from the shires and similar figures from boroughs. In the shires they were elected by all freeholders with land worth not less than £2 p.a. Before 1530 that meant, at 8d an acre, a farm of at least 60 acres. We have seen that, in 1545, there were very few such people in Bucklow Hundred. However, by 1640, with Cheshire land valued at 12s an acre, there were hundreds of voters. The members of the House of Commons almost all came from major gentry families, but they knew they had to maintain the support of their electors and thus a pluralist system had come into existence.

In the Law, events unrolled slightly differently. We have seen that some of the families with small farms were made rich enough by the rising value of land to educate their more talented children in the Law. Two examples are the Shuttleworths of Gawthorpe and the illegitimate Thomas Warburton of Northwich,[13] both of whose children became senior judges. Enough judges appear to have come from similar backgrounds to give the whole group a strong incentive to maintain an independent judiciary in order to protect the property of their families and friends. They were assisted in this task by the fact that the new small freeholder voters also composed the juries at the Assizes. When the Stuart kings tried to re-establish traditional European culture and absolute monarchy in the seventeenth century, Parliament and the Courts resisted and the Civil War saw the supporters of the new culture triumph. In the rest of Europe, absolute government and the traditional culture were victorious almost everywhere in the wars of the late sixteenth and seventeenth centuries. Only Holland, with help from England, held onto its new business culture and society. In France, the business society was given a stay of execution by the Edict of Nantes in 1598 which guaranteed the civil rights of the Huguenots and toleration for their religion. However, the Protestants remained under great pressure and 200,000 fled the country after the Edict was revoked in 1685.

13 See p. 199 and Foster, 2002, pp. 9–10.

The strong growth of the business society in north western England encouraged friendly relations to develop between the old major gentry and the business community. For example, the Norris family of Speke were an old major gentry family with an estate worth at least £700 p.a. which had been sequestered by Parliament in the Civil War.[14] At the end of the seventeenth century the family provided two MPs for the thrusting new port of Liverpool and they enjoyed most friendly relations with the businessmen. Nevertheless, their two nieces married a Leycester of Toft and a Warburton of Winnington.[15] We have seen that in the eighteenth century Peter Legh of Lyme was friends with Thomas Eyre, and Sir Peter Warburton persuaded the Quaker, Thomas Hough, to join a committee of Cheshire gentry to help upgrade the Weaver Navigation. Sir Peter's brother-in-law, heir to the Earl of Derby, the grandest family in the North-West, guided the Navigation's new Act through Parliament. He had earlier chaired the Committee on linen manufacture which reported on 26 April 1751. Perhaps the most striking example of the influence of the business culture on the major gentry in north-western society were the activities of the Duke of Bridgewater. Going much beyond the traditional role of landowners in developing the mineral resources of their estates, he built a canal to take his coal into Manchester and a second one across north Cheshire, to make a better waterway between the booming town of Manchester and the Mersey estuary at Runcorn.

Staffordshire and the West Riding of Yorkshire were two regions adjacent to Cheshire and Lancashire where communities developed which had all the features of the business culture that has just been described. With Staffordshire, we should include those parts of Warwickshire and Worcestershire that surrounded the town of Birmingham, just south of the Staffordshire border (see Map 4). In the north of Staffordshire were the coal-mines which supplied the brine salt boilers in Cheshire and a pottery industry which had grown steadily after 1650. From less than 20 potters in the area in the 1660s, there came to be at least 130 by the 1750s, so that north Staffordshire had the greatest concentration of potteries in the country.[16]

In the south of the county, coal and iron were found together in a number of places – particularly round Dudley[17] and iron-working was well established in the area by the middle of the sixteenth century.[18] This iron, however, was not suitable for making edge-tools (knives, scythes, etc.) so their main products were therefore

14 WM Box 1.
15 Ormerod, 1851, Norris pedigree.
16 Weatherill, 1971, pp. 4–9.
17 Plot, 1686, p. 158.
18 Court, 1938, pp. 36–42.

nails and blacksmiths' iron for a thousand common uses – ploughshares, cooking pans, horseshoes, etc. Wolverhampton specialized in the production of locks, and Newcastle under Lyme excelled in frying-pans.[19] They developed a particular expertise in all the metalwork required for horses – bridles, bits, spurs and so on. One of the reasons for this was that all these parts needed to be tinned to prevent them from rusting,[20] and the River Severn provided a cheap route for Cornish tin to reach Stourbridge. The industries that developed on the south Lancashire coal-field were different. Having no local iron, that area had to import it, principally from Spain. It so happened that this iron was suitable for hardening and tempering. Consequently it could be used for making edge-tools or springs and other watch and clock parts. This was one of the reasons why watchmaking became established in south Lancashire, rather than in the Birmingham area. Both areas were exceptionally active in developing these businesses because they both had large numbers of small capitalists on little farms.[21]

In the early sixteenth century, the largest landowner in that part of the West Riding producing woollen cloth was the Duchy of Lancaster's Honour of Pontefract. More land came to the Crown from the Dissolution of the Monasteries. Then, in 1536, the Pilgrimage of Grace led to the forfeiture of several gentry estates, so that the Crown became the major landowner in the area. In common with the tenants on other Crown property, these West Riding tenants were either found to be freeholders or became copyholders in the sixteenth century, as we saw in Chapter 3 (iv) above.[22] These numerous small landowners soon formed a society of small independent cloth makers. They obtained freedom from the restrictive practices of the rest of the English woollen industry in the Halifax Act of 1555. In contrast with the other two large cloth-making areas in England – East Anglia and the West of England – Yorkshire woollens steadily increased their markets until Leeds and Bradford became the world's leading centres.[23]

South of the woollen cloth part of the West Riding was the iron-working area around Sheffield. In the sixteenth century it was part of the great estates of the Talbot family, Earls of Shrewsbury. Coal and iron outcropped in their park at Sheffield. Following the traditional gentry practice of developing the minerals on

19 Plot, 1686, p. 335, 376.
20 Ibid., pp. 376–78.
21 Court, 1938, pp. 43, 92–93; VCH Worcestershire, Vol. 3, pp. 142–43 for Halesowen copyholds; Large, 1990, for a good detailed description of the vicissitudes of a copyhold manor near Kidderminster.
22 Smith, 1970; Raistrick, 1970, p. 78.
23 Heaton, 1920; Wadsworth and Mann, 1931, pp. 384–85 for the contrasting styles of the industry in the two areas.

322   *Comparisons*

their estates, the Earls opened coal- and iron-mines there in the fifteenth century. The iron was not suitable for making edge-tools, so the Earl's steward encouraged the importation of Spanish iron and the manufacture of cutlery. In the sixteenth century many of the Earl's tenants developed substantial businesses manufacturing inexpensive knives, and all his tenants seem to have become copyholders. This appears to be an example of a nobleman following the Crown's lead and not altering the rents or tenure of his tenants in the 1530s and 1540s. In the late sixteenth century the Earl leased the ironworks in his park to the old gentry family of Copley. This family and the Sitwells of Renishaw Hall controlled the supply of locally-made iron in the area in the first half of the seventeenth century.[24] However, after the Civil War, the small copyholders' iron-working businesses grew steadily. They took over the local ironworks from the old landowner families and came to dominate the industry in the eighteenth century. This change in the ownership and management of ironworks from landowners to businessmen may be compared with similar events in the rock-salt industry in Cheshire, described in Chapter 7 above. Important improvements in the qualities of tool-steels were made, the most famous innovations being associated with the name of Benjamin Huntsman. Peter Stubs of Warrington bought the material for his files in Sheffield. In the 40 years before the Civil War, Sheffield's vicar, the Reverend Thomas Toller, was a fervent Puritan. He was forced to resign by the Archbishop of York in 1635, but the area remained staunchly Puritan throughout the Civil War and the Commonwealth period. Many of the ministers were ejected from their livings in 1662, but they continued to enjoy the confidence of their congregations, who therefore became Dissenters or Nonconformists.[25]

There would probably be substantial agreement among historians that the heartland of the business community in the middle of the eighteenth century was the area stretching from Birmingham in the south, up through Staffordshire and Cheshire into Lancashire, and across the Pennines to the upland part of the West Riding of Yorkshire[26] – an area characterized by a high level of technical innovation and vigorous commercial activity. However, there would be less agreement about the reasons for this. Some would believe that it was principally the natural endowments of each area that determined its pattern of development. The view put

24 Hey, 1998, pp. 35–37.
25 Ibid., pp. 40–42, 86.
26 I have not attempted to identify a number of adjacent areas that may have been socially, culturally and technically part of the heartland region. For example, the Ironbridge area in east Shropshire was about ten miles west of the Staffordshire border. Derby and Nottingham were halfway between Sheffield and Birmingham. A business culture definitely existed in Scotland in the eighteenth century.

forward in this book is that there were other factors at work as three examples demonstrate:

1) It was possible for natural resources not to be exploited.
An example would be the great coal mines near Ales in the Cevennes in southern France which were scarcely developed before the Revolution for reasons suggested below, see p. 332.

2) Industries could succeed using only imported materials.
For example, the textiles for which Manchester became famous in the eighteenth century – the checks, the cotton prints and the cotton velvets – were composed entirely of imported materials. The cotton came from the West Indies, the linen yarn was grown and spun in Ireland and north Germany, and the dyestuffs were drawn from all over the world. It was the technical expertise and the commercial organization which had already grown up in Lancashire that made it the greatest cotton textile manufacturing centre in the world.

3) Entrepreneurial capital and skills could make industry flourish in unlikely places.
For example, the principal raw materials for high-quality ceramics in the middle of the eighteenth century were ball clay (pipe clay), china clay and flintstones. In Britain, ball clay was found in Devon and Dorset, china clay in Cornwall, and flint-stones on the south and east coasts. One might have expected the ceramic industry to be located near a port with a good supply of cheap coal – for example, Tyneside or Swansea. Potteries did indeed start up in a number of port towns, but the industry actually became concentrated on the coalfield at Stoke-on-Trent, 30 or 40 miles from the nearest port.

As an explanation of the last two examples, some historians have suggested that the existence of communities with long-established craft skills may explain the location of successful industries. This might help to account for Manchester's ability to develop new kinds of textiles or Stoke-on-Trent's skill in becoming the leading British centre for ceramics. However, in other situations, old skills seem to have been a handicap. East Anglia and the West of England had long traditions in the manufacture of woollen cloth, but the business migrated to Yorkshire as new technology appeared.

This suggests that it was the ability to innovate, both commercially and techni-cally, that was crucial, and so the importance of the number and quality of entrepreneurs is emphasized. Capital-owning entrepreneurs and their employees in craft-based industries often make small technical improvements, as anyone with production experience in small-scale manufacturing will know. Before 1750, technology was mostly craft based, so the cumulative effect of these advances became significant. Historical evidence of such innovations is rare but J. R. Harris has suggested 'that there was a very large craft element in many of the newly pioneered and progressively developed technical processes by which British industry was converted to the use of coal ... in the well over two centuries before 1790'.[27] These skills in coal fuel technology, unique in Europe, made cost savings in many English industries; we have already noticed how the use of coke for malting made this an important Warrington industry. My researches have also indicated a considerable improvement in the carrying capacity of carts between the 1670s and the 1760s, which was presumably due to 'craft' advances in their construction and in harnessing techniques.[28] Similar innovations were certainly made in the watch and tool industry of south Lancashire and in the Potteries.[29] It was probably the great number of small capital-owning entrepreneurs and the craft improvements they encouraged that created the success of a wide range of north-western industry.

The northern business societies we have examined were all in pasture country, where arable agriculture was kept to a minimum. Cattle and sheep were the produce of the farms, and the old medieval farms of 15 to 50 acres remained undisturbed. In arable areas to the east and south it was not the same. From the end of the fifteenth century onwards, the development of the market for grain in London and other towns produced a need for large commercial farms on which to grow it. The growth of these large farms concentrated capital into the hands of a small number of families – a situation which promoted gentry culture. An example is provided by the village of Chippenham, Cambridgeshire,[30] which is situated in flat country sloping gently down to a river and a fen. In 1544 there were 27 tenants with farms ranging in size from 13 to 111 acres. By 1636, there were only 13 farms over ten acres in size, the largest being 207 acres. By 1712 the number had been reduced even more, with only ten farms over five acres, the two largest being 472 and 461 acres respectively. There was now only one farm left of under 50 acres – a smallholding of just 15 acres.[31]

The manor of Chippenham was old monastic land which was sold by the Crown in 1544. In that year virtually all the 1,286 acres of tenanted land were copyhold. The lord of the manor bought out many copyholders so that, in 1636, he was letting 700 of the 1,286 acres at market rents. The more successful copyholders also bought

27 Harris, 1976, p. 180.
28 Foster, 2002, pp. 211–14 and above, p. 190. where loads improved from 11 cwts in the 1670s to 15–20 cwts in the 1760s.
29 Bailey, 1967, and Stoke-on-Trent Museum.
30 See Wrightson, 1979, pp. 6, 25–26; Gras, 1930; Beckett, 1989, pp. 59–69 and 92–99, Chibnall, 1965, pp. 87, 165, 187 and 239 for other examples.
31 Spufford, 1974, pp. 67–71; VCH, Cambridgeshire, Vol. 10, 2001, pp. 370–88.

copyhold land. In 1636 there were four large copyhold farms ranging in size from 50 to 199 acres. Two other farmers, who owned variously 50 and 30 acres of copyhold land, leased more land from the lord of the manor to make their farms 154 and 103 acres respectively. So six of the 13 large farmers in 1636 were substantial copyholders and seven were rack-rented leaseholders. In 1696 the lord of the manor bought out the remaining five copyholders. All the farmers henceforth were lease-holders paying market rents. Among the 60–70 households in the village, there was only one with significant capital invested in the land – that of the lord of the manor. This was in striking contrast with the position in Cheshire where, in the 1740s, in the four townships described in the first volume of this series, the three major gentry landowners owned only 40% of the capital value of the 8,682 acres and 194 other landowners owned the other 60%.[32]

Arable agriculture was the most important single activity in most regions of southern and eastern England. The culture that went with it was the dominant culture of the eastern, midland and southern counties. This culture was the gentry's culture because, by the eighteenth century, the gentry owned most of the capital involved in arable agriculture. They owned the freehold title to the land and were usually getting a market rent from it. Their wealth gave them both social and economic dominance.

iv) Bristol and the Severn Basin
The importance of culture in determining the rate of economic growth can be illus-trated by contrasting the experience of Bristol and the Severn Basin in the period 1650 to 1770 with that of Liverpool and the Mersey Basin. In 1700 Bristol was the second port of England. In that year 240 ships arrived in Bristol from foreign ports with just under 20,000 tons of goods. The population of the city was about 20,000. At that time Liverpool had only 5,714 inhabitants and the foreign trade of its port in 1709 was only 14,574 tons.[33] 60 years later the position was dramatically different. In the five years, 1759 to 1763, the average number of ships which entered Bristol from foreign parts was 341. They carried just over 30,000 tons of goods. By contrast, in those same five years, the number of ships entering Liverpool averaged 636 and their cargoes totalled over 48,000 tons.[34] Liverpool's trade was growing so rapidly that, by 1764, the number of ships entering the port had risen to 766 and their cargoes added up to nearly 59,000 tons. – almost twice Bristol's trade.[35] The main

32 Foster, 1992, pp. 11–14.
33 Minchinton, 1957, pp. ix, 5; Enfield, 1773, pp. 28, 67.
34 Enfield, 1773, p. 70.
35 Ibid., p67.

reason for this large difference was that Liverpool had captured a much larger share of the Irish trade. In 1764, 418 ships arrived in Liverpool from Ireland against only 79 returning to Bristol.[36] Manufactured goods were the main English exports to Ireland. Those produced in Liverpool's hinterland were evidently more desirable than goods which could be exported from Bristol. In the important trans-Atlantic trade, where English manufactures were again the main exports, Liverpool had 181 ships against Bristol's 137.[37] The strongest part of Bristol's trade in 1764 was its traditional business with Spain and Portugal. Since the sixteenth century Bristol merchants had sent ships to Newfoundland to collect fish, which they then sold in the Iberian Peninsula. With the proceeds they bought wine, fruit and iron which the ships carried back to Bristol.

In 1650, Bristol appeared to have every advantage over Liverpool. Its geographical position was greatly superior. The Bristol channel linked it to Somerset, Devon and south Wales. The rivers Severn, Wye, Stour and Avon gave access to a huge area, including the iron and coal industries near Birmingham and the salt-works at Droitwich. There were coal supplies in the upper Severn around Broseley, near Swansea on the coast of South Wales and just south of Bristol in north Somerset. There were districts producing linen and high class woollens were made by the famous west of England industry.[38]

The failure of Bristol to retain its lead over Liverpool in any foreign markets except the Iberian Peninsula suggests that the industries that developed in Bristol's hinterland were almost all inferior to those developed in the areas served by Liverpool. Was there some reason for this? There are a number of different problems which have to be overcome to ensure vigorous economic growth. By taking as an example the different responses of the two regions to a similar situation, we may be able to identify some of these problems, which may in turn suggest some answers to the question of why Liverpool eventually became more successful than Bristol.

36 Ibid., p71.
37 It appears not to have been much noted by historians that the Customs' figures contain major distortions. The 1660 Book of Rates was extensively revised between 1697 and 1701, but after that the categories and rates appear to have remained largely unchanged. But the technology and output of many manufactures changed dramatically. For example, by 1780, many families in America and the West Indies will have had a clock and some will have had one or more watches. These will have mostly been made in south Lancashire and will have been shipped fully assembled. They presumably passed through Customs as 'Brass, wrot', at £4.10s 0d a cwt (112 lb), as there does not seem to be any other suitable category, but they will have been at least ten times more valuable than that. The same problem will have applied to all kinds of tools such as pliers and saws, also to machinery, and to hinges, locks, screws, etc. See Schumpeter, 1960, pp. 71–72.
38 See Minchinton, 1954, pp. 69–89 for a fuller description of Bristol's hinterland and Morgan, 1993, for an extensive description of Bristol's trade.

The old salt industry in Droitwich was, as in Cheshire, originally enmeshed in a maze of legal rights which protected the interests of the numerous proprietors who had owned salt-works since the fifteenth century. It took the Worcestershire people much longer to break out of this medieval straitjacket. In the early 1690s, the area was producing less than 13% of the salt produced in Cheshire. The brine pits were modernized from the late 1690s onwards and production increased, but by 1730 their output was still only equal to about half of Cheshire's annual output.[39] The opening of the Weaver Navigation in 1733 so improved the competitive position of Cheshire salt that sales of all other producers started to decline relatively to Cheshire and the deepening of the Navigation in 1760 reinforced this trend. In order to compete, the Worcestershire community should have created a similar waterway long before the 1730s. Droitwich was close to navigable rivers and waterborne coal supplies.[40] In 1655 Andrew Yarranton proposed improving the rivers in the area and in 1665 he made part of the River Stour navigable. Lord Windsor built part of a canal in 1680[41] but the community failed to support these entrepreneurs and no canals were completed until the 1770s.

The failure to develop an internationally competitive salt industry at Droitwich had wider effects. While Liverpool-based ships were carrying salt into the Baltic to enable the Scandinavians and Germans to preserve their fish, Bristol merchants had little cargo to export to this area.[42] Between 1724 and 1783, 181 of the 248 ships that sailed from Bristol to the Baltic were either in ballast or carried 'plantation goods', things such as sugar, tobacco and cotton grown in the New World Plantations.[43] The vigour of the Warrington sailcloth industry no doubt owed something to the competitive position which had been obtained by Liverpool-based ships trading in the Baltic.[44] By contrast, the uncompetitive position of Bristol shipping in the Baltic damaged other industries based around Bristol in the Severn basin. Timber for building was more expensive than in Cheshire and Lancashire, as was hemp and flax for rope-making and the textile trades. Failure in one industry made progress in others more difficult. The success of the North-West and the adjacent areas was based on a wide range of competitive industries with the prosperity of each one aiding that of their neighbours.

The second area in which Bristol failed to match Liverpool was in improving their port facilities. In these two western ports the tides rise and fall by up to 30 feet

39 See Appendix 7.9
40 B.L. Add MSS 36914. Aston correspondence – report on Droitwich salt in the 1690s.
41 VCH Worcestershire, Vol. 2, pp. 260–61 and Vol. 3, p. 165.
42 Davis, 1962, p. 225.
43 Minchinton, 1957, p. xiv, note 2.
44 See Ch. 9 above.

(9 metres). This caused difficulties in loading and unloading larger ships and it also meant that such vessels could be damaged when they settled unevenly on the mud at low tide. Liverpool merchants responded to these problems by building one of the first Wet Docks in England between 1709 and 1720. Enclosed behind sea gates, the water level at the quays in this dock altered by only three feet (1 metre), so ships could easily be loaded. Shipping moored in the dock was also secure against storms, so this development reduced the risks for ship-owners as well as lowering the costs of using the Port (see Pls. 24 and 49). Bristol merchants did not follow this lead and so continued to receive complaints about vessels grounded at each tide.[45] The construction of Liverpool's Dock required two Acts of Parliament and it cost more than £15,000. This was a prodigious sum of money for a small town of 6,000 people (in 1709). Its successful completion was a technical, administrative and political triumph for the predominantly mercantile and Whig councillors who had gained control of Liverpool Corporation under the new Charter of 1695.[46]

These two examples show that the establishment of successful industries in an area involved solving a range of problems – technical, legal, entrepreneurial and political – which taxed the ability of the whole society. The reasons for failure are therefore to be sought in the structure of society and in its way of doing things – its culture. What was the dominant culture in the Severn estuary?

The south-west of England, like the North-West, is wetter than the eastern side of the country, so grass grows better. In some areas therefore there were small dairy farms similar to those in the North-West. The area was the home of Cheddar cheese and three-life leases were common on the estates there. There were also small farms in some of the linen textile producing areas. Much of the rest of the country was given over to arable farms with associated sheep walks on the hills. These were often large farms of several hundred acres.[47] These large farms were sometimes both owned and occupied by the same families, who were minor gentry. Other large farms were leased by larger estates to tenants at market rents. As on the eastern side of England, the arable areas had a gentry culture. So the South-West was a mixed area with islands of businessmen in a wider sea of gentry supporters. David Underdown found that the cheese and textile districts supported Parliament in the Civil War, while the arable areas were Royalist.[48] Whereas in the North-West the large new towns – Manchester, Liverpool, for example – exerted enough influence to carry the whole area into a business culture, there were no towns of this kind in the South-West. Bristol was an old city with many of the characteristics of Chester, the main

45 Bird, 1963, pp. 187 and 281.
46 Parkinson, 1952, pp. 78–82; Power, 2000, pp. 51–71.
47 Thirsk, 1967, pp. 64–80, 177.
48 Underdown, 1985, pp. 73–104.

centre of gentry culture in the North-West. Its leading merchants belonged to the Bristol Merchant Venturers, established by Royal Charter in 1552. This was a socially exclusive organization of rich, established families, whose main trading links across the Atlantic were with the gentry who owned plantations in the southern states of America and in the West Indies. Much of the west of England woollen cloth trade was in the hands of large clothiers belonging to similar families. It was organized on the 'putting out'[49] system, so many of its workers were without capital. They lived at subsistence level on their labour. This was different from the Yorkshire system where capital-owning families bought wool and sold the cloth they made from it. The culture of the small business communities of the South-West seems to have been submerged by the gentry culture of the landowners and the old established business families. It seems likely, therefore, that the economic development of the south western counties was delayed by the dominance of gentry culture, which prevented them from making many changes and improvements to their various enterprises.

v) Continental Europe

There seem to have been only three countries in continental Europe in the sixteenth and seventeenth centuries where much land was held by working families – Holland, which is described later in this section, Sweden and Finland.[50] Elsewhere much of the land was owned by kings, noblemen and the Church. However, the dominant culture in continental Europe was different to that of the English gentry in many ways. It should perhaps be called 'aristocratic culture', because titles were so numerous. In England under Queen Elizabeth there were about 60 members of the House of Lords. This number was increased to around 120 by the first two Stuart Kings, but titles remained rare in England compared with the continent. In Spanish-controlled Sicily, for example, the sale of titles ran riot. The first dukedom was created in 1556 and the first title of Prince was sold in 1563. In the 1620s the Government created 27 new princes, 7 new dukes and 17 marquises. By 1800 there were 142 princes, 788 marquises and about 1,500 other dukes and barons.[51]

Besides noblemen and the Church, the urban bourgeoisie was a significant landowning group in most of continental Europe where land was held under a great variety of legal systems and tenurial arrangements. Many peasants had 'ownership' rights to small properties, but taxes were so high that their properties were often not valuable (see below pp. 332–3). A few peasants had rights that made them pros-

---

49 See note 23 on p. 321 above and p. 116.
50 Andersson, 1956, pp. 124–25.
51 Smith, 1968a, p. 157; Smith, 1968b, p. 284.

perous; a few more were better off than most country families, but the majority of the workers who cultivated the lands of the owners were sharecroppers (*metayers*) or leaseholders (*fermiers*). The rents specified in these leases were mostly in money and the leaseholders' situation was usually better than that of the *metayers,* who paid in kind between one third and a half of the crops produced.[52] Not only did these agricultural families not own any of the capital invested in the land and the buildings of the farm, they frequently owned little or nothing of the working capital – the animals, the seed, the ploughs and other implements. Their contribution was their labour. How miserably poor and cowed such people were even in the 1920s in Sicily has been brilliantly described by an American anthropologist.[53] Whole families were living, with their goat and chickens, in one room without a window.

Here is an example of the distribution of land ownership in France in the eighteenth century. In 1750, the city of Toulouse in the south of France had a population of about 40,000. The civil diocese of Toulouse contained a total of around 120,000 people. The distribution of land among the social classes in 78 of the 214 communities in the diocese was as follows:

Nobles	44.4%
Clergy	6.5%
Bourgeoisie	25.2%
Peasants and artisans	22.5%
Commons	1.2%
	99.8% = 138,865 acres

The nobles had an average estate of 267 acres each, while the majority of peasants and artisans had holdings of between three and five acres. The nobles' estates were usually cultivated for them by servants or sharecroppers.[54]

We have to beware of one-word descriptions of people. The estates of many French noblemen would actually have been the equivalent of that of minor gentry in England. In France the owner of 50 acres or more was usually a nobleman, i.e., had a title, though for the less rich this was often only a *particule, de* or *d'*. The largest nobleman's estate in the Toulouse sample was 1,620 acres. This is likely to have been smaller than the landed estates owned by the Blackburne and Patten families of Warrington and less than a fifth the size of the estates of the Leicesters and Warburtons, none of whom were noblemen in the sense of having a peerage. If lists of this kind had been made in England in the middle of the eighteenth century (which they were not), the categories might have been – Gentlemen, Clergy, small-

52 Goubert, 1986, pp. 30–34; Scribner, 1995, pp. 74–75, 248–49; Herlihy, 1985, pp. 116–21; Abel, 1980, pp. 130–33.
53 Chapman, 1973, pp. 12–13.
54 Forster, 1960, p. 1, 34–38.

holders and almost all the land would have been owned by Gentlemen.[55] All the families we have examined in Part II were Gentlemen – including the salt-works owners, the Quakers and the sailcloth manufacturers. So the French nobleman, as property owner, was the equivalent of the English gentleman. The difference between them was in their culture. This is not the place to attempt a description of European noble culture but 'no-one, however, will deny that the social prestige of business was lower in France than in England, that the ideal of *vivre noblement* (that is of doing nothing) was stronger there, contempt for work more widespread'.[56] The richer noblemen of Toulouse normally spent their winters in town so as to enjoy the social life there, which included theatrical performances, concerts and religious spectacles. They went to their country properties in the summer to avoid the oppressive heat in the cities and to supervise their workers gathering and storing the harvest. The way of life of some of the less well-off seems to have had similarities with that of George Dockwra,[57] who dressed fashionably and passed his days at social gatherings, with cards and drinking, or at sports, such as fishing.

Aristocratic culture was traditional in Europe (including England) throughout the Middle Ages. Most French noblemen belonged to the *noblesse d'épée*, the calling of which was to fight for the king (so paying a 'blood tax' which exempted them from ordinary *direct* taxes). In the sixteenth century, it could have been modified on the continent as it was in England. Throughout Europe the decrease in population resulting from the Black Death, and the rapid rise of rents and land values as population recovered, could have altered the social structure and the culture.

Governments in Continental Europe, in the sixteenth century, reacted to the crisis created by the conflict between 'customary' rents and the rise in land values in a different way to the Tudors in England. The creation of copyhold and three-life leasehold tenures in Cheshire and Lancashire, which gave property rights to working families, has been described in Chapter 3 (iii) and (iv) above. Continental kings by contrast, seem to have enlisted the support of the Church and enlarged their bureaucracies to improve the collection of taxes so as to re-establish their economic dominance and the absolute nature of their rule. Neither kings nor their ministers realized the potential power of the new business society to increase wealth. Bishops and kings thought it was their duty to God to suppress heresy. They were not concerned that they might be restraining their populations from increasing trade and improving technology. The Tudors did not follow this path because of their rift with the Catholic Church. Henry VIII quarrelled with the Papacy over his

55 Foster, 1992, p. 15, Table 5.; App. 5.1.E above.
56 Crouzet, 1967, p. 158.
57 Foster, 2002, Chapter 6.

divorce from Catherine of Aragon, and his daughter, Elizabeth, was not recognized as Queen by the Papacy during much of her reign. Charles I followed the same tactics as the Continental monarchs, and encouraged Archbishop Laud to harass the Puritan opponents of his attempt to rule without Parliament. Charles II and James II persecuted the Nonconformists, but the English business society had tasted freedom under Elizabeth and had grown too rich through trade and technical innovation for the kings to succeed. Charles I lost the Civil War and his head, while James II lost his throne. The following three examples describe situations that may have occurred widely in Europe.

The first example relies on evidence that the rise in land values in the sixteenth century did result in the redistribution of land to working families in some parts of Continental Europe. Upland areas, away from the main estates of the noblemen and gentry, seem to have enjoyed unusual tenurial arrangements. For example, in the Cevennes in France, there were many small *alods* (freeholds) and other manorial tenancies with small fixed rents. The sixteenth century saw the rise there of a purely rural 'bourgeoisie'. In the triangle of Alès, Ganges and Mende, coal-mining was developed, mills were built and the silk industry was established. A large number of small businesses appeared in 'mining, weaving, milling and working in wood and leather'[58] and it is interesting to note that all these people became Huguenots (Protestants). By 1560 they were in a powerful position in the area and were launching political attacks on the old Church and its tithe income. Then came the Counter-Reformation and the area became embroiled in more or less continuous civil war for the next 40 years. The Catholic majority in France were victorious and, in the seventeenth century, these unruly non-conforming areas were slowly repressed, so that their small businesses withered. The great coal-mines near Alès remained largely undeveloped before the French Revolution. Local people continued to use wood as their main fuel until a Catholic mining entrepreneur appeared from Normandy in the 1770s.[59]

The second example uses another type of evidence which suggests that French landlords in other areas had similar difficulties to English landlords in raising rents when land became scarce in the sixteenth century. P. Goubert's great study of the Beauvais area, say 80 km (50 miles) north of Paris, provides detailed information on peasant life there between 1670 and 1730.[60] He tells us that a typical rent in the 1730s was about 1s 8d an acre, while Government taxes amounted to about 6s per acre.[61]

---

58 Le Roy Ladurie, 1974, pp. 69–70, 94.
59 Lewis, 1993, pp. 1–54.
60 Goubert, 1965, p. 155.
61 The rent is described as 9% of the wheat crop on one third of the acres of the farm. I have valued wheat @ 5s a bushel.

This was very different to Cheshire where the full market rent was around 10–11s per acre out of which central and local government taxes took only around 2s per acre.[62]

The difference in the total surplus generated on the land in the two countries (6s + 1s 8d = 7s 8d in France, compared with 10s–11s in England) was probably due to the different grain yields of the land described below. The different division of this surplus between the private landlord and the State measures the extent to which the French State was taking possession of the surplus created by the agricultural labour force. In England, more than 80% went to individuals, who might choose to invest some of it in better equipment, new farming technology or in some different business. In France the state took 78% so that only 22% was left for the private citizen, who was therefore much less well-off than his English counterpart. The imposition of these taxes in the sixteenth and seventeenth centuries appears to have been one of the ways in which the French government ensured that it remained in control, and the pattern in the Hapsburgs' Austrian dominions seems to have been similar to that in France.[63]

One consequence of the difference in wealth between English and Continental farmers seems to have been the technical competence of the former and the backwardness of the latter. Goubert tells us that the wheat yield on the best land in Beauvaisis was nine quintals a hectare. This converts to about 12 bushels an acre which was a much poorer yield than the 21.5 bushels the Arley home farm achieved in 1750–53, or the 15.8 bushel yield of the average farmer in the neighbouring townships.[64] The Beauvais area actually had some of the best grain-growing land in France. Arthur Young's enquiries in 1787–9 revealed that poor yields were general in France. He thought French yields overall compared with English in the proportion 18 in France to 28 in England.[65] These yields may provide a good general indication of the technical backwardness of European states, resulting from their aristocratic culture and the consequent poverty of their working families.[66]

62 Figures for a number of years in the 1740s to 1770s for my four townships are in WM Box 25, Folder 2. Land Tax is explained in Foster, 1992, pp. 50–55. It was usually under 1s an acre in these years and local taxes for the Poor, Highways, Church and Constable made up the balance.
63 Rebel, 1983.
64 Foster, 1998, p. 64.
65 Maxwell, 1950, p. 285.
66 The difference between English and French wheat yields resulted from a lack of manure in France. Patrick O'Brien has rightly opposed the 'animal intensive' farming of England (with its great quantities of manure) to the 'labour intensive' French cultivation. But keeping enough animals to allow adequate manuring in France would have required a revolution in their systems with much more capital employed in the ownership of flocks and herds, the buildings they occupied, the crops they ate and so on. How far the English systems were applicable to the different French regions is hard to tell and perhaps other technical solutions were better. For example, the Japanese, who had few

The third example is Vienna and its hinterland, Lower Austria, which were said to be solidly Lutheran before Archduke Ferdinand, brother of Charles V, came from Spain to succeed to the Hapsburg lands in 1521. The city of Vienna was an important trading centre and its council was in the hands of Protestant merchants with connections among the local gentry. However, from 1524 onwards, Protestant preachers were burnt and in 1527 an edict of the new sovereign made it illegal for citizens to be witnesses in court, to establish a business, to make a valid will or to enter into an inheritance, if they were Protestant heretics. In 1551 Ferdinand installed the Jesuits in Vienna. In 1577, despite such violent measures, there were still only two Catholic members among the 12 who formed the Inner Council of the city. But the Protestants slowly lost power and the pressures on them were increased by the Thirty Years War (1618-48). In 1625 it was decreed that all citizens must either profess their Catholic faith or emigrate and in the next few years up to 1,000 families a year emigrated. They were made to pay a tenth of the money they took with them for permission to leave, and in 1625 they together paid the huge sum of 24,446 florins. The loss of so many moneyed business families was to damage the development of Viennese trade and industry for two centuries.[67] This story of the intolerance of aristocratic society for the business community underlines one of the differences between aristocratic society and the gentry society of England, of which the merchants of London and Bristol were an integral part.

Continental Europeans carried their culture with them when they went to live in the New World. The Spaniards settled Jamaica in the middle of the sixteenth century. In 1655, when the English army arrived under General Venables (of Antrobus), the population was 'fifteen hundred Spaniards and Portuguese with about an equal number of mulattoes and Negro slaves'. There were twelve 'hatos' or estates 'owned by Spanish or Portuguese hidalgos' (minor nobles). 'Upon each of them was erected a mansion which the owner seldom visited.' Instead they preferred to pass 'a life of luxurious sloth in the town of St. Iago'.[68] The hidalgos exported only enough to pay for the things, like silks and swords, that they could not get their workers to produce on the island. By contrast, the British settlers quickly devoted their energies to producing sugar, which they had successfully produced in Barbados since 1641.

animals, maintained the fertility of their rice paddies by burying all kinds of green organic matter in the soil. The evolution of an efficient farming system in each area was done in England by the owner/occupiers of commercial farms between 1550 and 1780. This process does not seem to have been matched in Continental Europe. For examples in Cheshire see pp. 76–7 and 80 above and Foster, 1998, pp. 14–17 and 25–7, and for examples elsewhere see Best, 1857, Fussell, 1936, and Kerridge, 1967.

67 Barea, 1966, pp. 43–52.
68 Bridges, 1968, Vol. I, pp. 179–80, 184.

Holland was the only major country in Continental Europe where land came to be widely held by working families. This development occurred in the western part of the Netherlands in an unusual way.[69] In the early medieval period the western half of Holland was an area of low-lying marsh. The noblemen who owned it were determined to turn it into agricultural land. Their reclamation work was organized so that much of the local drainage had to be done by the farmers who came to live there. In order to attract these new settlers, the nobles had to offer them a secure tenure at a fixed rent. With the rise in rents in the sixteenth century, these lands became effectively freeholds. The proportion of the land owned in this way varied in different districts. Overall, perhaps as much as 50% was in the hands of owner-occupiers, who usually had farms of between 16 and 18 hectares (40 to 44 acres). The remainder was divided between noblemen, the Church and city dwellers.[70]

The noble families mostly had small estates of less than 100 hectares (247 acres) and there were only a few large estates with up to 1,900 hectares (4,693 acres). The bourgeoisie from the cities probably owned about 20% of the land. The large number of owner-occupier families with similar sized farms formed an unusually egalitarian society. As their wealth increased with the inflation of land values, these farmers became more and more occupied with trade. A growing part of this trade was to the Baltic, where Dutch manufactures were exchanged for bread grain. This allowed the farmers to concentrate on dairy farming, for which their lands were ideally suited. By the end of the sixteenth century, the cultivation of grain had virtually ceased. Trading thus became the major activity in these communities: 'There grew up in the midst of these farm populations a shipping and ship building industry, a colony of merchants ... and a service and petty trade sector.'[71] The Protestant religion quickly found adherents in this egalitarian rural business community. Lutheran ideas which allowed 'a man to form his own rule and judge for himself'[72] were popular in such a society, and they became part of its culture, ultimately leading to the creation of the Dutch Reformed Church. From these rural beginnings, the Dutch developed, in the sixteenth and seventeenth centuries, the most advanced commercial and industrial economy in Europe. There appear to have been many similarities as well as some differences with the advance of business society in England. Progress was much earlier in Holland because it was at the heart of the water transport system of Europe and close to the commercial capital of Antwerp.

69 Now the Dutch provinces of North and South Holland, Friesland, Groningen, Zeeland, and the western half of Utrecht.
70 de Vries, 1974, pp. 26–51.
71 Ibid., pp. 125–26.
72 Christopher Hill on Martin Luther in Hill, 1974, p. 24.

vi) Japan and China

To emphasize the importance of culture in the wealth-creating process I finish this book with two short sketches of these two great Asian societies which were so different to those in Europe. In the eighteenth century Japan was a country with a population of about 30 million. Edo, now Tokyo, with about a million inhabitants, was larger than any city in Europe. In the Tokugawa period (1600–1868) the government of the country was a military dictatorship. One fifth of the productive land was under the control of the *Shogun*, a member of the Tokugawa family. The rest of the land was owned by 266 *daimyo* or noblemen. In Europe, the great medieval nobles had 'enfiefed' their military supporters with land. Each knight had his own estate and found the serfs to cultivate it for him. He and his family and his men-at-arms were supported by the work of the serfs. In Japan, however, the villagers owed their tribute of rice direct to their *daimyo*. He decided how much each of his *samurai* should be given each year. This system concentrated the economic power of the country into the hands of only just over 300 men – the 266 *daimyos* and the 41 intendants who managed the various parts of the vast Tokugawa estate.

The samurai were a military caste who did no work. Their position in society was symbolized by the two swords they each always wore in public. Samurai households altogether comprised about two million people, around 7% or 8% of the total population. Villagers working the land were about 85% to 87%. Artisans may have been about 2% and the remainder were shopkeepers, traders, transport workers, priests, etc. In the villages the average family's landholding was about two acres. This was enough to support them because of the extraordinary productivity (by European standards) of rice grown in paddy fields, the typical yield per acre being around 40 bushels. After each family had given at least half their crop to the *daimyo*, there was still enough for them to live on.[73] This brief description shows that Japan had none of the four features of social organization required for technical innovation and wealth creation. Ownership of land was not widely distributed, the culture was militarist, the government was a dictatorship and there was little private property for the law to protect. It will not be a surprise to discover that much of their technology was primitive as can be seen by the following examples.

In Tokugawa times the Japanese were unable to build a masonry wall. The main reason for this was that there was virtually no lime in the country with which to make mortar. But mortar had been widely used on the mainland of east Asia for more than 1,000 years and it could have been obtained by trade were it not for the fact that the Tokugawas had sealed the country off from contact with foreigners.

---

73 Skene-Smith, 1937, pp. 7, 28, 31–33. For village life see Embree, 1946 and Dore, 1978, pp. 23–64.

An alternative material they could have used for walls was 'cob' – a mixture of clay and straw, which was used to make strong walls, two feet thick, in Devon and Normandy. This seems to have been unknown in Japan. The absence of walls that would allow the inside of houses to be kept warm in winter caused the northern parts of the country to be almost unpopulated. These were the latitudes in which they could have grown grass to feed cattle, sheep and horses. As a result there were few draught animals or wheeled vehicles in the country and there was no wool and no meat to eat.

The protein in Japanese diet was provided by fish, so fishing was a vital activity. Because of the mountains in the centre of the islands, most of the population lived on the coastal plains, so the transport of rice from outlying areas to the great cities of Tokyo and Osaka was another important nautical occupation. With these two big seafaring tasks to accomplish, one might have expected that Japanese coastal shipping would have been technically advanced, but that does not seem to have been the case. For example, the *daimyo's* rice, grown on the north-west coast of Japan, was all collected at Niigata for shipment to Osaka. The voyage south and west to Shimonoseki and then east across the Inland Sea to Osaka was some 800 miles. In the 1870s, the custom was for the fleet to set out in the late spring and to arrive in Osaka in the summer or autumn, three to six months later. After wintering in Osaka, the vessels returned to Niigata in the early spring. A full year was thus allowed for the whole trip.[74] By contrast, in the England of the 1680s, the cheese ships from Liverpool usually made a similar coastal voyage to London, a distance of over 700 miles, in 26 days. These cheese ships were able to make up to three and a half round trips a year.[75]

The technology that was well developed in Tokugawa Japan related almost entirely to the way of life of the *samurai,* and did not contribute to the economic development of the country as a whole. The manufacture of swords, of paper, of writing and drawing implements, of colours for painting, of lacquer work and of ceramics was all sophisticated. Their fine textiles of cotton, linen and silk were beautifully dyed and finished.

In contrast to Japan, the landowning pattern in China was more similar to that in England. By the sixteenth and seventeenth centuries, the farmers of China seem to have escaped from the bondage of the large rural estates and the typical farming family possessed a small freehold.[76] Small rural businesses in textiles, basketry and other handicrafts flourished everywhere and there was much trading up and down

74 Skene-Smith, 1937, p. 76.
75 Foster, 1998, pp. 17–18.
76 Eastman, 1988, p. 74.

the great rivers. But nothing at all comparable to the advances in technology and transport that occurred in England in the seventeenth and eighteenth centuries ever happened in China. Why not?

The most important reason appears to have been 'the orthodox Confucian ordering of social classes: scholar, farmer, artisan, merchant'.[77] (Soldier was not even listed as a respectable occupation.) Of central importance in the social structure was the status and prestige of the scholar – official class. No other career offered comparable rewards. To attain '*literati*' status by successfully participating in the civil service examinations, and thereby to gain a government post, was the ultimate goal of every clever young man. As soon as a family made enough money, they spent it on sending their sons to school and university so that they might do well in these exams. This education and these exams did not include any historical, commercial, technical or scientific subjects. They were solely concerned with a narrow scholastic study of the Confucian classics.[78] Only a few young men attained to high governmental office, many more becoming minor officials such as tax collectors. Even if they failed to obtain any post, young men who had spent five or ten years in higher education outside their villages were no longer willing to do manual work. In the 1930s detailed studies were carried out by sociologists in four Chinese villages. All had a similar social structure.[79] In one of these villages called Luts'un, 84 families owned land and 38 were landless. The richest 41 landed families each owned between one and four acres of good land. In virtually all of these 41 families the males did no manual work on their farms,[80] mainly as a result of the widely held belief that educated people should not do such work and the social custom allowing the men to send their wives and daughters into the fields. This social view was reinforced by the economics of the situation. At the time of the study in 1938, every acre of good land had an annual value of about Chinese $96 (C$96).[81] An agricultural labourer earned about C$40 a year, his usual wage being 10 cents a day. Why would a rich and educated man work in the fields for such a small reward?

Many of these idle men found life without work so boring that they took to gambling and opium smoking, habits which often reduced their families to penury, so they had to sell their land. New rich families bought the land and settled into the village. The source of the wealth of the new families was usually either a small business or the profits of some official post. However, when the new families

77 Ibid., pp. 101, 203.
78 Ibid., p. 153.
79 Fei, 1945, p. 300, Table 50.
80 Ibid., pp. 45, 74, 84.
81 One US dollar at this period was equal to between 4 and 20 Chinese dollars. Approximately, US$4 = £1 at that period.

acquired lands they ceased working and sent their children to school, so the cycle was repeated. The ownership of a small amount of capital, invested in land, did not lead to the accumulation of sufficient capital to develop larger businesses, as it did in Cheshire and Lancashire. The social customs – the culture – of traditional China caused the people to follow a different path.

Subsequent events have shown that these two Asian societies could have improved their technology and created great wealth for their populations centuries earlier. When, in the 1860s, the Japanese changed their culture, so that the pursuit of business success became the goal of the *samurai*, they caught up with many European countries within 80 years. We seem to be witnessing a similar transformation in China today.

Appendix 11.1 *The cult of the inventor*

Since the nineteenth century, the public and many historians have made much of 'inventors', who were almost always people who had obtained a patent and made a lot of money. My experience of creating new products gives a rather different picture of 'inventions'.

From 1970–87 I owned and ran a small engineering firm that made special tools for telecommunications. The man I bought the business from and one or two of his tool-makers were clever mechanical engineers, so that British Telecom (BT) engineers were in the habit of asking the firm to make prototypes for them. Sometimes the BT engineer provided most of the design, sometimes our tool-makers did; some tools were patented and others were not, but BT always owned any patent and their engineer would have been labelled the 'inventor' because they paid for all the work.

In my first eight years with the firm I spent a lot of the firm's money and my own time trying to develop a type of wire wrapping tool called a 'cut, strip and wrap tool'. Our clever tool-makers fairly quickly made tools that worked, but every batch we made always included many defective tools. I spent a large amount of time with one of the tool-makers testing and experimenting to try to find out where the faults lay. We asked the advice of BT engineers, other customers and friends. We made 'improvements' over 2 or 3 years, but there were always a significant number of defectives in every batch we made. Among the other tools we were making, an increasing number required 'grinding', a technology for which we had only primitive equipment in the factory. We subcontracted the work to a skilled grinder with whom we became friendly; finally we agreed to buy his machines so that he could come and work full time with us. He could make and measure things very accurately – at least ten times more accurately than the traditional equipment in the factory permitted. It was not long before he pointed out that one of the problems with our wrapping tools might be their size variation – in engineering language that our tolerances were too wide. We took his advice and over the next 18 months we redesigned the whole manufacturing process of the wrapping tools. We bought several new grinding machines and made a lot of special tools, fixtures and cutters. We then found that we could make wrapping tools which always worked, which cost much less than they ever had before and which turned out to be the best and cheapest in the world. We never patented them because the basic design was the same as we had been making when lots of them didn't work properly, and we didn't make our fortunes because telecom technology had moved on and wire wrapping was going out.

Who was the 'inventor' of these tools – the original tool-maker, the friends who suggested improvements, the grinder who revolutionized the manufacture or the firm who paid the bills? Is it not wiser to see new products as being 'developed' by a team that consists of one or more designers who work with an entrepreneur to produce something which is both technically and economically successful? Who owns the patent and makes the money is, of course, a different story – a legal story, not a technical or 'entrepreneurial' one.

Bibliography

(All books were published in the U.K. except where noted. Short titles.)

Abel, Wilhelm. (1980) *Agricultural Fluctuations in Europe.*

Abraham, J. J. (1933) *Lettsom: his life, times, friends and descendants*

Adams, A. (ed.) (1941) *Cheshire Visitation Pedigrees 1663*, Harleian Soc., Vol. 93.

Aikin, John. (1795) *Description of the Country from 30–40 Miles round Manchester.*

Allen, R. C. (1988) *The Price of Freehold Land and the Rate of Interest in the 17th and 18th centuries*, Econ. Hist. Rev., 2nd Series, Vol. XLI.

Anderson, Robert C. (1995) *The Great Migration begins: Immigrants to New England 1620–1633*, P-W, Vol. 3. New England Historic Genealogical Society, Boston.

Andersson, C. Ingwar. (1956) *A History of Sweden.*

Antrobus, Sir Reginald. (1929) *Antrobus Pedigrees.*

Armitage, G. J. and Rylands, J. P. (1909) *The Visitation of Cheshire 1613*, Harleian Soc., Vol. 59.

Arrowsmith, P. (1997) *Stockport: a history..*

Ashton, Robert. (1960) *The Crown and the Money Market 1603–1640.*

Ashton, T. S. (1939) *An Eighteenth Century Industrialist: Peter Stubs of Warrington, 1756–1806.*

Awty, B. G. (1957) *Charcoal Ironmasters of Lancashire and Cheshire 1600–1785*, H.S.L. & C., Vol. 109.

Bailey, F. A. and Barker, T. C. (1969) *The Seventeenth Century Origins of Watchmaking in South West Lancashire*, in John. R. Harris (ed.) *Liverpool and Merseyside.*

Barea, I. (1966) *Vienna: legend and reality.*

Barker, T. C. and Harris, J. R. (1954) *A Merseyside Town in the Industrial Revolution: St Helens 1750–1900.*

Beamont, W. (ed.) (1866) *Arley Charters.*

Beamont, W. (ed.) (1849) *Warrington in 1465*, Chetham Soc., Vol. 17.

Beckett, J. V. (1989) *A History of Laxton:, England's Last Open Field Village.*

Best, Henry. (1857) *Farm Account Book 1641*, Surtees Soc., Vol. 33.

Bird, James H. (1963) *Major Seaports of the U.K.*

Boyd, A.W. (1928) *The town-books of Sevenoaks and Newton-by-Daresbury, Cheshire*, L.& C.A.S., Vol. XLV.

Braithwaite, W. C. (1955) *The Beginnings of Quakerism*, ed. H.J.Cadbury (orig. 1919).

Braithwaite, W. C. (1961) *The Second Period of Quakerism*, ed. H.J.Cadbury (orig. 1919)..

Bridbury, A. R. (1955) *England and the Salt Trade in the Later Middle Ages.*

Bridges, G. W. (1968) *The Annals of Jamaica*, orig. 1828, reprint, Vols. 1 & 2.

Brooke, Richard (1853) *Liverpool as it was during the Last Quarter of the Eighteenth Century.*

Bulmer, J. R. (1980) *The Registers and Inscriptions of the Unitarian Chapel, Cairo Street, Warrington.*

Calvert, A. F. (1915) *Salt in Cheshire.*

Chapman, C.G. (1973*) Milocca.* U.S.A.

Chapman, S.D. (1970) *Fixed Capital Formation in the British Cotton Industry 1770–1815*, Econ. Hist. Rev., 2nd Series Vol. 23.

Chapman, S. D. and Chassagne, S. (1981) *European Textile Printers in the 18th Century,*

Chapman, S.D. (1969) *The Peels in the early English cotton industry*, Business History, Vol. 11.

Charley, W. (1862) *Flax and its Products in Ireland.*

Chibnall, A. C. (1965) *Sherington: Fiefs and Fields of a Buckinghamshire Village.*

Chipping Local History Soc. Lancs. (ed.) (2000) *The Diary of the Reverend Peter Walkden 1733–4.*

Churton, R. (1800) *Lives of William Smyth and Sir Richard Sutton.*

Clark, G. (2002) *Land Rental Values and the agrarian economy: England and Wales 1500–1914.* European Review of Economic History Vol. 6, Pt 3.

Clay, C.G.A. (1981) *Life leasehold in the Western Counties of England 1650–1750*, Ag. Hist. Rev., Vol. 29.

Clay, C.G.A. (1974) *The Price of Freehold Land in the Later Seventeenth and Eighteenth Centuries*, Econ. Hist. Rev., 2nd Series, Vol. 27.

Clemens, P. G. E. (1976) *The Rise of Liverpool 1665–1750*, Econ. Hist. Rev., 2nd Series, Vol. 29.

Cooper, J. P. (1967) *Social Distribution of Land and Men in England 1436–1700*, Econ. Hist. Rev., Vol. 20.

Corner, B. C. and Booth, C. C. (1971) *Chain of Friendship: Letters of Dr. John Fothergill 1735–1780*, Harvard University Press.

Court, W. H. B. (1938) *The Rise of the Midland Industries, 1600–1838.*

Cox, M. (1975) *History of Sir John Deane's Grammar School, Northwich 1557–1908.*

Craig, R. and Jarvis, R. (1967) Liverpool Registry of Merchant Ships, Chetham Soc., Third Series, Vol. 15.

Crosfield, George. (1843) *Memoirs of Samuel Fothergill.*

Crouzet, F. (1967) *England and France in the 18th century: a comparative analysis,*

Annales Vol. XXI, No 2, 1966, trans. J.Sondheimer in R. M. Hartwell, ed., *The Causes of the Industrial Revolution in England*.

Davenport, F.G. (1906) *The Economic Development of a Norfolk Manor 1086–1565*.

Davis, Ralph. (1962) *The Rise of the English shipping industry in the 17th and 18th centuries.*.

de Vries, Jan. (1974) *The Dutch Rural Economy in the Golden Age 1500–1700*, Yale University Press.

Dickinson, Henry W. (1936) *James Watt, Craftsman and Engineer*.

Dore, Ronald. (1978) *Shinohata*.

Durie, A. J. (1996) *The British Linen Company 1745–1775*, Scottish Hist. Soc., Fifth Series, Vol. 9.

Durie, A. J. (1979) *The Scottish Linen Industry in the 18th Century*.

Dyer, C. (1980) *Lords and Peasants in a Changing Society: The Estates of the Bishopric of Worcester 680–1540*.

Eastman, L. E. (1988) *Family, Fields and Ancestors: China's Social and Economic History 1550–1949*.

Ellis, Joyce. (1980) *The decline and fall of the Tyneside Salt Industry 1660–1790*, Econ. Hist. Rev., 2nd Series Vol. 33.

Embree, J. F. (1946) *A Japanese Village: Suye Mura*.

Enfield, W. (1773) *An essay towards the history of Liverpool*.

English, B. (1990) *The Great Landowners of East Yorkshire, 1530 – 1910*.

Farrer, W. (1912) *The Court Rolls of the Honor of Clitheroe, Vols. 2 & 3*.

Fei, Hsiao-Tung and others. (1945) *Earthbound. China*. University of Chicago Press.

Fischer, D.H. (1989) *Albion's Seed. Four British folkways in America*.

Fisher, F. J. (ed.) (1961) *Essays in Economic and Social English History in Honour of R. H. Tawney*.

Fishwick, H. (ed.) (1913) *Survey of the Manor of Rochdale in 1626*, Chetham Soc., 2nd Series, Vol. 71.

Fitton, R. S. (1989) *The Arkwrights: Spinners of Fortune*.

Ford, *Whitmore and Brunton of Birmingham Catalogue (1777)*.

Forster, R. (1960) *The Nobility of Toulouse in the 18th Century*, Johns Hopkins University.

Foster, C.F. (1998) *Cheshire Cheese and Farming in the North West in the 17th and 18th centuries*.

Foster, C.F. (1992) *Four Cheshire Townships in the 18th century*.

Foster, C.F. (2002) *Seven Households: Life in Cheshire and Lancashire 1582–1774*.

Foster, C.F. (1996) *History of the Gardens at Arley Hall*, Garden History, Vol. 24, No. 2.

Foster, Joseph (1891) *Alumni Oxonienses.*

Foster, Joseph (1873) *Pedigrees of the Families of England*, Vol. 1, Lancashire.

French, G. J. (1859) *Life and Times of Samuel Crompton*, reprint 1970, S. D. Chapman (ed.).

Fussell, G. E. (ed.) (1936) *Robert Loder's Farm Accounts 1610–1620*, Camden 3rd series, Vol. 53.

Gilboy, E.W. (1934) *Wages in Eighteenth Century England*, Harvard University Press.

Goubert, P. (1965) *The French peasantry of the seventeenth century: a regional example* in T.Aston, ed. *Crisis in Europe – Essays from Past and Present.*

Goubert, P. (1986) *The French Peasantry in the 17th century.*

Gow, H. (1928) *The Unitarians.*

Gras, E. C. and Gras, N. S. B. (1930) *The Economic and Social History of an English Village: Crawley, Hampshire*, Harvard University Press.

Gray, Charles. M. (1963) *Copyhold, Equity and the Common Law*, Harvard University Press.

Greene, J. P. (1979) *The Elevation of Norton Priory*, H.S.L.&C., Vol. 128.

Greig, James (ed.) (1923) *The Farington Diary*, Vol. 2.

Hadfield, E. C. R. and Biddle, G. (1970) *The Canals of North West England*, Vol. 1.

Hainsworth, D. R. (1977) *Commercial Papers of Sir Christopher Lowther 1611–1644*, Surtees Soc., Vol. 189.

Hall, D. S. (1989) *Richard Robinson of Countersett (1628–1693) and the Quakers of Wensleydale.*

Hamilton, Henry. (1926) *The English Brass and Copper Industries to 1800.*

Harris, John. R. (1964) *Copper King.*

Harris, John.R. (1976) *Skills, coal and British Industry in the Eighteenth Century*, History 61, June, pp 167–82.

Harte, N. B. (1973) *The Rise of Protection and the English Linen Trade 1690–1790*, in Harte, N.B. and Ponting, K.G. (eds.) *Textile History and Economic History*, pp 74–112.

Hartwell, R.M. (1967) (ed.) *The Causes of the Industrial Revolution in England.*

Hatcher, J. (1993) *History of the British Coal Industry*, Vol. 1.

Hawkins, E. (ed.) (1844) *Sir William Brereton's Travels 1634–1635*, Chetham Soc., 1st series, Vol. 1.

Heaton, H. (1920) *The Yorkshire Woollen and Worsted Industries.*

Heginbotham, H. (1882) *Stockport Ancient and Modern*, Vol. 2.

Herlihy, D. and Klapisch-Zuber, C. (1985) *Tuscans and their Families*, Yale University Press.

Hey, D. (1998) *A History of Sheffield.*

Hey, D. (1980) *Packmen, Carriers and Packhorse Roads.*

Heywood, T. (ed.) (1846) Norris Papers, Chetham Soc., 1st series, Vol. 9.

Hill, C. (1967) *Reformation to Industrial Revolution 1530–1780.*

Hinton, R. W. K. (1959) *The Eastland Trade and the Common Weal in the 17th century.*

Home, James. (ed.) (1899) *Lady Louisa Stuart – selections from her manuscripts.* David Douglas, Edinburgh.

Hopkins, E. (1962) *The Re-leasing of the Ellesmere Estates 1637–1642*, Ag. Hist. Rev., Vol. 10.

Hoskins, W. G. (1964) *Harvest Fluctuations and English Economic History 1480–1619*, Ag. Hist. Rev., Vol. 12.

Hoskins, W. G. (1968) *Harvest Fluctuations and English Economic History 1620–1759*, Ag. Hist. Rev., Vol. 16.

Hoskins, W.G. (1976) *The Age of Plunder: King Henry's England 1500–1547.*

Holdsworth, W. S. (1909) *A History of English Law*, Vol. 3.

Howell, C. A. H. (1983) *Land, Family, and Inheritance in Transition: Kibworth Harcourt 1280–1700.*

Hoyle, R. W. (1992) *The Estates of the English Crown 1558–1640.*

Hoyle, R.W. (ed.) (1987) *Early Tudor Craven: Subsidies and Assessments 1510 – 1547*, Y.A.S.R.S., Vol. 145

Hoyle, R.W. (1989) *Monastic Leasing before the Dissolution.* Y.A.J., Vol. 61.

Hughes, Edward. (1934) *Studies in Administration and Finance 1558–1825.*

Hunter, Joseph. (1819) *Hallamshire*, reprint 1869.

Iredale, D.A. (1965) *The rise and fall of the Marshalls of Northwich 1720–1917.* H.S.L.&C., Vol. 117.

Irvine, W. Ferguson. (1901) *A list of the Freeholders in Cheshire in 1578* in Miscellanies, Record Soc. L. & C., Vol. 43.

Ives, E. W. (ed.) (1976) *Letters and Accounts of William Brereton of Malpas*, Record Soc. L. & C., Vol. 116.

Ives, E. W., Knecht, R.J., Scarisbrick, J.J. (1978) *Wealth and Power in Tudor England.*

Jacobs, Jane. (1992) *Systems of Survival. A dialogue on the moral foundations of commerce and politics.*

Jenkins, Charles. F. (1923) *Tortola.* Friends History Soc. Journal Suppl. No. 13.

Kerridge, E. (1967) *The Agricultural Revolution.*

Kerridge, E. (1953) *Movement of Rent, 1540–1640*, Econ. Hist. Rev., 2nd series, Vol. 6.

Large, Peter. (1990) *Ombersley 1580–1700*, in John Chartres and D. Hey (eds.) *English Rural Society 1500–1800.*

Laslett, P. (1965) *The World we have lost.*

Latham, R. and Matthews, W. (eds.) (1971) *The Diary of Samuel Pepys*, Vol. 4.

Latimer, Hugh. *Sermons.* Everyman.

Laurence, Edward. (1730) Dissertation on Estates upon Lives.

Lawton, G. O. (ed.) (1979) *Northwich Hundred Poll Tax 1660 and Hearth Tax 1664*, Record Soc. of L. & C., Vol. 119.

Lee, Clive H. (1972) *A Cotton Enterprise 1795–1840: a history of M'Connel and Kennedy, Fine Cotton Spinners.*

Le Roy Ladurie, E. (1974), translated by J. Day, *The Peasants of Languedoc*, University of Illinois Press.

Levine, D. and Wrightson, K. (1991) *The Making of an Industrial Society: Whickham 1560–1765.*

Lewis, Gwynne. (1993) *The Advent of Modern Capitalism in France, 1770–1840.*

Lowe, N. (1972) *The Lancashire Textile Industry in the 16th Century*, Chetham Soc. 3rd series, Vol. 20.

Lysons D. and S. (1806). *Magna Britannia*, Vol. 2.

Macbeath-Calder, I. (1934) *The New Haven Colony*, Yale University Press.

Mansfield, H.C. and Winthrop, D. (eds.) (2000) *Alexis de Tocqueville: Democracy in America.* Chicago University Press.

Marshall J.D. (ed.) (1967) *Autobiography of William Stout of Lancaster 1665–1752*, Chetham Soc., 3rd series, Vol. 14.

Maxwell, C. (ed.) (1950) *Travels in France during the years 1787, 1788 and 1789 by Arthur Young* (orig. 1929).

McLachlan, H. (1943) *Warrington Academy*, Cheetham Soc., 2nd series, Vol. 107.

Minchinton, W. E. (1957) *The Trade of Bristol in the 18th Century*, Bristol Rec. Soc., Vol. 20.

Minchinton, W. E. (1954) *Bristol – Metropolis of the West in the Eighteenth Century* Trans. R.H.S., 5th series, Vol. 4.

Miles, M. (1981) *The money market in the early Industrial Revolution.* Business History, Vol. xxiii, No 2, July.

Money, L.G.C. (1910) *Riches and Poverty.* 10th edition.

Montgomery, Florence M. (1984) *Textiles in America*, W.W. Norton, New York.

Moore, J. B. (c1842) *Memoir of Theophilus Eaton.* New York Hist. Soc. 2nd series, Vol. II.

Morgan, Kenneth (1993) *Bristol and the Atlantic trade in the eighteenth century.*

Morgan, Kenneth (2000) *Slavery, Atlantic Trade and the British Economy 1660–1800.*

Musson, A. E. (1965) *Enterprise in Soap and Chemicals: Joseph Crosfield and Sons Ltd 1815–1965.*

Myddleton, W.M. (1931) *Chirk Castle Accounts, 1605–1753.*

Myers, A. R. (1963) *An Official Progress in 1476.* H.S.L.&C., Vol. 115.

Oliver, V. L. (1919) *Caribbeana*, Vol. 5.

Ormerod, G. (1882) *The History of the county palatine and city of Chester,* ed. T. Helsby.

Ormerod, G. (1851) *Miscellanea Palatina.*

Osterweis, R.G. (1953) *Three Centuries of New Haven 1638 – 1938.* Yale University Press.

Parkinson, C.N. (1952) *The Rise of the Port of Liverpool*

Peet, H. (1907) *Liverpool in the reign of Queen Anne*, H.S.L.&C., Vol. 59.

Penney, N. (ed.) (1920) *Household Account Book of Sarah Fell.*

Phillips, C.B. and Smith, J.H. (1994) *Lancashire and Cheshire from AD 1540.*

Phillips, C. B. and Smith, J. H. (eds.) (1985) Stockport Probate Records 1578–1619, Record Soc. L. & C., Vol. 124.

Phillips, C. B. and Smith, J. H. (eds.) (1992) *Stockport Probate Records 1620–1650,* Record Soc. L. & C., Vol. 131.

Plant, R. (1881) *History of Cheadle in Staffordshire.*

Plot, R. (1686) *The Natural History of Staffordshire.*

Power, M. (2000) *Creating a port: Liverpool 1695–1715*, HSL&C, Vol. 149.

Price, Richard (1771) *Observations on Reversionary Payments.*

Ragatz, L.J. (1929) *The Fall of the Planter Class in the British Caribbean, 1763 – 1833.*

Raistrick, A. (1953) *Dynasty of Iron-founders: The Darbys and Coalbrookdale.*

Raistrick, A. (1950) *Quakers in Science and Industry.*

Raistrick, A. (1970) *The West Riding of Yorkshire.*

Rebel, H. (1983) *Peasant classes: the bureaucratization of property and family relations under early Hapsburg absolutism 1511–1636.* Princeton University Press.

Renny, Robert. (1807) *History of Jamaica.*

Richards, John. (1739) *Annuities upon Lives.*

Richards, John. (1730) *The Gentleman's Steward.*

Richardson, R.C. (1972) *Puritanism in north-west England.*

Rimmer, A. (1852) *Ancient Halls of Lancashire.*

Robinson, M. (1998) *The Linen Industry of North Lancashire and Cumbria 1660–1830* in Roberts, E. (ed.) *A History of Linen in the North West.*

Rogers, J. E. T. (1882) *A History of Agriculture and Prices in England*, Vol. 2.

Rolt, L. T. C. (1962) *James Watt.*

Rose-Troup, F. (1930) *The Massachusetts Bay Company and its Predecessors*, New York.

Rylands, J.P. (1880) (ed.) *Lancashire Inquisitions 1603–1614.* Record Soc. L.&C, Vol. 3.

Rylands, J. P. (1882) *Visitation of Cheshire 1580*, Harleian Soc., Vol. 18.

Schumpeter, E. B. (1960) *English Overseas Trade Statistics 1697–1808*.

Scribner, Bob. (1995) *Germany: A New Social and Economic History*, Vol. 1.

Shaw, Simeon (1829) *History of the Staffordshire Potteries*, reprint David and Charles 1970.

Simpson, A.W.B. (1986) *A History of the Land Law*.

Singleton, F. J. (1977) *The Flax Merchants of Kirkham*, H.S.L.&C., Vol. 126.

Skeel, Caroline. (1926) *Cattle Trade between Wales and England from the fifteenth to the nineteenth centuries*, Trans. R.H.S., 4th series, Vol. IX.

Skene-Smith, Neil (1937) *Tokugawa Japan*.

Smith, Denis Mack. (1968a) *Medieval Sicily 800–1713*.

Smith, Denis Mack. (1968b) *Modern Sicily after 1713*.

Smith, Ralph. B. (1970) *Land and Politics in the England of Henry VIII: The West Riding of Yorkshire 1530–1546*.

Spufford, M. (1974) *Contrasting Communities: English Villagers in the 16th and 17th Centuries*.

Stephenson, Robert. (1757) *Inquiry into the State and Progress of the Linen Manufacture*, Dublin.

Stone, L. (1965) The *Crisis of the Aristocracy 1558–1641*.

Stone, L. (1973) *Family and Fortune*.

Styles, P. (1978) *Studies in seventeenth century West Midlands History*.

Swain, J. T. (1986) *Industry before the Industrial Revolution: North East Lancashire c1500–1640*, Chetham Soc., 3rd series, Vol. 32.

Tait, J. (ed.) (1916) *The Domesday Survey of Cheshire*, Chetham Soc., 2nd series, Vol. 75.

Tait, J. (1924)(ed.) *Taxation in Salford Hundred, 1524–1802*, Chetham Soc., 2nd series, Vol. 83.

Tawney, R. H. (1912) *The Agrarian Problem in the 16th Century*.

Thirsk, J. (1961) *Industries in the countryside* in F.J.Fisher (ed.) *Essays in the Economic and Social History of Tudor and Stuart England in honour of R.H.Tawney*.

Thirsk, J. (1967) (ed.) *Agrarian History of England and Wales*, Vol. IV, 1500–1640.

Thorne, R. G. (1986) *The History of Parliament, The House of Commons 1790–1820*, Vol. 3.

Thrupp, S. L. (1948) *Merchant Class of Medieval London*, University of Chicago Press.

Tomalin, C. (2002) *Samuel Pepys: the Unequalled Self*.

Tupling, G. H. (1927) *Economic History of Rossendale*, Chetham Soc., 2nd series, Vol. 86.

Turner, William. (1813) *Warrington Academy*, reprint Warrington Library 1957.

Underdown, David (1985)*Revel, Riot and Rebellion: Popular Politics and Culture in England 1603–1660.*

Venn, J.A. (1922–7) *Alumni Cantabrigienses.*

Wadsworth, A. P. and Mann, J. de L. (1931) *The Cotton Trade and Industrial Lancashire 1600–1780.*

Wardle, A. C. (1941) *The Early Liverpool Privateers*, H.S.L.&C., Vol. 93.

Wareing, J. (1980) *Changes in the Geographical Distribution of the recruitment of Apprentices to the London companies 1486–1750*, Journal of Historical Geography 6, No. 3, pp241–9.

Weatherill, L. (1971) *The Pottery Trade and North Staffordshire 1660–1760.*

Webb, William, and Smith, William (1656) *The Vale-Royal of England..*

Welch, Charles. (1908) *Register of Freemen 1551–1553.*

Wells, H. (1996) *A short history of Orford Hall.*

Whitaker, T. D. (1872) *History of Whalley*, Vol. 1. (revised, orig. 1802), ed. J.G. Nichols.

Wilkinson, J. (1994) *The Letters of Thomas Langton, Flax merchant of Kirkham 1771–1788*, Chetham Soc., 3rd series, Vol. 38.

Willan, T. S. (1980) *Elizabethan Manchester*, Chetham Soc., 3rd series, Vol. 27.

Willan, T. S. (1951) *The Navigation of the River Weaver in the Eighteenth Century*, Chetham Soc., 3rd series, Vol. 3.

Willan, T.S. (1936) *River Navigation in England 1660–1750.*

Willan, T. S. and Crossley, E. W. (eds.) (1941) *Three Seventeenth-century Yorkshire Surveys*, Y.A.S.R.S., Vol. 104.

Withersby, J. P. (1998) *Linen men*, M.A. thesis 9011, Sidney Jones Library, University of Liverpool.

Woodward, D. M. (1967) *Chester Leather Industry 1558–1625*, H.S.L.&C., Vol. 119.

Woodward, D. M. (1970) *The Trade of Elizabethan Chester.*

Wrightson, K. and Levine, D. (1979) *Poverty and Piety in an English Village: Terling (Essex) 1525–1700.*

Wrigley, E.A. (2000) *The Divergence of England.* Trans, R.H.S., 6th series, Vol. 10.

Wyke, J. (1758–1782) Catalogue, printed for Winterthur Museum by University Press of Virginia, Charlottesville, 1978.

Young, Arthur (1770–1771) *A Six Month Tour through the North of England*, Vol. III.

Subject index

Index of names and places